IN A WOUNDED LAND

Global Change / Global Health
CYNTHIA T. FOWLER AND ELIZABETH ANNE OLSON

IN A WOUNDED LAND

Conservation, Extraction, and Human Well-Being in Coastal Tanzania

VINAY R. KAMAT

THE UNIVERSITY OF
ARIZONA PRESS
TUCSON

The University of Arizona Press
www.uapress.arizona.edu

We respectfully acknowledge the University of Arizona is on the land and territories of Indigenous peoples. Today, Arizona is home to twenty-two federally recognized tribes, with Tucson being home to the O'odham and the Yaqui. Committed to diversity and inclusion, the University strives to build sustainable relationships with sovereign Native Nations and Indigenous communities through education offerings, partnerships, and community service.

© 2024 by The Arizona Board of Regents
All rights reserved. Published 2024

ISBN-13: 978-0-8165-5308-2 (hardcover)
ISBN-13: 978-0-8165-5309-9 (ebook)

Cover design by Leigh McDonald
Cover photographs by Vinay R. Kamat and Ververidis/AdobeStock
Typeset by Leigh McDonald in Warnock Pro 10.5/14 and Cassino WF (display)

Library of Congress Cataloging-in-Publication Data
Names: Kamat, Vinay R., author.
Title: In a wounded land : conservation, extraction, and human well-being in coastal Tanzania / Vinay R. Kamat.
Other titles: Global change/global health.
Description: Tucson : University of Arizona Press, 2024. | Series: Global change/global health | Includes bibliographical references and index.
Identifiers: LCCN 2023027590 (print) | LCCN 2023027591 (ebook) | ISBN 9780816553082 (hardcover) | ISBN 9780816553099 (ebook)
Subjects: LCSH: Ethnology—Tanzania—Mtwara Region. | Marine parks and reserves—Social aspects—Tanzania—Mtwara Region. | Gas wells—Social aspects—Tanzania—Mtwara Region. | Mnazi Bay-Ruvuma Estuary Marine Park (Tanzania)
Classification: LCC GN659.T3 K36 2024 (print) | LCC GN659.T3 (ebook) | DDC 304.209678/24—dc23/eng/20231023
LC record available at https://lccn.loc.gov/2023027590
LC ebook record available at https://lccn.loc.gov/2023027591

Printed in the United States of America
♾ This paper meets the requirements of ANSI/NISO Z39.48-1992 (Permanence of Paper).

For Kavita, Abhishek, and Aarti

CONTENTS

List of Illustrations ix
Preface xi
Acknowledgments xvii

Introduction: Conservation, Extraction, Dispossession 3

PART I. FRICTION

1. "Let's Build Our Nation!": Nation Building and Social Transformation in Southeastern Tanzania 47
2. "The Ocean Is Tired. It's on Leave.": Marine Conservation and Food Security 82
3. "In a Wounded Land": Natural Gas Development in Tanzania 118
4. "No Peace of Mind": Dispossession and Disenchantment 145

PART II. REPROACHMENT

5. "The Government Knows Best": Conservation, Extraction, and Environmental Justice 177
6. "Now We Are All Educated": Rethinking Environmental Subjectivities 213
7. "What Really Matters": Conservation and Well-Being 244

Conclusion: Conservation, Extraction, and Just Governance 275
Epilogue: Insurgency and Counterinsurgency 289

Notes 295
References 313
Index 339

ILLUSTRATIONS

FIGURES

1. Msangamkuu (Msemo) landing site in 2009 — 23
2. Main Street in Msimbati village in 2011 — 63
3. Three bungalows in Msimbati village — 65
4. Main Street in Nalingu village — 67
5. Grocery store in Msimbati — 98
6. Mkubiru village on a quiet afternoon — 109
7. Drilling for gas in Msimbati village in 2012 — 120
8. Gas pipeline along the Msimbati oceanfront in August 2014 — 137
9. The marine park's ticketing office and firebombed section — 138
10. VICOBA in progress — 151
11. A restaurant in Msimbati — 245
12. The baraza in Mkubiru village — 290

MAPS

1. East Africa and Tanzania — 4
2. The locations of the three marine parks in Tanzania — 6
3. Fieldwork villages in Mnazi Bay-Ruvuma Estuary Marine Park — 15
4. The Mtwara–Dar es Salaam gas pipeline — 19

PREFACE

GLOBAL EFFORTS TO conserve nature and prevent biodiversity loss have intensified in response to planetary-scale challenges: human-caused global warming, large-scale deforestation and habitat loss, mining operations, oil and natural gas extraction, and overfishing, among others. Accordingly, governments, intergovernmental organizations, international nongovernmental organizations, bi- and multilateral funding agencies, marine policymakers, scientists, and conservation interventionists have increased their efforts to promote marine protected areas (MPAs) as one of the interventions to prevent biodiversity loss in specific places that are often deemed as "hot spots." These ongoing efforts to increase the number of MPAs are likely to affect an ever-growing number of people across the world in terms of resource use as the rights and access to their sources of livelihood change. Hence, there are calls to document and understand how MPAs affect humans who depend on marine ecosystems, not just how MPAs affect or protect marine life. Policymakers and social scientists worldwide have repeatedly asked questions about the steps needed to ensure that MPAs successfully protect marine biodiversity while also safeguarding the livelihoods and well-being of humans who depend on the ocean and coastal ecosystems for their survival. However, natural scientists (e.g., marine biologists) have dominated the planning and implementation of MPAs using different intervention models.

Social scientists, including anthropologists, have only recently begun to create a niche in the marine conservation discourse and practice by calling attention to the importance of the "human dimension" in marine conservation. Their central message has been that if the ultimate goal is to conserve nature and minimize biodiversity loss, then paying attention to the needs of humans in conservation contexts is as important as focusing on nonhumans in ecological contexts. Such propositions are commonly presented in the social science literature as "win-win" ideals or outcomes—benefiting humans and marine life.

This book is about the human dimension of marine conservation in Tanzania. It has an added layer of complexity instantiated by the presence of a large natural gas extraction project in the core area of the Mnazi Bay-Ruvuma Estuary Marine Park in southeastern Tanzania—the country's second MPA and the ethnographic context of this book. The book's title *In a Wounded Land* is a plaintive phrase used by one of my key interlocutors to describe the environmental damage the gas project had caused inside the marine park. Over seven chapters, I illustrate what happens when impoverished people living in underdeveloped regions of Africa are suddenly subjected to top-down, state-directed conservation and natural resource extraction projects implemented in their landscapes of subsistence. I explore the role that state institutions (e.g., the Ministry of Livestock and Fisheries), stakeholder companies (e.g., Equinor, formerly known as Statoil), international nongovernmental organizations (e.g., World Wildlife Fund), aid agencies (e.g., Swissaid), global financial institutions (e.g., World Bank), and foreign governments (e.g., Canada and China) play in the siting and development of an extractive project in a globally recognized area of high biodiversity value, as well as the local responses to these interventions. I ask: How can the copresence of two very divergent and potentially antithetical projects—one designed to protect the environment and the other to extract resources from the same geographical area—be explained? Given the growing concern for preserving marine biodiversity, how can a natural gas extraction project be implemented in the same place? Is preserving marine biodiversity incommensurate with implementing a natural gas extraction project in the same area? How exceptional is this scenario? What is so troubling about it, and for whom? Could the copresence of the marine park and the gas project be read as emblematic of the neoliberal turn in conservation?

And if so, what are the implications for biodiversity conservation? More importantly, what sense do people living adjacent to these projects make of the copresence of a conservation project and an extractive project in their midst? These are some of the questions that animate this book, and I seek to answer them by drawing on ethnographic data collected over ten years (2009–19).

To this end, I provide ethnographic insights into some well-known theoretical concepts such as structural violence, social suffering, dispossession, governmentality, environmentality, incommensurability, social justice, environmental justice, food security, and well-being, among others. By examining the "nexus," i.e., the global connections, networks, and underlying ideological forces driving the expansion of natural resource extraction in protected areas, I also engage the politics of global governance over conservation initiatives and extractive projects. The book provides a social science perspective on the copresence of conservation and extractive projects, particularly in East Africa. Moreover, much of the social science literature on conservation and the extractive industry in the East African context pertains to terrestrial conservation, the tourism industry, mining (open-pit mining, artisanal mining, gold, diamonds, etc.), greenwashing, and so on. There is a growing body of literature on how extractive companies are greenwashing their environmentally harmful practices by supporting a conservation project on the side. The critical social science literature on marine conservation and the natural gas industry in the East African context is relatively new.

Drawing on rich case studies and vignettes, I show how state power, processes of displacement and dispossession, forms of local resistance and acquiescence, environmental and social justice, and human well-being become interconnected in the context of marine conservation and a natural gas extraction project. The book reveals the social implications of the copresence of a marine park and a gas project at a time when rural populations in several African countries are experiencing rapid social transformation brought about by internationally funded conservation initiatives and extractive projects.

When I began researching the problem through fieldwork in southeastern Tanzania, I believed that something improbable had happened. How could a natural gas extraction project be implemented inside an MPA recognized by the World Wildlife Fund and the UN? In due course,

I learned about the layered complexity that undergirded the copresence of these two projects. For one, blatant greenwashing was not at play because the marine park was implemented *before* the gas project. For another, the Tanzanian state had implemented both projects. They were state directed, not managed by an international conservation NGO (the marine park) or a multinational extractive company (the gas project). The people I worked with in the marine park villages displayed varying dispositions toward the two projects, depending on their imaginings, where they lived in the region, and whether the projects had directly affected them over time. Moreover, people's disposition toward the two projects changed significantly over the years. I document these changes in this book and reflect on their implications for marine biodiversity conservation, natural gas extraction, and human well-being.

Overall, in this book I tell a story of ongoing dispossession, structural violence, social suffering, and (in)justice at the margins, with significant historical, cultural, contextual, and analytic differences from similar stories told from the margins elsewhere in Africa and beyond. The book focuses on the local response to the marine park and the natural gas project, individually and as copresent interventions in the same area. More importantly, it examines how discourses and practices related to the two projects have shifted over the years with significant and continuing implications for local communities. Through this book, I hope to bring what happens in communities that are overly dependent on marine ecosystems for survival in the face of externally imposed extractive interventions to the attention of a global audience of researchers, policymakers, and scholars concerned with biodiversity and well-being.

I began my research in Tanzania in 2000 as a graduate student at Emory University with an interest in global health. As I describe in this book, while I trained as a medical anthropologist, I was drawn to the study of marine conservation in Tanzania following a chance introduction to the subject matter in 2009, during my first trip to Mtwara, in southeastern Tanzania. I had stopped in Ziwani (at the lake), a midsize village in rural Mtwara, about ten kilometers from Mtwara, a port city that the British colonial government of Tanganyika had planned and developed after the end of World War II. Ziwani lies at an important intersection, where the main road bifurcates—one leading toward Msangamkuu, a large fishing village near the Mtwara Port, and the other to

Kilambo, another large village on the banks of the Ruvuma River. The Ruvuma River is the "frontier"—the natural and political border between Tanzania and Mozambique. When I first arrived in Mtwara in July 2009, I read the dusty signage at the Ziwani intersection welcoming visitors to the Mnazi Bay-Ruvuma Estuary Marine Park. It sparked my interest in marine conservation. At the time, no signage indicated the presence of a natural gas extraction project in the region. As I would soon find out, the gas project was in the marine park's core area—only a few meters from the "pristine" beach that was advertised to attract tourists to the marine park. Artumas Group, a Canadian energy company, had drilled several gas wells and built a gas processing plant close to the beach.

Contrary to my initial assumption that a marine park was an unequivocally good intervention aimed at protecting biodiversity and something that local villagers would welcome, I was surprised at the vehemence with which residents of the area voiced their opposition to the marine park. "We just don't want the marine park. We want to have nothing to do with it. We don't even want to talk about it," they told me. I learned about the violence associated with their opposition to the marine park. The security forces beat up people and jailed many. I was drawn to the "why" question, in addition to finding out whether the marine park had a significant impact on food security and the livelihoods of the local people. Why were the local people so strongly opposed to the marine park? What had prompted their overall negative disposition toward the marine park? What was the likelihood that things would change over time? Was it a problem of inadequate awareness about conservation, which could be remedied through more judicious educational interventions? Was it a problem of poor governance that needed some critical reconsideration and a reset? Later, when I learned about the natural gas project, I was also curious about the local people's responses to it.

My initial ethnographic research addressed these questions, but my approach to understanding the problem was complicated in 2014 following the dramatic scale-up of the natural gas extraction project. It became impossible for me to ignore the presence of the gas project's infrastructure inside the marine park—the gas wells, the pipelines, the massive gas processing plant, and the expansive gated industrial compound (enclave) in its proximity—while I continued to document why local people were so strongly opposed to the marine park and its impact on their food security and livelihoods. This book, then, is an ethnographic account, a narrative of how things unfolded regarding the marine park and the gas project over ten years. It is about state intervention, power politics, and the social transformation occurring in Mtwara following the implementation of the two projects. More broadly, it is about state domination, dispossession, exclusionary politics, exclusionary techniques of environmental governance, and the negative consequences of all this for social life and human well-being.

The story I tell in this book about the marine park and the natural gas project in rural Mtwara does not have a clear beginning nor a coda; in fact, it starts somewhere in the middle, for by the time I began my research in rural Mtwara, the marine park had already been implemented for about eight years. What I have offered in this book is, therefore, a perspective, a representation of the research questions and issues I focused on and the theoretical and conceptual frameworks I used to gather and analyze the data. Needless to say, as with every ethnography, this book is a partial representation of what is, in reality, a far more complex and dynamic situation about the politics of conservation and extraction in Tanzania and East Africa and, more broadly, on the African continent. My primary goal in this book is not to offer a new theoretical framework for the study of marine conservation, resource extraction, or human well-being. Rather, I document and analyze the experiences of people who live on the margins in relation to these processes, so as to bring their experiences to the attention of a global audience. I hope to have adequately highlighted and brought to the fore the diversity of views held by marginalized communities in Tanzania, particularly those that are subjected to externally imposed conservation and extractive interventions.

ACKNOWLEDGMENTS

DOCUMENTING AND ANALYZING people's stories about their experiences with the marine park and the gas project over several years was made possible, principally, by the willingness and openness of the people of rural Mtwara to participate in my research. Over ten years, I conducted hundreds of interviews and dozens of focus group discussions with people from different villages inside the marine park. I did this in addition to engaging in participant observation and numerous conversations with my key interlocutors in the coastal villages. I learned about people's social lives, their everyday struggles, and about the multilayered complexities that people have to negotiate in their daily lives to "live in peace" (*kuishi imani*), amid deepening poverty, food and existential insecurity (*hali ngumu*) and the looming threats of violence and death from "terrorists" (al-Shabaab) on the Mozambican side (Cabo Delgado). I am grateful to the people of Mtwara for welcoming me into their villages, government offices, homes, and lives and for giving their responses to the questions I asked repetitively over the years—about the marine park, the gas project, and their well-being. I thank all my research participants for their patience in engaging with my endless questioning. I will cherish the friendships I developed with my key interlocutors over several years, especially in Msimbati, Nalingu, and Mkubiru. I have named several of my key interlocutors (some given names and teknonyms and some pseudonyms) in the book's substantive chapters, where I have documented their narratives. For reasons of confidentiality, however, I have not included photos of my interlocutors in the book. I want to thank my research assistants in Tanzania—Mariam Mohamed, Abdallah Njowele, Daniel Nyato, Arafa Abdallah, Mohamed Rajab, Gilbert Msangi, Enica Bwire, Tumaini Mtambo, and Abdallah Ntandu. And my field assistants from Sinde—Salum Mnovo and Rehema Njowele—who helped me with the logistics, interviews, and group discussions during various stages of the research. I would not have been able to build rapport with the residents of the marine park villages and gather the data I needed without my research assistants' help, commitment, sense of humor, and friendship. This book is as much a product of their labor as mine.

I am grateful to the government of Tanzania for allowing me to conduct research on a sensitive topic without any barriers; indeed, instructing regional and local government officials to provide me with all the support and cooperation I needed to conduct my research. I thank Mashuhuri Mushi and Sylvia Francis for always welcoming me into their office space at the Tanzania Commission for Science and Technology (COSTECH) in Dar es Salaam and for renewing my research permits every year with alacrity. I want to thank Rosemary Mwaipopo from the University of Dar es Salaam (UDSM) and Jackson Kaijage from Stella Maris Mtwara University College (STEMMUCO) for being there for me, as my research collaborators, and for guiding me through various stages of this study. I am also grateful to them for facilitating two productive knowledge mobilization workshops in 2017 on marine conservation and natural gas extraction.

This research would not have been possible without the generous funding I received from the Social Sciences and Humanities Research Council (SSHRC) of Canada in the form of two Insight Grants (430-2014-00248 and 435-2018-0448) and a COVID-19 Special Partnership Grant (1008-2020-0139). I am also grateful to the Canadian International Resource and Development Institute (CIRDI) for a generous grant in 2015, which made research on natural gas extraction and two knowledge mobilization workshops in Tanzania possible. Special thanks to Marie-Luise Ermisch, who patiently and cheerfully shepherded my research team and me through the process. I am also grateful to my colleague Philippe Le Billon for collaborating with me and bringing his expertise to the CIRDI-funded gas project study. I also want to thank UBC's Faculty of Arts for awarding me the Dean of Arts Fellowship, which made fieldwork in Tanzania possible during a full term in 2019. I want to express my heartfelt thanks to three world-class medical anthropologists: Mark Nichter, Marcia Inhorn, and Peter Brown, who have mentored me since 1992 and made me the anthropologist I am today. Thanks to Rashid Sumaila and Nathan Bennett for instilling the confidence that I can write a book about marine conservation, and to my colleagues in the Department of Anthropology, especially Gaston Gordillo for cheering me on and Andrew Martindale for expertly preparing the maps for this book.

My current and former graduate students Jan Lim, Younus Ahmed, Olivia Brophy, Josie Klein, Justin Raycraft, and Chung Liu have all contributed their ideas to this book during multiple readings of preliminary draft chapters and the manuscript. I thank them for their frankness in criticisms and for calling my attention to the limitations of my analysis, inconsistencies in my arguments, embarrassing omissions, and to the need to rethink, revise, and simplify what I want to say. Overall, their insightful comments have made this a better book.

The idea of writing this book originated in 2014 as I began to publish some of the data I had gathered in rural Mtwara on marine conservation and food security. I was eager to tell the story of what was happening in Mtwara—the empirical reality from an ethnographic perspective. However, I quickly realized that I needed to do much more fieldwork and data analysis before writing a book proposal, let alone a book manuscript. Funding from SSHRC for eight years made long-term fieldwork through intermittent visits, usually for three months during the summer break, possible. To plan and anticipate fieldwork over an eight-year period is a scholarly luxury that I was fortunate to enjoy. I am immensely grateful to SSHRC for supporting my research and the publication of this book.

At the University of Arizona Press, I thank Allyson Carter for her trust in me from the start, for encouraging me to work on the book manuscript. I thank Alana Enriquez for coordinating the manuscript reviews, Amanda Krause for expertly and calmly guiding me through the book's production process, Leigh McDonald for designing the beautiful book cover, Abby Mogollón and Cameron Louie for help with the book's promotion, and Kat Thomas for her excellent copyediting skills. I thank the three anonymous external reviewers for their frank criticisms, constructive feedback, and helpful advice on what I can do to push my analysis further and improve the manuscript. Thanks also to the Global Change / Global Health series editors Cynthia Fowler and Elizabeth Olson for their enthusiastic support for my book project.

Part 1 of the book draws on previously published material in the following articles: "'The Ocean Is Our Farm!': Marine Conservation, Food Insecurity, and Social Suffering in Southeastern Tanzania." *Human Organization* 73 (3): 289–98 (chapter 2); "Powering the Nation: Gas Development and Distributive Justice in Tanzania." *Human Organization* 76 (4): 304–14 (chapter 3); "Dispossession and Disenchantment: The Micropolitics of Marine Conservation in Southeastern Tanzania." *Marine Policy* 88:261–68 (chapter 4); and "Food Insecurity and Coping Strategies in a Marine Protected Area in Southeastern Tanzania." *Ecology of Food and Nutrition* 57 (3): 187–205 (chapter 2). I thank these journals' respective editors/publishers for giving me permission to use the ethnographic material. I have revised, updated, and reframed the text and references in light of the broader focus of this book—to present the data according to the period when they were collected. Part 2 of the book is based on previously unpublished data and analysis in that the material presented in this section is new. However, some overlap with the material presented in the previous chapters is inevitable. Earlier versions of these chapters were presented at annual meetings of the American Anthropological Association, Society for Applied Anthropology, and the Canadian Anthropological Society.

I wrote a significant portion of this book during my "stay-at-home" sabbatical in 2020 and 2021, which coincided with the COVID-19 pandemic, with all the public health restrictions, everyday anxieties, and fears that were associated with it. As my sabbatical arrangements and travel plans were scuttled, and everything, including conferences, moved online, the task of writing became increasingly lonely and challenging. Staying focused became additionally difficult. My wife, Kavita, kept encouraging me to finish the book no matter how many excuses I came up with to explain the delay, while our beloved feline family members, General Grey and Princess Kilu, kept me company and cheered me on. Together they guaranteed my well-being.

IN A WOUNDED LAND

INTRODUCTION

Conservation, Extraction, Dispossession

EAST AFRICA, COMPRISING Kenya, Tanzania, and Uganda, represents some of the world's most iconic and recognizable terrestrial and marine biodiversity hot spots. The region has also contributed significantly to advancing interdisciplinary scholarship on conservation, tourism, ecotourism, and extractivism.[1] In the popular imagination and in the media, East Africa is commonly associated with "wilderness" and the "African safari," expressions that conjure up media representations of the Serengeti National Park, the Ngorongoro Conservation Area, and Mount Kilimanjaro. These imaginaries often feature the Big Five charismatic wildlife species—elephants, lions, leopards, rhinos, and buffalos—and other wild animals that thrive in their natural habitats (Butt 2012; Nelson 2012). Along East Africa's coastline, also known as the Swahili Coast, the turquoise and azure-blue waters of the Zanzibar Archipelago (Unguja and Pemba Islands), the dhows with their lateen sails, and the alluring reefs of Mafia Island beckon tourists to the marine protected areas (MPAs)—marine reserves and marine parks.[2]

These idyllic representations exist alongside growing concern among environmentalists for the fragility of these biodiversity hot spots. Increasingly, environmentalists fear that poaching, unsustainable and destructive fishing practices, oil and natural gas extraction, and other human interventions could threaten the biodiversity of these locations. There is, therefore, a heightened sense of urgency to designate these areas as MPAs, with goals to conserve marine biodiversity, increase fish abundance, and improve the livelihoods of coastal communities through ecotourism. The governments of Kenya, Tanzania, and Mozambique have forged ahead with creating MPAs along the East African coastline, such as the Malindi Marine National Park and Reserve and the Watamu Marine National Park and Reserve on Kenya's coast.[3]

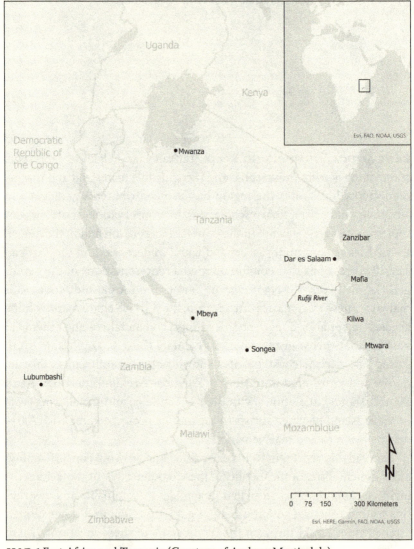

MAP 1 East Africa and Tanzania (Courtesy of Andrew Martindale)

Advocates of MPAs in East Africa and elsewhere have asserted that these MPA initiatives represent a so-called win-win opportunity for biodiversity conservation and poverty alleviation, arguing that MPAs help to protect marine ecosystems and increase fish biomass, or target species, and biodiversity, which in turn can improve the health and well-being of coastal populations (Cinner et al. 2014; Foale et al. 2013; Leisher, Beukering, and Scherl 2007). Others, however, have argued that win-win outcomes are challenging—and in some cases almost impossible to realize; in reality, unrealistic expectations, "compromise, contestation and conflict are more often the norm" (McShane et al. 2011, 970; see also Bennett and Dearden 2014; Fabinyi, Evans, and Foale 2014).[4] Still others have emphasized that there is nothing inherently good or bad about MPAs for coastal communities and that social impacts and outcomes vary depending on numerous factors. Expressly, Mascia, Claus, and Naidoo (2010, 1428) point out that "the social impacts of MPAs vary within and among groups and subgroups and across different indicators of social well-being." Simply put, MPAs are not static but dynamic interventions; they "are not introduced in a social, cultural, political, and legal vacuum," and their outcomes can vary greatly (Chuenpagdee et al. 2013, 235). Besides, as Jentoft et al. (2012) have emphasized, "MPAs are not politically neutral instruments for marine conservation. They interfere in people's livelihoods and social relationships. They tend to reconfigure the economic, social, and political action space of stakeholders, but in a way that does not necessarily provide equal opportunity for all" (2012, 195).[5]

Tanzania has fifteen marine reserves and three marine parks. The Mafia Island Marine Park (MIMP), established in 1996, is located approximately 120 kilometers south of Dar es Salaam—Tanzania's commercial capital—and 20 kilometers offshore from the eastern extent of the Rufiji Delta. It covers an area of 822 square kilometers (URT 2011b). The Tanga Coelacanth Marine Park (TACMP), established in 2009, is located on the northern coastline of Tanzania, north of Tanga City. The TACMP covers an area of about 552 square kilometers, of which 85 square kilometers is land and 467 square kilometers is water (URT 2011d).

The Mnazi Bay-Ruvuma Estuary Marine Park (MBREMP), which provides the ethnographic context for this book, was established in 2000. It is located in the coastal Mtwara Rural District on Tanzania's southern border with Mozambique, about 600 kilometers by road from Dar es

Salaam (see map 2). The park covers an area of 650 square kilometers (162,500 acres, or 65,000 hectares)—of which 220 square kilometers is land and the remaining 430 square kilometers is water—and is home to an estimated fifty thousand people living in twenty-three government-recognized marine park villages. A more detailed description of the marine park is provided in a later section.

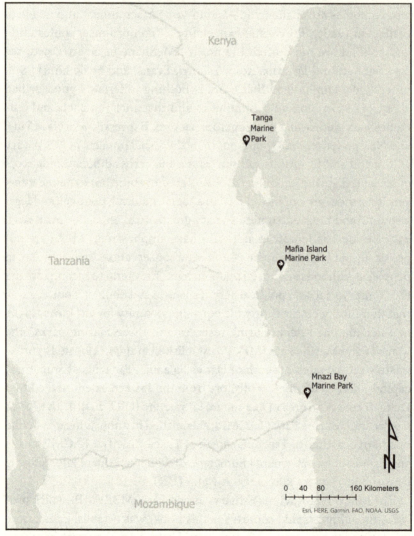

MAP 2 The locations of the three marine parks in Tanzania (Courtesy of Andrew Martindale)

This book examines the social complexities of marine parks. By social complexities, I refer to the interplay of factors such as social hierarchies, social identities, social relations, social exchanges, gender relations, community-level power politics, or the micro-politics, and perceptions of social justice that influence how people relate to and make sense of the conservation interventions implemented in their communities (see Fabinyi, Knudsen, and Segi 2010; Fabinyi, Foale, and Macintyre 2015).

The book explores the various social and cultural factors that determine whether a park is successful (or not) in preserving marine biodiversity and promoting human well-being. It also demonstrates how social complexities become even more entangled when the hydrocarbons industry begins to invest fossil capital and extract fossil fuels from sites legally designated as MPAs. Using the marine park in rural Mtwara as the ethnographic context, this book illustrates what happens when a large natural gas extraction project is implemented in an internationally recognized MPA. The book addresses questions such as: How did a legally designated marine park become the site of a large natural gas extraction project? What was the local people's response to the gas development activities and infrastructure development concerning the marine park? How did the gas project's presence in their midst affect local people's understanding of marine biodiversity conservation—did it challenge their environmental sensibilities? And if so, what did they do about it? What kinds of environmental and social justice concerns did these two projects raise for the local people? How did they negotiate their problems over time? In this book, I answer these and other related questions from an ethnographic perspective.

BIODIVERSITY CONSERVATION, EXTRACTION, AND HUMAN WELL-BEING

Conceptual approaches to terrestrial and marine biodiversity conservation have varied over the years—from "fortress conservation" to "community-based conservation" (CBC), and more recently, "new conservation" or "neoliberal conservation" of the Nature™ Inc. kind. The new conservation model is embedded in the ideology of neoliberalism and privatization. It privileges decentralization and the private sector's increased involvement in biodiversity conservation practices (Büscher and Fletcher 2020; Holmes and Cavanagh 2016; Holmes, Sandbrook, and Fisher 2016). All three models have their proponents and critics.[6] None is regarded as a panacea to deal with all the problems commonly associated with biodiversity conservation and sustainable development.[7] Moreover, in the real world, aspects of these models tend to overlap and vary over time because of multiple factors relevant to the local context. Specifically, as illustrated in this book, these models have been complicated by the implementation of industrial extractive projects (minerals, oil, and gas) in protected areas.

There are several overlaps between terrestrial conservation and marine conservation in terms of fundamental principles, styles of governance, types of responses, and the regulatory mechanisms that are put in place to conserve biodiversity (see Avery 2003; Carr et al. 2003). Yet, as Agardy, di Sciara, and Christie (2011, 226) have cautioned, "the uncritical application of models developed for terrestrial systems to the marine environment, which differs from land in terms of structure, scale, dynamism, and connectedness," poses some unique challenges, particularly with respect to scales and delineation of habitat boundaries. Still, it is useful to understand different conservation approaches, how these have evolved over the years, and the inherent problems in each approach.

Many transnational NGOs, government bodies, international protocols, scholars, and environmental activists have struggled to contend with questions such as: Should big-game trophy hunting and hunting concessions, which generate income for the government and local communities through hunting licenses, be encouraged to pay for projects that save wildlife and their environment? Put differently: Is it worth commoditizing wildlife and "selling nature to save it" through ecotourism (McAfee 1999; see also Holmes 2012; Igoe and Brockington 2007; Dempsey and Suarez 2016)? At the same time, others have asked whether "justice for people must come before justice for the environment" (Shoreman-Ouimet and Kopnina 2015, 320). In other words, if planners put too much emphasis on the social outcomes of conservation, such as human livelihoods and well-being, the primary objective of biodiversity conservation, which is to save species and genetic diversity, could be compromised (Martin 2017, 21).[8] Still others have asked whether the extractive industry should be allowed to extract minerals and fossil fuels from designated protected areas—including heritage sites, national parks, and marine parks—at all.⁹ If so, what are the social, economic, and political ramifications of such decisions? Who can allow or disallow extractive activities in protected areas? And finally, what are the environmental impacts of such decisions?

There are no clear answers to these critical questions because different countries have different laws that attend to these questions differently. Moreover, these laws tend to change over time. Governance styles also vary significantly across countries and under different governments. Therefore, the debates continue. In Uganda, for example, the Murchison Falls Protected Area is the site of an oil exploration project (MacKenzie et al. 2017). In Tanzania, the government boasts of having set aside between 40 percent and 42 percent of the country's terrestrial area (land base) for conservation purposes—including 16 national parks, 31 game reserves, 38 Game Controlled Areas (GCAs), over 30 Wildlife Management Areas (WMAs), and other forms of protected areas (Weldemichel 2020, 1501).¹⁰ At the same time, extractive activities in protected areas are legally allowed, provided the government has a stake in the operations (Holterman 2022). The state owns the subsoil resources, and historically, the state generally prioritizes resource extraction over protecting surface rights to land.¹¹

In Tanzania's southeastern region of Mtwara, there are two state-directed projects. One is a multiple-use MPA—the Mnazi Bay-Ruvuma Estuary Marine Park (hereafter marine park)—and the other is an extractive project, the Mnazi Bay gas project, also known as the Tanzania Petroleum Development Corporation (TPDC) project (hereafter, the gas project). Both projects are implemented in the same geographical space: the rural Mtwara peninsula. The "technological zone" (Appel 2019; Barry 2006; Willow and Wylie 2014) where the gas wells and processing infrastructure are located, and to which only certain people have access, is only a few meters away from the Msimbati-Ruvula beach—the park's prime tourist location—and the park's main office. A portion of the controversial Mtwara–Dar es Salaam gas pipeline is buried along the ocean front. In 2014, thousands of mature coconut and cashew trees belonging to local farmers were uprooted to prepare the fifty-foot-wide right-of-way for the pipeline. Moreover, a sprawling gas processing plant owned by TPDC, built on an eight-hectare site between Madimba and Mngoji villages, is also inside the marine park's boundaries.

SOCIAL DIMENSIONS OF MARINE BIODIVERSITY CONSERVATION

According to the UN's World Database on Protected Areas, which records MPAs submitted by countries, in 2023 there were more than sixteen thousand MPAs in the world. Some of these MPAs are as small as 18 hectares, and others as large as 1.5 million square kilometers, such as the Papahānaumokuākea Marine National Monument in Hawaii. Their numbers continue to grow as efforts are made to meet the lofty targets set by the UN Convention on Biological Diversity (CBD) at Aichi, in 2010. Target 11 aimed for the protection of "at least 17 percent of terrestrial and inland water, and 10 percent of coastal and marine areas" by 2020. The ambitious goal is to protect 30 percent of the world's oceans and marine ecosystems from human extractive activities by 2030. These initiatives and goals are part of the ongoing discourse on "crisis conservation" and the "great acceleration" in the so-called Anthropocene, or Capitalocene.[12]

While some marine parks are designated as multiple-use MPAs, others are designated as "no-take" MPAs, where fishing and marine extraction is strictly prohibited. MPAs are established with diverse goals, including "protecting marine biodiversity and habitats from degradation, replenishing depleted fish populations, regulating tourism and recreation, accommodating conflicting resource uses, and enhancing the welfare of local communities" (Fox et al. 2014, 208; Laffoley et al. 2019). Many of these MPAs are "real," in that the necessary governance systems and funding mechanisms have been put in place to monitor and implement their "protected status," but others are believed to be "paper parks" that exist only "on paper" to meet certain targets. Some of the existing MPAs have been regarded as "successful" in terms of achieving their initial objectives of protecting certain species of fish and increasing biomass and biodiversity, but others have been regarded as failures, particularly in regard to their social impacts on local human populations.[13] Unsurprisingly, there is a growing body of critical academic literature, which highlights the lack of serious attention to the human dimensions of marine biodiversity conservation in MPA design. This neglect, critics have argued, has led many projects to fail completely, or to deviate significantly from their original objectives.[14] Walley's (2004) ethnographic work on the Mafia Island Marine Park, Eder's (2005) work in the Philippines, and Bennett and Dearden's (2014) work on marine parks in Thailand provide illustrative examples of why MPAs that are not sensitive to the social and cultural aspects of conservation tend to fail in meeting their goals. Anthropologists in particular have argued for paying closer attention to the social and cultural dimensions of MPAs—especially when they are driven by nonlocal individuals' expert knowledge and political, economic, or environmental motives (Blount and Pitchon 2007; Eder 2005; Fabinyi, Evans, and Foale 2014; Gray 2010; Walley 2004).[15] Indeed, through empirical research in the Mozambican context, Rosendo et al. (2011, 64) have argued that if local residents in MPAs are presented with no-take zones (i.e., areas where fishing or other extractive activities are disallowed) as win-win solutions for conservation and livelihoods, they often feel that they have been misled. This can result in considerable frustration and antagonism within these communities.

The critical social science literature is replete with examples of the difficulties that local resource users face in MPAs. This is especially true in situations where MPA managers have alienated local communities and marginalized them further through top-down enforcement of restrictions and regulations. Concurrently, social scientists and marine biodiversity conservationists alike have argued that for MPAs to succeed, local communities' support is indispensable. In other words, unless there is significant involvement of local marine resource users and communities in the choice of marine conservation tools, MPAs may alienate local communities, thereby failing to alleviate poverty and promote sustainable resource use.[16]

Over the years, conservationists of various backgrounds have experimented with different conservation models or interventions to achieve socially and ecologically successful MPAs. Conservation interventions are policies, programs, and projects—often novel governance systems—designed to shape the behavior of specific actors and thus conserve natural resources (Mascia et al. 2017, 95). These interventions have involved restrictions, exclusions, the establishment of no-take zones, community-based conservation efforts, and a combination of these in protected areas. The results have been mixed—and in many cases inconclusive. The social impacts of MPAs continue to be poorly understood, and as Mascia et al. (2017, 108) note, "In many cases, conservation policymakers are shooting in the dark, not knowing which interventions work and which do not" (see also Gill et al. 2019, 349). Hence the need for more studies on the social and cultural dimensions of marine conservation that are grounded in local histories and contexts.[17]

This book explores the impacts of and the relationship between the marine park and the gas project in rural Mtwara and addresses specific questions about the copresence of these two projects. The ethnographic focus, more broadly, is on the estimated fifty thousand people who inhabit the rural Mtwara peninsula. The book documents how the peninsula's residents, most of whom self-identify as belonging to the Makonde (or Wamakonde) ethnic group or tribe (*kabila*), have been affected by (and have responded to) the two projects over an extended period. The other smaller ethnic groups that live on the peninsula are the Makua, Mwera, Yao, and Matambwe. As of 2023, the local residents live in twenty-three government-recognized villages of varying sizes, some of them created out of existing larger villages for administrative reasons. About ten of these twenty-three villages are coastal/seafront fishing villages, where many residents rely directly or indirectly on the ocean, as artisanal fishers and subsistence farmers, for their livelihoods. As I show later in this chapter, the majority of the households in these twenty-three villages, however, rely on subsistence agriculture and cashew and coconut farming (Mangora, Shalli, and Msangameno 2014). This book is a representation of the lived experiences, lifeworlds, and subjectivities of the people who live in the marine park villages, as they have been affected by the conservation and extraction projects implemented in the region. I address the larger sociopolitical matrix in which the two projects are embedded and their impact on the everyday lives of people whose cultural identity, well-being, and survival are intimately connected with the ocean and agricultural lands in southeastern Tanzania.

MARINE CONSERVATION IN TANZANIA —A BRIEF OVERVIEW

Compared with terrestrial wildlife conservation, the history and growth of marine conservation in Tanzania is relatively short and recent (Levine 2004). In the 1960s and 1970s, the government designated a few small marine reserves off the coast of Dar es Salaam, which existed without any active management of tourists or local fishers (Andrews 1998; Benjaminsen and Bryceson 2012). The catalyst for marine conservation was the Marine Parks and Reserves Act No. 29, ratified in 1994 (Levine 2007). It provided the legislative basis on which to establish MPAs in Tanzania, under the guidance of the minister responsible for the fisheries sector and the Board of Trustees of Marine Parks and Reserves. The act, under section 10, specifies the purposes of designating a marine park—mainly protecting biodiversity and promoting sustainable harvesting. Crucially, the act specifies that resident users should "be involved in all phases of the planning, development and management of that marine park or marine reserve, share in the benefits of the operation of the protected area and have priority in the resource use and economic opportunity afforded by the establishment of the marine park" (URT 2005, 8). As will become evident in this book's later chapters, this clause helps to identify the gap between the rhetoric of local people's involvement and empowerment and the reality of how MPAs are implemented in Tanzania.

The legislation for mainland Tanzania (which excludes Zanzibar) allows for the gazettement of three types of MPAs: marine parks, marine reserves, and national parks containing marine habitat. The overarching goal of these initiatives is to ensure the sustainability of Tanzania's aquatic biological diversity and ecological processes and to achieve this goal by ensuring the full participation of and consultation with local communities at all stages of the planning and implementation of the MPA. A key component of the legislation aimed at ensuring community participation in all stages of the MPA is the establishment of the Village Environment Management Committee (VEMC) and Village Liaison Committee (VLC), which play integral roles in achieving the MPA's goals. These important committees are constituted to fulfill a statutory requirement but tend to be meaningless if they are nonfunctioning or are dominated by the local elite.

The impetus to designate certain coastal areas as MPAs in the 1980s and 1990s came from international sources; the government of Tanzania subsequently endorsed them. Buoyed by encouragement from donor countries such as Norway (through its agency for development cooperation, Norad), as well as from global financial institutions, the World Bank and IMF, multilateral and bilateral development agencies such as the Food and Agricultural Organization (FAO) and United Nations

Development Program (UNDP), and conservation institutions, in particular the International Union for Conservation of Nature (IUCN) and the World Wildlife Fund (WWF), the government of Tanzania followed through with the idea of implementing MPAs as a strategy to encourage tourism and attract the foreign exchange it desperately needed (Andrews 1998; Gardner 2016; Walley 2004). The country's first MPA—the Mafia Island Marine Park—was formally gazetted in 1996. It was meant to serve as a prototype for future marine parks throughout Tanzania—an MPA where community participation in all stages of the initiative is seen as a prerequisite for its success and that "would encourage conservation *and* development through 'sustainable development' based on ecotourism" (Walley 2004, 2–5; see also Levine 2007, 564).

Tanzania's second marine park, the Mnazi Bay-Ruvuma Estuary Marine Park, which provides the context for this book, is located in the coastal Mtwara Rural District, on the southern side of Mtwara town, in southeastern Tanzania. The Ruvuma River forms the international border with Mozambique. The park is strategically located where the South Equatorial Current (SEC) meets the African mainland after crossing the Indian Ocean. It is the source point for the East African Coastal Current (EACC) and forms a critical node for the accumulation and dispersal of marine organisms for East Africa. Thus, the health of the reefs in the park is of critical importance to downstream areas in Tanzania and Kenya and adjacent areas in Mozambique (URT 2005, 17). North of the Ruvuma estuary are sand dunes of the highest quality on the East African seaboard, with plants species not found anywhere else in continental Africa.

The marine park is distinguished by two important characteristics. First, the terrestrial area is significantly larger than in other marine parks. This explains the large proportion of households inside the marine park engaged in farming for livelihood. The rationale behind incorporating so much land into the park's boundary was to constitute a buffer zone and establish control over human activities affecting the protected marine environment.[18] Second, the management plan requires the warden-in-charge to consider the well-being and livelihoods of the thousands of people who live inside the park and are directly affected by the park's implementation (URT 2005, 8). As will be discussed in this book's later chapters, the question of whether the warden-in-charge met the

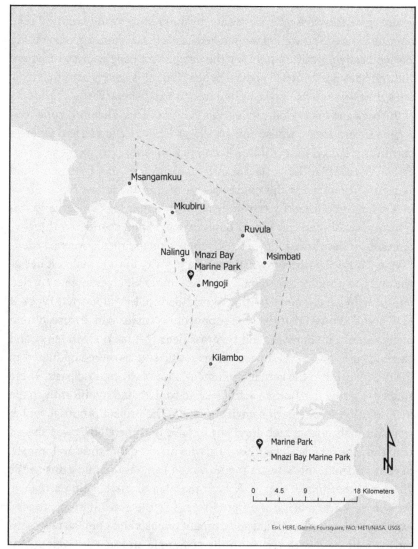

MAP 3 Fieldwork villages in Mnazi Bay-Ruvuma Estuary Marine Park (Courtesy of Andrew Martindale)

requirements of the management plan remains contentious and was at the core of some of the problems I documented during my fieldwork in the region.

The marine park's catchment area is divided into three types of zones. The first type is core zones, where no extractive use is permitted and where nonextractive uses are either prohibited or strictly limited (i.e., no-take zones). The second is specified-use zones, where a given activity is specifically permitted only for the designated beneficiaries or where cultural sites are afforded special protection. This covers artisanal fisheries zones, where fishing is limited to artisanal fishers who are residents of the park and engage only in legal fishing practices. The third zone type is general-use zones, where only legal activities are allowed and where a permit is required for outsiders to enter (URT 2005, 49).

The Mnazi Bay-Ruvuma Estuary Marine Park was first identified as a priority area for the conservation of global marine biodiversity in a report published by the International Union for Conservation of Nature (IUCN) and the World Bank in 1995. Soon thereafter, the government of Tanzania followed the report's recommendations by identifying Mnazi Bay-Ruvuma Estuary as a priority for marine park designation. The preliminary social and environmental assessments carried out prior to gazettement (with a World Bank/GEF–supported Block B PDF grant) showed that the area supports a complex and diverse system of coral reefs, mangroves, and seagrass beds (Muhando, Mndeme, and Kamukuru. 1999). Several baseline scientific studies were conducted in the region prior to the actual implementation of the marine park. These studies revealed that human activities had contributed significantly to the deterioration of the marine environment.[19] The project proposal, which went through several high-level consultations at the UNDP, was shared with the Mtwara District authorities, who believed that the development of ecotourism in the Mtwara region would bring economic gains to the district. Accordingly, they endorsed the idea of establishing a marine park in Mtwara. During the initial stages of the consultation process, expectations among regional government officials and political representatives were high with regard to the economic and social development that marine ecotourism would generate in Mtwara.

Following a series of consultations between the Marine Parks and Reserves Unit (MPRU)—headquartered in Dar es Salaam—and officials and representatives from local communities, the idea of starting a marine park in rural Mtwara received considerable support.[20] People believed that this initiative would ultimately improve the resource base—including fish abundance—and their livelihoods. In July 2000, MBREMP was gazetted as a Marine Park (Government Notice No. 285, published on April 8, 2000) (URT 2005, 6–7). The project was designed as a fifty-four-month, two-phased project, including an initial participatory planning phase (twenty-four months) followed by an implementation phase (thirty months).

The marine park officials laid out plans that initially generated high hopes among local communities in terms of the improvements they would see in their livelihoods through additional income from ecotourism activities and abundance of fish stocks. However, as will be discussed in detail in this book, these initial hopes and expectations soon fizzled out and the marine park became the target of sustained opposition from inhabitants of the park villages. Local representatives also realized that their lofty expectations were unrealistic and that they needed "to keep them consistent with the realities of what the project and the marine park could and could not provide" (Gawler and Muhando 2004, 7–8). The local situation became even more complicated starting in 2012 when the marine park's presence in the region was overshadowed by the implementation and dramatic expansion of the gas project—a topic I turn to next.

NATURAL GAS EXTRACTION IN TANZANIA —A BRIEF OVERVIEW

The marine park, as stated earlier, is also the site of a large natural gas extraction project. The gas project is currently operated by the French company Maurel & Prom (with a 48.06 percent stake), the Tanzania Petroleum Development Corporation (TPDC) (20 percent stake), and Wentworth Resources (formerly Artumas) (31.94 percent stake) as joint venture partners under the Mnazi Bay Production Sharing Agreement. Natural gas from the Mnazi Bay gas fields is fed into the National Natural Gas Infrastructure Pipeline (NNGI) that runs from Mnazi Bay to Dar es Salaam. Crucially, natural gas deposits were discovered in the Mnazi Bay area well *before* the government decided to implement a marine park in that location. In 1982, the Italian oil company Agip discovered natural gas in Mnazi Bay. The national media underreported this discovery at the time. The company drilled the "discovery gas well" known as Mnazi Bay #1 (MB-1) and conducted tests to demonstrate the commercial potential of the discovery. However, Agip suspended further development of the project, as the volume of gas discovered in the Mnazi Bay area was deemed commercially unviable for export or domestic consumption at the time. Agip subsequently relinquished the concession (RPS Energy Consultants 2019, 1–2).

In 2004, the Canadian energy company Artumas Group (Wentworth since 2010) acquired the license to the Mnazi Bay discovery well (MB-1).[21] Artumas drilled four more gas wells successively in the Mnazi Bay gas fields, on shore and near shore; these gas wells define the Mnazi Bay and Msimbati gas fields. Artumas's gas-to-power (GTP) project included the development of a gas reservoir, drilling and tie-in of sufficient production wells, an eight-inch gas pipeline to supply gas to an associated eighteen-megawatt electric power generation facility at Mtwara, a twelve-megawatt gas-fired power plant in Ruvula, and an upgraded power transmission system for local power distribution (RPS Energy Consultants 2019, 1–2).[22]

In the meantime, between 1995 and 1996, the MPRU of the Ministry of Fisheries, the government of Tanzania, the IUCN, the World Bank, the UNDP/GEP, and Fonds Français pour l'Environnement Mondial (FFEM) had identified the Mnazi Bay area as a prime location for the development of Tanzania's second marine park—the MBREMP (Gawler and Muhando 2004, 9). Consequently, the protagonists of the marine park were already aware that the proposed marine park would encompass an area with known deposits of natural gas that might one day be extracted for commercial purposes. In 2004, after Artumas was granted the license to explore and extract natural gas in the Mnazi Bay area, the scale of the operations was small and not considered a major threat to the immediate marine environment—although some marine conservationists did raise concerns regarding the gas project's detrimental impact on the coral reefs and marine life (see Gawler and Muhando 2004). Others saw the implementation of a gas development project (gas-to-power assemblage) inside the marine park's catchment area as a revenue-generating project that could directly and indirectly support the marine park's operations and the livelihoods of surrounding communities (see Tortell and Ngatunga 2007). The marine park's General Management Plan states: "The development of the Mnazi Bay gas reserves should continue and do so with minimum negative social or environmental impact, generating significant economic benefits to the region and beyond" (URT 2005, 26–27). Notably, the document does not mention how the two projects' potential incommensurability might be a concern; instead, the emphasis is on how the two projects could contribute to the region's economic development.

Excerpts from official documents reveal that expert conservationists were at odds regarding the benefits and dangers of implementing a natural gas project in the marine park's prime area. However, these documents

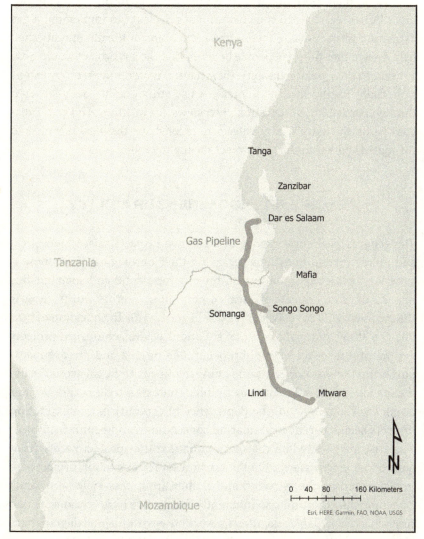

MAP 4 The Mtwara–Dar es Salaam gas pipeline (Courtesy of Andrew Martindale)

were published between 2004 and 2008, when the scale of the gas project was still relatively small. At this time, the project included five gas wells, a twelve-megawatt gas-to-electricity power plant in Ruvula, and a twenty-seven-kilometer marine and terrestrial gas pipeline to Mtwara town. The subsequent expansion of the gas project from 2012 onward transformed the nature and scale of the gas project's impact on the environment and its social and economic impact on the local communities.

Absent in all these documents is any reference to the local community's initial response to the government's decision to implement a gas extraction project inside the marine park. None of the documents shed light on whether the local people believed that the gas project would pose a threat to their personal safety, their natural environment, or, by extension, their livelihoods. In chapter 2, I use ethnographic data gathered through participant observation, interviews, life histories, and group discussions in the marine park villages to reconstruct the local response to the marine park and the gas project during the initial phase.

NEXUS AND INCOMMENSURABILITY

The geographical convergence of these two projects raises theoretical and policy-related questions regarding their ontological (in)commensurability or inconceivability and the environmental and social justice impacts of these projects on local communities. In other words, "how is the inconceivable conceived"? (Povinelli 2001, 320). The question of how one can study and make sense of situations where ecotourism projects and natural resource extraction occur side by side and are even supported by the state or the same company needs to be answered using the specificities of different ethnographic contexts (Davidov and Büscher 2013). On the one hand, the copresence of ecotourism and extraction projects seems paradoxical; marine conservation and ecotourism projects are implemented on the assumption that they protect nature from anthropogenic pressures. On the other, resource extraction projects are implemented on the assumption that they are necessary for economic development—they are also inherently destructive interventions, which result in irreconcilable and often irreversible environmental degradation. However, scholars who have studied the problem of incommensurability have argued that such coexistence is, in some cases, normal, easily explainable, and in congruence with the sentiments of national governments and the local populations (Davidov and Büscher 2013; Enns, Bersaglio, and Sneyd 2019). Indeed, as neoliberal ideology's influence on conservation and development policies grows, the copresence of, or "partnerships" between, conservation and extractive projects is increasingly common (Adams 2017; Holterman 2022, 113–14; Le Billion 2021).

Davidov and Büscher (2013, 13) assert that "the coexistence between ecotourism and extraction is not a fluke, an aberration, or a temporary paradox arising out of 'sustainable' and 'unsustainable' development trajectories vying for dominance in a particular place." Indeed, the authors contend that "beyond their seeming incommensurability, ecotourism and extraction are actively connected by 'real' actors, ecosystems, ethnoscapes, and a myriad of political-economic, social, and cultural flows" (19). They have gone so far as to emphasize the need to problematize and "defetishize the ontological and epistemological incommensurability engrained in the ecotourism-extraction nexus" (21).[23] In the same edited book, Dressler also notes that "the fact that ecotourism increasingly emerges adjacent to, or out of, various extractive industries, is neither contradictory nor coincidental" (255). In fact, MacKenzie et al. (2017, 329) point out that "paradoxically, tourism and extractive industries are often found in the same locations. Oil extraction co-exists with tourism in the national parks in Belize, Cameroon, the Democratic Republic of Congo, Rwanda, Ecuador, and Uganda." Using the example of oil exploration in Uganda's Murchison Falls Protected Area, MacKenzie et al. (330) have argued that "neoliberal capital accumulation as a conservation policy actually makes protected areas more vulnerable to industrial exploitation . . . because nature is commodified, allowing economic value and profitability of land uses within the PA to prioritise how nature is exploited within the PA" (see also Holterman 2014a; Holterman 2022).

This book reflects Davidov and Büscher's (2013, 3) call to "conceptualize and empirically analyse the 'ecotourism-extraction nexus' within the context of broader rural and livelihood changes in the places where both these activities occur" and anthropologist Anna Willow's (2014, 222) call for "the need for ethnographic studies of the tumultuous social and physical transformations resulting from, and produced by, an unfolding frontier of energy production that unsettles social, economic, and ecological landscapes."

In this book, I use the situation in rural coastal Mtwara as the historical and ethnographic context to examine the question of "incommensurability" in the ecotourism-extraction nexus. I also use it as a moot point to discuss the social complexities surrounding the two projects in the larger context of Tanzania's unique socialist past and neoliberal present and the southern region's status as a historically "backward" and neglected "Cinderella region of a Cinderella territory" and aspects of dispossession and environmental and social justice.[24] The book explores, from an ethnographic perspective, how two seemingly incommensurate conservation and extractives projects have differentially affected the social, cultural, economic, and political lives of the people who live on the rural Mtwara peninsula. To this end, the book examines the perceived impacts, individually and collectively, within and across different villages inside the marine park. It also examines how dominant discourses (at the national, political, and government levels) and alternative discourses (at the local, community, and regional levels) on marine biodiversity conservation, natural gas extraction, and development (*maendeleo*) have been articulated and circulated. In other words, I seek to analyze how these discourses about marine conservation and natural gas extraction have flourished, diminished, and shifted over the years.

The discovery of gas deposits off the coast of Mtwara in 2012 generated a discourse regarding the unprecedented prosperity that the gas bonanza would bring to the region and the country. By 2016, however, this discourse had given way to dashed expectations and local grievances of neglect and worsening poverty. Thus, I examine the significance of the shifting discourses and practices for East Africa, a region known for conservation, ecotourism, and extractive projects; for Tanzania, a postsocialist neoliberal nation-state keen to become a middle-income industrializing economy, and for Mtwara, the peripheral historically neglected frontier province.

In this book, I show how attention to social complexities at the community level can reveal diverse dispositions and responses to an extractive project that has dispossessed some, while benefited others. I demonstrate why we cannot assume that those dispossessed by extractive projects will indefatigably oppose them because of social or environmental injustice concerns. On the contrary, I illustrate, using ethnographic data, why those affected by an extractive project such as the gas project in Mtwara might support the project, despite experiencing state-directed violence and perceived social and environmental injustice.

DISPLACEMENT AND DISPOSSESSION ON THE PERIPHERY

As mentioned in the preface, I became interested in the social dimensions of marine conservation during an exploratory trip to Mtwara in July 2009. Abdallah Njowele, one of my research assistants in Dar es Salaam, had invited me to visit his family in Sinde village, on the rural Mtwara peninsula, which lies across from the Mtwara Port.[25] At the time, two privately owned motorized small wooden boats (*mitumbwi*) served as a ferry—plying the seven hundred meters between Kivonkoni, the landing site on the mainland, and Msemo, the landing site on the peninsula known as Ras Msangamkuu.

FIGURE 1 Msangamkuu (Msemo) landing site in 2009

A few motorcycle taxis (*boda boda*) and three-wheel autorickshaws (Bajaj) would be parked at both landing sites. From Msemo, a ten-minute motorcycle ride through the bush and coconut palm trees was the fastest way to get to Msangamkuu, the nearest village settlement, of about seven hundred households, bordering the Indian Ocean. The motorcycle ride to Sinde took between twenty to twenty-five minutes. Maharuf, my designated boda boda driver, carefully balanced the motorcycle, meandering through the sandy and dangerously slippery pathways created over the years while dodging the low-lying branches of endless rows of cashew trees, which locals had planted along the coast. Motorcycle accidents were common on these narrow sandy paths—partly because boda boda drivers often carried three or four passengers on the back seat, when they were legally allowed to carry one, and partly because the incoming motorcycles were difficult to see. However, they offered people the fastest mode of transportation to get from one place to another; the alternative was to take a privately operated minivan (*dala dala*) by road from Mtwara town—a journey that averaged an hour and a half to two hours.

During long walks with Abdallah through different coastal villages, I learned that until a few years ago, some of the villages on the peninsula had sat much closer to the oceanfront on the Mtwara Port side. The villagers, I discovered, had been dispossessed of their land, homes, and orchards and were resettled farther away. Park boundaries had been marked with whitewashed milestones, "TPA" (Tanzania Port Authority) written in black letters across their faces. Everything on one side of the dirt road now belonged to the TPA. Abdallah showed me what was once the village soccer field close to his mother's house. The goalposts were still standing, abandoned and overgrown with dry grass. The foundation lines of several houses, torn down during the resettlement process, were still visible.

In due course, I learned from some village elders that their dispossession and displacement were part of the Mtwara Development Corridor (MDC) project. This intercountry spatial development project involved the expansion of the Mtwara Port, with spillover effects on the people living in and around the peninsula.[26] The villagers lamented the poor compensation (TSh6500, or about $4 USD at the time) that the government had paid them for each coconut, mango, and cashew tree they had lost to the project. Here, it is essential to note that all land in Tanzania is public and vested in the president on behalf of all citizens. Furthermore, the Land Acquisition Act of 1967 grants compensation only for "improvements" of the land, not for the land itself. This has, over the years, disadvantaged customary rights holders—who have found it difficult to demonstrate the improvement of land value (see Pedersen and Kweka 2017, 219; Pedersen and Jacob 2017).

Daranga, a fifty-one-year-old resident of Msangamkuu village who served as village executive officer (VEO), provided a detailed rendition of how the MDC had displaced and dispossessed the villagers of their livelihood assets, which consequently led to food shortages and increased poverty in his village. He complained that when the compensation amount was decided in 1996, the government had based it on a law that was passed in 1972. The actual payments were made out even later, in 2008 and 2009; by then, the value of the Tanzanian shilling had gone down considerably, and the compensation was worthless. "People bought bed frames, mattresses, tables, chairs and finished the money. It only worsened the poverty in the villages," he told me. I explore the subject of compensation-related grievances in the marine park villages in detail in chapters 3, 4, and 5.

Hela, a forty-four-year-old VEO of a neighboring village, explained how the MDC project officers had told the villagers that once the Mtwara Port and the shipping container storage facility—a warehouse (*godowni*)—expanded, there would be plenty of employment opportunities for the community. These jobs never materialized. He lamented: "The years have just gone by, and people are becoming poorer. The MDC has done nothing good. It has only brought us hurt [*imeleta zulma*]. We have become increasingly poor. It has not helped us. They paid us very little. We were angry, but they said that they have no choice. They were simply following the law." These initial conversations, interviews, and narratives of dispossession, injustice, poverty, and suffering set the tone for my research over the next several years.

Through conversations with residents, I learned about the travails that people in some of the villages were facing because of the marine park's restrictions (*vikwazo*). The people included residents of Msangamkuu village, where I first started my fieldwork, which lies inside the marine park's buffer zone (see map 3). As I was new to the politics of marine conservation, I did not initially understand why nearly everyone I spoke to in the villages I visited expressed strong resentment toward the marine park. "We just don't want the marine park! We want it to go away!" they declared. People told me they were angry with the officials representing the marine park; they made emphatic statements to suggest that they would rather the marine park be discontinued and that the officials leave the people on the Mtwara peninsula alone, so that they could carry on with their traditional fishing activities and return to their everyday lives. Fishing, they asserted, had become less important in the park villages because of the park's restrictions, and farming had become stressful in villages where the land had been taken from the local people as part of the Mtwara Port's expansion.

Unpredictable and diminishing rains also made life difficult for those farming food grains. "The land is not fertile" (*Rutuba hamna*) was a common refrain. In such situations, there was an even greater dependence on fishing for survival—but the marine park authorities had placed restrictions on fishing and marine-extractive activities. With their food security threatened, an increasing number of women had taken to gleaning (*kuchokoa*) bivalve mollusks (clams), crabs, octopus, and other resources for food in the intertidal flats. They summarized their sentiments by reiterating: "What's the use of conservation if we have to remain hungry? The ocean is our farm. If you take the ocean away from us, what will we eat? Why has the government sold our ocean to the Europeans [*wazungu*]?" Later in this book, I use elements of these expressions to represent in detail the local response to the marine park during the early years of its implementation.

POVERTY, RESENTMENT, AND DESTRUCTIVE FISHING PRACTICES

Tanzania's decision to implement a marine park in coastal Mtwara was prompted not only in recognition of the area's high biodiversity value but also by the government's desire to put an end to destructive and unsustainable fishing and coral degradation practices—especially dynamite fishing, which was widely practiced in the region.[27] This form of fishing involves the use of dynamite sticks or homemade explosives, made by mixing kerosene and ammonium nitrate or sulfur, to kill or stun and capture marine fish. The immediate and long-term destructive effects of dynamite fishing on hard coral reef structure and marine life are lethal and often irreversible. Dynamite fishing can also result in serious physical injuries and invite social disapproval and public condemnation.[28] As will become evident in later chapters, dynamite fishing was one of the most contentious issues in the marine park villages where I conducted fieldwork. On the one hand, the marine park authorities blamed local residents for destroying the marine environment and shielding the perpetrators. On the other hand, local residents accused the park authorities of corruption, overzealous enforcement of restrictions, and the confiscation of fishing boats and nets—which perforce left local fishers, who were dispossessed of their fishing gear, to resort to dynamite fishing. Although I was introduced to the problem of dynamite fishing during the early stages of my fieldwork, it took me several months to appreciate its complexity. The following experiences were revelatory.

One bright afternoon in September 2010, Hassan, a fifty-one-year-old chairman of Msangamkuu, offered me a tour of the village while narrating its history. As we arrived on the beach, a speedboat roared in the distance, zigzagging through the waters at such high speeds that I thought it must be in hot pursuit. Hassan chuckled and said, "They're *pono* [soldiers in green fatigue, or *askari wa doria*]. They're just showing off. They're warning people not to go into the ocean and toss dynamites into the water to catch fish."

"Do people engage in dynamite fishing here?" I asked. "Of course!" Hassan said nonchalantly. What was new, he said, was the context in which people were continuing to use dynamite or homemade bottle bombs to do their fishing—despite the marine park authorities explicitly prohibiting the use of blast fishing. In chapter 6, I revisit the problem of dynamite fishing and other destructive fishing practices in the marine park villages and discuss how and why people's ideas and practices regarding destructive fishing practices changed over the years.

That same evening I had scheduled an interview with the chairman of Mnomo village, a sub-village of Msangamkuu. We met in the village government office, which was close to the beach. At the time, I was recording the oral history of the village and the life histories of some of its elderly residents. The chairman offered me his chair. As he pulled another from behind the desk, his cell phone rang, and he left the room without saying a word. Assuming he had to attend to something urgent, I waited. He returned an hour later, looking distraught, with a glaze in his eyes as he said, "My grandson has died."

"Oh *pole sana*, (I'm so sorry)," I said. "What happened?"

"He had gone to the ocean," the chairman said. "He drowned." Apologizing for being unable to do the interview, the chairman left the office. As I stepped outside, I saw a small crowd—men and women of all ages. They were huddled together and talking loudly about the tragedy that had just occurred. One of them said: "He had gone there looking for fish. He was helping those dynamite fishers [*wapigaji wa baruti*]. He must have stayed below the water for too long [looking for a school of fish where the dynamite fishers could toss their explosive]."

"Maybe he forgot he was under water," another commented.

"How old was he?" I asked one young man who was standing nearby.

"Just fifteen," he said.

I would soon learn that it was primarily young men who engaged in dynamite fishing, using rudimentary diving gear, including locally made glass face masks, to catch a lot of fish in the shortest time possible.

A VIOLENT VILLAGE

An abundance of literature demonstrates that conflict, and sometimes violence, is inevitable in establishing and maintaining terrestrial and marine protected areas (Duffy 2014; West, Igoe, and Brockington 2006, 260). In the context of the marine park, researchers have indicated how violent conflicts between the marine park managers and the local fishermen (the purported beneficiaries) threatened the park's long-term sustainability (Gawler and Muhando 2004; Robinson, Albers, and Kirima 2014). Nalingu, one of the large sea-bordering villages inside the marine park's catchment area, was emblematic of the complexities underlying the reasons local people do not support marine parks. In fact, during the marine park's early years, consultants who conducted baseline household surveys and midterm evaluations excluded Nalingu from their studies, citing the villagers' uncompromising and combative response to visits by outsiders. They depicted Nalingu as "a violent village"; villagers were described as uncooperative, using threats of physical violence against marine park staff, as well as against any outsider (especially foreigners) representing the marine park who entered the village (Malleret-King 2004; Malleret-King and Simbua 2004; Gawler and Muhando 2004).

Delphine Malleret-King (2004), who conducted the first socioeconomic baseline assessment of the marine park, called attention to the intransigence among the people of Nalingu to cooperate with the park authorities, stating that "no information could be collected on this [Nalingu] village because *villagers refuse to participate in Marine Park activities and have violently threatened the Marine Park team despite attempts to improve relations*" (Malleret-King 2004, 4; emphasis mine; see also Malleret-King and Simbua 2004, 4). In their midterm evaluation, Gawler and Muhando (2004, 14) also characterized Nalingu as a difficult village. They wrote: "Riots broke out in Nalingu after the visit of the District Commissioner in June 2003, and three people were arrested. When the villagers went en masse to the police to protest these arrests, 14 more people were arrested. They spent two weeks in custody and are now out on bail, waiting for their cases to come to court." As I discuss in chapters 2 and 6, such violence stemmed from miscommunication, misunderstandings, betrayal, fears of food insecurity, anger toward the marine park authorities for their overzealous enforcement of restrictions, and confiscation of fishing gear and boats.[29]

The people I spoke to, however, assured me that while the inhabitants of Nalingu were vehemently opposed to the marine park, they were unlikely to stop me from doing research in their village as I was not from the marine park or one of the international NGOs (WWF) involved in marine conservation in that area. Salum Mnova, from Sinde village—Abdallah's next-door neighbor whom I had hired as a paid field assistant in rural Mtwara—played a crucial role in facilitating my research in Nalingu and other villages on the Mtwara peninsula. Early on, Salum told me that he had already spoken with Issa, the chairman of Nalingu village at the time, about my research interests. I found the idea of doing research in Nalingu compelling but equally daunting in light of the villagers' well-documented and violent opposition to the marine park and their belligerence toward the marine park staff.

Apprehensive, I delayed visiting Nalingu for a year and continued my fieldwork in other coastal villages. Finally, in July 2011, I made my first visit to Nalingu. At the village office, Salum introduced me to Issa. After entering my details in the quintessential "visitors' book," I submitted the research permit that the government of Tanzania had issued to me to Issa.[30] He dismissed it with a wave to indicate that he did not care and asked me multiple questions about my intentions and my fluency in Kiswahili—which I had developed in Dar es Salaam during fieldwork over several years. He agreed almost immediately to offer his cooperation and encourage the people of Nalingu to participate in my research; he even volunteered to be interviewed that same day. Abdallah's and Salum's family connections, social networks, and resourcefulness—and their goodwill in Nalingu and other villages—were crucial in facilitating my research.[31]

BOOMTOWN VIOLENCE

In 2013, after the new gas discoveries in the region, the political situation in Mtwara took an unexpected turn. Mtwara, which was a historically neglected peripheral region (Liebenow 1971; Lal 2015; Seppälä and Koda 1998), suddenly became central to the national political discourse on development. The Tanzanian government had hurriedly prepared a draft national gas policy in 2013 in anticipation that the country would become a major gas producer in the East African region. Jakaya Kikwete, Tanzania's president at the time, spoke of Mtwara becoming a prosperous boomtown; in Mtwara, there was a flurry of infrastructure development, including laying the gas infrastructure. Pipelines were piled up on the roadside and guarded by government security guards with automatic firearms; numerous specialized trucks plied the dusty roads, carrying construction equipment, shipping containers, pipes, earthmovers, and building materials.[32] As Appel (2019, 210) has observed in the context of the discovery of commercially viable hydrocarbon deposits in Equatorial Guinea, the discovery brought in innumerable infrastructure and construction companies from across the world and also "countless oil services companies . . . offering seismic studies and exploratory drilling; plant construction and rig rental; well heads, casings, and completion services; transport and shipping, submarines, and fireboats; catering and accommodation; and the list goes on." The situation in Mtwara was similar to Appel's description of the "infrastructure" in Equatorial Guinea. Taking photos of the pipes that had been piled up along the road was, however, prohibited, as I found out when a guard with an automatic rifle suddenly appeared from behind the bush and told me politely but firmly in English to delete all the photos I had taken.

The discovery of large deposits of natural gas on and off the coast—and a $1.2 billion loan from China through its Export-Import (EXIM) bank—dramatically changed the landscape in Mtwara. Everyday conversations about regional development had also changed. New bank branches and luxury hotels with swimming pools were built alongside motels, lodges, and guesthouses in anticipation of international investors, visitors, and migrants. A logistics company had promptly taken over one well-known restaurant-hotel in the center of Mtwara town and converted it into a dormitory for its employees. Men with high-visibility orange suits and hard hats of different colors became a common sight in Mtwara town. On the rural peninsula, the physicality, materiality, and high visibility of the gas project's expanding infrastructure were impossible to ignore. An expansive gated residential enclave was being built to house workers, many of whom were from China, at the new gas processing plant in Madimba—with large banners in Chinese and English declaring the Chinese government's lead in the development of the gas project.[33]

My interlocutors were less interested in talking about the marine park and more eager to talk about the greatly expanded gas project and its impact on their lives. They explained that the gas project signified their hopes, aspirations, and expectations; they were optimistic about the benefits they would gain from the project, such as electricity, infrastructure development, and jobs. At the same time, they narrated their lived experiences—their frustrations, struggles, and successes—in the wake of the displacement and dispossession they had experienced because of the gas project. President Kikwete, cabinet ministers, and high-level bureaucrats who visited the region buttressed people's high expectations. Many people summed it up as election propaganda, saying that once the elections were over in October 2015, all the promises of jobs and infrastructure development would amount to nothing. As I will show in this book's later chapters, their skepticism was justified.

STATE VIOLENCE

On May 22, 2013, people across Mtwara protested the proposed 540-kilometer-long pipeline designed to transport gas from the Mnazi Bay gas fields to Dar es Salaam. The Tanzanian security forces responded with live ammunition, killing several protestors in Mtwara town (BBC 2013). That same night, in Msimbati village, the marine park's newly refurbished gate office was firebombed and destroyed. It was an obvious unguarded soft target. As of this writing, no one has been apprehended in connection with the firebombing; its motivation remains unknown.

Three or four hours after the office building was bombed, several military trucks filled with personnel from the Tanzania People's Defense Force (TPDF)—whose security forces were stationed at the garrison in Mtwara town to quell the protests—arrived in Msimbati village and unleashed physical violence and terror on the villagers. Men and women fled the village in the darkness with their children; many were caught and mercilessly beaten by the security forces. The TPDF's indiscriminate brutality shocked many villagers into silence—they had never imagined they would experience this form of state-directed violence in their village.

Haki—one of my key interlocutors, who was in his late forties at the time—told me that the violence had made him at once sad and angry and that he had become fearless of the government. He had vowed to take the cause of the people of Msimbati and Ruvula to the Tanzania parliament, in Dodoma. I detail this event and people's narratives regarding the state-directed violence in Msimbati village in chapter 3, which focuses on the politics of the gas project. Even two years after the incident occurred, when I asked some villagers about what had happened that night or who might have been behind the firebombing, many changed the topic, appeared uninterested in my question, or remained silent.

One afternoon in August 2015, as I began documenting and analyzing local perceptions and responses to the copresence of the marine park and the gas project, I sat down with a group of village elders on the veranda of a house near the entrance to Msimbati village. Jamali, an octogenarian living in the neighboring house, approached me and gave me a mock military salute; laughing, we talked about the marine park and the gas project. The other village elders who were present remained reticent or looked unconcerned. Haki, who had recently been elected as the chairman of Ruvula village (the site of the gas wells and the gas processing plant), was also present—but he remained a quiet spectator. Jamali, a staunch supporter of the marine park and the gas project, reiterated that the government had implemented these two projects in the best interest of the people of Tanzania.

"These are international projects meant to benefit everyone. The government is doing the right thing and we must support the government," he emphasized. I turned to the other elders sitting on the veranda and asked them what they thought of Jamali's proposition supporting the two projects. After some hesitation, a few of them spoke up nonchalantly. They had little to say about the projects in terms of environmental damage and environmental justice—but they had a lot to say about social (in)justice and the dispossession, displacement, and inadequate compensation they had received from the gas company for the assets they had lost to the project. After all, they said, it is an extractive project of national importance, which the government had implemented in a top-down manner. I surmised from their conversations that the gas project's presence inside an MPA was not as serious a concern for the people of Msimbati as I might have thought.[34]

A close analysis of the situation revealed that multiple factors were at play in determining why local residents did not oppose the gas project's presence inside the MPA—even though they had been subjected to brutal state-directed violence. Even those who complained about the gas project did so for reasons other than the fact that the project had damaged their natural environment, including the uprooting of thousands of planted trees. Their main concerns were economic in nature: dispossession, inadequate compensation, and negligible employment opportunities for local people on the gas project. Later in this book, I elaborate on this issue by juxtaposing the theoretical literature on incommensurability and the ethnographic data I gathered.

I continued with my research in other villages on the Mtwara peninsula. Most people in these villages did not see the marine park and the gas project as incommensurate or paradoxical—inconceivable—development initiatives. Instead, they saw both as initiated and managed by one entity: the state/government (*serikali*). The ruling party, Chama Cha Mapinduzi (Party of the Revolution), had historically persuaded Tanzanian citizens to support and obey rather than oppose its infrastructure projects and development initiatives. People in the villages I surveyed had many reasons for not supporting the marine park, including the restrictions the park authorities imposed on the villagers, which they believed were unreasonable. By contrast, they were more positively inclined toward the gas project, which they thought—at least initially—would bring prosperity to their region.

CONSERVATION AND WELL-BEING

My interest in documenting and analyzing local understandings and experiences of well-being in the context of the marine park and the gas project emerged from a deeper analysis of the narratives of suffering that the people of Msimbati and Nalingu communicated to me during my fieldwork in the coastal villages. Their narratives contrasted with the statements made in the marine park's General Management Plan regarding the priority that would be given to community participation and well-being (URT 2005, 8). At the time, several of my key interlocutors told me they felt constrained by the marine park and the gas project through displacement and dispossession and that they felt their lives had worsened over the years. The burgeoning literature on conservation, well-being, and ecosystems helped me to sharpen my focus on what people believed was most important for living a life that they felt was fulfilling, including the steps they took to ensure their well-being at a time when the marine park and the gas project had disrupted the lives and livelihoods of many on the peninsula.

The impetus to study human well-being and human capabilities, rather than the causes underlying human poverty and underdevelopment, came from scholars in the United Kingdom who proposed that human well-being should be studied as a multidimensional concept, that it should take into account objective conditions of people and their subjective assessments of their lives—including how much emphasis they put on freedom—what they value doing and being.[35] Marine conservation research conducted by social scientists has demonstrated the usefulness of the concept of well-being in making sense of why people do what they do and what they value most—freedoms and their hopes and aspirations for the future (Abunge, Coulthard, and Tim Daw 2013; Coulthard,

Johnson, and McGregor 2011; Mahajan and Daw 2016). Other scholars, particularly Woodhouse et al. (2015, 2017) and Woodhouse and McCabe (2018), have demonstrated the usefulness of using the three-dimensional concept of well-being to study and better understand how conservation interventions affect communities. Since then, a profusion of studies have sought to demonstrate the usefulness of certain methodologies for data collection on well-being and even quantifying well-being in conservation contexts (see Baker et al. 2021; Ban et al. 2019; Nowakowski et al. 2023; Rasheed 2020). I researched local understandings of well-being in eight of the twenty-three marine park villages, and I discuss the theoretical literature and my findings in the book's last chapter.

HISTORICAL AND ETHNOGRAPHIC CONTEXT

An Overview of East Africa's Swahili Coast

This book concerns East Africa, in particular the coastal region known as the Swahili Coast. The Swahili Coast and its inhabitants continue to be the focus of historical, anthropological, archeological, and linguistic studies and debates—adding to a deeper appreciation of the region's role in world history, long-distance trade, and slavery. As the anthropologist-historian John Middleton (1992, ix) has clarified: "We cannot understand the Swahili present without understanding their past, nor can we understand that past without an ethnographic knowledge of the present." Historically, those living along the Swahili Coast have been referred to as the *waSwahili*, the "people of the coast." However, not everyone or every community that lives in this polyethnic geographical region identify themselves as Swahili (Caplan 2007). Islam provides a sense of unified cultural identity (Middleton 1992, 162)—but here too, not all Muslims who live on the Swahili Coast identify themselves as Swahili (Eastman 1994, 86; Keshodkar 2010, 2013; Horton and Middleton 2000; McIntosh 2009; Middleton 1992).

Over the years, especially since the 1980s and 1990s, the Swahili Coast has been an important region for international tourism. However, a consistent theme in the scholarly literature on international tourism is the perceived and real imbalances in tourism's benefit to the local people, given that tourism in the region is "controlled by European entrepreneurs and their African partners, who are virtually never Swahili" (Middleton 1992, 53; see also Walley [2004] and Keshodkar [2013] for similar comments on tourism on Mafia Island and Zanzibar).

Mtwara and Its Peoples

The southeastern region of Tanzania, which forms part of the Swahili Coast, comprises two coastal provinces: Lindi and Mtwara. In 1971, the Lindi-Mtwara Region (*mkoa*) became two separate regions, or provinces. The Mtwara Region is divided into seven administrative districts—Mtwara Urban, Mtwara Rural, Masasi Urban, Masasi Rural, Newala, Tandahimba, and Nanyumbu. The Mtwara Region borders the Lindi Region to the north, the Ruvuma Region to the west, and the Indian Ocean to the east and is separated by the Ruvuma River from Mozambique in the south.

In 2012, the population of the Mtwara Region was 1,270,854, and the population of the Mtwara Rural District was 228,003.[36] The overall socioeconomic profile of Mtwara Rural is very poor; the area lacks access to basic infrastructure and resources, and nearly 40 percent of the population of Mtwara Rural lives below the basic needs poverty line (URT 2016; see also Becker 2019). Only 4.1 percent of rural households had access to piped water, and more than 92 percent of the population used traditional pit latrines. Of the twenty-nine regions that constitute Tanzania (including Zanzibar), the Mtwara Region has the highest percentage of its population working in agriculture of any region in the country, with 87 percent of individuals ages ten and above primarily employed in agriculture (URT 2016). Mostly, agriculture is practiced for subsistence and supplemented by only a few cash crops, particularly cashews and coconuts. In 2012, infant mortality rate had reached 45.2 deaths per 1,000 live births. Mtwara had one of the lowest school-attendance rates in the country, with only 18.8 percent of individuals over age five attending school. Given Mtwara Region's unimpressive statistical profile, it is unsurprising that the region is commonly described in the literature as "the periphery" (cf. Lal 2015; Seppälä and Koda 1998), with its historic, economic, and social importance often neglected in the past and current literature.

The waMakonde Peoples of Tanzania

The Makonde, or waMakonde, people constitute the majority population in the Mtwara Region. They are the third largest of the 120 ethnic groups of Tanzania and commonly trace their ancestral origins to the Makonde (spelled Maconde in the academic literature) from Mozambique (Msumbiji), who live on the southern side of the Ruvuma River. Both groups, from either side of the Ruvuma River, are Bantu-speaking—traditionally matrilineal but patrilocal in practice (Liebenow 1971). The Maconde people from the Mozambican side inhabit the northeastern part of Mozambique, in the Cabo Delgado Province. They are mainly concentrated in the Piano Alto de Mueda region, a high plateau rising to about six hundred meters above sea level from the southern bank of the Rovuma River. The Makonde people who live on the Tanzanian side are also concentrated along the Ruvuma River and have their traditional homeland on a similar high plateau in the Mtwara Region, known as the Makonde Plateau (Sætersdal 1999).

In Tanzania, the Makonde are concentrated in the Mtwara and Newala Districts. They are commonly divided into three main subgroups: the Nnima, who live in the northwest of the plateau; the Ndonde, who live on the southwest of the plateau; and the Maraba, who live near the Ruvuma River and along the coast, as well as on the eastern part of the plateau. The Maraba are commonly associated with the Swahili coastal culture, which determines their cultural and historical identity, along with their Makonde origin. This is reflected in their religion (Islam), fishing practices, dress, and language, which is strongly influenced by Kiswahili (Krall 2005, 1).[37] Most Makonde people living in villages where I conducted fieldwork trace their ancestral origins to Mozambique; many are believed to have settled on the Tanzanian side following raids conducted by the Ngoni from southern Africa that prompted many to flee across the river. The Mozambican War of Independence from Portugal (1964–74), known as the "dirty war" (Nordstrom 1997), also contributed to an influx of migrants and refugees. The majority of Makonde people who live in the coastal villages on the Tanzanian side are engaged in small-scale farming and subsistence fishing. They grow maize, paddy, cassava, sorghum, and different types of lentils and peas, but also cashews and coconuts, widely recognized cash crops. Artisanal fishing is a significant activity but a secondary occupation in most households (Malleret-King and Simbua 2004; Mangora, Shalli, and Msangameno 2014, 271). Throughout my fieldwork, I came across only a few individuals who said that their primary occupation and sole source of livelihood was fishing, even in sea-bordering villages.[38] Although farming was the primary occupation for the vast majority of the local residents (only a minimal number of people had changed their primary occupation), people in the park villages were engaged in more than thirty different occupations. There were masons, carpenters, tailors, cashew traders, small business owners, shopkeepers, schoolteachers, street vendors, charcoal makers, boda boda drivers, bicycle mechanics, and so on (Kamat et al. 2019). Baseline surveys conducted in the proposed marine park villages revealed that more than 85 percent of the households were involved in farming. Artisanal fishing, while a substantial livelihood occupation in seafront villages, was a secondary occupation. Nonetheless, many of my older interlocutors told me that although farming was their primary occupation, they had started their lives as fishers.

Most marine park villagers were Muslim. Some interlocutors were devout, praying five times a day as prescribed by the tenets of Islam. Many of these individuals were deeply involved in the Eid al-Fitr celebrations marking the end of the holy month of Ramadan as well as the Maulidi festival marking the birth of prophet Muhammad. During my fieldwork, I attended several Maulidi celebrations, which brought the entire village together in one place. Children were given special attention during these celebrations and showered with gifts. Initially, I served as the unofficial photographer at such events. My role eventually became redundant as locals began inviting professional photographers and videographers from Mtwara town to document the momentous occasions. This was also true for weddings. Those I attended were by Tanzanian rural standards lavish—with full-fledged music systems and professional videographers.[39]

In summary, this book documents the shifting discourses and practices about marine conservation and natural gas extraction in the Mtwara Region, as I documented them over ten years. Instead of providing an overarching theoretical framework encompassing all the key concepts I wish to engage with in the book, I have discussed the empirical data in different chapters by drawing on one or two key concepts, such as dispossession, incommensurability, environmentality, well-being, and so on. Nonetheless, conservation, and extraction-related accumulation by dispossession, and well-being in the Mtwara Region are discussed throughout. Therefore, each substantive chapter may be read as a stand-alone or in conjunction with the others. Each chapter raises key questions and answers them in the context of contemporary anthropological and interdisciplinary scholarship through narratives, vignettes, and case histories contextualized by ethnographic data.

The overarching argument I make in this book is that the win-win goals of marine conservation through MPAs are laudable but often fail to achieve their objectives because of the challenges posed by social complexities. Therefore, those who implement MPAs must anticipate and continuously negotiate social complexities to ensure that the goals of biodiversity conservation are pursued in conjunction with human well-being. While this is not an original argument, it still bears reiterating and reemphasizing given the gaps that are commonly observed between statements of intent in MPA policy documents and master plans and their actual implementation on the ground (see Bennett and Dearden 2014; Christie 2004; Fabinyi, Evans and Foale 2014; Walley 2004). Sustainable marine biodiversity conservation demands a thorough understanding of the social and political complexities that affect the everyday lives of those who depend on the ocean and marine resources for their livelihoods and social identity. A governance strategy developed to be responsive to people's livelihoods, food security concerns, gender relations, social hierarchies, aspirations, and well-being is, therefore, indispensable for sustainable marine biodiversity conservation.[40]

An anthropologically grounded ethnographic approach is key to developing insights into the social complexities that often influence sustainable biodiversity conservation and extractive interventions (see also Büscher and Davidov 2016; Gilberthorpe and Rajak 2017; Walley 2004). Attention to social complexities foregrounds the heterogeneity of communities, the micropolitics of social relations, and community-level diversity in subjectivities and responses—all of which are key to the successful implementation of marine conservation interventions.

Exploration and extraction of oil, gas, and minerals in protected areas is legal in Tanzania, provided certain conditions are met (Holterman 2022; MacKenzie et al. 2017; Pedersen et al. 2016). Nonetheless, the immediate and long-term impacts of environmental damage, dispossession, and displacement of local people and land alienation cannot be downplayed, ignored, or justified on the grounds that national interests are incontrovertible. These undesirable environmental and social impacts should be anticipated, problematized, ethnographically documented, and mitigated to ensure that those directly affected by an extractive project are provided the environmental and social justice they deserve—a form of justice that includes recognition, dignity, fair compensation, preferential employment opportunities, alternative livelihood opportunities, food security, and hope. In sum, good or just governance should be a fundamental tenet in the rendering of environmental and social justice.

CHAPTER OUTLINES

Chapter 1, *"Let's Build Our Nation!": Nation Building and Social Transformation in Southeastern Tanzania,* highlights the broader historical and political context in which the country's conservation and extractive sectors emerged. This chapter also provides insight into how inhabitants of coastal villages in rural Mtwara experienced different periods of social transformation—reflecting different ideologies and styles of governance under five different presidents who governed the country from 1961 to 2021. In this chapter, which has two sections, I discuss why an appreciation of Tanzania's socialist past and its transition in the 1990s to a multiparty democracy and the adoption of neoliberal economic policies is critical for our understanding of the shifting discourses and practices related to conservation and the resource extraction sectors. I also focus on people's articulations of hopes and trepidations for the present and the future in the context of their remembered past.

Chapter 2, *"The Ocean Is Tired, It's on Leave.": Marine Conservation and Food Security,* examines the local response to the marine park in rural Mtwara during the early years of its implementation. This chapter also examines the impact of the marine park's early interventions on food security in the coastal villages. The chapter has two sections. The first section elaborates on the general ethos in the park villages—the miscommunications, resentments, and violent confrontations that characterized the marine park following its implementation in 2000.

The second section focuses on local perceptions of food availability and accessibility, changes in modes of food acquisition, experiences of food insecurity (food deprivation, insufficient food), and the potential health impact of food insecurity—particularly on women and young children—following the implementation of the marine park and its encompassing territorialization, restrictions, and regulations.

Chapter 3, *"In a Wounded Land": Natural Gas Development in Tanzania*, provides a brief history of the origins and development of the gas project, located in the same geographical area as the marine park. It provides the background information to questions such as: How did the marine park become the site for a gas project? What were the antecedents that resulted in this decision? The chapter examines the gas project's social impact on the people who live on the rural Mtwara peninsula—and, more broadly, on the people of the Mtwara Region. Through ethnographic data, I highlight differing perspectives on the gas project, including lived experiences of exclusion, indignation, humiliation, injustice, powerlessness, or, in some cases, an ambivalent attitude toward the project and its significance to the project-affected people. I illustrate how the process and scale of the gas project and the speed with which it was implemented represents what scholars have variously called "accumulation by dispossession," "accumulation by displacement," and a "regime of dispossession"—as well as similar processes in neoliberal environments.

Chapter 4, *"No Peace of Mind": Dispossession and Disenchantment*, explores in greater depth the micropolitics of the implementation of the marine park at a time when the gas project was being significantly expanded, compounding the ongoing processes of displacement and dispossession in the marine park villages. By juxtaposing the narratives of marine park supporters with those of detractors, the chapter highlights inter- and intra-village perceptions of the marine park's impacts and significance. Highlighting the micropolitics of local responses to the marine park illustrates the importance of reiterating that communities are heterogeneous, constitutive of different voices and perspectives on key issues and mundane, everyday concerns. Thus, the chapter's focus is on "social diversity within the community" and the village communities' "internal differentiation" as it relates to marine conservation.

Chapter 5, *"The Government Knows Best": Conservation, Extraction, and Environmental Justice*, examines elements of environmental and social justice embedded in people's everyday discourses and elicited narratives by centering people's understandings of the notion of "incommensurability" (*kutowezekana*) or "incompatibility" (*kutokubaliana*). This chapter also examines individuals' understandings of, and responses to, perceptions of environmental (in)justice and social (in)justice, specifically in relation to the gas project implemented inside the marine park. The chapter examines why environmental justice pertaining to the gas project did not appear as a priority concern among most of the people on the rural Mtwara peninsula. It also examines why an overwhelming number of people in the study area did not see the marine park and the gas project as incommensurate. The chapter concludes by emphasizing the need for increasing awareness of land issues among the people who live in park villages to minimize potential misunderstandings and conflicts over matters of compensation and the sale of land.

Chapter 6, *"Now We Are All Educated": Rethinking Environmental Subjectivities*, focuses on how discourses and practices surrounding marine conservation in the coastal villages of rural Mtwara have changed and shifted since the marine park was implemented in 2000. Beginning sometime in mid-2016, the discourse began to shift to one of either general indifference toward the marine park (i.e., there was no overt resistance) or of support for the project marked by a ubiquitous refrain: "Now we are all educated," or "Now we have understood the importance of marine conservation and recognize the benefits of caring for the environment." This chapter analyzes and explains the underlying meaning and significance of these expressions and considers what factors might have prompted this discursive shift in people's discussions surrounding the marine park.

Chapter 7, *"What Really Matters": Marine Conservation and Well-Being*, examines local conceptions and experiences of well-being (*ustawi*) in the context of the marine park in rural Mtwara. Through personal narratives, this chapter explores whether the marine park has played a meaningful role in improving people's lives, particularly their well-being. The chapter concludes by emphasizing some of the methodological limitations of studying well-being in rapidly changing contexts. At the same time, it validates the importance of human well-being, in all its dimensions, for the success of marine conservation interventions and human development on a sustainable basis.

The conclusion, *Conservation, Extraction, and Just Governance*, reiterates some of the key issues emerging from the substantive chapters surrounding the "ecotourism-extraction nexus" and the "incommensurability" of the copresence of the marine park and the natural gas project in the same geographical space. In doing so, this chapter summarizes the book's contributions to scholarship and calls attention to the way forward in making marine ecosystem conservation interventions and extractive projects sensitive to, and integrative of, environmental and social justice. In discussing the way forward, the chapter elaborates on just conservation and just governance, which entails giving importance to local understandings of justice, human well-being, and capabilities—what people value most in their lives beyond food and economic security.

In a brief epilogue, *Insurgency and Counterinsurgency*, I use vignettes to describe my departure from the field in September 2019 and my return three years later (post–COVID-19 pandemic) in August 2022 to resume fieldwork and document the changes that had taken place in the marine park villages. The epilogue introduces a potential new line of research: how the threat of cross-border insurgency and terrorist attacks by al-Shabaab from the Mozambican side was affecting peoples' livelihoods, food security, and well-being.

PART I
FRICTION

1

"LET'S BUILD OUR NATION!"

Nation Building and Social Transformation in Southeastern Tanzania

TANGANYIKA (TANZANIA SINCE 1964) was part of German East Africa from 1885 to 1918. It became a British League of Nations mandate between 1922 and 1946 and a British United Nations Trusteeship Territory between 1946 and 1961. On December 9, 1961, Tanganyika gained independence from the British, and in 1964 it merged with Zanzibar, a former British protectorate located thirty-seven kilometers (twenty-three miles) from the coast of the mainland, to become the United Republic of Tanzania (Lal 2015).[1] Mainland Tanzania shares its border with eight other countries—Kenya, Uganda, the Democratic Republic of Congo, Rwanda, Burundi, Malawi, Zambia, and Mozambique. The country is administratively divided into thirty-one regions (*mikoa*), and each region is further divided into districts (*wilaya*) and wards (*kata*).

Tanzania is a multiethnic, multicultural, and multilingual country; Kiswahili is the official language spoken by all Tanzanians. Compared with some of its immediate neighbors, in particular Kenya, Uganda, and Rwanda, Tanzania has prided itself on the peaceful coexistence of people with different ethnic and religious identities. As Lofchie (2014, 10) points out, "Tanzanians do not perceive or describe their political process as one in which ethnic communities are pitted in win-lose adversarial relationships against one another" (see also Kelsall 2002, 598).

Although Tanzania is a multiparty constitutional democracy, the ruling party—Chama Cha Mapinduzi (CCM)—the then Tanganyika African National Union (TANU)—has remained in power since the country's independence in 1961. CCM has singularly formulated policies related to all sectors of the economy through centralized control, including within the natural resources sector—encompassing conservation, tourism, and the extractive sector (Nelson, Nshala, and Rodgers 2007). Opposition political parties remain weak and underresourced and under constant threat of being banned from holding rallies and participating in national elections. This was especially the case during Tanzania's former president John Magufuli's time in power—from November 2015 to his death in March of 2021 (Cheeseman, Matfess, and Amani 2021).[2]

This chapter provides a brief overview of Tanzania's political, economic, and social history, highlighting the broader historical and political context in which the country's conservation and extractive sectors have emerged and transformed over time. It sheds light on how inhabitants of the coastal villages that are now inside the marine park in rural Mtwara experienced different periods of social transformation in Tanzania—reflecting different ideologies, economic and social policies, and styles of governance under five other presidents who governed the country from 1961 to 2021. The chapter also considers how people's experiences with government policies in the past inform their current experiences with top-down interventions, such as the marine park and the gas project in their region.

In this two-part chapter, I demonstrate why an understanding of Tanzania's socialist past, its transition from a one-party rule to a multiparty democracy, and its adoption of neoliberal economic policies in the 1990s is crucial to our understanding of its conservation and resource extraction sectors. Section 1 of this chapter focuses on Tanzania's transition from a single-party state to a multiparty democracy in the 1990s. As a single-party state undergirded by President Julius Nyerere's *ujamaa* (familyhood) philosophy, Tanzania engaged in the nationalization of land, mining, housing, health, banking, transportation, and other sectors. However, after the country transitioned to a multiparty democracy, Tanzania embraced neoliberalism and the reappropriation of land for agriculture, tourism, and protected areas. By definition, neoliberalism, or neoliberalization, refers to an ideology and the multifaceted, dynamic processes that are geared toward significantly reducing the state's role in managing the economy while ensuring a more significant role for nonstate actors (mainly NGOs), private enterprises, and market forces to determine a country's economic trajectory and development policies and outcomes. In the conservation context, neoliberalization leads to the "reregulation of nature through commodification, the spread of free markets to manage these commodities . . . ; it involves the opening up of areas of land for capital accumulation under the paradoxical assumption that the tense relationship between capitalism and the environment can be solved through the latter's complete integration into the capitalist system, resulting in growth, improved efficiency, development, democracy and sustainability" (Green and Adams 2015, 98–99; see also Büscher et al. 2012; Fairhead, Leach, and Scoones 2012; Harvey 2005; Kelly 2011). In the Tanzanian context, the neoliberalization of its economy and its conservation sector has led to the entrenchment of green (land) and blue (ocean) grabbing—processes that have resulted in the displacement and dispossession of historically marginalized citizens (see chapters 3 and 4).

Section 2 of this chapter draws on ethnographic data from life history interviews to shed light on the people's everyday lives in six villages on the rural Mtwara peninsula during the postcolonial period. Most notably, this section reflects on the period from 1961 to 1985, when Julius Nyerere was president. During this period, Tanzanian citizens experienced dramatic transformations in their social and political landscape. Additionally, I use oral histories gathered from two large villages—Msimbati (an "original" village, *kijiji cha asili*) and Nalingu (an ujamaa village)—where I conducted extended fieldwork to highlight individual and collective memories of everyday life during different ideological shifts in Tanzania's history and the social transformation that ensued. I use these two villages as case studies to compare and contrast their unique histories, socioeconomic profiles, and the local residents' overall response to the marine park and the gas project. I discuss why some residents of the marine park villages described their lives as having improved over the years, while others felt that their lives had become more difficult. I illustrate how their affective experiences reflect the country's larger political shifts. These affective experiences contextualize the village elders' varied responses to conservation and extractive projects implemented in Mtwara.

SECTION 1: FROM AFRICAN SOCIALISM (*UJAMAA*) TO NEOLIBERALISM (*MAGEUZI*)

Tanzania has, for the most part, maintained its global reputation as a "peaceful" country in a region of Africa that has witnessed some of the worst interethnic conflicts in living memory—including the genocide in Rwanda in 1994 and the postelection political violence in Kenya in 2007–8. This does not mean that Tanzania has not had its fair share of political and economic foibles, including a costly war with Uganda in 1978–79, known as the Kagera War. But the nation has succeeded in avoiding interethnic conflicts, arguably through nationalistic policies that favor unity (*umoja*) and development (*maendeleo*).

Since its independence, Tanzania has experienced four major ideological or sociopolitical national policy shifts. The first of these was the Arusha Declaration (Azimio la Arusha) of 1967, in which Nyerere, Tanzania's founder-president, articulated his ujamaa policy. This policy ultimately led to the nationalization of the various sectors of the economy, including land, housing, mining, and the industrial sector. The second was the implementation of Operation Vijiji (villagization)—the ujamaa villagization (Ujamaa wa Vijijini) scheme—during the late 1960s and early 1970s. This scheme involved the mass resettlement of millions of Tanzanians in rural areas. During this period, Tanzanians experienced some of the most drastic changes in their lives.

Third, Tanzania's economy and politics dramatically shifted in the 1970s and 1980s following economic crises and the subsequent IMF/World Bank–supported structural adjustment program (SAP). This period saw the first signs of Tanzania abandoning its socialist ideals. The country experienced one economic crisis after another and became reliant on loans from the IMF, the World Bank, and numerous donor countries to see itself through. The fourth shift was a period of economic liberalization (*mageuzi*), starting in the early 1990s. During this period, Tanzania formally abandoned its commitment to ujamaa, replacing the one-party state with a Western-style multiparty democracy that was committed to market reforms. In due course, the economy was restructured to encourage private enterprise in all sectors—including natural resources and tourism—following the tenets of neoliberalism.

In the following sections, I briefly review the literature on these four sociopolitical shifts, contextualizing Tanzania's existing conservation and extractive sectors' policies and practices. These sections also outline the consequences of these policies—and of the social and political ethos in Tanzania—on the lives of the people there.

The Arusha Declaration (1961-1967)

There is an abundance of literature on the role and impact of the country's founder-president, Julius Nyerere, who governed Tanzania for twenty-five years—from independence in December 1961 until the end of 1985 (Lofchie 2014, 4–5; Schneider 2004, 346). Nyerere was widely admired and respected nationally and internationally as a visionary committed to improving the lives of his fellow citizens through his version of African socialism, ujamaa (Sanders 2008, 30; Blommaert 2014). The Tanzanian scholar Isaa Shivji (2012, 103) has described Nyerere as "a great thinker [who] stood intellectually head and shoulders above most of his political contemporaries. He could be truly described as a philosopher-king." Others have gone even further. Paget (2017, 155) notes that "Julius Nyerere... assumed a position of saint-like virtue in the popular imagination, an image that played a key role in legitimizing nation and party alike." By contrast, other scholars such as Saul (2012) and Schneider (2004, 2006) have, in their writings, depicted Nyerere as an intolerant autocrat and have characterized his famous policy of ujamaa villagization as draconian and antidemocratic. Regardless of the different representations of Nyerere's persona, virtues, and politics in the academic literature, across Tanzania he remains immensely popular and the well-respected Father of the Nation (Baba wa Taifa), even after his passing in October 1999 (Fouéré 2015).

Nyerere first articulated his philosophical and ideological commitment to national development and national identity through his belief in ujamaa in the Arusha Declaration of 1967 (Nyerere 1968). As the oft-told story goes, in 1962, during a short visit to his native Zanaki village in northwest Tanzania, Nyerere wrote and later published a small pamphlet titled *Ujamaa: The Basis of African Socialism* (Stoger-Eising 2000, 118; Hunter 2008, 475). In this essay, which was written in English, Nyerere described a non-Marxist socialist society in which everyone worked and cared for one another. Such a society, he wrote, was much like precolonial traditional African society.[3] As the Tanzanian historian Yusufu Lawi (2007, 73) has observed, "Nyerere had hoped to revive egalitarianism which he believed was a central characteristic of all precolonial African societies that decades of colonial intervention had destroyed." Nyerere's principles became the core ideology of the Tanganyika African National Union (TANU), founded in 1954, when the national executive committee (NEC) of the party adopted the Arusha Declaration on February 5, 1967, putting the country firmly on the path of socialist development.[4] As Issa Shivji (2012, 107) notes, unlike the 1962 ujamaa pamphlet, which was written in English, "the Arusha Declaration was of a different genre. It was written in Kiswahili, perhaps the best, yet understandable, linguistic articulation. It inspired, it mobilized. It was a call for a revolution, yet not a call to arms." The Arusha Declaration effectively outlined the newly independent nation's core values.

The broad goals of the Arusha Declaration and the associated ujamaa were "to allow a planned utilization of land and other local natural resources, to enable the government to provide social and economic services more efficiently and, above all, to organize communities spatially and politically so that they could engage successfully in the collective improvement of their own social and economic wellbeing" (Lawi 2007, 69). As Hunter (2008, 475–76) has observed, "The aim was both to build a nation which would rely on itself and not be dependent on the vagaries of international hand-outs, and to ensure that within this nation wealth was allocated justly. It, therefore, set out a moral vision within which to debate a just ordering of society."

One of the most immediate results of the Arusha Declaration was the emergence of a highly centralized state that placed itself at the center of the development agenda (Tripp 1997). Adopting the Arusha Declaration marked a turning point in Tanzania's political and economic history; it was an "economic manifesto," a blueprint for Tanzania's socialist construction (Townsend 1998, 14). "The Declaration introduced a thoroughgoing economic transformation, in the sense that the country would basically withdraw from the economic world market and focus its economy on national self-reliance [*kujitegemea*]" (Blommaert 2014, 27–28). The discourse on *ujamaa na kujitegemea*, or ujamaa and self-reliance, was meant to provide Tanzanian citizens with a new narrative that would give them the courage and confidence to take control of the country's destiny—and achieve the economic justice anticipated since the pre-independence period (Hunter 2008, 479). In sum, it was meant to radically restructure Tanzania's economy and polity through self-reliance; the one-party state emphasized manufacturing and agricultural production within the nation, for the nation, with self-reliance (*jitegemea*) as the primary goal (Sanders 2008, 30). Relatedly, the Arusha Declaration called for a complete stop to the accumulation of private wealth by leaders in the dominant party and the government. The declaration indicated the party's desire to prioritize rural development, enabling a more effective utilization of domestic (as opposed to foreign) resources.

In 1967, when the Arusha Declaration was adopted, few could have predicted Tanzania's dramatic economic downfall in less than a decade. Despite attempts at self-reliance, Tanzania ultimately became one of the heavily indebted poor countries (HIPC) that desperately needed its sovereign debts to be forgiven. In the 1960s and the 1970s, however, the political leadership was still determined to disseminate the ideals of ujamaa and ujamaa politics throughout the country. This included making Kiswahili (Swahili) Tanzania's national language as an important strategy to achieve national integration and social cohesion (Blommaert 2014; Topan 2008).

Operation Villagization (1967-1974)

Following the adoption of the Arusha Declaration in 1967, Tanzania embarked on what is considered by many scholars to be one of the greatest experiments in social engineering on African soil. In the first ten years of independence, with nearly 90 percent of the country's population living in rural areas, the government launched what became known as Operation Vijiji—which led to the burgeoning of ujamaa villages in the countryside. These villages were initially developed on an experimental and contingency basis in select locations; they were to serve as prime examples for the population—models for the rest of the country to emulate independently, without government assistance. Persuaded by political education and by example, rural people were encouraged to live together in villages, to work together in communally owned fields, and to share the product of their collective work. The villages were to be democratically run by local community members, and production decisions were to be coordinated with regional and national economic development plans (Barker 1979). Notably, at the local level, there was no obligation to establish collective production—although local leaders could urge and indeed require this to be done. At the national level, development villagization was a policy aimed solely at nucleating rural settlements into villages on or adjacent to roads, to facilitate the distribution of productive and social service infrastructure.

Ujamaa villages were intended to serve as the foundation from which Tanzania's countryside would move from low-level production and poverty to high-level production and prosperity (Townsend 1998). There was a high degree of idealism and voluntarism involved in this vision of society, and the leadership understood that there would be difficulties with the implementation of the ujamaa policy (Hydén 1980). Nyerere and other leaders emphasized that ujamaa villagization was not simply a return to traditional living. Instead, it was a strategy to improve the quality of life for people in rural areas. Progress toward socialist agricultural production would follow, as it was hoped that people would come to see the wisdom of cooperative production (Mascarenhas 1979).

The scale of the operations in terms of the number of affected people, the number of villages established, the resources invested, and the campaigns required to start ujamaa villages was remarkable. By 1973, over two million Tanzanians were reported to be living in such villages, though these figures were not entirely accurate. In August 1973, Nyerere announced that with the ruling party's ratification, it would be compulsory for all rural people to live in ujamaa villages by the end of 1976 (Kikula 1997). Over the next three years, large numbers of rural households were forced to relocate into villages. These villages soon acquired legal status (as incorporated entities) and were governed by elected councils along with government-appointed civil servants. As legal entities, the villages could manage local trading stores and communal farms (Sarris and van den Brink 1993). Although people were not forced to move far when relocated, they had to agree to abandon their previous residence and land. Where people refused to accept this condition, coercion was applied by forcibly moving them to ujamaa villages. In his case study of the peoples of Eastern Iraqwland (present-day Manyara Region), Lawi (2007) has described the forced manner in which the Operation Vijiji was implemented.

Operation Vijiji involved the largest number of people in the history of African resettlements.[5] Estimates vary regarding the number of people who were moved during the villagization program. According to one estimate, more than nine million people, or 70 percent of the total population, were moved (see Nyerere 1977, 41). Villagization resulted in the abandonment of traditional scattered, semipermanent settlements and the adoption of concentrated and permanent settlements (Kikula 1997). By 1976, it was declared that practically all rural Tanzanians were living in new development villages.

The creation of ujamaa villages was intended to slow the pace of urbanization by discouraging rural-urban migration, promoting economic and social development in rural areas, encouraging national economic self-reliance, and increasing wealth equality in Tanzania overall. In sum, ujamaa was a means to overcome the major problems hindering Tanzania's development and to promote nationalism (McHenry 1979).

Over the years, scholars have debated the merits and demerits of the villagization program—particularly the forced manner in which the program was implemented between 1973 and 1976. As Greco (2016, 27) has perceptively noted, "Forced and voluntary resettlement of rural populations is far from being a thing of the past. In present-day Tanzania, resettlement is still considered as a viable development policy, for example, for the purposes of environmental conservation." There is a consensus, however, that the effects of the villagization program were both positive and negative. Although the villages provided services, the disruption caused by the land tenure arrangements negatively affected agricultural production. While the villagization program seriously disrupted the social fabric within the villages (Seppälä 1998, 17), the villagization policy was sensitive to gender issues, especially concerning land distribution, land rights, and land inheritance rights (see Koda 1998). Moreover, as Green (2014, 109) points out, the villagization program "was successful in its restructuring of governance and the modality through which rural communities were incorporated into the state."

As we will see in section 2 of this chapter, the lived experiences of people during the ujamaa period varied significantly within and among different villages, as well as across generations and gender. Critically, these experiences of the remembered past affected how people in the marine park villages, especially some of its elderly residents, responded to the implementation of the marine park and the gas project on the peninsula. Their past experiences with the government and the Chama

Cha Mapinduzi party and their acknowledgment that the government had command over natural resources and citizen subjects imbricated their justification of the projects' implementation in their region. They were convinced that the government had implemented these projects in the people's best interest—and indeed, in the national interest.

Structural Adjustment Programs (1974-1985)

In the mid-1970s, Tanzania spiraled into economic decline and stagnation. Both domestic failures and adverse international structures were synergistically responsible for an economic crisis that necessitated major economic and political changes in response. The start of the economic decline coincided with the peak of Operation Vijiji and lasted until President Nyerere's resignation in 1985. During this period, agricultural production stalled, industrial production faltered, and development goals were not met. The protracted economic crisis led to a shift in state policy toward the centralization of state power and a top-down approach to governance.[6] Operation Vijiji would eventually assist with the implementation of more top-down approaches—despite having initially been designed to empower rural, low-income residents.

The first oil shock in 1973, which led to the quadrupling of world oil prices, necessitated sharp increases in import expenditures and a decline in export proceeds (Sarris and van den Brink 1993). Recurring droughts in 1973–74 were followed by the breakup of the East African Community (Kenya, Tanzania, and Zambia) in 1977, which placed further economic pressures on the Tanzanian state (Sarris and van den Brink 1993). The second OPEC oil crisis, in 1979, the subsequent world recession, the war with Uganda (Tripp 1997), the rapid depletion of international reserves (foreign exchange) following the end of the coffee boom in 1978, and the abortive import liberalization that same year all resulted in a fiscal deficit that plunged the Tanzanian economy into crisis. The country's agricultural production dramatically declined over the years (Lofchie 1988), and its foreign debt skyrocketed, quickly becoming unmanageable. External debts developed rapidly, and after the end of Tanzania's war with Uganda, foreign inflows fell dramatically as the government clashed with donors over macroeconomic policy. From the late 1970s onward, Nyerere strongly resisted the IMF/World Bank pressures toward economic liberalization (Baregu 1994). The dialogue with the IMF broke down in 1978–79 when President Nyerere vetoed an IMF agreement that included a 15 percent devaluation of the Tanzanian shilling. Because of Nyerere's resistance, foreign exchange supplies for Tanzania dried up. Critical of Nyerere's legacy up to this point in Tanzania's political and economic history, Kelsall (2002, 608) notes: "The period 1963–1976 witnessed the consolidation of the Tanzanian state under *Mwalimu* Julius Nyerere's leadership.... Political expression outside the channels of *Chama Cha Mapinduzi* (CCM), the single party, was stifled."

In the 1970s and 1980s, Tanzania was only one of many African countries whose worsening economic situations forced them to accept the structural adjustment programs (SAPs) prescribed by the World Bank and the IMF. These SAPs leaned heavily toward increased economic liberalization and privatization of the economy, coupled with political reforms such as the institutionalization of Western-style multiparty democracy. They also included stabilization (increasing interest rates, reducing cheap loans, and raising taxes) and privatization programs.[7]

Eventually, the Tanzanian government had little choice but to return to the IMF. An agreement with the IMF was reached in July 1986 in which the IMF provided Tanzania with a structural adjustment facility (1987–90) (Tripp 1997, 75). Tanzania reluctantly accepted the World Bank/IMF–recommended SAPs, which operated on "the principle that less government intervention in the economy is better; that economies will work best, and most efficiently, if propelled by market forces rather than bureaucrats" (Sanders 2001, 163; Lockhart 2008). This contradicted Tanzania's previous focus on self-reliance through a centralized state. It was in the context of these SAPs and Tanzania's worsening economic woes that international financial organizations and donor countries persuaded the Tanzanian government to consider developing its tourism sector, with a focus on terrestrial and marine ecotourism, as a strategy to attract the foreign currency that it needed to service its debts.[8]

Economic Liberalization, Privatization, and Multiparty Democracy (1986–1990s)

On November 5, 1985, Nyerere announced his decision to step down as president—making way for Sheik Ali Hassan Mwinyi to become Tanzania's second president.[9] Nyerere's resignation did not result in the diminishment of his political influence. He remained very popular among Tanzanians. Not surprisingly, at Mwinyi's request, Nyerere retained his powerful post as chairman of the CCM—the only political party in Tanzania—for five more years (Townsend 1998; Fouéré 2014).

In March 1991, President Mwinyi recognized the inevitability of political and economic adjustment. In 1992, the government conceded to external and internal pressure (coming from urban areas) and approved a multiparty political system, which effectively initiated a process of political reform from above. Among the ingredients of this reform was freedom of organization for opposition parties and the separation of state and state party (CCM) at various levels (Tripp 1997). The Zanzibar Declaration of 1991 officially marked the end of socialism in Tanzania. Mwinyi formally announced that the state had rejected the Arusha Declaration; in its stead, Mwinyi adopted the reforms of structural adjustment required by the IMF to finance Tanzania's transformation into a post–African socialist society (cf. Weiss 2002; Lofchie 2014).

On July 1, 1992, Tanzania legally became a multiparty state—after twenty-seven years under the heavy influence of a one-party system. Previously, the CCM and its predecessors held an exclusive monopoly on formal power and authority, wielding enormous influence on almost every aspect of the social fabric of Tanzania (Ngware 2003). The shift from African socialism to the adoption of Western-style multiparty democracy brought about significant changes to Tanzanian society, particularly between 1990 and 1995. Tanzanian scholars used the term *mageuzi*, meaning "a complete turnaround," to refer to this period. The public reaction to this shift was mixed.[10]

Tanzania's political and economic liberalization brought about the opening of various sectors of the economy, including mining and tourism. This resulted in greater flows of direct foreign investment into key sectors of the economy, which also spurred increased levels of "corruption, rent seeking and a political system that increasingly relies on patronage in the absence of any guiding ideology that enjoys popular legitimacy, as was the case in the 1960s and 1970s" (Nelson 2012, 363; see also Benjaminsen et al. 2013; Green and Adams 2015; Neumann 1995).

Tanzania held its first presidential and parliamentary multiparty elections on October 29, 1995. Predictably, the CCM won the elections. Benjamin Mkapa, the new president, took office in a peaceful hand-over from President Mwinyi and headed a more market-friendly political settlement among the CCM's leadership, international capital, domestic private sector operators, and a politicized bureaucracy (Bofin, Pedersen, and Jacob 2020). Mkapa, a native of the Mtwara Region, was reelected in the second multiparty elections held in October 2000, with a substantial lead over the opposition.[11] His chosen successor, Jakaye Kikwete—a former lieutenant colonel in the military—was elected president in 2005 and reelected in October 2010. During Kikwete's two five-year terms, the CCM became increasingly associated with major corruption scandals, especially in the energy sector.[12]

John Magufuli, a low-profile minister who was nominated as the "compromise" candidate in 2015, was elected president with a much narrower margin against a united opposition party. From the outset, Magufuli positioned himself as what some have called a "populist" president, with an anticorruption platform. He underscored his ideology extolling the importance of hard work instead of idle talk and indolence (Paget 2017, 2020) during the 2015 election campaign, emblazoned by the slogan *Hapa kazi tu*, meaning "Here there is just hard work." Opposition politicians and some scholars accused him of showing authoritarian and dictatorial tendencies (Poncian 2019); they criticized Magufuli and the CCM for suppressing dissent, harassing the opposition, and arbitrarily circumscribing the freedoms of leaders of the opposition parties. Taking a cue from his predecessor Jakaya Kikwete and his rhetoric about the permanence of the CCM party, Magufuli declared that the CCM would rule Tanzania "forever." Magufuli was reelected on October 30, 2020, following a controversial election process in which he won 85 percent of the popular vote—reinstating the CCM's dominance of the political landscape in Tanzania.

As Lofchie (2014, 220) has pointed out, a key feature of Tanzanian political history is the CCM's political resiliency and its leaders' determination to remain in power at all costs. Even some leaders of the opposition parties acknowledge that "the CCM has been willing to allow relatively fair elections only so long as it seemed assured of victory" (Lofchie 2014, 221). The 2020 national elections—held during the peak of the COVID-19 pandemic, in which CHADEMA, the main opposition party, was decimated even in its traditional strongholds—epitomized the CCM's determination to remain in power "forever" at all costs. There are several reasons why the CCM dominates the political landscape. For one, the CCM was the only political party in the country for more than five decades; therefore, it enjoyed huge electoral advantages against novice opposition parties. As Lofchie points out, when the multiparty system was adopted, the CCM already had more than fifty years of political experience and a nationwide organization that was embedded even in remote villages in the rural hinterlands. At the same time, the organization relied on the country's business elite to finance its expensive nationwide campaigns and cash payments for party supporters (Lofchie 2014, 221). In exchange for the financial support it provided to the party, the business elite itself relied on the CCM to further its own economic interests. Not surprisingly, "Tanzanians who have risen to positions of wealth in Tanzania have done so through their connections to the political process.... Wealth and power in Tanzania are so inextricably interconnected that it is impossible to have one without the other" (Lofchie 2014, 25; see also Kelsall 2002, 612). For example, Mohamed Dewji, one of Tanzania's best-known businessmen and billionaires, was a member of parliament for ten years—from 2005 to 2015—during which he made the bulk of his fortune.

Expectedly, members of the political-economic oligarchy are willing to go to great lengths to remain in power—even going so far as to use state police and security forces to unleash violence against the opposition (Lofchie 2014, 25–26). Contrary to its global image as a "peaceful country," then, a close reading of the political ethos in Tanzania suggests that it is not significantly different from its neighboring countries of Rwanda, Uganda, Burundi, Mozambique, and the Democratic Republic of the Congo—all of which are governed by electoral authoritarian regimes of one variety or another. "Though these regimes differ from one another in many ways, each benefits from the presence of neighbors that champion authoritarian development" (Paget 2017, 154).

The following section considers the relevance of these scholarly observations and discussions to the everyday lives of the people who live in rural Mtwara. Section 2 focuses on the oral histories of Msimbati and Nalingu: two large villages inside the marine park where I conducted sustained fieldwork. I examine the narrative representations of how people in these villages experienced their lives during Tanzania's different ideological periods and political shifts—from ujamaa to mageuzi—under different presidents—and how these experiences inform village residents' current life experiences.

SECTION 2: NATION BUILDING AND SOCIAL TRANSFORMATION IN RURAL MTWARA

Between 2010 and 2012, I interviewed local leaders and a few older men and women in six coastal villages on the Mtwara peninsula—Msangamkuu, Namera, Sinde, Mkubiru, Nalingu, and Msimbati—to elicit oral histories of their respective villages. I began documenting Msangamkuu's oral history and the life histories of some of the older village residents. Taking cues from the village chairman regarding the local protocol, I first met with Bibi Malango, a village elder, and asked her for permission to do my research in the village. I then requested that she tell me Msangamkuu's origin story. What followed was the telling of a well-known story of a migrant (Bibi Malango's great-grandfather) from Mueda (Cabo Delgado Province), in Mozambique, who in 1918 found a sandy location (*mchanga mkuu*) to settle down, and that's how the new village got its name.

In 2010, there were seventeen government-recognized villages inside the marine park's boundaries, with an estimated total population of forty-four thousand. As mentioned in the introduction, these seventeen villages were further divided over the years for administrative reasons. By 2016, there were twenty-three registered villages on the peninsula that were also included in the marine park's borders.[13] The life history interviews I conducted were particularly useful in understanding the origin stories and histories of the marine park villages. For example, as I detail below, people's life histories revealed that Msimbati was an "original village" (*kijiji cha asili*)—some of the older interlocutors claimed the village had a history stretching back more than three centuries. By contrast, Nalingu was a quintessential ujamaa village—a small new settlement in a forested area, which was subsequently inaugurated as an ujamaa village in 1967–68.

In the next section, I present a brief profile of two large villages that were most consequential to the marine park—Msimbati and Nalingu—especially during the early stages of planning and implementation of the marine park, and I contextualize local residents' opinions regarding the state and the government in the context of Tanzania's social and political history outlined in section 1 of the chapter.

Msimbati—The "Original Village"

Msimbati is a large oceanfront village located on the southeastern side of the Mtwara peninsula. It is about forty-one kilometers from Mtwara town by road—part of which is paved asphalt, but most of which is an unpaved, dusty dirt road cut through the bush. The two-hour bus journey from Mtwara town to Msimbati is unpredictable; it was not uncommon for the bus to break down somewhere in the middle of the trip. The bus was often the fodder for jokes among travelers. "This bus looks new, but only the body is new; the engine is from an old lorry," a fellow passenger wryly told me. In June 2011, when I first traveled to Msimbati, it took me more than two hours to reach the village in an overcrowded dala dala minibus from Mtwara town. On that day, the last bus back to town from Msimbati had left at 4:00 p.m., so I had no option but to get on the back seat of a boda boda. The hour-and-a-half motorcycle ride was bumpy and backbreaking, the road unpaved, with jutting rocks and dangerous potholes. Throughout my fieldwork in rural Mtwara, I relied on the boda boda drivers for my ethnographic mobility—to take me from one village to another—often via treacherous shortcuts and ditches. My research assistants would borrow or rent a motorcycle from a neighbor for their travels.

Msimbati has an estimated population of twelve thousand—though some residents put that number at fourteen thousand to fifteen thousand. I was initially struck by the size of the village and its population; despite its remoteness from Mtwara town, Msimbati was impressively large. Msimbati is an island (*kisiwa*) connected to the mainland (*bara*) with culverts and a small bridge. It is surrounded by marshy land and mangroves, mango trees, cashew trees, and coconut trees. During high tide, water from the ocean surrounds the village; during low tide, however, Msimbati appears to be fully connected to the mainland. The village primary and secondary schools, as well as the health center (*zahanati*), are located outside the main village. They were substantially upgraded in 2012. In 2016, villagers took it on themselves to build a second primary school in Mtandi to accommodate the growing number of children in the village; men and women had volunteered their labor (*kujitolea*) for the sake of their children's education. "Otherwise, where will our children get an education?" they asked rhetorically. The gas project has covered a portion of the construction cost as part of its corporate social responsibility.

In 2010, owing to its large population, Msimbati and Mtandi, which had been part of Msimbati, became two separate administrative units—each with its own elected chairperson, government-appointed village executive officer, and village office building. In 2014, Ruvula, the main site of the gas project's infrastructure, also became a separate village. Residents of Ruvula, however, continue to identify themselves as residents of Msimbati and use Ruvula as a qualifier. In 2017, Mnuyo, a section (*kata*) of Msimbati, became yet another separate registered village; in everyday conversations, however, residents commonly refer to the entire island region as Msimbati to suggest their common social history and cultural and familial ties.

The entrance to Msimbati is deceptively narrow for the size of the village. A large tree serves as the main bus stop, and a few grocery stores,

FIGURE 2 Main Street in Msimbati village in 2011

modest restaurants, and a licensed pharmacy (Duka la Dawa Muhimu) are clustered near the village entrance. Surprisingly, considering the large size of the village and its prime location inside the marine park, Msimbati did not have a resort hotel or a "guesthouse" (hotel) where visitors could pay to stay. The "tourist hotel" inside the marine park was nonfunctional and had a reputation for being badly maintained. As one local resident told me when I inquired about staying in a *gesti* (guesthouse), "rats and cockroaches are running around there." Abdallah, my research assistant, had suggested that I stay with one of his cousins, whose house was close to the marine park's ticketing office—only to find that the cousin had torn down his house and was rebuilding it with dead coral, mud, and wattle.

The sandy road that runs through the center of the village is impressively wide and flanked by a few small houses—some with thatched roofs, others with corrugated metal sheets for roofs. The neem trees (*mwarobaini*) that line both sides of the main road serve as *baraza*—a hangout place where residents (always men) meet to chat, socialize, or just relax in the open. In June 2011, most houses in the village were made of wattle and daub or blocks of dead coral, with thatched roofs made from palm fronds. Some wattle and daub houses were plastered with cement on the outside and many were half finished, with missing doors or windows. The marine park's gate office, a single-story concrete building, was located close to the police station, near the beachhead. At the time there were no fishing boats on the beach and no fishers in sight.

Near the entrance to the village are three strikingly large identical two-story concrete bungalows, which stand out in contrast with the surrounding structures. I was curious to know who had built these identical structures in a village that was so far away from Mtwara town. On a later visit, as we stood outside the village office waiting to greet Msimbati's chairman, I asked Salum, my field assistant, about the three bungalows. He laughed awkwardly and said, "I'll tell you all about it, but later. It's a long story." As it turned out, the long story was about Msimbati's history of prosperity and its close ties to the sea cucumber (*holothuria scabra*, or *jongoo*) trade, a topic I will explore in more depth later in this chapter.

Haki, the politically active and intellectually engaging chairman of Ruvula, had taken a keen interest in documenting the oral history of Msimbati. Ruvula, where he lived, was home to the marine park's prime beach. It was also home to another tourist attraction—the ruins

FIGURE 3 Three bungalows in Msimbati village

of a house called Wind's Whisper, which had once belonged to Latham Leslie-Moore, a retired British civil servant who claimed that Msimbati was his sultanate—a micronation in the 1950s (see the following paragraph). Haki's story of Msimbati was based on what some elders had told him about the village's origin. According to Haki, the first reference to the name Msimbati was in 1922, in a government gazette. Three hundred years before, however, the island had belonged to King Mngosi, who lived in Kitutila, in the famous modern-day Kilwa. The people of Msimbati remember King Mngosi in their annual *matambiko* (rituals). About a hundred years ago, some Arab merchant sailors lost at sea found themselves marooned in Msimbati; they married and settled down in the village. One of these sailors died during a major flood (*gharika*), which divided the village into two; one part of the village went under the ocean (*ukazama baharani*), while the other was covered with sand (*ukafukiwa na mchanga*). Jamali, one of the oldest residents of Msimbati village, gave me his version of Msimbati's origin stories in August 2014. "This is a very old village. Our ancestors started it. It is not an ujamaa village. We are several generations after those who started this village, but historically we know that one of our great-grandmothers was called Mtiti. Bibi Mtiti started this village. After Bibi Mtiti died, her granddaughter inherited her role. She is still alive. She lives here in Msimbati. If there is an inheritance ceremony, she is the one who tells us what to do, and she is the one who goes to pray to the spirits. We accept her decision."

Msimbati's oral history is entangled with Leslie-Moore's story. In 1959, after declaring himself as the sultan of Msimbati, Leslie-Moore submitted a petition on behalf of the people of Msimbati to Dag Hammarskjöld, the general secretary of the United Nations at the time, that the island be recognized as a micronation. The ruin of Wind's Whisper, the stone house that Leslie-Moore had built for himself close to the Ruvula beach, still stands. Although believed to be "infested with snakes and spiders," it is among the tourist attractions inside the marine park. When I spoke to some of the elders in Msimbati about Leslie-Moore, they told me they did not know much about him, as he allegedly did not allow the local people to tread on his property—except when he wanted them to work on his farms in Ruvula. In 1962, under Nyerere's orders, Tanzanian security forces escorted Leslie-Moore out of Msimbati. A Tanzanian Indian named Dosanjh bought his farmland. During the ujamaa period, however, people from Mnoyo were allotted plots of farmland in Ruvula that Leslie-Moore once claimed he owned. Significantly, the island that Leslie-Moore once claimed was his own private sultanate is now Tanzania's most productive gas field—as will be detailed in chapter 3.

Nalingu–An Ujamaa Village

Nalingu is a large coastal village inside the marine park with a population of more than five thousand. It is about twenty kilometers from Mtwara town and a kilometer from the fishing village of Mnazi. Nalingu is a quintessential ujamaa village. Many of its original physical features are still intact—wattle and daub houses originally built in the 1960s and 1970s, arranged in straight, neat rows; a market with kiosks in the village center; a communal warehouse (*godowni* or *ghala*) near the entrance to the village; thousands of planted coconut and cashew trees; an upgraded village dispensary; and an upgraded municipal school, among other features. Close to the village market are two abandoned tube wells sunk by the Finnish International Development Agency (Finnida) in the 1970s as part of its Mtwara-Lindi Rural Water Supply Project.

When I first visited Nalingu in August 2011, I was struck by three village features. First, Nalingu's population density is high relative to its smaller geographical size. This is reflected in the large number of schoolchildren playing and laughing on the unpaved main road. After some playful exchanges with a group of children who had gathered in front of a small grocery shop, I asked if I could buy them *pipi* (peppermints) from the store. "Yes!" said some delightedly, while others shouted in a chorus: "No, give us money to see *picha* [a movie]!" One of the huts on the main road served as the movie theater in the village, showing dubbed DVDs of foreign films, European football (soccer) matches, and "today's special"— charging TSh100 for children, TSh500 for adults. Of course, I yielded to their requests. Second, I noted the gridded layout of the village, with thatched huts in neat rows on both sides of the sandy dirt roads (*mtaa*) that ran through the village. Finally, an impressive upgraded health center caught my attention. It was very busy that day. A nurse on the veranda

FIGURE 4 Main Street in Nalingu village

was weighing babies and young children and chatting with the parents (mostly mothers) in good humor. A doctor attended to several patients seated outside the main clinic.

I elicited origin stories of Nalingu village from several of my interlocutors. These men and women belonged to different generations—those who were physically present when Nalingu had started as a small village and those who came during the later stages of the village's development and expansion phase. Many of those who had participated in the establishment of the village had died, but their children, grandchildren, and great-grandchildren still resided in Nalingu. While most of the residents were decedents or relatives (kin) of those original ujamaa villages, a significant number of residents had arrived during the last decade—as I learned during my fieldwork.

A DEFENSE UJAMAA VILLAGE

Maukilo, a bearded man with a deep voice, was one of Nalingu's oldest residents. He was well known in the village as someone who had actively participated in the planning and implementation of the marine park and its restrictions. He was also known in the village as someone who had suffered the wrath of some of his fellow villagers as a result. In 2012, residents of the village threw acid on Maukilo's face in response to his enforcement of the marine park's restrictions, leaving him nearly blind (see chapter 4). In 2014, I interviewed Maukilo to document his life history.

Maukilo was born in 1929 in Kitaya, on the banks of the Ruvuma River. He spent much of his youth in Mahurunga, located a few kilometers from the river. In 1966, Maukilo accompanied his older brother to settle in the ujamaa village that would eventually become known as Nalingu in 1967–68. He served as the village ambassador (*mbalozi*)—one of the leaders who represented ten households in the village during its initial years. Maukilo recalled the names of those who had taken the lead in starting the village: Hamisi, Ahmed, and Humbu—they were the village's founders (*waliokuwepo hapa waanzilishi*). At that time, the area was forested (*msitu*), so the early settlers, including Maukilo, decided to clear the forest and build the village in its place. "We developed a system of measuring everything [for the grid-like layout—laying the gridded lines according to the ujamaa villages guidelines and prototype]. After that, I became a ranger [*mgambo*] in the village. We started cultivating a village farm here ... then the soldiers came to train us in self-defense [*mafunzo ya mgambo*]. Fortunately, their activities were not political. The soldiers were good to us, and they gave us the training we wanted. Their training was focused on preparing us to protect our village [from intruders]." Here, Maukilo was referring to the Mozambique Liberation Front (Frelimo, formerly FRELIMO), or the warring factions from the Mozambican side during the war of independence from the Portuguese, and the South African–backed Resistencia Nacional Mozambiqueña (Renamo, formerly RENAMO).[14]

Maukilo's reference to the self-defense training that he and others in the village received sheds light on the larger political context of the region—specifically, the war on the other side of the border and the incursions across Tanzania's border with Mozambique—in which Nalingu and other coastal villages became ujamaa villages with government support. Frelimo was formed in Tanzania, with the backing of Nyerere, to help the group fight the Portuguese government forces. These ujamaa villages were, in this context, de facto defense villages. None of my interlocutors, however, mentioned that anyone from their respective villages had engaged in an encounter with Portuguese soldiers or Frelimo fighters from the Mozambican side.

Older adults from Nalingu corroborated Mauliko's recollections of when and how the village was established in a forested area and with his description of the gridded layout as specified in the prototype ujamaa villages. As people moved into the new village, they cleared the forest to build their homes, plant coconut trees and cashew trees, and participate in communal farming. In due course, Nalingu became a large fishing village because of its proximity to Mnazi village and the ocean.

Mnazi, a picturesque village, is a productive fishing and landing site, with many inhabitants dependent on the ocean for their livelihoods, fish protein, and other marine resources. Not surprisingly, when the marine park was implemented, the people of Nalingu were among the first to vehemently oppose it because they believed they would no longer be allowed to fish in the ocean—one of their main sources of food security. As described in the introduction, over the years, Nalingu had developed a reputation of being a "violent village" among outsiders, especially as described by marine park representatives (and their international consultants) in their reports. Nalingu residents countered such labeling as false and emphasized that their village was founded "in peace"—it was an ujamaa village.

NO COERCION

Contrary to what many scholars have written about Nyerere's high-handedness, as well as the violence and coercion that became an integral feature of operation villagization (in particular Lal 2015; Lawi 2007; Schneider 2004; Scott 1998; Shivji 2012; see also Kikula 1997), none of my interlocutors in Nalingu spoke of their experiences of resettlement as marked by coercion. Mussa, who was seventy-four when I interviewed him in 2014, clarified this. He detailed how most of the people who came to live in Nalingu were from other villages nearby; they came in small numbers to start a new life in Nalingu, and the village began to expand over an extended period. Before coming to Nalingu, Mussa lived in the neighboring fishing village of Mnete, along with his parents and grandparents, who had migrated from Mozambique several years earlier. For Mussa, it was a short walk from the fishing village of Mnete to Nalingu. He described how people from Mnete, Dihimba, Mngoji, and other villages had come to Nalingu to build their huts and to start working on the communal farm. Those who had come from a village called Nalingu had decided to give this new village the same name.

As more people came in to join the village, the village chairman allotted land to the newcomers on which they could work, build their huts, and grow their food. Importantly, Mussa emphasized that those who started their new lives in Nalingu had come of their own accord. They were not coerced into joining the new village by the government or by the militants and vigilantes that some scholars (e.g., Lal) have described in their writing on the ujamaa period. "The process was voluntary and not compulsory. There was no coercion," he averred.

Nalingu's founding as an ujamaa village occurred when Operation Vijiji was first announced. At the time, Operation Vijiji was a popular movement, and Nalingu was probably regarded as a trailblazer ujamaa village in rural Mtwara—as evidenced by the location of the health center and the two tube wells (now defunct) in the village. The fact that there was no coercion in Nalingu during the ujamaa resettlement period is noteworthy because it provides a different perspective from the large body of literature that emphasizes Operation Vijiji's coercive features, especially after November 1973, and its failure (Shivji 2012). In 1973, when forced villagization began, the settlement process in Nalingu (which started between 1967 and 1968) had been nearly completed—sparing its people from possible coercion.

A PEACEFUL VILLAGE

Before 1967, sixty-two-year-old Aisha lived with her parents in Milamba, a coastal village not far from Nalingu. Her parents had decided to move to Nalingu with their children to start a new life in the new village. For Aisha, life was difficult before Nyerere came to power; people were on their own (*maisha yalikua ya kujitegemea*). "But when the order [*amri*] from the government came to build the nation [*kujenga taifa*], people decided to give up living on their farms, and start living together in larger villages to build the nation. They started looking for a good piece of land to build their houses in neat rows [*ila nyumba ziwe kwa mistariki*] and make it into a large village—an ujamaa village." She recalled how the chairman of her village had announced one day: "Let's go and select the land to start a new village." This, in her view, was how people from Milamba had decided to clear up the forest area and establish the new ujamaa village of Nalingu. "But we were young children then. Although we understood what was happening, we could not analyze it [*ila tulikua tunaelewa hatuwezi kuchanganua*]," she said.

Aisha recalled: "At the time, Shija was the ward secretary [*katibu*], but he lived in Msimbati, and Nasoro was the chairman. They were the ones who said, 'Let's build a good village,' because they were the ones who had gone to an educational seminar on how to build an ujamaa village and they returned to explain to us about it." A *mbalozi* had gone to the government to announce that people from Milamba had decided to start a new ujamaa village and that they needed help from the government—including grains, seeds, and seedlings to start a coconut farm.

Importantly, as with all the older residents of Nalingu, Aisha asserted that there was no coercion involved in establishing Nalingu. She described Nalingu as an ujamaa village where people had come to start new lives—the resettlement was a peaceful process and there were no arguments or quarrels among the villagers. "We were living in peace. It was a peaceful village. We built a dispensary and also a school. Since then, we have seen a lot of development. For example, now everyone in Nalingu owns a cell phone." Aisha's narrative reveals the enthusiasm that Tanzanians of her generation had for the spirit of ujamaa—and that, at least initially, it was a successful initiative in Nalingu. Indeed, Nalingu residents held Mwalimu Nyerere in high esteem.

People held different perspectives based on their individual experiences with the ujamaa experiment; they articulated what they remembered and were willing to reflect on in their interviews. As Lal (2015, 178) has presciently emphasized in her study of ujamaa in Mtwara, recovering a coherent narrative of villagization from the numerous elderly villagers she interviewed proved to be difficult. Her analysis of the elders' narrative accounts produced a disjointed composite—a patchy mosaic—instead of a clear, seamless portrait of the past.

Nonetheless, Nalingu residents were consistent regarding certain information: to begin, Nalingu had started as a new village in 1967–68 and was registered as an ujamaa village after the Villages Act of 1975 was passed. People from different villages had come to join Nalingu over time; its population had increased with the autochthonous population of descendants and new migrants. To reiterate, in contrast to several accounts of heavy-handed tactics and "forced villagization" described in the literature (Kikula 1997; Lal 2015; Scott 1998; Shivji 2012) none of those who told Nalingu's origin stories said that the resettlement process was in any way forced or that it had resulted in social and physical dislocation. Instead, they emphasized that the process was voluntary and peaceful—done in the spirit of nation building in response to Nyerere's call: "*Tujenge taifa letu!*" (Let's build our nation!).

The two large villages of Msimbati and Nalingu, then, differed significantly from each other. They had unique histories, socioeconomic profiles, and occupational structures. Msimbati was a far more prosperous and occupationally diverse village, with a long, spontaneous history and an autochthonous population. By contrast, Nalingu was a relatively new village purposely created in the 1960s as part of Operation Vijiji. The people of Nalingu were poorer and more reliant on the ocean for survival than were the people of Msimbati. Although the inhabitants of both villages were living on the same peninsula and inside the marine park's boundaries, the lived experiences of the people of Nalingu during and after the ujamaa era differed significantly from the lived experiences of those residing in Msimbati. Critically, as will be detailed in subsequent chapters, the people of Msimbati were directly affected by the gas project, which dispossessed them of their land and trees. By contrast, the people of Nalingu had benefited from the gas project, gaining access to electricity without being subjected to dispossession. Nonetheless, the people of Msimbati and Nalingu were united in their concerns around state violence, state domination, and the top-down manner in which projects were implemented in their region. Next, I will discuss how people narrated the changes they had experienced in their lives by dividing them into a then-and-now dichotomy.

From Ujamaa, to Ruksa and the Mageuzi Era

Consistently, narrators told their stories in terms of "then" and "now." They reflected on life during the Nyerere era compared with the eras of Mwinyi and his democratically elected successors. Additionally, they compared these past eras with their present lives, emphasizing different events and experiences, even within the same village—suggesting that while some people were "nostalgic" about the past as a time when "things were cheap" and "life was good," others in the same village recalled a life of hardship during those same periods.[15] Residents of some villages, particularly those from Msimbati, spoke of the past as a time when there was food and income security in the village—while for some people from other villages on the Mtwara peninsula, the past was a period of struggle. "*Maisha ilikua magumu sana*" (life was tough) was a common refrain. These people described the present as a happier time, with better access to various foods, transportation, and health care. Thus, even at the village level, individual experiences of *ujamaa* varied significantly.

MSIMBATI: FROM GOOD LIFE TO A MICRO-ECONOMY IN PERIL
In Msimbati, sixty-eight-year-old Juwazi painted a dark picture of how people led their lives during the pre-independence era. As Juwazi plaintively put it, before Nyerere came to power as Tanzania's first president, "We were like slaves [*mtumwa*]. Someone would 'buy you' and you went to work for him." Recalling her own experience, she narrated how, as a young girl, she left her parents to work. "I did not know what I would eat, and where I would sleep. I would make *uji* [porridge], nibble on whatever

was available, and sleep. Life was just like that. But Nyerere brought us freedom, and he brought us out of the shell. We started wearing clothes, seeing food in the shops, seeing public transport. We started seeing money. We are grateful to live like that still today—wearing clothes—we did not suffer as we did before Nyerere's time, the colonial period." Similarly, Mwanajuma, a soft-spoken fifty-eight-year-old who had lived her entire life in Msimbati, described how before Nyerere became president, men would wear *shuka* (a white calico cloth) and women would wear *kaniki* (calico, a plain-woven textile, often from cotton that has not been fully processed). "They did not wear underwear, not even a skirt [petticoat] inside, no bra or blouse like *kanga*." When Nyerere came to power, things improved. The prices of essential commodities in the shops were very low. "With just one shilling, you were able to buy one kilo of sugar, and some snacks as well, and with that same money, you could also buy a kilo of maize [*sembe*] and rice [*mchele*] . . . just one shilling was enough to buy the day's groceries and necessities, but now, you cannot even buy a piece of cassava with that much money. You have to take twenty thousand shillings to be able to buy rice, oil, and sugar [because of inflation]." Mwanajuma described President Mwinyi as a big blessing (*alikua alihamdulahi*). "Life was good during his regime. If you did some work, you could get money. Now we don't have enough money to buy our necessities [*maisha yametubana*]. If we wake up in the morning and have nothing [food] to give to the children, then it is obvious that our life has been squeezed, constricted."

The past as a time when things were cheap—when people could buy their day's rations with just one Tanzanian shilling—was frequently set against the present, when those same groceries cost TSh20,000. Access (i.e., availability) to clothes was another recurring point for many village residents, who explained that in the past, colorful clothes were not available; women had only a kaniki to wear, and men had only one *dhoti*. They would wash and wear the same dhoti every day; at night, they would give the dhoti to the children to cover themselves. In the present, however, the market is full of colorful clothes that don't run color; new and secondhand clothes from *ulaya* (the West).

As noted earlier, the people of Msimbati had been engaged in a prosperous sea cucumber trade between the Tanzanian and Mozambican sides. During the war in Mozambique, people from the Mozambican side could not sell sea cucumbers and other sea creatures on their side of the border because of the risk of being caught in the cross fire between Frelimo fighters and Portuguese government forces, and later between Frelimo and Renamo forces. In the past, Msimbati had served as a government customs check post for people crossing the Msimbati channel—especially those coming into Tanzania by sea from the Mozambican side. Although Msimbati is located at a significant distance from Mtwara town by road, the distance between them by sea is much shorter. Two brothers and a neighbor, who built the three separate concrete bungalows near Msimbati's entrance mentioned earlier in this chapter, had run a thriving business in sea cucumbers with people from the Mozambican side. Fishers from Mozambique would bring their marine resources to Msimbati in their fishing boats (*machuas*)—especially jongoo—in exchange for food grains, plastic chairs, buckets, and sundries from the Tanzanian side. Sea cucumbers were in great demand among the Chinese community in Tanzania and in China. They were exported by middlemen, who made enormous profits through the trade.[16] Sea cucumbers were being sent out of Msimbati by truckloads and in shipping containers.

In 2016, the government of Tanzania banned the trade of sea cucumbers and canceled the licenses of all those trading in these and other sea creatures brought from Mozambique. The ban significantly affected the economic and social lives of the people of Msimbati, upending a microeconomy based on the sea cucumber trade. Some residents migrated to Mozambique and began conducting business from the Mozambican ports or landing sites. The three concrete bungalows underscored Msimbati's history as a once prosperous village whose economy had been threatened by the trade ban.

Haki told me that while the people of Msimbati earned a lot of money in trade (people also rented their homes and sold food to fishers and traders from Mozambique), there were few opportunities for productive investments. "People did not know what to do with the money in terms of their own development and their village's development. But now it's different . . . it's difficult for money to come by, but people are seeing the benefits of investing in their development. . . . Now if I want to do something, I know I can do it. But in the past, even if I wanted to do something, there were no opportunities," he said.

Zainabu, a forty-two-year-old mother of four children, was one of my key interlocutors in Msimbati. She described how, especially during the Mwinyi era, the people of Msimbati became more aware of business opportunities at the village level. "So life was good," she said, "but then people did not know what to do with their money. So many youth who made a lot of money doing business with people on the Mozambican side simply wasted their money on drinking alcohol." Following the government's decision in 2016 to stop issuing permits to sea cucumber (and other) traders from the Mozambican side, the local economy built around this trade suddenly stopped. Still, as Zainabu explained, "Now, it's different, you can see that young men have become more aware of the value of money—and they are investing their earnings in building a house or upgrading their existing house—now every young man can build a house for himself if he wants to. Things have changed. The ocean has changed, too. It has run out of its supplies, and farming has also become a difficult undertaking these days because the land is no longer fertile and it is unproductive." As with Zainabu, nearly all my interlocutors couched their explanations for poor crop yields and low fish catches to "hot weather" (*joto kali* or *hali ya hewa*), unpredictable rains, and God's will (Mwenyezi Mungu), and not "climate change," more broadly.

The people of Msimbati had prospered through their trade with the people of Mozambique, especially during the war in the northern province of Cabo Delgado. The trade in sea cucumbers and other marine creatures had created a micro-economy of its own in Msimbati, with cash circulating within the village. The jongoo business provided temporary wage labor to the local people—opportunities to sell water, firewood, and food. When the Tanzanian government canceled all licenses related to the trade in sea cucumbers and marine creatures from Mozambique, Msimbati's growing communal prosperity suddenly ceased. Life precipitously became hard for the people of Msimbati. As I discuss in the book's final chapter, several of my interlocutors described their lives as having become hard, saying that "life is hard" (*maisha magumu*) had become something like a national anthem (*wimbo wa taifa*).

NALINGU: WHEN LIFE WAS GOOD

Mussa (introduced earlier), from Nalingu, remembered and reflected on his life during the Nyerere era and under the presidents who came in after. He expressed his gratitude to Mwalimu Nyerere for liberating Tanganyika from the British and for bringing freedom to the people of the new nation, changing their lives significantly. "Life before Nyerere was tough," he said. But during Nyerere's era, people could go to the ujamaa stores and buy sugar, salt, clothes, garden hoes, etc. all in the same shop. "There was only one shop in the village," he recalled. Mussa spoke of the difficulties people experienced in getting access to clothes even during the ujamaa years—there was a real shortage of clothes and footwear in Tanzania—but said that things began to improve when Mwinyi became president. "People were covering themselves with jute sacks, even when they came to political meetings, because they did not have proper clothes to wear . . . he [Mwinyi] just opened the road [economy] and after that people had access to plenty of secondhand clothes [*mitumba*] in shops, and shops started filling up with kangas." Those who had the money were able to buy the clothes they needed. "Yes, Mwinyi shed good light on our lives," he concluded.

Mussa revered Nyerere for bringing freedom to the people of Tanzania and improving their lives through his ujamaa policy and related infrastructure at the village level. At the same time, he remembered Nyerere's rule as a time when the country had a real shortage of clothes. Under Mwinyi's presidency, Tanzania saw the economy open. Mwinyi allowed Tanzanian citizens to import goods, including secondhand clothes. For Mussa, Mwinyi's liberalization policies had a significant impact on people's lives—they gave them access to secondhand, discarded, and donated clothes from the West.

Hadija, a sixty-six-year-old woman from Nalingu, shed light on the social dynamics and complexities associated with the implementation of the ujamaa villages. She recalled that the village had a communal farm (*shamba la umma*) on which people worked. Each *mbalozi* had a group of ten households who helped him start a coconut farm and plant millet (*mtama*) and peas (*njugu*), which they would harvest as a community and hand over to the government shop. People built an ujamaa shop in the village and ran it as a cooperative store. They invested the earnings in buying livestock—goats and cows, which reproduced and multiplied. "It was all good. But then after some time, the shop closed, and the goats and cows started disappearing. Our leaders were corrupt. They emptied the shop, ate the goats and cows, and that was it—it was the end of ujamaa and the start of a hard life for us." Hadija's recollections are consistent with reports of corruption and incompetence, especially among the village leaders in villages elsewhere in Mtwara during and after the ujamaa period (see Lal 2015, 199). People did not reflect on how these developments had affected the social relations among the residents—whether this had resulted in enduring animosity and other interpersonal tensions. The village population at the time was significantly smaller than present-day Nalingu. In Hadija's case, after ujamaa, her husband returned to his previous life as a fisher, and Hadija went to work on a small plot of land to grow food for her family. As Lal (2015, 218–19), in her study of ujamaa in Mtwara, notes: "When a rural woman claims that *ujamaa* was a positive force in her life, she is not necessarily demonstrating a false consciousness or betraying a rote internalization of official discourse. Her comments likely correspond to the actual ambivalence of her experience, in which she was able to benefit from aspects of life in *ujamaa* villages even though her initial move was traumatic."

In remembering and reflecting on their lives during different periods (*kipindi*)—especially during the Nyerere-led ujamaa era—people often compared their memories with their present lives. Sixty-one-year-old Salama, one of my key interlocutors in Nalingu, explained how people were mostly on their own before Nyerere became president. During Nyerere's time in office, however, people began to have a sense of belonging and unity; they began cooperating. At the same time, like other interlocutors, Salama recalled that people did not have proper access to clothes or food during Nyerere's presidency compared with the grain and clothing options available today. "Today, we are thankful to God that we don't have to live in our black kaniki; we can wear bright and colorful kangas that do not fade" she concluded.

Sofia, a fifty-four-year-old resident of Nalingu, focused her narrative on the changes she had witnessed over time regarding the social relations in her village and elsewhere. "During Nyerere's time, life was good. It was stable, there was no volatility, and there were no political or government distractions or hassles. Food was plentiful, and people had compassion and sympathy in their hearts, and there was a willingness to help out, but now people have lost their sense of compassion. Their hearts have been filled with rage, hate, animosity. You come across a fellow villager or kin who is in trouble and is upset about it. Still, you don't help that person."

As with several other narrators, for Sofia, the Nyerere era was peaceful, a time of social cohesion in her village and the country at large. As she put it, "People had compassion and sympathy in their hearts"—however, there was a shortage of everyday necessities, including tea and sugar. Now, things are different. People have become more self-centered, but the market is full of clothes and other necessities—a legacy of the presidents who came after Nyerere.

These narratives suggest that the neoliberalization of the Tanzanian economy and society has significantly affected people's perceptions of social relations and social cohesion in their communities. People's access to material goods such as clothes, cell phones, cement, and corrugated metal sheets to build their houses had significantly improved. Still, they were concerned that their fellow villagers were becoming increasingly self-centered and less caring and giving. As I detail in chapter 7, with neoliberalization, responsibilization, and the financialization of everything, villagers equated their overall well-being with money and, more specifically, their financial well-being.

CONCLUSION

The brief overview of Tanzania's political, economic, and social history presented in this chapter provides a necessary backdrop for our understanding of the changes that have taken place in the country's conservation and extractive sector over the last several decades. It gives us the information needed to understand why conservation and extractive projects in Tanzania are centralized and continue to be implemented from the top down, despite the rhetoric of people's participation and empowerment in policy documents. As Greco (2016, 36) has observed, "The administrative and political institutions of present-day Tanzanian villages are very much a legacy of the institutional reforms brought about by villagization . . . there is also continuity between past and present authoritarianism, centralized decision making and top-down policies."

Moreover, the chapter highlights how and why, despite the sociopolitical and ideological shifts that occurred in the country under five different presidents over more than fifty years, the ruling party (CCM) has remained in power since its inception. The chapter addresses the consequences of this continued rule and how it affects people's expectations of their government.

The chapter also focused on the changes that took place in rural Mtwara during the ujamaa era and the lived experiences of those who were present during Nyerere's presidency—which encompassed Tanzania's transition to a multiparty democracy with a neoliberal agenda. The oral histories of Msimbati and Nalingu revealed their divergent histories. Msimbati was an old village, while Nalingu emerged as a new village during the ujamaa period. Though very real for people in both villages, the experience of Operation Vijiji had faded into the past. The forces of social transformation in Mtwara had varied over the years, and people had moved on with their lives. People from both villages recalled the changes they had witnessed in their lives and villages over the years; many spoke positively of their experiences as part of Operation Vijiji, while others recalled unpleasant experiences, such as corrupt leaders using up scarce supplies from the ujamaa shops in Nalingu and the constant shortage of essential items in the shops in Msimbati. People were neither completely admiring of the ujamaa era nor entirely scornful of it. As Lal (2015, 209) has observed in her work on a reconstructed history of ujamaa in Mtwara, "Mtwara villagers' conceptions of their relationship to the Tanzanian government and evaluations of the *ujamaa* project were—and are—complex, sophisticated, and profoundly ambivalent." The narratives of people from Nalingu and Msimbati bore this out. Residents did not provide a consensus but highlighted different experiences, despite having lived in the same villages during the same periods.

The Nyerere-inspired ujamaa developments of the 1960s and 1970s had significant impacts on the country's social fabric, as did the political and institutional changes that took place in and after the 1990s. From ujamaa to *ubinafsishaji* (privatization), these ideological shifts directly affected the decisions that government actors made in the realm of conservation and extraction. State-owned conservation institutions and extractive projects became increasingly privatized from the 1990s onward, leading to very different contractual arrangements between the state and ordinary citizens (see Gardner 2016).

As will be illustrated in the book's later chapters, the land (ownership) question became a contentious topic for the people of rural Mtwara—especially those who were displaced and dispossessed by conservation and extractive projects. In Mtwara, these consisted of the marine park, the gas project, and the MDC project. Questions around land and compensation harken back to the ujamaa era, when land was nationalized and the president was constitutionally made the custodian of all land in Tanzania on behalf of its citizens.

Overarchingly, people described having moved on from the past to live in "modern" times (*wakati wa kisasa*). This exemplified their sentiments with statements such as: "Now we have different kinds of colorful clothes to wear"; "Everyone in the village now has a cell phone"; and "Now people can travel to Mtwara town in minivans and on motorcycles and come back home the same day." Still, as will be described in the next chapter, people were worried about their livelihoods and about their food security. As Lofchie (2014, 207–8) has emphasized, despite the fact that the Tanzania government has introduced numerous social and economic programs over the years, economic growth has not improved the lives of "the overwhelming majority of Tanzanians, who continue to be rural, agricultural, and desperately poor. . . . The conditions of life for Tanzanian small farmers, who still comprise about 75 percent of the population, have barely changed, if at all, during the past twenty years. Most continue to live in the perilous margin between bare survival and near-famine conditions caused by periodic crop failures." In light of this background, the next chapter discusses some of the key insecurities that people face in the context of the implementation of the marine park in rural Mtwara.

2

"THE OCEAN IS TIRED. IT'S ON LEAVE."

Marine Conservation and Food Security

WHEN I STARTED my fieldwork in August 2010, the marine park in rural Mtwara had already completed the first two phases of its implementation. Consultants had conducted a terminal evaluation of the project. They concluded their report on an optimistic note, suggesting that with sustained funding and government support, the marine park would likely achieve its objectives endorsed by the primary funder—Global Environment Facility (GEF) (Tortell and Ngatunga 2007). At the time, Msimbati had a reasonably well-developed infrastructure to cater to potential tourists, including a small beach hotel, a ticketing office, a tollgate, and a stipulated entry fee ($20 USD for international visitors). The beach, accessible only with a ticket, was depicted in the promotional brochures as pristine. To use Levine's (2007, 575) characterization, Msimbati was a "showcase village," meant to impress visitors and international donors and used for publicity purposes. The park's second gate office was in Kilambo, near the Ruvuma River, which defines the Tanzania-Mozambique border. Kilambo did not have Msimbati's infrastructure or tourist-attracting beachfront views. Instead, the Kilambo gate office focused on the mangroves in Litembe village as a primary tourist attraction.

At this time, the marine park's policies and patrolling activities had already begun to affect some of the fishing villages on the Mtwara peninsula, including Msangamkuu, Sinde, and Namera. These villages were in the park's "buffer zone," just outside its boundaries. Fishers from these buffer zone villages continued to venture into fishing grounds inside the marine park, despite being aware of the park's restrictions. Some were allegedly engaged in illegal and unsustainable fishing practices, including dynamite fishing inside the protected area and no-take zones. As a result, they became the subject of complaints from the park's warden-in-charge and the people of Msimbati.

Households in sea-bordering villages dependent on fishing and marine-related activities for their subsistence most directly and severely experienced the negative impacts of the marine park's restrictions—in terms of access to fishing grounds and threats to food security.[1] Because the marine park was implemented in a staggered manner, more villages and sub-villages were incorporated into the park's catchment area over the years, with varying degrees of cooperation with authorities. Differences in the occupational structure of the villages and the duration of the marine park's involvement in their communities affected how individuals and households from these villages cooperated with the marine park authorities.

Not all those who were living in marine park villages had experienced the park's impact uniformly; not all villages inside the park's boundaries were "fishing villages." In Kihimika, for example, a park village several kilometers away from the coast, households mainly relied on farming and only occasionally took to fishing. While seafront villages such as Msimbati, Nalingu, and Mkubiru were directly affected by the park's restrictions, predominantly agricultural villages such as Mtendachi and Namidondi were less directly affected by the restrictions. As will become clear, the food security situation in the marine park villages was complex and varied across villages over time. Later in this chapter, I present a case study of food security in Mkubiru village to provide a nuanced analysis of the complexities underlying food security—availability, accessibility, affordability, and culturally accepted responses.

This chapter examines the overall local response to the marine park during the first ten years of its implementation. It focuses on the nature of local peoples' opposition to the marine park and on the food security situation in the region.[2] MPAs are known to boost fish abundance by implementing no-take zones and other restrictions on local fishers. In the process, however, they tend to disrupt local fishers' access to fish and other marine resources, leading to food insecurity and related disappointment among local communities. As Fabinyi, Dressler, and Pido (2017, 117) have argued, the relationship between MPAs and food security is "multi-faceted and complex, with various local contextual factors that mediate between fish and food security." Drawing on evidence from fishing communities in San Vicente, Palawan province, in the Philippines, the authors highlight specific linkages between fish and food security—how fishing contributes to food security through its primary role as a main source of income used to buy other essential foods. Understanding the MPA's overall impact on the local population's food insecurity, therefore, necessitates detailed research involving multiple methods of data collection and analysis.[3]

As noted in the introduction, the marine park's stated goal is to contribute to marine ecosystem sustainability—while equally improving the livelihoods of local communities through alternative livelihood projects and the promotion of ecotourism in the area. The General Management Plan (URT 2005, revised in 2011) clearly emphasizes the importance of community participation as key to the project's acceptability and success.[4] In this chapter, however, I show how, despite the initial consultations with stakeholders, the actual implementation of the marine park in the Mtwara Region proceeded in a top-down manner, i.e., with minimal proactive consultation and engagement with the local residents.

Narratives elicited from a cross-section of people in six coastal villages provide insights into how the marine park led to displacement and dispossession and directly and indirectly contributed to food insecurity in the region. These narratives show how top-down implementation, which often involved displacement and violence, intensified residents' feelings of distress, suffering, disempowerment, humiliation, anguish, despair, and extreme resentment toward the marine park. In essence, these narratives illustrate social suffering within the context of the park's implementation. Social suffering refers to the lived experience of social dislocation enacted by those in power on the least powerful—primarily through exclusion (Farmer 2004; Kleinman, Das, and Lock 1997). In this context, social suffering refers to how large numbers of individuals collectively experience suffering and how they narrativize and articulate their sentiments about their experiences with dispossession and displacement caused by the marine park. These adverse effects were especially pronounced among female-headed households. This was due to their increasing poverty, lack of economic support (either from other family members or the government), marginalization, social disarticulation, and worsening everyday food insecurity. I discuss the intensification of these forms of distress and suffering later in this chapter and in more detail in chapter 4.

This chapter has two sections. Section 1 explores the ethos in the park villages, detailing the miscommunications, resentments, and violent confrontations that characterized the local response to the marine park following its implementation in 2000. Section 2 delineates how the marine park's implementation led to significant changes in food access and security for the coastal villages. In section 2, I focus on local perceptions of food availability and accessibility as well as villagers' experiences of food insecurity and changes in modes of food acquisition. Altogether, this chapter demonstrates that without the necessary social safety nets and alternative livelihood options in place, the implementation of the marine park increased community opposition and undermined economic and social development. As a corollary, the chapter illustrates why improving food security should be a key component of marine biodiversity and conservation interventions. The goal should be to make these interventions genuinely collaborative and sustainable in terms of both social equity and ecological effectiveness.

SECTION 1: DISPLACEMENT AND FOOD INSECURITY—THE INITIAL YEARS

During preparatory fieldwork and later through interviews with coastal villagers on the Mtwara peninsula regarding the marine park, I found that people were generally aware of the marine park's presence in their region and its emphasis on marine conservation (*hifadhi*).[5] However, few people were aware of the process involved in planning and implementing the project in its initial stages. As noted in the introduction, I was first introduced to the problems associated with the marine park in Msangamkuu, a fishing village that lies in the buffer zone just outside the park's boundaries. Despite its location outside the park, Msangamkuu was subjected to the same regulations and restrictions that applied to villages inside the park.

Roots of Resentment: Msangamkuu

It was Hassan, the fifty-one-year-old chairman of Msangamkuu, who, earlier in this book, had related the history of dynamite fishing in the coastal Mtwara Region. In September 2010, Hassan explained to me why Msangamkuu, despite being a large fishing village on the Mtwara peninsula, was not included in the marine park's boundary. He remembered the day a delegation from the Ministry of Natural Resources and Tourism came to Msangamkuu. The delegation had explained the government's rationale for implementing a marine park in Mtwara: to protect the marine environment and promote ecotourism in the region. Members of the delegation had tried to convince the people of Msangamkuu to become part of the marine park, but local elected leaders did not feel they had sufficient details about the project—neither were they convinced that the park would bring them any tangible benefits. Some had heard from relatives and friends on Mafia Island that Tanzania's first marine park—implemented there in 1996—had made their lives difficult, especially for fishing households.[6] "Eventually," Hassan told me, "the leaders decided to cooperate, but the villagers refused to cooperate with the marine park authorities because they were not convinced that it would bring them any benefits." For this reason, Msangamkuu was not included in the marine park's boundaries.

However, while Msangamkuu remained outside the marine park's official boundaries, fishers from this village were still subjected to the park's regulations. Park officials knew that fishers from Msangamkuu were "fishing the line," or freely venturing into the fishing grounds of the park villages. This included entering the strictly demarcated no-take zones near Msimbati village to catch fish and other sea creatures—including turtles. Officials also knew that fishers from Msangamkuu engaged (by their admission) in dynamite fishing in the protected areas.

Rashidi, the thirty-seven-year-old village executive officer (VEO) from Msangamkuu village, was more forceful than Hassan in explaining why the people of Msangamkuu had refused to be included in the park's boundaries. He recalled that representatives from the marine park had come to Msangamkuu to tell the people that the park was "the *sheria*" (law) but had failed to explain what this law comprised. Instead, they began apprehending people for "illegal" fishing activities and sending them to the police station, court, or jail. "There's a lot of fighting going on," Rashidi explained to me then and continued. "Because of the marine park, politics has increased. Maybe the government wants to do what it thinks is best for the people, but they did not do sufficient research before implementing the project. The project's goals are not bad, but the way they have implemented it is a problem." For Rashidi, the problem was with the government officials advocating for the marine park. In his experience, their poor communication strategies had contributed to the ongoing tensions between local fishers and marine park authorities.

Evidence of villagers' widespread mistrust of park authorities became clear during my first visit to Msangamkuu, in 2010. I was strolling on the beach and approached a group of young fishers sitting under the shade of a fishing boat being repaired. I asked them if I could photograph the colorful reef fish they had caught and piled up in a basket. Angrily, they refused and dispersed. I later learned that they thought I was there on behalf of the marine park to take incriminating photos of their illegal catch. In due course, I was able to gain their trust; the young fishers learned from their parents and grandparents, whom I had interviewed, that I was a researcher—that I was a *mwalimu* in Canada and that I was there to gather information about the marine park's impact on the local people. More importantly, seeing me with my research assistants—Abdallah and Salum, in particular—helped to reassure the youth in Msangamkuu. Salum was, after all, their childhood friend.

Throughout my fieldwork in Msangamkuu, people expressed sentiments like those of Rashidi. They explained that the intentions behind the government's decision to implement the marine park were good—that the project itself was not bad but that the way the project had been implemented (in a top-down manner, without "educating" people or increasing awareness about the project's goals and strategies, rules and restrictions) had resulted in a lot of fear and consternation among the local people.

Daranga, the fifty-one-year-old VEO from Msangamkuu, sought to contextualize the overall negative disposition of villagers toward the marine park. Daranga said the real problem was the gap (*pengo*) between what the marine park authorities wanted and what the local people expected. The locals, he said, had nothing in terms of assets; the marine park authorities had confiscated fishing nets from local fishers without giving them legal nets or alternative employment opportunities in exchange.[7] As Daranga explained: "The elderly people and women in particular have suffered the most; they can't go and catch octopus, squid ... so people are suffering. Large nets are costly. People can't afford to buy them."

As Chuenpagdee et al. (2013, 235) have emphasized, the significance of "step zero"—the "initial stage when the idea was conceived, communicated, and discussed among stakeholders"—is crucial for the broader acceptance of marine parks among local communities. In the marine park's case, the organizers faltered at step zero of the project. Even immediately after that, organization was flawed; the project began a year later than was planned and two and a half years after the park was gazetted in 2000. As Gawler and Muhando (2004, 8) observe in their evaluation report, "The delayed start had serious implications for implementation and is one of the root causes of the problems linked to high expectations encountered in this initial phase" (see also Tortell and Ngatunga 2007, 11). The delayed start contributed to people's frustration and mistrust and to a loss of the initial enthusiasm they had shown for the park—especially in Msimbati.

Roots of Disenchantment: Msimbati

In its early years, the local response to the marine park in Msimbati was mostly positive. The marine park's main office was in Msimbati—the largest village included in the park's boundaries. In return for their cooperation and welcoming attitude, the people in the village were promised a share of the park's gate fees (formally known as benefit sharing)—though this promise, like many others, was never met. People in Msimbati were initially optimistic about the benefits the park would bring to the village; the proposed implementation plans received a more positive reception in Msimbati than they had in Nalingu. Soon, however, the initial optimism devolved into suspicion and disappointment.

Bi Mkubwa was fifty-eight years old when I first met her in 2012. Born and raised in Msimbati, she had spent her entire life in the village. Bi Mkubwa had been married and divorced four times and had four sons and a daughter. Two of her former husbands were originally from Mozambique. When they decided to move back, she chose to get divorced rather than live away from her aging parents. Moreover, she was afraid of the ongoing war on the Mozambican side. Bi Mkubwa had taken a keen interest in marine conservation. She was the most well-known female protagonist of the marine park I met during my fieldwork. Bi Mkubwa had participated extensively in the marine park's planning stages. She had attended all of the park's initial consultation meetings and workshops and had served as one of the interlocutors for the marine park's periodic external evaluations, which independent consultants conducted (see Gawler and Muhando 2004; Tortell and Ngatunga 2007). She was also among the first group of female volunteers (*kujitolea*) from Msimbati village to participate in the marine conservation activities undertaken by the Marine Parks and Reserves Unit (MPRU) and the World Wildlife Fund (WWF) in the Mnazi Bay area in support of the marine parks during its initial years.

At the time, Bi Mkubwa was working as a part-time volunteer ranger (*mgambo*) for the park. "My job," she explained, "is to protect mangroves, to plant mangroves, to patrol mangroves, to patrol tortoises, to set up turtle nests, to find out when turtle babies come out, and to prevent people from catching the turtles . . . that's my job. My work is in the ocean. At the end of the month, they pay me enough to buy some soap." She said this laughingly, suggesting that she volunteered at the marine park not for compensation but because she genuinely believed in the importance of conservation. Bi Mkubwa wore the Tanzania Marine Park and Reserves' official light blue shirt; a logo embroidered above the shirt pocket depicted two sea horses.

Bi Mkubwa recounted the uncertainties, rumors, miscommunications, and misunderstandings that marked the initial contact period between representatives of the MPRU and Msimbati's residents. She recalled:

> One day, someone came running to us and said: "*Jamani!* [My goodness!]. They have entered the island of the white man [*kisiwa cha mzungu*], and now they will sell us like slaves to the white man!" They spread rumors like this one. None of it was true. Representatives from our villages were taken to Mafia Island on a study tour to learn about the marine park there. When they came back, they told us very little about what they had seen and learned

about the marine park in Mafia. The truth is that there was nothing called the "island of the white man." They even invented the names of Europeans. They said that the European who wanted to buy us as slaves, his name was Paki Wadeni [park warden], and the name of his boss was Wadeni Nchaji [warden in-charge]. They just spread baseless rumors like this one in the village. But then, people soon learned that these were all false rumors. They realized that the marine park was a government project, so there was no problem. Still, many initially thought that the marine park had been implemented to stop people from accessing their traditional fishing grounds, which was untrue. And so, that's how the marine park first entered our village.

Bi Mkubwa narrated this story jocularly, laughing as she told it. It was a well-known story. In their report on the terminal review of the marine park, Tortell and Ngatunga (2007) mention that they were made aware of these rumors to draw attention to the miscommunication that had colored the initial periods of the marine park's presence in rural Mtwara. Bi Mkubwa dismissed these rumors about the "white man's island" and the "slave-buying Europeans" because she had been involved in the planning process that preceded the Mtwara Declaration on the marine park in April 1999. She had participated in workshops where she had met with MPRU officials, bureaucrats from the Mtwara Development Council, and leaders from other villages. As a result, she was well informed about the marine park's goals and objectives.

Most residents of Msimbati, however, were not consulted during the planning and implementation of the marine park. People repeatedly lamented the government's decision to "impose" the project on them without "educating" them (i.e., providing more detailed and specific information) about the policy and the project's goals. People were critical of park officials for not holding an open meeting in their respective villages to inform locals about the park's details—including its restrictions. Many complained that their own leaders had let them down. They specifically alleged that ten to fifteen leaders from different villages had met with representatives from the MPRU in Dar es Salaam, where they had "secretly" signed and stamped the acceptance papers (*waliiba iba sahihi na mihuri*). Villagers alleged that their leaders had informed park authorities that the "entire village had accepted the project," when in fact they had not consulted with the village residents. Yusuf, a sixty-seven-year-old resident of Msimbati said: "Our leaders betrayed us. They were in the hands of the government, and we did not have the strength to oppose the decision. Even if we had opposed the project, they would have coaxed us into accepting the project, because ultimately, it's the government's decision to implement the marine park here."

Some village leaders, including Kadude, who went by the nickname Tostao, expressed their disappointment with the marine park authorities. Kadude was in his late forties when I met him in September 2011. He was the chairman of Msimbati village, a confident, friendly, and extroverted leader. That day, he was wearing a white T-shirt embroidered with the MPRU's logo (two sea horses). Pointing to the logo on his T-shirt, he asked me, "Do you know what this represents?" He didn't wait for my response. It was a rhetorical question; Kadude proceeded to give an impromptu monologue on the importance of marine conservation. He spoke of the iconic prehistoric coelacanth fish found in the Tanga region and its symbolic importance for marine conservation. Kadude's monologue was meant to impress not only me and my research assistants but also a group of villagers that had begun gathering around him. When speaking publicly, Kadude compellingly relayed what he had learned from participating in WWF-sponsored workshops. The interview he gave that day, however, was less impassioned. Short and matter of fact, Kadude's thoughts on the marine park were unenthusiastic: "Initially they told us that they only wanted a small area along the coast to protect marine life and that they would mark that area as a 'no-fishing zone' with marker-buoys. They said that tourists will come to watch fish, and local fishers could go about their fishing activities a little further away. We thought it was a great idea, so we welcomed them, but now they have taken most of Msimbati, all the way till Ruvula. They have also not given out legal fishing gear. We are not happy. Our enthusiasm for the marine park has dissipated." Kadude had participated in several WWF-sponsored workshops and seminars on marine conservation and supported the marine park. Over the years, however, he had become disillusioned with the park managers. Park authorities had failed continuously to live up to their promises to local leaders—promises of tangible benefits to their communities.

Rehema, a loquacious and engaging forty-three-year-old single mother with two children, was one of my key interlocutors in Mtandi/

Msimbati village. She was a vocal critic of the marine park and echoed Kadude's sentiments. Rehema was particularly frustrated with the park authorities because they prevented her from selling a plot of farmland she had inherited from her father. The plot was inside the marine park's gated section. Rehema recounted a narrative widely shared among the people of Msimbati—that initially, the people of Msimbati had welcomed the marine park.

At the outset, park authorities claimed that they intended to protect only a small area near the oceanfront (protecting a small area is known as *tengefu*), including the mangroves (*mikoko*). They would restrict people from fishing in that area for only two or three years—until the fish had recovered and were in abundance. Park management had told the local people that they would use mooring buoys to indicate the boundary of the protected ocean area, so that the borders would be clear. "After a few months, however," Rehema told me, "they said that they did not need to put the mooring buoys because now they were protecting the entire ocean. We were shocked. Then they said they were also protecting the dry land [*nchi kavu*], our farmlands, and the forests [*misitu*]. They said that we could not sell our land to anyone because it was inside the marine park. That's when we all got angry with the marine park and wanted it to go away."[8]

The lack of transparency or consultation with the community—and the insufficient information regarding the marine park's goals and objectives—amounted to deliberate miscommunication about the project's scope. This led to feelings of mistrust, exploitation, and betrayal among Msimbati's residents. While they had been initially optimistic about the project, these villagers developed an increasingly negative disposition toward the marine park authorities.

When asked about benefits (*faida*) or losses (*hasara*) brought by the marine park, people emphatically stated that they had not seen any tangible (economic) benefits—not in their individual lives nor in their respective villages. This was contrary to what the marine park officials, district-level bureaucrats, and politicians had promised: that the marine park would cause tourism to flourish in the region, generating jobs and economic opportunities, better roads and transportation (including a reliable motorized ferryboat), and electricity. Some attributed this disparity to the fact that the marine park was still in its initial stages—any benefits would not be seen for some time. The most common response, however, was that in the next few years, people's lives would change for the worse. The marine park restricted people's access to traditional fishing waters, but crop yields declined because of unpredictable rains and depleting soil quality. This made farming—as an "alternative" means of livelihood—even more difficult for households relying primarily on fishing.

Roots of Indignation: Nalingu

Because of the opaque manner in which the park was implemented, there was increasing cynicism and hostility among the local residents toward anyone connected with the project. People from all six villages where I conducted fieldwork expressed similar resentment. Nalingu village residents were particularly vocal about their criticism. "We want to have absolutely nothing to do with the marine park," they said emphatically during my first meeting with a group of local residents—men and women. "We don't even want to talk about it."

The implementation of no-take zones had put the park managers in direct conflict with fishers in key fishing villages. Park officials were accused of calling in security personnel to physically intimidate people who violated the park's restrictions. The punishment for infractions of park rules included confiscating nets and boats, which led to further impoverishment among local residents (Robinson, Albers, and Kirama 2014). During focus group discussions in Nalingu, elderly fishers would often digress from the topic at hand to express their distress. They would angrily repeat the same statement: "They have confiscated our nets!" (*Wame nyang'anya nyavu!*). In August 2011, when I visited the marine park's office in Ruvula, I saw dozens of confiscated fishing nets piled several meters high in the front yard, along with four or five small wooden fishing boats (*mitumbwi*) that were slated to be destroyed.

Salama, the daughter of Nalingu's first chairman, generally supported the marine park. Nonetheless, she recalled how the initiative had started unpleasantly. Salama vividly remembered two men—strangers—who had come to live in Nalingu. As Salama described: "They did not tell us who they were and why they had come to live in Nalingu, but we knew they were soldiers, that they were spies [*wapelelezi*]." The two newcomers had rented a house in the village for a month. Deceptively, they had gone about the normal activities, like farming and going to the beach in Mnazi village to catch fish. "But we knew all along that they were spies sent by the government to spy on us," Salama said. One day the two "spies" went to Mnazi village and rounded up fishers who were using homemade bottle bombs to catch fish. The two men brought the fishers to the chairman's office in Nalingu to beat them up. There was a commotion (*mtafaruku*) in the village; a crowd had gathered before the chairman's office. Salama's father, who was the village chairman at the time, decided not to punish the fishers. The crowd of villagers had threatened to beat up the two "spies" if the punishment was carried out. Salama explained: "The soldiers had even beaten an elderly person from the village that day. They humiliated him by making him dance. The old man was fasting but asked for water to drink because he was exhausted. A police van came in the evening and took away all those who were apprehended. We did not see those two men again." It was a terrifying experience for Salama and her fellow villagers. The security personnel's stratagem had undermined the little trust the local people had placed in the marine park. Residents felt they were being dominated by the security forces sent by the marine park authorities—that they had been betrayed. Salama's conclusion highlights the lasting impact of this betrayal: "Even if you wake me up from sleep today, I will be able to remember what happened that day. It was terrifying."

Embedded in the participants' narratives was a common theme—of broken promises and feelings of betrayal. Many villagers saw the marine park as a threat to their livelihood. Nalingu residents had adopted an openly confrontational stance against marine park authorities since the project's inception. Following violent confrontations between the park-employed security forces and Nalingu residents, the local leadership resolved to disregard the park's restrictions. One thirty-eight-year-old woman from Nalingu explained:

> They say that the people of Nalingu are ignorant. We don't understand, we are recalcitrant, violent and dangerous, we don't cooperate. That's not true. We have a school, a health center, a government office, a warehouse, so it's not true that we have not cooperated with the government. But we don't want to have anything to do with the marine park or the people who work for the marine park because we don't like the project. The ocean is our farm

[*bahari ni shamba letu . . . kilimo chetu ni bahari tu*]. If we are not allowed to fish in the ocean, where will we get the money to buy food and send our children to school?

The above perspective is a corrective to the widely held perception that the people of Nalingu have a violent disposition toward the marine park. Instead, as this speaker explains, they are loath to comply with the marine park's restrictions because they have no alternative but to rely on the ocean for their food and livelihood.

Issa, the chairman of Nalingu at the time, was particularly vocal in his condemnation of the marine park officers' heavy-handedness in dealing with Nalingu's residents. When I interviewed Issa in July 2011, I asked him why the people of Nalingu were so against the marine park. He had this to say:

The marine park people tell us that our fishing methods are not good. We use nets that destroy corals and small fish and eggs . . . but that's not true. They have only theoretical knowledge. They don't have practical knowledge like we do. . . . We also use beach seine [*tandilo*] to catch fish. They say that it's illegal [*haramu*]. We once asked the marine park people to go to the sea with us so that they could see how we use the tandilo, but they refused and kept insisting that it is illegal. Because of all this misunderstanding, many people here are angry and have deliberately decided to use dynamite explosives for fishing.

Later that day, Issa invited me into his house—a small hut with a thatched roof. He asked me to take photos of him with one of his granddaughters and to make sure to give him print copies as a keepsake. Issa urged me to notice the living conditions in the village: "Look around, look at my hut, look at my possessions, that old, rusted bicycle there . . . do you think I'm rich [*tajiri*]? Do you think I've become the chairman of this village to become wealthy? We are poor people here. Our wells have dried up. We don't even have electricity in the village, and we rely on the ocean for our livelihoods. The ocean is small [bay—*bahari ndogo*]. The marine park people should leave us alone." In calling my attention to his poverty, even though he was the village chairman, and to the fact that the entire village was underprivileged with poor infrastructure, Issa justified the reasons why the villagers were opposed to the marine park: the restrictions would result in the further impoverishment of the people of Nalingu. This, in turn, explains his plea to the marine park authorities to allow the people of Nalingu to continue with their livelihoods.

A repeating theme regarding marine parks is the disconnect between the dominant, institutionalized discourse promoted by marine conservationists and international NGOs regarding the need to protect marine life from overfishing, destructive fishing, and marine extractive practices and the community-level discourse regarding the need to give credence to local knowledge, practices, and concerns.[9]

Significantly, the most prevailing response toward the marine park in all the coastal villages at the time was negativity and cynicism. For example, Masudi, from Mkubiru village, who was in his late sixties, said that although the marine park had been implemented several years ago, he had not seen any development from its activities. On the contrary, he said, the police had apprehended people (mainly the youth) from Mkubiru and sent them to jail. He explained: "Those people from the marine park patrol have confiscated people's fishing nets and their boats, so people are afraid. Many are in jail and cases are still going on in the courts. People have become increasingly poor. They are not fishing. They don't know what else to do. What's the use of conservation if it will make people hungry?"

People could not state specific ways in which the marine park had brought them *any* benefit; "no benefit" (*hamna faida*) was the collective response. I elaborate on this dissonance with more illustrative examples in chapter 4. Local discourses were predominantly focused on how the marine park had disrupted people's livelihoods and identity. As noted earlier, people commonly ended their emphatic statements with rhetorical questions such as: "What's the use of conservation if it's going to make life more difficult for us?" and "What's the use if it's going to make people hungry?" People directed these rhetorical questions at the marine park authorities, holding them morally responsible for causing hunger and food insecurity in the park villages.

Conservation and Double Discourse

I first met Musa, who was in his early fifties, in September 2011. He was the chairman of Mtandi village. Musa was amicable and well liked by his fellow villagers and spoke very dignifiedly with others. He had participated in some of the training programs and workshops organized by the WWF in collaboration with the marine park authorities. These workshops were intended to provide key leaders in the marine park villages with the necessary background information on the marine park's goals and objectives and the country's larger goal of marine conservation.

Musa described to me the initial confrontations in Msimbati and other fishing villages between government agents (patrols) and villagers—especially the youth, who were using dynamite for fishing. According to Musa, the confrontations eventually stopped, as people began to understand the marine park's importance. Local leaders (including himself) had done their best to educate their fellow villagers about the importance of marine conservation. Musa explained: "But people here are poor, they have small nets, so they cannot go fishing in the deep ocean, they get only small fish. . . . It has brought them hunger, and also problems with sending children to school." He also pointed to the marine park authorities' unrealistic expectations of the local villagers. For example, the park authorities had given the community three fishing skiffs with outboard motors. These skiffs were intended to be split between thirty fishers, who were expected to work in groups of ten. In reality, however, more than ten thousand people were living in Msimbati and Mtandi. The donation of three fishing boats did not have a significant positive impact on people's livelihoods. "They had promised alternative fishing gear and income earning opportunities," Musa said, "but nothing has happened. . . . At first, we thought the marine park would give us modern seaworthy boats and nets, and we would go out into the sea and get lots of fish, money and food, but nothing of that has happened. There is no development, and people are hungry. . . . Life has become very hard."

In the same breath, however, Musa continued: "But there are several benefits of the marine park. For example, people here used to eat turtle meat and turtle eggs, but after interactions with the marine park staff and WWF, we have given up eating turtle meat and their eggs. . . . We protect them, and the turtles return to the sea." He ended his narrative by expressing his uncertainty regarding the future and what it would look like for the people in his region. Musa said life was likely to get harder, and the climate may also change.

Elected village leaders who had participated in meetings and workshops organized by the WWF, like Musa and Kadude, were better informed about the marine park's goals and activities. As local leaders, however, they typically engaged in a double discourse of the kind embedded in the preceding narratives. They simultaneously emphasized that although the marine park had not brought any noticeable economic benefits to the local residents, it was significantly affecting the conservation of marine life. Musa and Kadude mentioned that the marine park had noticeably reduced dynamite fishing and the use of destructive fishing gear and noted that the ocean looked beautiful, the beach looked clean, and fish stocks had improved. Feelings of frustration, persecution, and anger among the villagers, however, had peaked.

To sum up, while the marine park's declared strategy is "collaborative management through community participation" (URT 2005, 30), the project unilaterally created new physical boundaries and restricted people's access to coastal waters, traditional fishing grounds, and, in some cases, ancestral farmland. The implementation of no-take zones and "buffer zones" as part of the conservation strategy put marine park

FIGURE 5 Grocery store in Msimbati. None of the food grains are locally grown.

managers in direct conflict with the park's purported beneficiaries, who believed that they were being unfairly prevented from accessing their traditional fishing waters (see also Gawler and Muhando 2004; Robinson, Albers, and Kirama 2014). Without alternative livelihood opportunities, both men and women experienced impacts on their daily lives because of restrictions placed on fishing and marine resource extraction. Overall, there were significant tensions between villagers and marine park authorities in the early years of the marine park's implementation, tensions that were related to the marine park's perceived disregard for the well-being of local residents and their concerns around access to fishing and farming—in other words, their food security.

Section 2 of this chapter reviews the relevant literature on marine conservation and food security. This section provides a background for the empirical data on food security as it relates to the implementation of the marine park in rural Mtwara.

SECTION 2: MARINE CONSERVATION AND FOOD SECURITY

Mascia, Claus, and Naidoo (2010) showed increased food security within twenty MPAs in eleven countries. Reflecting on the reasoning behind the MPA–food security argument, Gjertsen (2005) notes that increasing fish biomass can lead to larger catches, resulting in increased fish consumption and higher income from sales among fishers. Thus, "it would be logical to expect noticeable improvements in child nutritional status in the fishing households" (Gjertsen 2005, 201). However, numerous empirical studies have shown that the impact of MPAs on food security and the health of local populations is not straightforward or linear. Moreover, the relationship between MPAs and food security is not readily measurable. It is complicated by a range of mediating, historical, political, socioeconomic, ecological, seasonal, cultural, and contextual factors.[10]

For example, in the context of the Solomon Islands, Aswani and Furusawa (2007, 561) have illustrated how well-governed MPAs can foster food security and health by providing people with access to more abundant marine-derived protein (see also Weiant and Aswani 2006). Researchers have found the correlation between MPAs and food security in other contexts to be speculative and inconclusive. Some studies specifically examining the relationship between MPAs and food security among coastal communities have suggested that marine reserves and MPAs do not necessarily influence household food security. These studies measure household food security by protein consumption, diet diversity, food-coping strategies, and child nutrition (cf. Darling 2014; Gjertsen 2005). Contrastingly, studies conducted in Tanzania have documented that MPAs in fact have deleterious effects on human food security and nutrition.[11]

The links between MPAs and food security/human nutrition are neither self-evident nor causally related in all contexts. Darling's (2014) study of marine reserves on the Kenyan coast, for example, revealed that fishing livelihoods and household wealth more strongly influenced food security—with fishing families and wealthier households demonstrating higher food security than non-fishing and poorer households. Moshy, Masenge, and Bryceson (2013), on the other hand, found significant undernutrition among children under five years of age in the fishing communities they studied on Mafia Island. Their study revealed that since the establishment of the Mafia Island Marine Park (MIMP), decreased family income, food insecurity, changes in gender roles, and increased responsibilities for women had become key underlying problems contributing to higher levels of undernutrition among children in the study area. In follow-up research, Moshy, Bryceson, and Mwaipopo (2015) revealed that food quality had further deteriorated, including lower consumption of vegetables and smaller meals. Their findings echo Walley's (2004) work on Mafia Island conducted a decade earlier. It also revealed mothers' concerns regarding a growing need for cash, increased food insecurity, an inability to access fish for household consumption, and the diminishing quality of diets for their children. All these concerns were attributed to the displacement caused by the MIMP's presence on the island.

The restrictions imposed by the marine park authorities on Mafia Island had contributed to food insecurity both directly and indirectly in the form of decreased fishing, fish catches, fish consumption, and income for purchasing foods. By contrast, Darling's (2014) research findings showed that the benefits of MPAs in Kenya neither increased nor decreased food security. On Mafia Island, however—in response to the MIMP's operations—most fishers had abandoned fishing and were farming to produce their food (Moshy, Bryceson, and Mwaipopo 2015, 542).[12]

In sum, the causal effects of MPAs on food security are not easily discernible because they are indirect and long term. Therefore, in situations where there is no robust baseline data or longitudinal monitoring interventions, eliciting and analyzing individual narratives can provide important insights into the relationship between MPAs and people's perceived food security. Furthermore, the impacts of MPAs (whether positive or negative) are not uniformly felt across all households in coastal communities. Inter- and intracommunity variations exist in how food security is perceived, experienced, and acted on over time. Households that depend more on the ocean for food security and have *less* access to cash are more likely to experience higher levels of food insecurity. Regardless of these variations, as Chuenpagdee et al. (2013) have argued, food security should constitute an important concern—and an integral component—in MPA planning and implementation. The emphasis on food security concerns in relation to MPAs is significant because of the ethnographically visible impacts that conservation projects often have on people's access to food following displacement and the enforcement of restrictions.[13]

Changing Food Availability, Accessibility, and Utilization

During my initial fieldwork in the coastal villages, I focused my attention on the extent to which the restrictions imposed by the marine park authorities could have affected residents' food security. At the time, there was no baseline data available on food security in the region, so I relied on participant observation, everyday conversations, and narratives recorded through interviews to get a sense of the marine park's impact on food security in the study villages.[14] Importantly, people in the coastal fishing villages associated their food security not just with the ocean but also with their farmlands. Those who had lost their farmlands to the Mtwara Development Corridor (MDC) project—described in the introduction—spoke of difficulties resulting from the state-led dispossession. They complained about the poor cash compensation they had received from the government, which had led to their further impoverishment.

Hamisi, a seventy-two-year-old resident, summed up the food security situation in the region by saying: "In the past, we used to celebrate important events by organizing different kinds of *ngoma* dances. But now there's no ngoma. It's over. No one is organizing them because people don't have the food [surplus] and other resources to celebrate an event." According to Hamisi, in the past, people were food secure. Food insecurity had become a major concern in the region only recently.

Nostalgic representations of a past when people from the coastal villages of Tanzania were food secure—when they could afford to eat three meals a day—are not uncommon (see Moshy, Bryceson, and Mwaipopo 2015; Tobey and Torell 2006). None of my interlocutors described feeling food insecure in the past. They commonly expressed that "life was good, crops and food grains were in plenty, especially during the ujamaa era." As noted in chapter 1, people described the ujamaa era as a time when, although they did not have proper clothes and footwear, they had plenty of food to eat. The land was fertile and productive, the rains were more predictable, the population density was low, the ocean was full of large fish, and the fishing grounds were uncrowded—minimizing conflicts among fishers. Altogether, during the ujamaa era, the people on the rural Mtwara peninsula were food secure.

In 2010, however, food insecurity had become a key topic of conversation. People made emphatic statements such as: "There's a drought, so life is tough. There's food shortage.... Yes food is available, but it's all in the shops [grocery stores], and I don't have the money to buy food from the shops. Life has become very hard.... Things have become very expensive." Others lamented: "There's no fish left in the ocean.... The ocean is tired, it's on leave [*Bahari imechoka, iko likizo*]. The ocean is no longer productive. It's messed up [*Bahari imegoma*]. These days, if you go to the ocean to catch fish, you come back home empty-handed."

Importantly, people only sometimes drew a direct relationship between the marine park and their food security. More often, they described multiple factors as having an impact on their situation. Drought (*ukame*), food insecurity (*wasi wasi wa chakula*), and life of hunger (*maisha wa njaa*) are not uniquely recent phenomena in the rural Mtwara Region—nor in the southeastern region more broadly (see Lal 2015). Even so, people emphatically stated that until very recently, food was sufficient, even if it was not plentiful; they had, in the past, been able to eat well.

Now, when asked about the number of full meals (*milo*) they usually ate daily, nearly all interviewees said they were able to eat only two meals (breakfast and early dinner) instead of three (breakfast, lunch, and dinner). They would usually eat deep-fried cassava (*muhogo*), boiled red kidney beans (*maharage mekundu*), *chapatti*, or a sweet fried bun (*mandazi* or *vitumbua*) as snack (breakfast) in the morning, along with black tea (*chai kavu*) or thin porridge (*uji*) made from cornmeal. In the afternoon, they would chew on raw cassava and finish with an early dinner—usually regarded as the day's "real meal." This meal was typically thick porridge made from maize flour (*ugali*) or occasionally cooked rice (*wali mweupe*).

Fish was served as a relish rather than the main dish. As Hassan from Msangamkuu explained, "In general, all fishers sell 90 percent of the fish they catch and keep the remaining 10 percent for self-consumption. There are no cold storage facilities in this area and fishers have to sell their fish so that they can buy food—sugar, maize flour, millet, rice, soap, kerosene, cooking oil, and other sundries. Fish is not the staple food in this area. It is a side dish [*mboga, kitoweo*]."

A large majority of the people from all six villages where I conducted fieldwork were very concerned about their accessibility to food during the last five or six years (i.e., before 2011 and 2012). They asserted that, on the one hand, there had been a precipitous decline in the availability of fish in their traditional fishing waters; on the other, crop yields had also worsened. This led them to rely on store-bought food grains, cereals, and flour. Because of the declining access to locally grown food, an increasing number of people were eating only one or two meals a day instead of three, and their meals consisted mainly of starchy food such as cassava. As a result of changing food availability and accessibility in the region, people had adopted significant changes in their traditional diets and food consumption practices.

Amina, a thirty-four-year-old single mother of three young children from Msangamkuu village, spoke about food insecurity: "Our children are used to it. If we tell them that there's nothing for dinner tonight, they don't complain. They understand. They drink some water and go to sleep . . . they're used to it." When I followed up with Amina about her representation of food insecurity, she added that children often return home from school and find no food. The children would drink water instead of eating, search for food in the bush, climb a coconut tree and bring down one or two coconuts to share with their friends. Amina also elaborated that food security in her village was seasonal: people were far more food insecure during the rainy seasons than during the dry seasons when there was fish in the ocean to catch and sell. People offered several possible reasons for the decline in crop yields in their villages. Oft-repeated comments stated that the land had lost its fertility, that the land was no longer fertile, or that the land was sleeping.

Hawa, a soft-spoken fifty-one-year-old mother of nine (all of whom were now adults) from Sinde village, explained:

> You see, here we till the land with our hands and a hoe [*jembe*]. We don't have tractors and [artificial] fertilizer, so we can do only so much. We have no irrigation, so we rely on the rains. The rains have become erratic and unreliable, and they are insufficient. A few years ago, if we worked on two acres of land, we would get enough food to last us for six months, but now we get enough for maybe three months. So we must rely on buying food from the grocery shops in the village or Mtwara town. For that, we need money, and we don't have money.

Hawa was relatively well-off compared with most people I knew in Sinde. She lived in a reasonably good house by local standards and owned several acres of agricultural land and cashew trees inherited from her former husband. Her social network was extensive, and she commanded much respect from her fellow villagers; both men and women held her in high esteem. Hawa also hosted the annual *maulidi* celebrations in her front yard.[15] All told, her social capital was impressive. Despite her land and standing in the community, Hawa said she still did not feel food secure. It was not food availability that concerned her but rather food accessibility. Hawa expressed sentiments similar to those expressed by others in her village. Her narrative points to the increasing reliance on store-bought food and the resulting need for cash.

Similarly, thirty-nine-year-old Waziri, who held a leadership position in Msangamkuu, attributed the food shortage problem to land and soil degradation, poor fertility because of overuse, and population increase in the villages. He said that these days, people were eating food "the size of a passport photo"—a commonly used local expression for something very small. Not only had the land lost its fertility, but the ocean, too, had become less productive, yielding smaller catches. Waziri explained that until recently, there had been about 30 fishermen working in the traditional fishing grounds. Now there were 130 fishers using the same area. "The ocean is tired [*Bahari imechoka*]," Waziri said. "It's on leave. It has changed [*Bahari ikolikizo. Bahari imegoma*]. Everyone is fishing in the same area, and there are too many boats, so it is chaotic."

Waziri's statement highlights how the land and the sea are interconnected with locals' livelihoods. The agricultural land had lost fertility, people were squeezed into smaller plots of infertile land because of dispossession and displacement, and the population had also increased. At the same time, at sea, fishers were finding it challenging to catch sufficient fish for consumption and sale. The fishing grounds were overcrowded because of restrictions set by the marine park, the competition was intense, and the fish stocks had drastically depleted.

The region's growing poverty and limited access to fish and other marine resources had accentuated the involuntary out-migration of men, albeit temporarily (cf. Bunce, Brown, and Rosendo 2010; Raycraft 2019). Artisanal fishers, who travel to different places, including Kilwa, Mafia, Dar es Salaam, Tanga, Zanzibar, and Mozambique, to find a livelihood as temporary migrant fishers were particularly affected. A vast majority of the households from all the villages where I conducted fieldwork had at least one male person who had recently migrated elsewhere or was engaged in fishing or some other livelihood activity away from Mtwara for two to three months before returning home. However, long-term out-migration was seen as a risky decision, socially and economically. The restrictions affected women, especially single mothers, who depend on the ocean and harvest fish and other marine resources in the nearshore areas using small fine-mesh nets and cloth for household food security and sale.

People were pessimistic about the food situation, emphasizing that it would worsen as time passed. To reiterate, however, not everyone directly connected the marine park's implementation with their deteriorating food security. This was in part because, at the time when I was collecting data on food security, the marine park was not fully established in all of the fifteen villages (in 2011; twenty-three villages in 2016) that were within its boundaries. It had not affected all the sea-bordering villages equally. Furthermore, even within villages directly affected by the park's regulations (including no-take zones, surveillance activities by marine park rangers, and the confiscation of dugout canoes [*mitumbwi*] and illegal fishing gear), a significant proportion of the villagers were subsistence farmers; there were not many fishers who relied exclusively on the sea for their livelihood. Those who were solely reliant on fishing and marine extraction saw a direct connection between the implementation of the marine park and their deteriorating food security. They explained that the marine park's restrictions on their fishing and marine extraction activities had limited their access to cash, as they could no longer catch and sell fish. This, in turn, had limited their access to foods like flour, oil, and vegetables and other necessities that they would normally buy from the shops.

Daranga, the VEO of Msangamkuu village, expressed his concern by saying that most of the people in Msangamkuu relied on the sea. If villagers were prevented from fishing in their traditional waters, without being given alternative means of livelihood, they would be hungry. Children would be malnourished and unable to go to school or do well in their studies. He said: "So what's the use of saying that the conservation [*hifadhi*] has been successful, when people here are hungry?" Daranga's question had become a slogan in the marine park villages where people opposed the park or its top-down implementation. Their sentiments resonate with what some social scientists who champion the social dimensions of marine conservation have cautioned against: biological successes at the cost of social failures (Christie 2004, 162).

The complaint that marine conservation had taken precedence over people's food security was pervasive in villagers' everyday discourse. Elaborating on a similar concern, Asha, a thirty-nine-year-old mother of six children, highlighted the problems people in her village associated with the marine park. She said,

> These days, if we go to the sea, the marine park people chase us away, and they take away our fish. And if we try to cultivate the land, the Mtwara Port people say that the land belongs to the government. People have become desperate. Some have even started stealing coconuts from other people's farms because they are hungry and have nothing to eat. We have become like goats, chewing on what we get today because there's no guarantee that we will have enough food tomorrow.... The marine park people have destroyed

my husband's boat and confiscated his net. The children suffer. They don't get enough food to eat, so they become malnourished and don't do well in school because they are hungry.

Asha's comment—that some people had taken to stealing coconuts in a place where they grow in abundance—is a moral commentary on the consequences of hunger and desperation. In the local moral world, stealing coconuts from a neighbor's tree or farm is frowned on as an act of disrespect and desperation. Throughout my fieldwork, I heard similar stories of not only hungry children but young adults in other villages being labeled as hooligans (*wahuni*) for stealing coconuts and selling them for cash. This they would use to fulfill their betting habits: playing billiard pool, a favorite pastime in all the villages in the region (see chapter 4). Asha's self-deprecating remark, "We have become like goats," further speaks to the abjection that people experience because of food insecurity. Many others corroborated Asha's statement with similar stories, saying that harassment from marine park authorities has negatively affected their well-being.

The case of Bi Musa, a thirty-two-year-old woman, illustrates the cumulative effects of external conservation and development interventions on people's food security and well-being. In June 2012, when I interviewed Bi Musa, she lived with her husband, their four children, and four of her younger siblings. Her mother, an enterprising businesswoman, had unexpectedly died of a heart attack a few months earlier, and Bi Musa's siblings had been left in her care. Bi Musa's father, who had also died recently, was a prosperous man who had owned large tracts of land and planted hundreds of coconut trees and cashew trees. He had lost all of his agricultural land to the MDC, which plunged the family into a spiral of vulnerability and suffering. Bi Musa was unwell then; she had been prescribed medicines for anxiety and hypertension.

Bi Musa explained that before the MDC project and the marine park were implemented, she and her family would eat three or even four times a day, thanks to the abundant fruits and vegetables they planted and harvested on their farms. Now they would eat only two times a day, including tea and a snack in the morning. This shift occurred because her father had lost all his land to these projects. Moreover, the marine park authorities had confiscated his boats and nets. "It was a huge piece of land, with 200 coconut trees and 130 cashew trees. Now if I want to buy a small piece of land to build my own house, it will cost me TSh200,000 [$150 USD]. Where can I get that kind of money? I'm very worried. I'm suffering from BP [hypertension]," Bi Musa said, showing me her medication tablets.

I interviewed Bi Musa in the VEO's office because it provided a quiet venue for audio recording. After the interview, Bi Musa invited me to her home. She lived with her family in a single room she had rented in a larger house. Her husband was an artisanal fisher. The room had a double bed, a mosquito net, and other meager belongings. Aluminum pots, pans, and a winnow of unhusked rice were stored in one corner of the room. Near the entrance was a pile of more than thirty plastic buckets, which Bi Musa had saved to store water. At the time, there was a severe shortage of potable water in the village. Children could be heard frolicking outside on the large veranda; she used a hearth in the porch to cook food.

Mkubiru–A Case Study

Mkubiru is a picturesque village inside the marine park, located only a few meters from the oceanfront. The beach, however, is cluttered with mounds of shells of edible mollusks and leftovers from fish and shellfish. During high tide, children—many in their school uniforms—enter the water with their spears (*mdeki*) and hunt for fish, mainly puffer fish, which is a local delicacy. Many households in Mkubiru fully or partially depend on the ocean for their livelihood. However, rather than purely an oceanfront fishing village, Mkubiru may be best described as a subsistence fishing-farming village. About a kilometer from the beach is a valley with large tracts of paddy fields and clusters of planted cashew trees. A large freshwater pond in the middle of the paddy fields is a resting place for a large flock of black seabirds.

I chose Mkubiru as the focus for an in-depth case study of food security because of its status as a representative midsize coastal village inside the marine park and because it was close to Sinde village, which was my home base at the time. Mkubiru is home to approximately 460 households (*kaya*) and 1,540 people, all directly affected by the marine park's interventions and the following restrictions. These included a ban on dynamite fishing and the use of illegal fishing nets and the confiscation of

FIGURE 6 Mkubiru village on a quiet afternoon

illegal fishing gear and small dugout and planked fishing boats. Mkubiru was among the villages where certain households had benefited from a gear exchange program, which the marine park had implemented in 2008 to eliminate destructive fishing practices (Robinson, Albers, and Kirima 2014). It was also one of the villages where people were vehemently opposed to the marine park and had been particularly opposed to it during the project's initial phase. Mkubiru was a section (*kata*) of Mnawene village at the time. It became a separate village in 2008.

Through an analysis of mainly narrative data supplemented with quantitative survey data, I examined the local responses to food security concerns—particularly among those whose lives were directly or indirectly connected to subsistence farming and fishing. I aimed to document the food security–related effects of the fishing and marine extraction restrictions commonly put in place by MPAs on local communities. From Mkubiru village, 120 women participated in the study; they were interviewed during July and August 2012 and June and July 2013, with the help of Mariam, my female research assistant. I chose to interview only women for this study because of the significance of gender for household food security, which has been extensively documented in the literature.[16] Men's perspectives on food security were obtained through interviews and group discussions.

In the sample of 120 households, the head of the household was typically male, except for 14 percent of the respondents, who were single-mother-headed households. In 42.5 percent of households, men were primarily engaged in fishing; 27.5 percent were engaged mainly in farming but also relied on marine resources to supplement their income; 7 percent were involved in business or held a salaried position in the village administrative office; and 3 percent were schoolteachers. Among women, 91 percent of the respondents said that their primary occupation was subsistence farming; 6 percent were engaged in small business; 2.5 percent described their primary occupation as gleaning (*kuchokoa*) for shellfish and intertidal invertebrates; and two of the surveyed women worked in the village administrative office. Excluding the seventeen female-/single-mother-headed households, in 27 percent of the households, the husband and wife were both engaged in farming as their primary occupation. Overall, the majority of men were involved in subsistence fishing, and the majority of women were engaged in subsistence farming.

Most of the respondents (92 percent) grew their own food, particularly grains, lentils, and tubers, such as cassava (*muhogo*)—however, they also bought food from a grocery store in the village. Only 8 percent of the respondents said they bought all their food from a grocery store. As mentioned earlier, fish is not considered central to the everyday discourse on food security. Commonly considered a side dish or used to prepare relish (*mboga, kitoweo*), fish is not consumed as the primary food item to "fill one's stomach" (see also Walley 2004, 148).

While 41 percent of the respondents said that they often worry their food will run out before they can get the money to buy more, 37 percent said that they do not worry. The remaining 22 percent said that in their case, their worries were often related to seasonal factors—vagaries of the weather and rains—and access to cash income. Halima, a forty-five-year-old single mother of one dependent child said: "We are not happy with the food situation because we are unable to get the food we need from the ocean, and the village population has been increasing by the day and the availability [*upatikanaji*] of food has declined."

Other narratives revealed multiple themes related to various dimensions of food insecurity, such as monotony ("We just eat *ugali* every day"), affordability ("We cannot afford it"), food shortage ("We don't get enough to eat"), and a lack of opportunity to eat a balanced diet ("We go without eating a fruit for a month"). Most respondents were concerned about the monotony of their diet; as much as 44 percent of the respondents said they often ate the same thing for several consecutive days because they did not have enough money to buy different types of food. Coping strategies included "making do" with what was available at home, spacing out meals, tolerating hunger, eating less, and eating uncooked food—such as raw cassava.

Food supply and financial insecurity were equally common concerns among the respondents. As much as 76 percent of respondents said they worried that the food they bought or had in stock would not last (food insufficiency) and that they did not have the money to get more; 15 percent said they did not have that problem; and the remaining 9 percent said that their situation would often depend on a range of circumstantial factors. Respondents spoke of the limited opportunities to earn money in the village; even going to the ocean in search of fish, octopus, and other intertidal invertebrates was unreliable because of fear of harassment by marine park rangers who would confiscate their fish. And 74 percent of respondents said they could not afford to eat a full, balanced meal—which most respondents described as "being able to eat three meals: breakfast, lunch, and dinner," regardless of the variety of food items on the plate.

Respondents often equated food insecurity with financial insecurity and hunger. Two-thirds of respondents said they were often hungry and ate less than they wanted to because they did not have enough money for food. Only 6 percent said they were not usually hungry, and 28 percent said their situation was fluid and varied with circumstances. Fatu, a twenty-nine-year-old mother of two children, said she could not afford to buy enough food for all three meals. Even when she was hungry, she would tolerate her hunger until evening, eating only one or two meals daily to budget food. Fatu explained: "If I have the money, then I buy enough food to have three meals; if I don't have the money, I don't eat food regularly or till I am satisfied."

By contrast, Francisca, a thirty-three-year-old mother of three children, whose husband was a schoolteacher (very few people in the study villages were schoolteachers) with a regular monthly salary, said that she was not worried and that her situation was different because she had a budget for the month. Francisca would stock up on food for the entire month and worried about food only sometimes because of her limited monthly budget (her husband's salary). "I do some small business," Francisca elaborated, "to get some small money—but not much. I don't have enough money to buy everything. The budget constrains me." Francisca's situation in terms of food security was unusual because her husband had a salaried job. This helped her to buy the month's ration on her husband's payday. Nonetheless, she was not entirely food secure, as there were other commitments and contingencies requiring money.

The impact of hunger and food insecurity is often most visible among children under five; children are, therefore, often the focus of studies that measure the impact of food availability and accessibility on growth rates (Moshy, Masenge, and Bryceson 2013). When respondents were asked if they were unable to give their children a balanced meal with a variety of foods because they could not afford it, 56 percent said yes; 14 percent said they were indeed able to provide a balanced meal to their children; and the remaining 30 percent said that in their case, sometimes they could afford to give their children a balanced meal and sometimes they could not. One respondent explained that the children suffer the most because they are dependent on their parents. If parents don't have enough food, they are unable to give enough to their children, who end up hungry and malnourished. She continued: "Life has become difficult. Today I want rice, flour, sugar, cooking oil, and kerosene. Flour is TSh1,500. Sugar is TSh2,500 a kilo. If you have six children as I do, what can you feed them? I'm really worried about food security."

Food "availability" was not a major concern for the people of Mkubiru or the other study villages because of their proximity to Mtwara town; the local grocery shops were well stocked with food grains. However, the respondents' comments highlighted "accessibility" to food (as in the ability or inability to "buy" food with cash) as an everyday concern for most of the households. People were often worried about their food security not only because they could not grow or harvest sufficient food but also because they did not have enough money to buy the foods they needed, in sufficient quantities, from the shops.

As seen in this chapter, the impact of MPAs on the food security of local communities is not obvious, straightforward, or one-dimensional. A multitude of factors mediate and compound the impacts of MPAs in either direction—whether improving or diminishing food security. Baseline data are crucial if reliable conclusions are to be drawn based on before-after research designs (see Aswani and Furusawa 2007).[17] In the present case, people's interpretations of food security were broad; eating three meals a day to defeat hunger was key, regardless of the nutritional value of the meals eaten. The narratives examined in this section suggest that food security in the study villages was closely tied to financial security or access to cash income. Food security was synonymous with access to sufficient cash to buy food from the grocery shops.

Even in villages directly affected by the marine park's restrictions, not everyone attributed their food insecurity to the park rules. In the fishing villages, people were as concerned about the vagaries of the weather and rainfall, the diminishing quality of the soil, the low crop yields, and the limited employment opportunities in the region as they were about the restrictions placed on them by the marine park authorities.

CONCLUSION

The overall disposition among the residents of the six study villages toward the marine park during the first two phases of its implementation was overwhelmingly negative. People codified their negative sentiments by asking the oft-repeated rhetorical question: "What's the use of conservation if people are going to be hungry?" In other words, villagers directly or indirectly dependent on the ocean for their livelihood saw the marine park as a hindrance to their food security and survival. This led to considerable frustration and anger among locals, leading to protests and threats of violence against park officials. People's attitudes toward the marine park had become increasingly negative because of their repeated experiences with dispossession, including the confiscation of fishing gear.

Locals also felt deceived by the park authorities after being told that only a small portion of the ocean would be protected—only to be told, after welcoming the project, that it would restrict their access to the entire ocean and even the dry land. Given these experiences, people did not believe that the marine park project would improve their livelihoods or bring "development" to their communities. The marine park's interventions (restrictions), coupled with the farmland taken over by the MDC, had resulted in "a coastal squeeze" (Bunce, Rosendo, and Brown 2010, 422) because an ever-increasing number of people were being squeezed into smaller spaces. At the same time, access to land-sea areas was significantly reduced, leading to worsening food insecurity, anxiety, and related social suffering.

In the marine park's catchment area, only a small fraction of those directly affected by the project had benefited from alternative income-generating projects, such as fish farming, beekeeping, goat rearing, and fishing gear exchanges, including larger boats and nets. This was contrary to the park management's promises at the start of the project. The increasing out-migration of young men to fishing grounds in Kilwa and Mafia or on the Mozambican side had increased the vulnerabilities of women, children, and the elderly—in terms of not only physical insecurity and nutritional vulnerability but also common emotional and mental health concerns, such as insecurity-induced depression, stress, and anxiety.[18]

The marine park officials had assumed control of determining what was good for marine life and, by extension, for the people who live in the park's catchment area. Social theorists and anthropologists have described the kinds of regulatory controls the marine park has implemented "in the name of life and health" as representative of a biopolitics of the population, as "practices of intervention that are desirable, legitimate and efficacious" (Rabinow and Rose 2006, 197). Phrased differently, they are representative of "an orientation to intervene in populations to enhance their health and wellbeing" (Li 2009, 66; see also Fletcher 2010). As highlighted in the book's later chapters, the people of Msimbati countered the regulatory controls by criticizing the park officials for blatant corruption, incompetence, and negligence.

Despite severe consequences faced by individuals who flouted the marine park's regulations, villagers were not entirely lacking in individual and collective agency—the ability to act with freedom and intention. Both men and women tried to overcome domination by the marine park. They demonstrated their resistance and resilience by continuing to fish in prohibited waters, deliberately engaging in dynamite fishing in defiance of the restrictions and even threatening violence against marine park officers and NGO representatives who entered their villages. This was especially true in the case of Nalingu, which was at the forefront of the opposition to the marine park during its initial years. However, overestimating the agency of people who have been systematically marginalized and subjected to state-directed violence, which manifests in various forms—dispossession, worsening poverty, food insecurity, and deprivation of education and employment opportunities—presents unique challenges (cf. Farmer 2004; Raycraft 2020). In chapters 3 and 4, I detail how the marginalization of the people in rural Mtwara persisted in the marine conservation and industrial extractive sectors despite continued resistance.

The marine park had not gone unchallenged. The people of Msangamkuu, for example, refused to be included, despite visits from high-profile government officials to persuade the villagers to participate. The chairman of Nalingu village dismissed the marine park officers' claims about destructive fishing practices in the coastal villages—both in protest against the park rangers, who were known to harass fishers from Nalingu, and to highlight the park authorities' failure to provide gear and support services to enable fishers to engage in sustainable fishing practices. Similarly, the people of Msimbati were dismayed by the actions of the marine park officials, who they believed had deceived them by making them cede large tracts of land along the coast and their traditional fishing grounds to the marine park.

As it is in most rural Tanzania, food insecurity is an important concern in Mtwara. The data suggest that the problem of food insecurity in rural Mtwara requires a more nuanced analysis and explanation than simply correlating the increasing food insecurity with the implementation of the marine park and the MDC project in the region. While the park's restrictions on fishing and marine extraction have undoubtedly contributed to some villagers' perceptions of their impoverishment, disempowerment, vulnerability, and further marginalization, other effects must be factored into the analysis. These include the increase in the local population, unemployment, faltering rains, excessive utilization of land (often without crop rotation or fertilizer, which has contributed to a loss of land fertility), poor crop yields, and diminishing access to food. Still, while ascertaining the cause-effect relationship among such factors and the prevalence of food insecurity in the study villages is important, it is equally important, in the present context, to acknowledge people's subjective interpretations of their social condition—particularly their food security concerns in relation to the marine park.

The Mkubiru case study, which focused on the food security situation in one of the key villages within the marine park's catchment area, revealed that while most of the households were food insecure, the data did not reveal a linear cause-effect relationship between the MPA's implementation and precarious food security in the study village. This was mainly because the people of Mkubiru did not rely primarily on fish for their food security; instead, their definition was broader and had more to do with whether they had access to food grains. Fish, or "the ocean," featured less in people's discourse surrounding food security in comparison with farming and access to cash to buy food grains and flour from grocery stores. The people of Mkubiru would instead be assured of three starchy meals a day for themselves and their children than just one meal consisting of a variety of foods (such as fish, meat, vegetables, lentils, legumes, and fruits). These findings challenge assumptions that increased fish biomass through marine conservation will automatically increase food security in coastal regions.

The marine park's presence in rural coastal Mtwara had not positively affected people's perceived food security. It certainly had not improved people's access to more, or more-nutritious, food. If the situation in Mkubiru was representative of other fishing villages inside the marine park, then the marine park had not contributed positively to improving food security in the catchment villages—and by extension, had not contributed positively to people's well-being (see also chapter 7). The proposition that MPAs improve people's food and nutritional security needs to be reconsidered. The ability of MPAs to improve food security and social well-being can become a reality only if MPAs are accompanied by interventions that are specifically aimed at improving food security and alternative livelihood opportunities—in sum, interventions that take into consideration the multiple factors affecting income security in an MPA's affected region (see Fabinyi, Dressler, and Pido 2017, 186).

How the marine park was implemented serves as an example of how the global drive to establish MPAs and marine parks based on biological, scientific, and political-economic goals can potentially lead to unfeasible and poorly designed management interventions that fail to consider inter-stakeholder conflict, local ecological knowledge, and institutional constraints as integral to the planning process (Rosendo et al. 2011, 64; Christie et al. 2009; Voyer, Gladstone, and Goodall 2013). Clearly, the success of conservation initiatives is contingent on how people perceive the relevance and value of these initiatives to their own lives. The people living in the coastal villages of Mtwara had adopted an antagonistic stance toward the marine park because they believed it had brought them more harm than good. There was a palpable sense of dispossession, economic deprivation, insecurity, and powerlessness. While the causal link between the implementation of the marine park and people's experiences of poverty, food shortages, and other hardships is mediated by many confounding factors, addressing people's resentment and hostility toward the project is crucial. Understanding people's subjective interpretations and experiences of acute negativity toward the marine park is vital to the project's sustainability.

This chapter has clearly shown that at step zero and beyond, local stakeholders must be provided with a greater sense of ownership over the marine park. They must be convinced that their well-being is constitutive of the park's policies. Locals must believe that their concerns will be respectfully remedied through conflict resolution mechanisms and that investment will be made in successful alternative income-generating activities to alleviate poverty and food insecurity and promote sustainable resource use.

3

"IN A WOUNDED LAND"

Natural Gas Development in Tanzania

IN JUNE 2012, I interviewed Bi Mkubwa in the marine park's newly furnished gate office in Msimbati. It was fitted with brand-new high-quality chairs, tables, filing cabinets, and an encased display model of the coelacanth fish. Loud sounds from the generator and the drilling rig used to drill a new gas well (MS-1X) nearby punctuated the interview. As we stepped out of the office, Bi Mkubwa pointed to the rig about one hundred meters away from where we were standing. She said that the gas flare from the rig was polluting the air and causing shortness of breath among some local residents. Bi Mkubwa continued: "It's making everything hot here. Even the coconut trees have become poisoned. The coconuts are falling on their own, all dried up. It's because of the gas [flaring]. They are also drilling and injecting chemicals into the soil. Our land is wounded . . . we are living in a wounded land."

I took a few photos of the rig from the marine park's gate office and later walked to the drilling site to take some closeup photos. The area had been cordoned off with a fence. Two white engineers, dressed in regular clothes, were busy discussing something while looking at the rig and the heavy crane that was parked inside the fence. They were wearing white safety hard hats with a company logo. A single armed security guard, dressed in khakis, was guarding the heavy machinery; there was even a sentry box. I decided not to go any farther and did not take any photos, fearing that the guard would stop and question me.[1] Instead, I returned to the gate office and took photos of Bi Mkubwa, at her request. She was in her marine park uniform that day.

Bi Mkubwa's thoughts on the drilling rig encapsulated the concerns of many Msimbati residents regarding the gas project. People were worried about air pollution, noise pollution, and the poor health of their intergenerational coconut trees, cashew trees, and farmlands. As well documented in the East African context, for many coastal households, coconut trees constitute an important source of livelihood, food security, and cultural identity (see Abuya 2013). Bi Mkubwa described the gas project as having significantly altered the physical landscape and wounded the land on which people have lived and relied for generations. Her evaluation was a moral commentary on the disruption and hurt that villagers were experiencing because of the gas project. Bi Mkubwa's words underscored how people who may not be physically displaced could still experience a sense of displacement in the form of environmental degradation (Willow and Wylie 2014, 226; West 2016). Drawing on Deborah Davis Jackson's (2011) conceptual distinction between displacement and *dysplacement*, Willow and Wylie (2014, 226) note that "even when people are not physically displaced, the sensory experience of environmental degradation can lead to equally damaging displacement." In this and subsequent chapters, I focus on the lived experiences of dispossession and displacement experienced by people living in the marine park villages. They were not necessarily physically relocated but were displaced nonetheless in their own villages because they had lost access to their livelihood resources.

Between 2012 and 2013, the historically neglected peripheral Mtwara Region became a key focus in the national political discourse on development. The discovery of new large recoverable reserves of natural gas inside the marine park, both onshore and offshore, led to a shift in the region's long-standing low status in the national imagination. Mtwara's position became one of importance for the national economy. President Jakaya Kikwete called the nation's attention to the Mtwara Region's important role in powering the nation—metaphorically and practically—through economic growth and power generation. In media interviews and political speeches, he emphasized that the Mtwara gas project would catapult Tanzania from a low-income, aid-dependent country to

FIGURE 7 Drilling for gas in Msimbati village in 2012

an industrializing middle-income country (MIC) by 2025.² The political ethos across the Mtwara Region was rife with debate about the gas project—and its importance for the people of Mtwara in terms of their development. In due course, the presence of gas also attracted the attention of Tanzanian and international scholars. Scholars examining the gas discovery in Mtwara focused their analysis on four key topics: resource nationalism, or resource sovereignty; local content; corporate social responsibility and social license to operate; and perceptions of injustice concerning the promise of gas for development.³

The story, however, is far more complicated than the Tanzanian government's public pronouncements about the gas project's role in national development. As Pedersen (2015, 40) points out, the gas discoveries in rural Mtwara did not initially result in a greater domestic demand for gas—neither in the industrial sector nor in homes and restaurants (as cooking gas, for example). The idea of expanding Mtwara's gas exploration and extraction activities took hold only after the government decided to use the gas to produce electricity for local consumption.⁴

In addition to using the gas for domestic consumption, power generation, and industrial development, Tanzania boldly stated its desire to become a leading liquefied natural gas (LNG)–exporting country in East Africa.[5] To that end, the government initiated plans for investors to build a multibillion-dollar LNG project in Likong'o village, in the Lindi Region.[6] As Gustafson (2020, 98) reminds us, unlike oil, which can be moved "in a barrel or in massive supertankers, gas in its gaseous form has a high volume to value ratio and is dependent on pipelines for transport, with the spatial limitations on profitable marketization that that supposes. Yet with higher prices and new technologies, natural gas can now be piped to a coastline, superchilled to liquid form, and then shipped in ocean tankers like the mobile commodity that oil is."

Residents were initially optimistic about the discovery of gas; they hoped the gas finds would radically transform the Mtwara Region. These hopes fizzled, however, as they learned that the gas extracted in Mtwara would be transported out of the region. The gas would not be processed in Mtwara to generate electricity and develop local industries—nor would it provide jobs to the people of Mtwara. In May 2013, peaceful organized protests against the government's decision to transport the gas out of Mtwara to Dar es Salaam suddenly turned violent.[7] Protestors in several towns in Mtwara set fire to police stations, police vehicles, government buildings, and even a pharmacy. They were met with police brutality; security forces used live ammunition against the protesters, resulting in the deaths of several citizens. The government's drastic response to the protests shocked the people of Mtwara; they had never witnessed anything like it in their living memory. As I detail in this chapter, despair surrounding the gas project dominated everyday conversations in the marine park villages for several years.

This chapter focuses on the gas project infrastructure that is located inside the marine park and its effects on the people of Mtwara. It provides a brief history of the origins and development of the gas project. With the necessary background information, I address the following questions: How did the marine park become the site for a gas project? How did residents inside the marine park respond to the gas project during its implementation? What was the gas project's initial social and economic impact on the people of Mtwara, and how did the project unfold over time? This chapter also provides historical grounding for chapter 5, which further explores how local residents perceived the potential incommensurability, or contradiction, of the marine park and the gas project's copresence in the region and how their ideas and sentiments about the gas project changed over the years. Using ethnographic data gathered in rural Mtwara's coastal villages, I contextualize and examine local understandings of, and responses to, the gas project during its initial phase of expansion (2012–14).[8] I highlight differing local perspectives on the gas project, including lived experiences of exclusion, indignation, humiliation, injustice, powerlessness, or, in some cases, ambivalence toward the project and its social impact.

As the Tanzanian scholar Japhace Poncian (2019, 78) has stated, despite pronouncements regarding the importance of consultations with local stakeholders, "the government has consistently repressed community efforts for their engagement in gas governance." I show, in this chapter, how unprecedented levels of state violence in the region marked the implementation and expansion of the gas project in 2012 and 2013.

ACCUMULATION BY DISPOSSESSION

The process and scale of the gas project—and the speed at which it was implemented—represents what Harvey (2004), Hall (2013), Holden, Nadeau, and Jacobson (2011), as well as other scholars, have variously called "accumulation by dispossession," "accumulation by displacement" (Araghi 2009), and "regime of dispossession" (Levien 2013) and similar processes in neoliberal environments (Benjaminsen and Bryceson 2012). Collectively, these concepts "theorize the historical specificity and the predatory character of capital accumulation processes under neoliberal globalization" (Araghi 2009, 135). Dispossession, broadly and bluntly conceived by Paige West (2016, 24), "is a taking, a theft of sovereignty over lands and bodies. When the thieves use the stolen land and bodies (usually as labor) to make money for themselves, you have accumulation by dispossession."

Scholars who have theorized the processes of accumulation by dispossession in contemporary contexts draw their inspiration from Karl Marx's explanation of "original" or "primitive" accumulation. Here, people are dispossessed of their land, means of production, and livelihood through various mechanisms, including predation, fraud, and violence (Glassman 2006; Hall 2013). In this formulation, "the poor located in the peripheries of society are systematically deprived of their means of making a living and forced to look for work from the rich and powerful" (Holden, Nadeau, and Jacobson 2011, 142). Consequently, the dispossessed have no option but to sell their labor in the wage-labor system to survive (Marx [1867] 1975, 847; West 2016, 13).[9] Nonetheless, "the processes by which land and other resources are enclosed, and their previous users dispossessed, for the purposes of capital accumulation are central to both" (Hall 2013, 1583). Moreover, as Hall (2013, 1583) points out, "the role of the state in capital accumulation and dispossession, too, is at the core of both the theorization of primitive accumulation and accumulation by dispossession and of land grab research." Scholars who have examined the relevance of accumulation by dispossession in empirical contexts have concluded that the processes are often violent, especially in developing countries where opposition from the affected communities can be strong. As will be illustrated later in this chapter, the state often resorts to active repression, even to the point of low-level warfare (Harvey 2005; Holden, Nadeau, and Jacobson 2011, 157; see also Kelly 2011).

In examining the gas project's social impact on the people of Mtwara, I underscore how people make sense of and give meaning to their traumatic experiences by telling their stories. Elicited through oral histories, their narratives highlight "how people as 'experiencing subjects' make sense of violence and turbulent change" occurring in their lives (Eastmond 2007, 249). This was especially true about state violence, the powerlessness that characterized people's encounters with security forces, and the meanings individuals ascribed to their individual and collective experiences. Local narratives illustrate how "violent expropriations play a role in capital accumulation" (Hall 2013, 1586) and how the state uses "extra-economic coercion to expropriate means of production, subsistence or common social wealth for capital accumulation" (Hall 2013, 1593; see also Glassman 2006).

GAS DISCOVERIES

As mentioned in the introduction, natural gas reserves in Tanzania were discovered in 1974 by Agip (Tanzania), the Italian oil company, in which the Tanzania Petroleum Development Corporation (TPDC) had a 50 percent stake. Gas was first discovered on the Songo Songo Island, in the Kilwa district, near the mouth of the Rufiji River.[10] In 1982, further reserves were discovered by Agip in Mnazi Bay, in rural Mtwara—where the marine park is currently located. Agip was focused on oil and did not have markets for gas. As a result, the company rescinded all of its Tanzanian licenses back to the Tanzania government (Artumas 2004, 16).[11] It was not until 2004 that gas production for domestic consumption began in earnest (Anyimadu 2016, 24; Pedersen and Bofin 2015, 9).[12] Encouraged by several new gas discoveries between 2009 and 2012 in the Mnazi Bay area, which put the country's natural gas reserves at between forty-six and fifty-five trillion cubic feet, the country's political leadership was highly optimistic about gas extraction in the region.

Some academics, lawmakers, and Tanzanian civil society representatives sought to dampen the excitement surrounding the "gas bonanza"—arguing that it might become the "Dutch Disease"—a situation where one sector develops rapidly at the expense of other sectors, which becomes counterproductive to the economy's holistic development, a "resource curse" that would hurt rather than boost Tanzania's economic growth.[13] Tanzanian scholars cautioned the government that the gas discoveries could worsen corruption levels and inequalities.[14] Their concerns persuaded Tanzania's policymakers to revise the country's existing petroleum policy, to circumscribe the risk of unscrupulous rent-seeking and elite capture and ensure that natural gas was utilized for the benefit of all Tanzanians. To that end, the Tanzania government passed several legislations and put an elaborate policy, legal, and institutional framework in place to address several extractive resources governance issues.[15]

In public speeches, President Kikwete promised that after decades of being economically marginalized, the people of Mtwara would soon see unprecedented levels of prosperity and subsequent lifestyle changes. Uninterrupted electricity, new factories, paved asphalt roads, dependable transportation, infrastructure, hospitals, schools, hotels, and more were promised. Kikwete also assured locals that the gas project would generate plenty of jobs for youth. There would be dramatic reductions, he said, in poverty levels in the region. At the time, the proposed Dangote Cement Factory in Mikindani was heralded as the harbinger of the anticipated industrialization of the Mtwara Region.

Unsurprisingly, people's expectations from the gas project's anticipated development were high. They expected not only improvements in the region's physical infrastructure but also improvements in their development—their individual economic development and well-being. Their expectations were not met. Instead, what followed was unprecedented levels of state-directed violence against citizens and suppression of protests.

Broken Promises

On May 21, 2013, Sospeter Muhongo, the minister of Energy and Minerals, made a budget speech in Parliament. He stated that the gas extracted from the Mnazi Bay area would be transported via a 540-kilometer pipeline to Dar es Salaam, the country's commercial capital, and beyond. The pipeline was owned and operated by the gas supply company Gasco—a subsidiary of TPDC—and funded by a concessionary Chinese credit of $1.2 billion USD through its Exim Bank. The loan was conditional: the lead contractor was the China Petroleum Pipeline Bureau (CPPB), a subsidiary of the China National Pipeline Corporation (CNPC), a state-owned integrated-energy company (Bofin, Pedersen, and Jacob 2020, 16). Construction was officially launched on November 8, 2012. As expected, the China Petroleum Technology and Development Corporation (CPTDC)—a subsidiary of CNPC—constructed the pipeline. People's initial elation about the gas project quickly turned to antagonism. Violent protests broke out in several towns in the Mtwara Region. In a speech given initially in February 2013, President Kikwete had promised that 84 percent of gas from the fields in Mtwara would remain in the region (Ndimbwa 2014), where it would be used to generate power and provide employment opportunities. When this promise was broken three months later, people expressed deep resentment toward the government's decision to transport the gas out of the region.

The ruling party's leadership publicly accused the opposition parties of deliberately spreading misinformation and inciting violence. Protesters were labeled traitors and secessionists. Consequently, paramilitary forces known as the Tanzania People's Defense Forces (TPDF) were deployed to quell the protests. As noted in earlier chapters, the TPDF's use of live ammunition resulted in the deaths of several individuals and widespread property damage. The national and international media reported extensively on these protests and their underlying causes.[16]

The protests received substantial scholarly attention as well; scholars alluded to the "longstanding sense of marginalization from 'national' development that is prevalent in southern Tanzania" (cf. Ahearne and Childs 2018, 3; Barlow 2022; Elbin 2021) and the "natural gas mismanagement and subsequent leadership framing that exacerbated group grievances" (Must 2018, 85). The mismanagement allegations were complicated because a few years before the Mtwara protests, the country's energy sector had been mired in protracted controversies and major corruption scandals (Anyimadu 2016). In 2006, then prime minister Edward Lowassa forced the Tanzania Electric Supply Company Limited (TANESCO) into an emergency power purchase agreement with Richmond—a briefcase company registered in the United States with no experience in this sector or in any other (Cooksey and Kelsall 2011). As the scandal's details began to unravel between 2006 and 2008 it became impossible for the prime minister to continue denying his implication. Ultimately, Lowassa was forced to resign, and then president Kikwete dissolved his cabinet as required under the Tanzania Constitution (Cooksey 2017). Moreover, in 2008, rights to the Mnazi Bay north exploration block were awarded to Hydrotanz Limited, a company that shared an address with Pan African Power Limited. A firm founded in 2008, Pan African Power Limited ultimately bought out Independent Power Tanzania Limited (IPTL) in one of "Tanzania's greatest ever corruption scandals" (Bofin and Pedersen 2017; Bofin, Pedersen, and Jacob 2020, 13; Cooksey 2017; Gray 2015).

In the wake of the minister's budget speech, leaders representing the people of Mtwara threatened to secede from the Tanzanian state over the question of natural gas extraction and its distribution. They claimed they had been historically neglected and deprived of investments that would lead to economic and social development in the region. Demonstrators protested the political leadership's broken promises, claiming their entitlement to benefit directly from the natural resources extracted from their lands (Poncian 2014; for similar scenarios in the Bolivian context, see Painter and Castillo 2014 and Gustafson 2020). As Lal (2015, 128) notes, "The turmoil in Mtwara brought older and deeper questions about citizenship and development to the surface of national politics in ways that both suppressed and revived the historical dynamics."

In his speech to the people of Mtwara, President Kikwete emphasized that as with all natural resources, the natural gas found in Mtwara belonged to the entire nation—not to the people of Mtwara alone. He reiterated that the resource would be used to improve the socioeconomic well-being of all Tanzanians. Kikwete also emphasized that most of the natural gas would be utilized to generate electricity and facilitate power generation for new industries in the Mtwara Region, which would generate employment opportunities and economic and social development. Alluding to provisions articulated in Tanzania's natural gas policy, he reassured the people of Mtwara that there had been a misunderstanding or miscommunication of the facts. He clarified the "facts" about the percentage of gas that would remain in Mtwara and that 0.3 percent of the revenue would be given to the Mtwara Region for its development. By November 2014, the construction of the gas pipeline infrastructure had gone ahead full steam, with much of the midstream work undertaken by the Chinese state-owned giant CPTDC.[17]

The speed with which an environmental and social impact assessment of the project was undertaken in 2014 and completed and published on the internet by Maurel & Prom (2014) revealed the project's underlying political expediency. The project had to be completed before the general elections in October 2015; it was a prestigious national project, and President Kikwete, whose term in office was rocked by numerous corruption scandals, was keen to demonstrate to the people of Tanzania that he had indeed delivered on one of his important promises. Kikwete inaugurated the gas pipeline on October 10, 2015, just two weeks before the general elections on October 25, 2015. The ruling Chama Cha Mapinduzi party, with John Magufuli as its presidential candidate, won the elections, albeit, as noted in chapter 1, with a significantly smaller margin than had been its historical trend.

Social License to Operate

In 2005, when Artumas began its drilling operations in the Mnazi Bay area, local residents were open to the project; Artumas had offered to adequately compensate villagers for their livelihood assets. Artumas had declared its intention to follow the policies and guidelines of the Tanzania government and the World Bank; it had promoted itself as a sustainable development initiative (SDI) in the Mtwara-Lindi Regions, calling "for the participation of bi-lateral and multi-lateral development institutions to form partnerships to advance sustainable development in the Mtwara-Lindi region" (Artumas 2004, 5). Furthermore, it announced its corporate social responsibility (CSR), focusing on health and safety, the environment, employment, and education.[18] Artumas had also promised to refurbish roads and schools, upgrade the dispensary, and provide free electricity to all the households in the affected villages. This electricity would come from the twelve-megawatt gas-fired power plant that the company would build in Ruvula to serve Mtwara and Lindi. Moreover, the company had promised to create employment opportunities for 600 people during phase one of its operations, 480 of whom would be Tanzanian nationals—although it was generally acknowledged that most of these jobs would be low paying and of a temporary nature (Artumas 2004, 2005, 2006).

During phase two of its operations, Artumas had originally planned to fully develop the Mnazi Bay gas field by drilling five new wells, installing production facilities, constructing a 27-kilometer pipeline, and installing and operating a 30-megawatt power generation facility. It would also upgrade the existing transmission and distribution system—approximately 205 kilometers of transmission infrastructure and 400 kilometers of distribution system. Artumas promised that during this second phase, it would employ about 3,000 workers—2,000 of whom would be Tanzanian nationals (Artumas 2004, 4). Once the project was fully operational, Artumas planned to employ 2,000 workers—90 percent of them Tanzanian citizens (Artumas 2005, 19). Assured of its social license to operate, Artumas completed the reentry, completion, and testing of the Mnazi Bay #1 well and began to drill a few exploratory wells both offshore and onshore. Artumas also laid an 8-inch, 27-kilometer land and marine pipeline from the Mnazi Bay well site to power generation facilities in Mtwara. All the gas wells, except MS-1X, had been drilled inside the marine park's gated section in Msimbati. They were heavily guarded by armed security personnel.

Local Responses and Corporate Social Responsibility

During my fieldwork in the marine park villages, I found that not everyone living near the gas project was opposed to it. Many spoke in its favor, despite widespread opposition to the government's decision to transport gas from Mtwara to Dar es Salaam and the violence that had erupted in its wake. I found that there were a variety of views and opinions among local people regarding the gas project in general.

Jamali, a resident of Msimbati village in his early eighties, was a vocal supporter despite having lost nearly all his farmland to the gas project. I interviewed Jamali twice in 2014 and engaged in informal conversations with him several times during my fieldwork. He repeatedly told me that he did not regret losing his farmland to the gas project; he considered it a sacrifice he had made for the nation's good.[19] Jamali had worked as a security guard at the gas plant. As he said: "My last job was to finish closing the gas plant every day [security]. When I finished my job, I returned to Msimbati."

Jamali recalled a meeting with Artumas's president and CEO Steven Mason, along with other village elders. During the meeting, he learned about the national and international significance of the gas project. Mason had assured the villagers: "Msimbati is soon going to twinkle [*utameremeta*] with electricity." "I think his thoughts were very good," Jamali told me. He bemoaned the people in his village who did not understand the project's significance—and who he felt wrongly believed that the government was playing an unfair game. "That's not true," Jamali asserted, adding that the gas project had brought many tangible benefits to the village. He lamented that, unfortunately, many people from his village were unnecessarily suspicious of the government's good intentions. Jamali explained:

> Gas, it has helped us a lot, and people get a lot of work in this village. All these houses you see, is because of gas, they work there, they earn money, they build houses, they buy a motorcycle—all because of the gas [project]. My parents did not teach me anything other than farming, and I have held on to doing agricultural work to this day. They did not tell me anything in particular as I was growing up, except that I should live peacefully with my fellow villagers and respect the government [*kuheshimu serikali*]. But today's children [young adults] are not afraid of the government. They don't listen to it.

Here, he was referring to the youth, who, in an open show of truculent defiance, were known to flaunt their allegiance to the opposition liberal party—the Civic United Front (CUF)—while openly condemning politicians from the ruling Chama Cha Mapinduzi party as corrupt and incompetent. By contrast, Jamali's deference to the government was evocative of his lived experience during the ujamaa era and his long-term loyalty to the CCM and its ideology.

Similarly, Hamisi, a fifty-four-year-old resident of Mtandi village, said he viewed the gas project favorably because of Artumas's public promises regarding community development. Hamisi was convinced that Artumas had come to help the people of Msimbati. He recalled that Mason had told the residents of Msimbati that Artumas would build an all-weather asphalt road from Msimbati to Ruvula. Hamisi elaborated: "But the government interfered, saying that it was for TANROADS [Tanzania National Roads Agency] to make decisions on road construction." Nonetheless, he said that he had appreciated Artumas's help in refurbishing the primary school and the kitchen in the secondary boarding school before a different company—Maurel & Prom—took over the operations in the gas fields.

Mau Mau, a sixty-four-year-old resident of Msimbati village, praised Artumas but expressed his disappointment with the government's interference. Mau Mau felt that the government had ultimately deprived the people of Msimbati and Mtandi of free electricity. He explained: "Artumas had agreed to 'throw in' [*mtupe*] free electricity as part of the compensation because we had lost our land and trees to the project. But the government intervened and said it was TANESCO's [Tanzania Electricity Supply Company] responsibility to provide electricity, not Artumas's. We had agreed to support the gas project because Artumas had promised to provide electricity to the entire village free of cost. . . . Artumas had even brought one generator exclusively for us, but TANESCO sent it elsewhere [to Masasi]." Mau Mau was one of the wealthiest residents of Msimbati village; he was living in a large concrete house and he owned sizeable tracks of farmland—some of which he had lost to the gas project. He was the only person in the village with a small car parked in his front yard—although the vehicle belonged to his son. Still, he felt betrayed by the government, rather than by Artumas, regarding access to free electricity.

Msimbati residents such as Hamisi and Mau Mau were doubly disappointed that government interference had "tied the hands" of a foreign company—one that was willing to fulfill its corporate social responsibility (CSR) in return for the social license to operate. The promise of free electricity had prompted many who had lost their assets to the gas project to acquiesce to Artumas's compensation offer without protest. The narratives of these three older men from Msimbati and Mtandi village align with Artumas's declared intention to fulfill its CSR by using revenue and power generated from the gas project to benefit the local village community. These benefits included free electricity, fair cash compensation for land and trees lost to the project, and an improved village infrastructure (Artumas 2005).[20]

As will become evident in this chapter, many villagers expressed disappointment with the government's interference in the gas company's intentions to fulfill its CSR. In other words, while companies engaged in extractive activities are encouraged to fulfill their CSR, the process may be complicated by potential "misinterpretations" of the respective domains of authority—as occurred between Artumas and the Tanzania government (Nuhu et al. 2020).

However, the praise and support that Jamali, Hamisi, and Mau Mau expressed for Artumas was rare among those who participated in my study. At the time (2013–14), many of my interlocutors were ambivalent about the gas project. Some of the older women said, "I have no idea what this gas project is all about." Many also spoke negatively about the project and its destabilizing effects. Through their narratives, residents provided insights into their subjective experiences and their struggle to make sense of the dispossession and discontinuities caused by the gas project.

NARRATIVES OF SACRIFICE AND HOPE

Between 2013 and 2014, many Msimbati residents asserted that they were willing to lose their land and trees to the gas project in return for the compensation they knew was meager. This was because residents believed in President Kikwete's promise that the gas project would generate thousands of jobs; they believed it would provide their grown-up children with long-term employment and regular cash income. Villagers saw themselves sacrificing their immovable assets in anticipation of wage-earning opportunities for themselves and their children. Such sacrifices are understandable, given that, at the time, most youth in the study villages were unemployed. Many of them would have been fishers but were deterred by the marine park's restrictions.

Both men and women expressed these sentiments in their understanding of the gas project. Katundu, a forty-four-year-old resident of Msimbati, was active in the village and had taken on a leadership role at a young age. He was one of the few individuals from Msimbati who had participated in the early workshops organized by the MPRU and other NGOs during the planning stages of the marine park. Katundu said that the gas company was responsible for creating employment opportunities for the village because many households in Msimbati had lost their farmlands and trees to the project. He said that contrary to what was promised, the gas company had employed only about ten people from Msimbati—and even those jobs were temporary. Most of the youth, he said, "just wander around in the village like hooligans [*wahuni*]." The default occupation for the youth was artisanal fishing to earn a living. However, given the restrictions that the marine park had put on certain fishing practices in the region, the youth were mostly left to their own devices. Some parents blamed the marine park authorities for creating conditions for the village youth becoming hooligans (see chapter 4).

From Katundu's perspective, it was the gas company's social and moral responsibility to generate employment for the hundreds of youths who, because of lack of employment, had become "hooligans." Several other interlocutors echoed Katundu's comments that it was incumbent on the gas project to provide gainful long-term employment to the village youth. In their view, if the youth in the village remained unemployed, they would become hooligans—an insulting, stigmatizing label and a source of constant worry and embarrassment for parents and the village community in general.

As seen in Katundu's statement, villagers felt morally entitled to employment opportunities because of the losses they had incurred following the permanent dispossession of their livelihood assets. They believed the government's moral obligation was to provide them with jobs after the gas project had resulted in their displacement. They cited their displacement for undermining their livelihoods and causing in extensive financial loss. As a result, they not only suffered economic loss but also experienced moral injury from the failure to receive promised jobs. In sum, local residents felt betrayed by their government, escalating their antagonism against the gas project.

Artumas had fulfilled its promise to employ hundreds of local villagers on the gas project. However, several villagers told me that nearly all the new jobs created during the project's initial stages were temporary and short in duration. Mwema, who was in her midsixties, reflected on this issue. Most of the youth in the village, she said, were unemployed and living with their parents, which in her view was evidence that the gas project had not brought development to the people of Msimbati. Gesturing with her hands, she said: "We haven't seen any development from this project so far. We are occupying the lowest rung [*Sisi tumeisha kalia chini*] because although this project is based here, most people working on this project are from outside of Mtwara. So how can we say that this project has brought us benefits?" Mwema's rhetorical question reveals her skepticism of claims that the project would bring development to the village or its individual residents. In her view, the government and the gas company had marginalized the local people and unfairly placed them on the lowest rung of the ladder regarding jobs, development, and prosperity. Effectively, Mwema's frustration with being marginalized in relation to the gas project is reminiscent of the region's long history of neglect.

When I interviewed Zainabu, the forty-two-year-old mother of four children from Msimbati, in August 2014, she expressed her frustration regarding the gas project, saying that it had not provided employment opportunities to the local people. Instead, as she put it, "the gas project has come only to humiliate us [*tumenyanyasa*], to kill us [*wanakuja kutuuwa tu*]. My family members nor I have benefited in any way from this gas project. We have been completely marginalized [*Tutakuwa tumedidimia kabisa*]." Zainabu's frustration with the gas project—and her feelings of being marginalized, humiliated, and threatened by the project's presence in her village—was expressed in her use of caustic language. She spoke against the project's excesses, indicating her sense of abjection and abnegation resulting from domination. Zainabu's statements of vulnerability underscore the suffering experienced by residents because of asymmetrical power relations between gas project officials and the local population.

The negative disposition of several interlocutors toward the gas project, and the vehemence with which they voiced their feelings about the project, must be understood in relation to "the social and political contexts that have shaped and continue to shape the circumstances of their lives" (Eastmond 2007, 252). Their statements must be understood and analyzed in the context of the cultural memory of state violence, which was still fresh in their minds.

Nearly all those interviewed said that they had not benefited from the gas project in any way. Most people who had received cash compensation for the land, trees, and crops they had lost to the gas project asserted that they did not see the cash compensation as a benefit. Instead, they saw it as a loss because it was woefully inadequate. In their perspective, a "benefit" would have been finding employment on the gas project; this applied especially to those who had lost their livelihood assets. Many did not even consider electricity as a benefit they had derived from the gas project, as they had to pay for the electricity, wiring, and meters at the same rate as people paid elsewhere in Tanzania. To reiterate, at the time when the gas project was first implemented, Artumas had assured the local people that they would be provided with electricity free of cost. This promise was not fulfilled.

One middle-aged male resident from Ruvula blamed electoral/party politics in the region for the neglect. He said that the government had done nothing to help the people of Ruvula and Msimbati because these villages did not support the CCM (the ruling party)—instead, they supported the CUF (the opposition party). He expressed that political leaders did not bother to come and discuss anything with the people of Ruvula or Msimbati because they knew that no one from the villages would receive them. The participant said: "So they drive past us to the gas plant. We are suffering here because party politics have squeezed us. If we were CCM supporters, instead of CUF, then of course, we would have seen development in our lives because in places where people have supported CCM, they are thankful, they have seen development, but here, no one remembers us, no one cares for us." Many of my interlocutors echoed this individual's sentiments framing "party politics" (CUF versus CCM loyalty) as the reason they had not seen tangible benefits from the gas project. Others, who were mainly CCM supporters, dismissed this interpretation by pointing to the fact that many of the CUF-dominated villages on the peninsula had indeed received electricity and other infrastructure developments, including piped water supply.

NARRATIVES OF BETRAYAL

Residents of villages near the gas field, like Ruvula, Msimbati, and Mngoji, weren't the only ones paying close attention to the project; people from villages several kilometers away were also affected. Mohamed, a sixty-five-year-old resident of Mkubiru village, explained the context for the hype surrounding the gas project and development: "In his speech, our president said that the people of Mtwara should get ready to witness dramatic developments in the region. He said that the gas project would result in the construction of big hotels, big houses, a bigger port, a bigger airport and about fifty-one new factories, including cement and fertilizer factories, where the youth will find employment, and women, too, will find work. He promised us that the gas project would bring income earning opportunities for men and women." Here, Mohamed alludes to President Kikwete's representation of development as not only about enlarging the region's infrastructure but also about bringing individual-level prosperity through employment. Moreover, both men and women would benefit materially from the gas project, providing employment opportunities for the local youth while indirectly facilitating gender equality through expanded employment opportunities for women. In sum, the gas project would be a win-win investment—a successful solution for the social issues in Mtwara—such as low employment for youth and women.

Mohamed added that the president had told the people of Mtwara that "if they worked hard, they would be able to fulfill their desires, like owning bicycles and motorcycles from their earnings." People were initially delighted with the president's promises. However, they became disgruntled once they learned that the gas would be transported to Dar es Salaam and would not be used to generate electricity or facilitate jobs in the community. "That's when the angry protests started," Mohamed said. Embedded in Mohamed's narrative is a repeated theme in Tanzania's southeastern context: that of being betrayed by political leaders. This is exemplified by the president himself, who had "gone back on his promise" (*aka geuza*) of bringing unprecedented development to the people of Mtwara. In addition to being unhappy with the government for transporting the gas to Dar es Salaam, Mtwara residents were also troubled by their loss of farmland to the initiative. They felt they had been shortchanged by the cash compensation, which was paid to mitigate the effects of displacement. They expressed their despair and disillusionment with the gas project through their narratives.

Haji, a forty-six-year-old resident of Mtandi village, had initially acquiesced to the gas company's decision to dig trenches on his land to bury the pipeline. Haji explained how his initial perception of the project had changed. In contrast, he had initially been satisfied with the compensation he had received, but he grew shocked and disappointed with the project as it was scaled up, specifically as it continued to destroy the local environment. Haji elaborated: "If you go to the oceanfront, where they have buried the pipeline, you'll see that they have uprooted hundreds of coconut trees that our forefathers had planted. One coconut tree can live up to seventy-five years or more, and if I harvest the coconuts, I can get up to TSh200,000 [$100 USD] per year from each tree—every day I can harvest five to six coconuts from each tree, and at the end of the month I can sell up to sixty coconuts from each tree. So, it's a big loss."

In addition to expressing his despair over the permanent damage caused to the oceanfront, Haji called attention in his narrative to the thoughtfulness of the villagers' forefathers in planting coconut trees. These trees, planted years ago, would ensure decades of guaranteed economic and food security for future generations. His characterization of the destruction of the landscape as an irreversible "big loss" and his valuation of a coconut tree are at once an expression of his economic insecurity and a moral commentary on the project's destructive effects. In sum, those who had lost their farmland and intergenerational trees to the gas project were concerned not only about the economic loss they had incurred but also about the obvious environmental damage the gas project had caused. However, they could do little to nothing to prevent the gas project from continuing to expand. Over time, they even trivialized the environmental damage and spoke in favor of the gas project, often in the context of their sentiments toward the marine park, as I detail in chapter 5.

AN EXPLOSION OF VIOLENCE

Late in the evening on May 22, 2013—the same day that the gas protests had erupted in Mtwara town, Mikindani, and Masasi—security forces

FIGURE 8 Gas pipeline along the Msimbati oceanfront in August 2014.

arrived in Msimbati village after receiving the news that someone had firebombed the marine park's office with a homemade bottle bomb or explosives—commonly used for blast fishing. The destroyed office building had been refurbished in 2012 with funding from the World Wildlife Fund (WWF). I had used the office space to conduct some of the life history interviews with my key interlocutors in Msimbati. I had also taken photos of the building and its impressive interior. The firebomb had destroyed the building and its contents beyond recognition. In July 2013, when I returned to do my fieldwork in Msimbati, Mohamed, the young local resident who was managing the park's gate office, told me that the blast was so loud people had heard the explosion in Litembe, more than ten kilometers away. Surprisingly, the blast had not damaged the ticketing office, which was adjacent to the new building that had been destroyed.

The marine park's gate office was close to the gas pipeline and the gas well known as MS-1X. Unlike the gas project's infrastructure, which was heavily guarded by security personnel with submachine guns, the marine park's office was an obvious, easily accessible, unguarded soft

FIGURE 9 The marine park's ticketing office and firebombed section

target. The firebombing of the marine park office—and the individual actions of the perpetrator—would result in a collectively traumatic experience for the entire community of Msimbati. Mwanaidi, a thirty-three-year-old resident of Msimbati village, recalled her experience: "It was late in the night and my neighbor told us that someone had tossed a bomb inside the marine park office and destroyed it. After some time, the soldiers [TPDF] came and started beating up people randomly until they fell to the ground. They beat people mercilessly as if it was a punishment [*walipigwa na adhabu*]. It took up to a month for those who were beaten to recover from their injuries. Others ran into the forest, but I did not. I had one child on my back and one in my hand. I will never forget what happened that day." This excerpt from Mwanaidi's narrative reveals the shock, scale, and intensity of the physical violence that the TPDF unleashed on the people of Msimbati. It also shows the long-term negative impact of this traumatic event on Mwanaidi's memory. She was one of many who believed they were being collectively and unfairly punished for a crime that an individual (or individuals) had committed.

Hadija, a sixty-four-year-old woman from Msimbati, recounted her experience with the TPDF when they arrived in Msimbati village late that night.

> I had taken one of my grandchildren outside to the toilet when I saw people running helter-skelter. I stood there and watched, until my neighbor yelled at me: "Don't you see us running? The soldiers are here. Run!" I rushed inside, and my children and I picked up the grandchildren, and we also started running blindly into the forest. I carried two of my grandchildren. I was terrified by the soldiers. We hid in the bush. Then we started running into the woods with my grandchildren and there were dry thorns everywhere. My grandchildren still have scars on their faces. I lost my balance and hit my head on a rock while running. We were all soaked in blood. There were many others, and we were all running blindly in the forest. We did not even have any proper clothes on us. The next day we heard that the soldiers had left the doors of all houses in the village open. They had announced that women and children were free to return, but we were too scared and decided to stay away for three days until the violence in the village had died down completely. I think I'm going to take this memory to my grave.

For Hadija, the TPDF's descent into the village was a traumatic experience. As with several other village residents, she distrusted the TPDF and was too scared to return home despite their assurances. Her narrative of the event is a moral reflection on the "why me or why us" question, as in, "What have we done to deserve this? Why did we have to run away from our homes and survive in the forest with our young children?" Hadija's coda indicates the long-lasting psychological effects of violence-related trauma. As Harvey (2003, 74) asserts, "The state, with its monopoly of violence and definitions of legality, plays a crucial role" in the process of accumulation by dispossession. In the context of the gas project, the Tanzanian state displayed its asymmetrical power over the people of Mtwara in May 2013.

Lichumbu, from Msimbati, who was in his midthirties, recalled his ordeal with the security forces in May 2013, of the beatings he endured to the point of exhaustion. He described the incident by contextualizing it within the gas pipeline–related protests that had broken out in several towns in Mtwara. The police had intensified the clampdown, and the government had called in the army; soldiers had overwhelmed the citizens. The security forces were able to quickly arrive in Msimbati following the blast at the marine park's office because they were already stationed at the Mtwara Garrison to deal with the impending gas pipeline protests. The marine park's office was one of many government structures and properties destroyed on May 22 and May 23. Lichumbu explained: "The soldiers arrived in the village in four armored personnel carriers and seven trucks. They came here at three a.m. Initially, we did not think too much about why they were here [most people were asleep]. Those who had caused the problem ran away. We had our families, so we couldn't run away anywhere. Those who could run away, escaped to the Mozambican side."

No one was apprehended after the blast; no one in the village could tell whether the perpetrator was a single individual or a group. It is difficult, therefore, to ascertain whether the primary motive behind the firebombing of the marine park's office was to vent anger against the marine park or the gas project—or whether the anger was directed at "the government" more broadly. Those involved likely saw the protests in Mtwara as an opportune moment to express their anger toward the government's treatment of their communities.

CONCLUSION

The new gas discoveries in Mtwara had brought Tanzania's southeastern region to the center of the political discourse around development and nation building (Lal 2015). A region historically depicted as developmentally stunted, Mtwara was saddled with the power to wrest the Tanzania nation from the grips of poverty—freeing it from overdependence on foreign aid and transforming it into a self-sufficient MIC by 2025. As Lal (2015, 230) notes, the resurgence of the ujamaa idiom of self-reliance (*kujitegemea*), self-development, and optimism articulated in political speeches, the popular press, and the country's *Vision 2025* document is reminiscent of the nationalism and optimism that characterized much of Julius Nyerere's post-independence ujamaa era. Thus, starting in 2010, the dominant political discourse in Tanzania was replete with optimistic statements about the "gas bonanza" in rural Mtwara and how it would be a "game-changer" for Tanzania and East Africa (Poncian 2014). Despite this overwhelming optimism, many cautioned state actors and policymakers about the pitfalls of the resource curse and grand corruption.[21]

The gas project is obvious in terms of its infrastructure in the Mtwara Region, as well as in the national imagination and media representations. Consequently, the process of accumulation by dispossession in the region (which is still ongoing) has put an extra burden of ideological legitimation on the state. The political leadership has continued to paint the dispossession of the people of rural Mtwara as unavoidable given the gas project's significance to national economic growth.[22] Indeed, as Lal (2005, 5) notes, Tanzanian leaders have gone so far as to justify the displacement and dispossession of people in rural Mtwara by "invoking the welfarist logic of villagization," claiming that the expropriation of the land for the gas project "is intended to benefit rural people according to the socialist principles of the past."

The Mtwara gas project, and all it entails, is thus emblematic of the process of accumulation by dispossession in Tanzania's neoliberal economic environment (Harvey 2004; Holden, Nadeau, and Jacobson 2011). The Tanzanian state has explicitly justified blatantly visible expropriations with an ideological (and legal) claim to be serving the "common good" or a "public purpose"—typically cloaked in the language of "development" (Levien 2013, 402). As Agrawal and Redford (2009, 2) have emphasized, "The usual defense of displacement lies in arguments about how critical those projects are to national economic growth. Progress in achieving economic growth is viewed as capable of generating a sufficient surplus for the entire population that will offset losses by those who are displaced."

As discussed, between 2013 and 2014, most people living in Mtwara's gas-producing region felt despair over the project's negative impact on their lives. Ordinary people told stories imbued with desolation and hopelessness. Their narratives revealed how the project had dispossessed many households of their ancestral farmlands and had directly threatened their livelihoods and food security. Many villagers felt that instead of creating job opportunities for local residents, the gas project would likely push the people of coastal Mtwara toward further hardships and insecurities. The most common themes emergent in local narratives were exclusion, humiliation, and powerlessness. At the same time, narrators held on to hopes that local youth would find regular employment on the gas project or its related industries. As Tanya Li (2009, 69) reminds us, "There is another dynamic, however, that is potentially more lethal: one in which places (or their resources) are useful, but the people are not, so that dispossession is detached from any prospect of labour absorption."

People felt betrayed by political leaders who had failed to live up to their promises of unprecedented development in the Mtwara Region. Women were dismayed at the physical violence the state security forces had unleashed on them, their men, and their children in May 2013. At a time when mechanisms to seek redress for grievances were either limited or absent, villagers felt marginalized. Recognizing that the Tanzanian state has far more power than ordinary citizens, most of the interlocutors acknowledged that they were in a structurally weak position. As a result, they had adopted an attitude of resignation and were unmotivated to engage in further protests. Some participants described themselves as having become physically or emotionally too weak to engage in any meaningful dialogue with the government (see also Pedersen 2014). The potential for more deadly violence had fed into their anxieties. Soon people would come up with a new slogan, "Cashew is our gas," to indicate that they had to continue relying on cashew production for economic development (see also Barlow 2023). In other words, they had decided to "let go" of their expectations from the gas project and, more broadly, the authoritarian state.

The violence unleashed by the state apparatus on the people of Mtwara in May 2013 underscored the lengths the government was willing to go to subdue its citizens. This traumatic event sent a clear message that the government would privilege the gas project—in the name of national development—over the rights of its citizens on the periphery. The narratives in this chapter reveal the consistent patterns of violent dispossession associated with the extractive industry (Holden, Nadeau, and Jacobson 2011, 157). These patterns underscore the tensions inherent in the extractive industry's relationship with local communities in Tanzania and elsewhere (Ablo and Asamoah 2018; Nolan, Goodman, and Menga 2020; Painter and Castillo 2014; West 2016). Gustafson (2020, 20), for example, has written about the effects of violence, terror, and resistance on the ground in the context of the gas project in Bolivia and ethnographically documented "the constant tension between the intensification of nationalist sentiment, and its aspirations for an imagined unity and shared history, and the intensely regionalized ways that struggles over gas rents and its sequiturs create other intense claims on a share of the excess." Tanzanian scholars have also long recognized the importance of judiciously using the nation's natural resources to bring the country's millions out of abject poverty through comprehensive, sustainable interventions, investments in health and education, social protection, and employment opportunities—especially for youth (Moshi 2014; Shanghvi and Jingu 2013). While there is no dearth of well-meaning ideas aimed at bringing the benefits of gas extraction to poor and marginalized citizens in Mtwara, the challenge is to implement measures that translate these good intentions into tangible programs that will genuinely benefit the affected communities.

The gas project's long-lasting impact on local communities is not exceptional, especially regarding state-led violence and the state-mediated dispossession of intergenerational livelihood assets. On the contrary, there are several similarities between the situation in rural Mtwara and other sites of natural resource extraction in East Africa, such as the titanium mines in Coastal Kenya and the large-scale gold mining operations in Northern Tanzania (Abuya 2015; Holterman 2014b; Holterman 2020; Smith 2022). The fundamental problems of distributive justice are encountered with predictable regularity in all these extractive sites.[23] Ahearne and Childs (2018, 15), however, argue that perceptions of gas development–related injustice in Mtwara are rooted in long-standing perceptions of differentiated citizenship and discrimination. These are further complicated by "a sense of injustice in which community access to information is lacking . . . and government corruption remains problematic."

More broadly, in East Africa, the gap between rhetoric and reality in the energy sector remains wide. The reasons are complex and do not relate to "greedy" corporations and "incompetent" authorities. Instead, the gap is related to the very nature of the political economy, which hinges on a set of historically embedded cleavages and political processes that keep local communities marginalized within local and national projects of resource-driven development.

At the time of my research, the dominant discourse focused on the gas project's potential to transform Tanzania's economy and the nation's future. Alternative oppositional discourses about the irreversible damage done to those on the margins of rural coastal Mtwara remained largely suppressed. In this chapter, I have highlighted the views from the margins that have received very little attention in the media or scholarly works. As Willow and Wylie (2014, 226) have emphasized in the context of their ethnographic research on hydraulic fracking in the United States, "We need to tell real stories that speak to real people's experiences, to give voice to views that may otherwise remain unheard." I have provided ethnographic insights into the social drama of dispossession that unfolded in the rural Mtwara Region up until 2014, the local expressions of indignation, the embodied effects, and the broader human experiences of dispossession, disempowerment, vulnerability, and suffering. Collectively, these insights could be read as a corrective to the top-down, repressive, and violent manner in which extractive projects are implemented in Tanzania and elsewhere in the world, i.e., extractive violence (Ferguson 2006; Gustafson 2020; Jacka 2018; Smith 2022; Watts 2004). In other words, despite the presence of institutions such as the Extractive Industries Transparency Initiative, of which Tanzania is a signatory, the on-the-ground situation in extractive sites leaves a lot to be desired (Poncian and Kigodi 2018). The corrective in this case would be for the Tanzanian state to acknowledge and demonstrate responsiveness to local people's demands for better compensation in the spirit of social and environmental equity and justice.

4

"NO PEACE OF MIND"

Dispossession and Disenchantment

THE DRAMATIC EXPANSION of the gas project within the marine park's boundaries in 2014 intensified the dispossession and displacement processes on the rural Mtwara peninsula. Villagers whose agricultural land and traditional fishing grounds were within the park boundaries were forced to reconsider their fishing strategies and livelihood options. In tandem, the marine park and the gas project had doubly dispossessed and displaced the residents of Msimbati in particular. Some villagers had begun to question why the government allowed onshore and offshore drilling while restricting local fishers from engaging in subsistence fishing in the same locations. Local discourse around the two projects vacillated during my fieldwork in the marine park villages; some of my interlocutors were ambivalent or inconsistent in their opinions, as the following case example illustrates.

Athumani, a seventy-five-year-old fisher turned cashew farmer, had lived most of his life in Msimbati village. He commonly wore a lungi (sarong), a half shirt, and an embroidered *kofia* (skull cap) on his head. In August 2014, when I first met Athumani and recorded his life history, he spoke about his parents, siblings, two wives, and six children (five boys and one girl)—all living in Msimbati. His father and his paternal grandparents had migrated to Mtwara from the Comoros islands; his grandparents on his mother's side were from Msimbati. Athumani also described his life experiences as a fisher for over fifty years, the hardships he had endured, particularly during the colonial period, his knowledge about marine conservation, and his understanding of why the marine park was implemented in Mtwara. Toward the end of the interview, he said: "Two of my children work for the gas company; they conduct [seismic] surveys . . . they get money. I get food. . . . Regarding the marine park, I have not seen any loss, for me or for us, because the marine park is training and education (*mafunzo na elimu*). [They say], 'You can catch fish here, but not there. It's a protected area,' and after a few years, they will protect this area. [They say], 'There are some very small fish here, don't catch them.' We don't catch them. It's all to our advantage. So as far as the marine park is concerned, it's all for our benefit."

Athumani, who had recently undergone hernia surgery, spoke thoughtfully, punctuating his vignettes with humor. Later that day, I invited Athumani to a group discussion with five other participants. One of them was his age, two were older than he was, and two others were in their late forties. Athumani became emotional during the discussion, stating that if the marine park had been a private company, the villagers would have "driven it away a long time ago." Still, because it was a government project (backed by the state's repressive power), they felt powerless to take such drastic action. Athumani asserted that rather than bringing in the promised conservation-related development, the marine park had stood as a bulwark against people's access to their traditional fishing grounds and farms. Effectively, it had jeopardized their livelihoods and their food and nutrition security.

Athumani's statements during the group discussion were in complete opposition to what he had said in his interview earlier that day. Most likely, he was unsure of my status then and was "playing it safe" during the interview by articulating a positive picture of the marine park and the gas project. Not everyone in the group agreed with him—especially Jamali, a staunch supporter of the marine park and the gas project. Bwamkuwa, a forty-seven-year-old fisher, had set the tone in the group discussion for speaking against the marine park; he launched a litany of complaints, stating that the marine park had destroyed his life. Bwamkuwa blamed the park not only for his food insecurity but also for his inability to send his children to school. He explained that he did not have the money to pay for school fees, uniforms, and books. "My life has become tight in every 'sector' [he used the English word]," Bwamkuwa said.

There is substantial academic literature on why some people support the implementation of a marine park in their community, while others oppose it. In the East African context, the long history of opposition to wildlife parks and protected areas has been well documented in the domain of terrestrial conservation in Tanzania (Gardner 2016; Neumann 1998). However, the academic literature on the social dynamics of opposition to MPAs in Tanzania and elsewhere is relatively scarce (see Walley 2004; Moshy, Bryceson, and Mwaipopo 2015). As mentioned in previous chapters, Christie et al. (2009, 370) have emphasized that "conflict and controversy are a predictable part of MPA design and implementation... [and] conflict is associated with the generation and equitable distribution of benefits derived from an MPA." In East Africa, as elsewhere, numerous scholars have documented repeated historical conflicts between local social norms of marine use governance and government-backed, national-level management systems (Benjaminsen and Bryceson 2012; Cinner et al. 2014; Fabinyi, Knudsen, and Segi 2010; McClanahan et al. 2009). In Tanzania, Walley's (2004) ethnographic study of the early years of the Mafia Island Marine Park (MIMP) revealed that local residents' overall response to the MIMP was marked by antagonism. Moshy, Bryceson, and Mwaipopo (2015) also found that while people appreciated the benefits of conservation in the MIMP in principle, they decried the noninclusive nature of its implementation. Similarly, as noted in previous chapters, there was tension during the marine park's initial phase among the various stakeholders involved in establishing the park. Nalingu residents, for example, had threatened to use physical violence against park officials and NGO representatives to undermine the park's viability (Katikiro, Macusi, and Deepananda 2015; Robinson, Albers, and Kirima 2014; Tortell and Ngatunga 2007).

This chapter explores the micropolitics—or local-level politics—associated with the marine park's implementation at a time when the gas project was being significantly expanded in rural Mtwara (2013–14). Together, these projects compounded people's experiences of dispossession and displacement in the region. In emphasizing what anthropologists have known for years, that "communities are far from being homogeneous" and that a "political ecology approach does not always account adequately for cultural specificities or community-scale politics that may influence communities' engagement with environment and development issues," Leah Horowitz has advocated for the use of a "micropolitical ecology" approach. As Horowitz (2011, 1381–84) states: "One of micropolitical ecology's contributions is to highlight the complexities of social groups, and ways that contemporary political and economic stakes increase this complexity." This approach "entails recognizing such resource conflicts within and between communities, and between communities and the state, while analyzing these tensions within their broader historical, social and politico-economic context" (Horowitz 2008, 261; see also Hemer 2016, 280). In this chapter, I shed light on the village-level micropolitics behind locals' support for or opposition to the marine park. I juxtapose the narratives of those who supported the marine park for several years after it was gazetted in 2000 with those of villagers who consistently opposed it on various grounds.

This chapter highlights inter-village and intra-village variation in the marine park's perceived significance and continuing impacts. By highlighting the micropolitics and heterogeneity of the local response to the marine park, the chapter reiterates that communities are not spatially bounded, homogenous, or static structures (as is often the case in policy documents, including the marine park's General Management Plan). Instead, they are heterogeneous configurations encompassing different and often oppositional voices and perspectives.[1] This is especially critical when examining local responses to key issues such as economic security, food security, political convictions, the environment, and even mundane everyday concerns.[2]

The chapter underscores the need to pay more attention to the local-level micropolitics, social complexities, social hierarchies, internal differences, and agreements and disagreements within coastal communities. While these processes have been acknowledged and deemed integral to calls for the scale-up of MPAs around the globe, such discourse demands moving beyond the rhetoric of community engagement toward an in-depth consideration of village-level micropolitics and social relations.[3] I show how historical experiences and village-level micropolitics were tied to differences in people's perceptions of the marine park—and their relationships with the park's representatives. Additionally, I elaborate on what I have termed "gendered suffering," or "gendered narratives of suffering," by highlighting women's experiences of emotional distress and hurt associated with the marine park.[4] I conclude the chapter by emphasizing key concerns emerging from the analysis and reiterate the need to pay close attention to the social complexities underlying the diverse perspectives of residents living in MPAs. In chapters 5 and 6, I discuss how these positions changed, i.e., those strongly opposed to the MPA had begun to support it (or at least were no longer overtly opposed). Additionally, this chapter introduces the reader to the early responses to the copresence of the gas project and the marine park. I detail this in chapter 5, which focuses on local perceptions regarding the incommensurability of the copresence of the gas project and the marine park.

NARRATIVES OF SUPPORT

Scholars who have documented the negative effects of MPAs on local communities have highlighted the nature and magnitude of the opposition to MPAs among fishers and marine resource users from coastal communities in different parts of the world. These studies shed light on the socioeconomic dynamics that have led to tensions, hostility, and violent confrontations between those who represent the MPAs and those who believe that their livelihoods are negatively affected by these conservation efforts.[5] Poor planning, overambitious goals, top-down governance structures and management styles, lack of engagement with local populations, physical displacement and forced relocation of local populations, violent approaches to enforcement/infringements of regulations, lack of trust, and poor communication have all been identified as reasons why MPAs fail to represent win-win scenarios—which refer to a situation where both biodiversity and human well-being are realized.[6] At the same time, it is worth noting that dissenting opinions or intracommunity disagreements among community members are not absent; instead they tend to persist, making the local response to marine conservation messy, inconsistent, and shifting. As is often the case, the processes put in place to mitigate stakeholder conflicts often determine whether MPAs can achieve their goals.

On the Mtwara peninsula, residents dependent on the ocean for food security were overwhelmingly against the marine park's continuing presence in their villages. The park had upended their livelihoods, lifestyles, and cultural expectations—that young men and women from fishing households would grow up being socialized into fishing in the ocean or that women would use *tandilo* to catch small fish and collect firewood from their farms and the mangroves to cook food for the family. The marine park's restrictions had frustrated these cultural expectations and practices. People's complaints (*malalamiko*) against the marine park included the unsympathetic implementation of fishing restrictions, the confiscation of fishing nets and boats, the prohibition on women collecting firewood from the mangroves and from their farmlands, the failure of park authorities to share park revenues with the community, and corruption. Those who argued forcefully against the park were fishers, people from fishing households, and people who owned land inside the marine park's boundaries. This was especially the case in Msimbati and Ruvula. In contrast to certain villagers' strong opposition to the park, other residents were ambivalent about their disposition toward the marine park. While they decried the park's top-down governance, they also felt the park had significantly reduced destructive and unsustainable fishing in their villages—particularly dynamite fishing. As a result, they wanted the marine park to stay and continue its work.

As will become evident in the next section, those who spoke equally forcefully to support the marine park and its continuation were mainly village elders. These elders had participated in the initial planning and implementation meetings held between 1999 and 2002 (discussed in the introduction) and had shared sentiments about the government's good intentions behind the marine park. Many were subsistence farmers who earned their livelihoods by harvesting coconuts and cashews from their farms. They were not necessarily fishers or the village economic elites or political leaders. Instead, they were mainly people who had participated in meetings and workshops on marine conservation organized by the World Wildlife Fund (WWF) or the Marine Parks and Reserves Unit (MPRU). Because of their participation in these workshops, they were better informed about the rationale behind the implementation of the marine park.

"A Government Project with Good Intentions"

Bi Mkubwa was one of the park's most ardent supporters. In July 2012, when I recorded Bi Mkubwa's life history, she explained that she

FIGURE 10 VICOBA in progress

supported the marine park for environmental and economic reasons. Bi Mkubwa said that before the marine park was implemented in Msimbati, she had had no idea about the importance of conservation, nor about how to conserve the environment. "People were catching turtles and eating their eggs and meat with complete disregard for their conservation," she explained, throwing up her hands. Additionally, Bi Mkubwa explained that Msimbati residents had not established any savings group to improve their livelihoods. With the help of the WWF, the marine park assisted Msimbati residents in setting up a village community bank—VICOBA.[7] The park also helped residents to buy the VICOBA savings box—a large metal trunk, usually painted green, with a lock.

Bi Mkubwa described how the marine park had sent experts to teach a group of women in Msimbati how to manage the VICOBA. Similarly, experts were sent to teach local women how to build the sheds needed to install a special oven, whose innovative curing process preserved fish for extended periods. They sent experts to help local women build an aquatic fish farm in the village and to support local villagers in learning about beekeeping.

For Bi Mkubwa, the marine park had transformed her life through tangible benefits. In her narrative, she illustrated how marine conservation was not just about protecting marine species but also about improving the livelihoods and socioeconomic well-being of people whose lives depended on marine resources. Bi Mkubwa's best friend, Siwema, with whom she had partnered to start a flourishing business in roasted fish that they sent daily to Mtwara town, echoed similar sentiments in her interview in July 2012. Siwema was sprightly and spoke very rapidly. She was only two years younger than Bi Mkubwa but looked several years younger than her actual age; she had had very different life experiences. As with Bi Mkubwa, Siwema had also spent her entire life in Msimbati. Siwema echoed much of what Bi Mkubwa had said about the need to support the marine park and the benefits of its presence. Siwema explained: "Really, they have lifted us, we have drawn a lot from them, and they have engaged with us." Entrepreneurial women such as Bi Mkubwa and Siwema benefited financially from their association with the marine park and had good reason to speak in the park's favor. Other residents of the park villages, who had not directly benefited from the marine park, spoke in its favor regardless. Jamali was one such resident who believed in the government's noble intentions.

Jamali was in his eighties and had once owned a lot of farmland in the Msimbati-Ruvula area under customary tenure. He had lost most of his land, trees, and crops to the gas project inside the gated section of the marine park and had been given cash compensation according to the Land Acquisition Act of 1967 and the Village Land Act of 1999. Importantly, neither Jamali nor anyone else in Msimbati was given an alternative piece of land as compensation for their lost land. In addition to receiving cash compensation (which most recipients believed was inadequate), Jamali was employed at the Artumas gas project's camp in Ruvula (Mnazi Bay), where he was paid an equivalent of $2 USD a day. His work involved taking care of the workers' laundry and ensuring that all camp doors were locked at the end of the day.

In August 2014, Jamali stressed that the marine park was a project of national and international importance—stating that "the government had implemented it with good intentions." Jamali alluded to the fact that the government was aware of the illegal poaching, illegal trade in sea cucumbers (*holothuria scabra*), and predatory practices of foreign fishing vessels in Tanzanian waters. "The government studied the problem very carefully and then decided to implement the marine park to protect the local communities," he said. Jamali also alleged that outsiders (non-Tanzanians) were taking away marine resources that belonged to the local communities. While these outsiders prosper, local communities become poorer without their traditional resources. Accordingly, Jamali said, the government had implemented the marine park as an antipoaching intervention—"to secure the ocean and the marine resources that the people of Tanzania have been blessed with."

Jamali specifically mentioned China, Hong Kong, and Singapore, alleging that they had fished all the food from their ocean and were now fishing in Tanzanian waters. He said these countries wanted to enrich themselves by using up the resources from the waters belonging to Tanzanians. According to Jamali, this kind of illegal fishing and poaching had prompted the government to establish a marine park in rural Mtwara to protect Tanzania's sea life. He cautioned: "While they were prospering, we were being robbed of our precious marine resources"—and reasserted that "the government's intentions are good." Jamali had most likely received this information through the Tanzanian media—radio and TV—which reported well-documented cases of foreign trawlers and illegal fishing in East African coastal waters. Foreign trawlers engaged in illegal tuna (*jodhari*) fishing and shark finning in Tanzanian waters, seized by the Ministry of Livestock and Fisheries, were often impounded near the Mtwara Port, as I would find out during my fieldwork.

Jamali also stated that the government was keen to help the villagers by attracting foreign tourists to the marine park. Increased tourism would contribute to the local cash economy, with tourists buying products from the local people. Moreover, villagers would also receive a share of the marine park's fee collection. Drawing parallels between the marine park and wildlife national parks (*mbuga*), such as the Mikumi National Park near Morogoro, Jamali said that the two projects were the same—in that the government had started them to protect wildlife for tourists and local communities and that the country had benefited from both parks. He then lamented: "But people here don't understand the significance of the marine park project. They complain that the government is preventing them from accessing the ocean and the marine resources, including the mangroves, but that's not the government's intention. The government wants to protect the resources for our future generations, so we should cooperate." Jamali reiterated that the marine park was not bad; it was, in fact, a positive government project that was meant for the good of the local people. "That's my opinion," he concluded.

In his lengthy narrative, Jamali invoked numerous points to justify the marine park's presence in Mtwara. He expressed the project's need for support and appreciation from his fellow villagers, and he reinforced that the government had initiated the marine park with the best interests of the Tanzanian people in mind. As a village elder, he not only saw himself as more knowledgeable about the rationale behind the marine park but also hinted at the urgent need to educate his fellow villagers about the marine park's significance and benefits and the government's good intentions.

Jamali was a government loyalist—and wanted his fellow villagers to be the same. He repeatedly stated: "My parents did not teach me anything besides farming. But they told me that I should live peacefully with my fellow villagers and respect my elders and the government."[8] As a village elder who had lived through Tanzania's transition from a former British colony to an independent nation—and the ujamaa era—Jamali was a great admirer of Julius Nyerere and a staunch supporter of the ruling CCM party. He was convinced that the government had implemented the marine park and the gas project with good intentions—to bring development to the people of Mtwara and prosperity to the entire country.

"We Should Blame Ourselves"

Sadala was in his early sixties when I first met him in Msimbati. He was a short, soft-spoken man who lived in a modest house in Msimbati. He would often be seen in the village, wearing either a white *kanzu* with a kofia and flip flops or a lungi with a shirt and a short black coat. Occasionally, he would use a walking stick. Sadala had participated in the planning and implementation of the marine park right from its inception—including the 1999 conference that led to the Mtwara resolution on the marine park. At that time, he was the village chairman. He explained why he continued to support the marine park's presence in the area.

Sadala saw no reason why the marine park should be discontinued. On the contrary, he wanted it to remain in Mtwara to continue its important work. Similar to Bi Mkubwa, Sadala spoke of the important educational activities that the marine park authorities had undertaken to educate people on environmental conservation. He attributed the significant reduction in destructive fishing practices in Msimbati and other marine park villages to the work the marine park staff was doing. Sadala gave a specific example to illustrate his point, explaining that the sea level had risen (*bahari limefukia*) and that the ocean had already swallowed a lot of the coastal land. He attributed this change not to "climate change" but to Msimbati residents' actions in the past—including his own—specifically to the extraction of corals (*matumbawe*) from the coastline to build houses and to make *choka* (white powder from burnt corals) to paint them.[9] Following the marine park's interventions, people had stopped extracting even dead coral from the ocean, and things had started to get a little better. Sadala said: "Even though there are no corals or stones left, at least we know the cause [*chanzo*, or source] of the coastal erosion—we were using the coral from the ocean to build our houses."

Sadala's statements countered the criticism that was common among people from his and neighboring villages against the marine park. His statements underscore the importance he saw in the marine park's educational role—in teaching the people of Msimbati and other fishing villages about why and how they should conserve the environment. In his example of rising sea levels, Sadala took the blame on himself and his fellow villagers who, for several decades, were extracting coral from the beachfront to build their houses. In the process, Sadala believed that they had jeopardized their own lives by accelerating coastal erosion.[10] As a protagonist supporter of the marine park, he wanted his fellow villagers to see its value and the benefits it brought to his community.

"We Should Laud the Marine Park"

Haki, who became the chairman of Ruvula village in 2015, also believed that the marine park should remain in Mtwara. He argued that the marine park minimized environmental damage by preventing potential investors from buying land/property and setting up hotels and bars on the beach. Haki's perspective, however, was not popular with other residents. An oft-told story in Msimbati and Ruvula concerned a local resident who owned a plot of land inside the marine park's gated section. Vodacom, the cellular network company, was interested in installing a cell phone tower inside the marine park's gated area and had offered the plot owner one million Tanzanian shillings upfront, plus a monthly rent. However, much to the disappointment of the plot owner and his fellow villagers, the marine park authorities had disallowed him from selling or leasing his plot of land to Vodacom. As noted elsewhere in this book, villagers decried the marine park's policy of not allowing them to sell their farmlands or parcels of land—even if they needed the money to deal with a health emergency or to pay their children's school fees. This was one of the many reasons why those who owned land inside the catchment area opposed the marine park; they wanted the park to relocate.[11]

Haki argued that many people do not support the marine park because they feel it is focused only on conserving and protecting the environment; they need to see how it benefits the local people. As Haki said, "People feel that the marine park is here to restrict them from carrying out their livelihood activities, when in fact, all that the marine park is asking people to do is to engage in livelihood activities that are legal and contribute to improving the environment, not harming it." As a licensed subsistence fisher and someone who had actively participated in the conservation measures implemented in the region, Haki sought to provide a more "judicious" view of the marine park's importance in the region. However, his views were not popular with most marine park villagers. Unlike Sadala and Bi Mkubwa, he was not involved in the planning and implementation of the MPA during its early years. Nonetheless, in his new position as the chairman of Ruvula in 2015, Haki had the opportunity to attend numerous government and NGO-led meetings, workshops, and seminars at the district level. During these meetings, as the village chairman, he had the opportunity to learn about the importance of his stewardship in promoting proconservation measures.

"It's Difficult to Criticize the Marine Park"

Adamu was in his midsixties when I first met him in 2012. He was relaxing in a chair outside his house, wearing shorts and a loose shirt—an uncommon attire for someone his age in the village. I soon learned that he had recently returned alone (his wife had died) to Mkubiru, his ancestral village, after working for more than twenty years in Dar es Salaam at a tourist hotel attached to one of the marine reserves. He had worked there as a recreational boat driver, taking tourists to local snorkeling spots. Adamu told me he found it difficult to criticize the marine park because of his previous exposure to marine conservation and international tourism. Instead, he praised the marine park and clarified that the park authorities had not prohibited fishing in the protected waters. Rather, they wanted fishers to catch larger fish instead of small fish, like *dagaa*. He said the marine park authorities wanted to prevent local fishers from "fishing like poachers, like those who use bombs for fishing—they destroy the corals where the fish live." Adamu described an occasion when marine park staff had come to Mkubiru to distribute large fishing nets to help local fishers legally catch big fish. "I have one of those nets," he said. "They gave them to us for free, and if we had formed groups, they were willing to give several more nets, ropes, boats, and outboard motors. In my view, they have done a very good thing by helping people in this village to engage in alternative fishing methods and lead a good life."

In his narrative, Adamu highlighted the marine park authorities' good intentions and their gestures to support local residents' engagement in sustainable fishing methods (which would theoretically improve their living conditions). Adamu's previous exposure to marine conservation and tourism was an important factor in his understanding of the marine park's principles and his positive stand on the restrictions in the park's catchment area. Additionally, he had personally benefited from the fishing gear distributed by the park representatives in his village, which made it difficult for him to criticize the project.

A year later, however, when I met Adamu again, he acknowledged that he needed to figure out what to do with the large net he had received, as he was not a fisher. He had sold the net to someone in Mtwara town; he explained that he had returned to Mkubiru to lead a retired life. More importantly, Adamu explained that the net he had received was too large for any of the local fishers to put to good use. Neither he nor any fishers in Mkubiru village owned a fishing boat or skip that was big enough to accommodate the legal fishing net—nor were their boats equipped to go out into the deep waters where larger fish were found. This was a common complaint regarding the park's net exchange program, especially during its initial years—large nets were doled out without ensuring that the recipients were active fishers or that local fishers had suitable fishing boats to put them to good use (see also Katikiro 2016).

"People Will Return to Dynamite Fishing"

Forty-three-year-old Sofia from Nalingu gave her perspective on why she supported the marine park and did not want it to relocate. She forcefully asserted that if the marine park were no longer present in the village, destructive fishing practices, such as dynamite fishing and *kokoro* nets, would return—despite people's knowledge of the dangers and side effects of unsustainable fishing practices. Sofia was convinced that many people in the village would defy village leaders and return to destructive fishing and that arguments and fights would break out over the issue. She was skeptical of the claim that the people of Nalingu were making—that they were not engaging in dynamite fishing because they were self-monitoring. In truth, she believed, people had stopped openly engaging in dynamite fishing for fear of being apprehended by park authorities or the police. "If they see that no one is patrolling their activities," Sofia said, "they'll engage in dynamite fishing again. Suppose they see that there is only one person who is telling them to stop; they'll say, 'Oh, it's only Sofia, so why bother?' They're not going to heed my advice. So there's no point in abandoning the marine park now. It's better if the marine park remains here and protects the environment." As someone who had spent her entire life in Nalingu—where a significant number of people rely on fishing for their survival and livelihoods—Sofia's comments are noteworthy. She did not trust her fellow villagers to refrain from engaging in destructive fishing activities—like dynamite or kokoro—if the marine park was discontinued.

In summary, up until 2014—when the dramatic scale-up of the gas project changed the everyday discourse in the villages—I found that support of the government and the marine park as expressed in the preceding narratives was rare in the marine park villages. Most people were dismissive of the marine park and spoke of it negatively. In the next section, I provide examples of oppositional discourses in the study villages regarding the marine park—when the gas project's expansion inside the marine park's core area further complicated the local discourse about dispossession and development.

NARRATIVES OF DISPOSSESSION AND DISENCHANTMENT

Since Msimbati is a small island with a large population, agricultural land is scarce. Nearly all the land has been converted into cashew farms, coconut farms, and rice (*mpunga*) and millet (*mtama*) farms for subsistence—though most people in Msimbati relied on store-bought food grains and flour for their survival. Not surprisingly, following the scale-up of the gas project, land prices in Msimbati (outside the gated park area) had increased significantly in a short period. The discovery of new gas deposits in the region and the subsequent expansion of the natural gas project—with migrant workers coming to live in Msimbati—hiked up land prices even higher. Residents of Msimbati and Ruvula, whose farms were inside the marine park's gated section, were angry. Park representatives had not told the villagers that once the marine park was implemented, they would be unable to sell their farmland directly to a buyer from outside the village. The prerogative to make decisions on land sales would remain with park officials. People alleged that park officials would deliberately quote exorbitant prices for the land inside the marine park as a strategy to prevent any land sales from happening.

"There Was No Consultation"

Forty-six-year-old Hassani owned a small plot of land inside the marine park's gated section in Msimbati but earned his livelihood mainly as a mason/bricklayer (*fundi*), while engaging in small side businesses. He was a vocal critic of the marine park. On the question of the park's control over the land in its catchment area, he said: "Initially, we had good relations with the marine park people because we thought that we'll be receiving some concrete benefits. We welcomed them. We did not think that they were going to take away our land, but that's what they did—they put restriction on our fishing activities, and they also took away our lands. The project took over the land that customarily belonged to the local people and made it government land—the land, of course, really belonged to the government."[12] But there was no consultation between the project and the local people, as they would have liked. Residents of Msimbati, Mtandi, and Ruvula alleged that the marine park authorities had betrayed the people by failing to disclose the scope of the park's remit, sphere of activity, and authority. The marine park authorities had failed to consult with local residents on matters related to land ownership. As a result, villagers were disenchanted with the project, even though they had initially agreed to support it.

"They Don't Allow Us to Sell Our Land"

Rehema, a forty-five-year-old single mother of two children and one of my key interlocutors in Mtandi, elaborated on the restrictions that marine park authorities had put on the local people. Rehema's main issue with the marine park authorities concerned a two-acre plot of land she had inherited from her deceased father. The plot was inside the marine park's gated section, and Rehema wanted to sell it and use the money to cover the cost of sending her children to secondary school. She also wanted to use some of the profits as seed money to start a new business—an enterprise based on buying clothes from Mtwara town and selling them to her fellow villagers on credit. In August 2014, she justified her frustration and reiterated a widely shared concern among the people of Msimbati regarding the park: "The marine park is, after all, the government, and we are just citizens, so we agreed to their initial promises, schedule, and plans. Once they entered the village, things started to go badly, because the marine park took over everything from the dry land [*nchi kavu*] to the ocean. It's different from when they first entered the village. They did not tell us that if we needed to sell our land or farm [*shambaa*], which is inside the marine park, we should be going through them." Drawing on her own experience in trying to sell her plot of land, she explained that marine park authorities would place so many conditions on the potential transaction that it would become impossible for the sale to go through. Rehema alleged that marine park staff deliberately quoted a price to the potential buyer that was five or six times higher than what she would have estimated. Unsurprisingly, potential buyers failed to make the purchase. As she put it: "Even though you own the land, you don't have the right to know what the marine park told the potential buyer. Ultimately, you are unable to sell your land, even if you want to get some money to send your children to secondary school or if you need money to treat someone in the family who is very sick and needs expensive medical treatment."

Rehema concluded by saying that this was one of the reasons why many people in Msimbati disliked the marine park. Rehema's allegations in this regard were not unfounded. No land inside the gated section of the marine park had been sold during the time I was doing my fieldwork in Msimbati. The single tourist hotel inside the marine park's gated section was barely functioning. The gated section of the park in Msimbati did not even have a restaurant.

Rehema's feelings of betrayal by the marine park authorities were widely shared among the people of Msimbati and Mtandi—who were most directly affected by the marine park's interventions and, in due course, those of the gas project. Only a select few older villagers, such as Bi Mkubwa and Sadala, continued to believe that the park authorities were genuine in their intentions to support the residents of rural Mtwara.

"They Should Have Educated Us Better"

In Mkubiru, the relationship between the villagers and the marine park representatives was similarly strained. Mpojola—in his early forties, was the chairman of Mkubiru village at the time (August 2014). He was living with his wife and children in Mkubiru. Mpojola was very friendly and outspoken and always willing to engage in political discussions and talk about the issues that mattered to him the most: the livelihoods of those who live in the coastal villages on the Mtwara peninsula. He was born in Mkubiru in 1975 and had spent his entire life in the village. He had been fishing since he was a young child. More recently, because of the marine park's restrictions, he had switched to farming—including growing cashews on a subsistence scale. Mpojola justified his standpoint and Mkubiru residents' opposition to the marine park by explaining that park authorities should have provided residents of his and other fishing villages with alternative livelihood opportunities first, and only then implemented the project. As he explained: "What they have planned is indeed good and beautiful, but they should have educated us better on what they wanted to do with the ocean. Instead, they have hurt us by confiscating our fishing gear and apprehending us for using illegal fishing gear." Like Mpojola, most villagers appreciated the rationale behind the park; however, they were quick to say that they were disappointed with the way the project unfolded in their villages. Mpojola reemphasized the root cause of the tension between the marine park authorities and the local people: that the marine park representatives had failed to consult with the villagers early on and had neglected to educate them about the conservation strategy. In other words, the main problem lay with the marine park's top-down implementation, rushed through without a thorough consultation process involving a wide range of the local residents (see also Katikiro, Deepananda, and Macusi 2015).

"Double Standards and Corruption"

Many residents admitted that while they wished the marine park would "go away," they knew that they did not have the power to seriously challenge the project or its governance. They expressed their sense of frustration with the marine park by highlighting the double standards, hypocrisy, and corruption they had experienced in their dealings with marine park officials. Bwamkuwa alleged that the marine park officials had confiscated illegal nets and small boats, only to sell them back to fishers for a small fee. He exclaimed: "So, what's the point in saying that they are confiscating our nets because they are illegal, while also telling us that if we pay them TSh20,000 [$10 USD], they'll let us take back our net and our boat? It doesn't make any sense." Everyone, including staunch park supporter Jamali, corroborated Bwamkuwa's allegation, stating that his statement was true.

While the extensive corruption and rent-seeking practices among state officials in the domain of terrestrial conservation—in Tanzania's northern tourist circuit, and in the wildlife management areas in particular—has been well documented (Benjaminsen et al. 2013; Brockington 2008; Gardner 2016; Nelson, Nshala, and Rodgers 2007; Sachedina 2008), rumored allegations of corruption in the domain of marine conservation and sustainable fishing are relatively less common (Samoilys and Kanyange 2008). In her ethnography of the Mafia Island Marine Park, for example, Walley (2004, 35) reports of "explicit charges that government officials were accepting bribes to ignore dynamiting or were even cooperating [*wanashirikiana*] with the dynamiters." What is more, in an audit report published by the government of Tanzania's National Audit Office (March 2018), the controller and audit general states specifically in reference to the Mnazi Bay-Ruvuma Estuary Marine Park (MBREMP):

"According to parks officials, there were breaches of patrol confidentiality such that when surveillance plans are made and patrols are planned somehow culprits were able to find prior information. This resulted in failing to capture them in action and, in most cases, they fled and abandoned their gears" (26). In other words, independent auditors substantiated local residents' allegations of corruption and incompetence among the marine park authorities.

In addition to allegations of double standards, some people in Msimbati and Mtandi were cynical about the park's presence in rural Mtwara. In 2013 and 2014, when the gas project was expanded in the region, they began to question the government's decision to implement an extractive project in an area that had been declared a protected area. At the time, I was unsure how widespread these sentiments were in Msimbati. I had not gathered data specifically focusing on the nexus question, which is the topic of chapter 5. Even then, only a few people I interviewed spoke of the double standards related to the copresence of the gas project and the marine park. They frequently mentioned the large pipe-laying ship that was anchored opposite the marine park's main office—off the main beach—to underscore their point.

Bwamkuwa, who expressed exasperation with the marine park's "double standards," said that the marine park's main goal was to have control over the land, and in turn, to give it to the gas company. In other words, the marine park was only a pretext; its real goal was to grab the land in Msimbati for extraction, i.e., ocean grabbing and land grabbing in the name of conservation and development. "If they could," Bwamkuwa said angrily, "they would evacuate everyone from Msimbiti and relocate us somewhere far away because they have found a lot of gas here and want to drill many more gas wells inside the marine park."

The dramatic scale-up and high visibility of the gas project, which local residents had witnessed since 2012 (see chapter 3), caused residents—particularly fishers like Bwamkuwa—to assert that the marine park was an excuse, enabling gas companies to carry out their resource-enclaving practices and extraction activities in an unhindered manner. Periodic visits by prominent politicians and journalists to the gas project and discussions about the project in the Tanzania Parliament had also contributed to the belief that the gas project was far more important to the government than the marine park.

To sum up, while a small number of mostly older villagers spoke favorably about the marine park, many more villagers were unhappy with the marine park's presence in their respective villages. Those who opposed the park did so because of the restrictions on their marine extraction activities, because they were prevented from selling their plots of land, and because they believed that the marine park personnel were incompetent and corrupt. Moreover, many villagers were frustrated by the dispossession of their farmlands and coconut and cashew trees—originally planted along the coast by their ancestors.

The gas project's presence alongside the marine park represented a double disappointment for some of the region's residents; the gas project compounded their predicament as many more villagers lost their farmlands and trees to the gas project for little recompense. Notably, those who had lost assets to the gas project did not distinguish between the gas project and the marine park. As will be explored further in chapter 5, they conflated these two projects as representations of state power and domination—in short, *serikali*, or the government—against which they felt powerless. Because of their feeling of powerlessness, residents largely refrained from engaging in any organized protest. The marine park's presence in rural Mtwara had both divided opinions in the fishing villages as to the project's value and contributed to inequalities between those who had benefited from the project (e.g., Bi Mkubwa) and those whose lives had been upended by the restrictions. The park had also exacerbated intra-village conflicts—in other words, conflicts between the small number of people it had empowered and the majority (in the same village) it had dispossessed and displaced—a topic to which I now turn.

INTERPERSONAL VIOLENCE

As noted in the previous chapters, the marine park's engagement with Nalingu was strained from the project's inception. It was marked by miscommunication, distrust, noncooperation, villagers' outright refusal to follow the park's regulations, and physical violence (Gawler and Muhando 2004; Tortell and Ngatunga 2007). Nalingu's reputation as a "violent village," where marine park rangers and NGO representatives "dare not enter," persisted for several years (Robinson, Albers, and Kirima 2014). Significantly, marine park–related violence in Nalingu occurred not only between the villagers and the security personnel protecting the marine park's interests but also between a small minority of villagers who supported the marine park and the majority who opposed it. The following case exemplifies the intra-village tensions that prevailed in Nalingu during the course of my fieldwork.

Maukilo, a well-known elderly resident of Nalingu, had been trained by the MPRU in Nachingwea and Tanga in the 1990s to serve as the park ranger for Nalingu village. Maukilo had decided to work for the marine park as a park ranger because he wanted to do something to protect the ocean/marine environment from destructive fishing practices. He was also a key member of SHIRIKISHO, a community-based organization with the mandate to end dynamite fishing in Mtwara. Maukilo recalled that illegal fishing and dynamite fishing were rampant in coastal Mtwara in the 1990s. As a result, some people had decided to do something about it. "There were violent conflicts—*vurugu vurugu*," Maukilo said, "so we formed an initiative called Shirikisho Hifadhi ya Mazingira ya Bahari Kanda ya Kusini.[13] There were twelve people in that group—we were divided between Lindi and Mtwara."

Maukilo continued: "We used to consult with each other and seek guidance from the marine park people on matters related to natural resources [*mali ya siri*]. I used to go there to consult with them periodically and report on the work we were doing to stop [*wasimamizi*] illegal marine harvesting practices." Maukilo worked as a park ranger for seven years. During that time, he was able to work without any hassles. The MPRU had sent him and some of his colleagues to Tanga for training in aquaculture, fishponds, and crab-fattening ponds. When he came back to Mtwara after his training, Maukilo shared his experiences with the people of Nalingu. He recalled: "So the fishers found out that this marine park was a real thing, and I was the designated park ranger in this village, but the villagers did not want the marine park because they thought that they would lose their livelihoods and also access to their food source."

In December 2014, Maukilo narrated how a group of young men had harassed and attacked him for enforcing the marine park's regulations. He spoke haltingly and recalled the traumatic incident:

You see this damaged [left] eye? I wasn't born like this. This happened because someone threw battery acid on my face. They [the village youth] did this because I was supporting the marine park and working for SHIRIK-ISHO as a park ranger [*mgambo*]. They said that I was interfering with their livelihoods and that I was spying on them and giving information about them to the marine park authorities. They thought that I had gone to the police station to complain about them and to urge the soldiers to come and apprehend the people in this village. So, one day when I was going to the VICOBA meeting at the school, they said: "Hey old man, where are you going?" I said I'm going to the VICOBA meeting. They said, "Okay, this will be the last time you'll be going to the VICOBA." I replied to them saying, "No, I will go there tomorrow, the day after, and as often as I want." They then wrote a letter to me saying that I should stop supporting the marine park and leave the village in five days, or else the angry youth in the village will take the law into their own hands and force me out of the village. I just ignored their letter. I have lived in Nalingu since 1967. I stood my ground. Five days later one of them forced his way into my house late in the evening and threw battery acid on my face and ran away. My wife had gone to the mosque and I was sitting on a chair. It was a hot day. My son and neighbors rushed me to the village dispensary. The doctor there did what he could, but by then the acid had completely damaged my left eye.

No one was arrested following this incident. Maukilo suffered because of his commitment to saving the marine environment from destructive fishing practices; he said that he stopped serving the marine park after the incident. Significantly, however, Maukilo said he did not regret his role in protecting the marine environment. He believed he had played an important part in minimizing destructive fishing practices in Nalingu and the neighboring fishing villages. In September 2017, I met with Maukilo to ask him about his thoughts on the changes he had witnessed in Nalingu—particularly relating to destructive and unsustainable fishing practices—over the last five to ten years. He said that things had changed for the better; illegal and destructive fishing practices in Nalingu, Mnete, and Mnazi had stopped. Maukilo had grown very frail. He was able to give only a short interview before he decided to get some rest. His resolve to remain committed to protecting the environment against all odds was rare.

GENDERED SUFFERING IN MARINE PARK VILLAGES

The literature on how women in particular are affected by MPAs is relatively scant in the African context (cf. Baker-Médard 2016; Mwaipopo 2008; Walley 2004). During my fieldwork, however, I found that in general, women across all the fishing villages were far more vocal about their disenchantment with the marine park than men were. Decreasing access to resources, including gleaning, tandilo, and firewood from their own farms, was a common reason for their disappointment in the marine park. They narrated evocative stories, calling attention to experiences of emotional distress and hurt associated with the marine park. They had harsh words for the park officials, accusing them of oppressing the villagers and preventing the citizens from claiming their basic rights (*haki ya misingi*). These women commonly used the term *wametutenga*, as in, "sidelined" or "don't care," to suggest that the marine park had separated them from the ocean and their ancestral land. Others used the expression *wametunyenga nyenga*—literally "they have dominated us, coerced us, and violated us"—and *wametudhoofika*, meaning "they have weakened us." Still others expressed their frustration with having been betrayed by the park's management.

In August 2014, fifty-two-year-old Rukia, from Mtandi-Msimbati, who was a vocal critic of the marine park, complained that park rangers were preventing women from collecting firewood from their own plots of land inside the marine park's gated section. Rukia said: "They confiscate the firewood and tell us to go back to the village, empty-handed." Rukia described her personal troubles with the marine park authorities when she wanted to sell her plot of land, located inside the park's boundaries: "When the marine park officials heard that I wanted to sell my land, they promptly came to my house and told me that I cannot sell my land because it is inside the marine park. They say that the entire Msimbati village is inside the marine park, starting from this ocean, including the dry land where we have our farms and also the little forest that we have on the edge of the village. We really do not know what portion of the land the marine park has left for us. There is no peace of mind for us, really." Rukia's narrative reveals the kind of aggravation and despair that women were experiencing in their encounters with the marine park rangers. She asserted that ongoing dispossession, harassment, and insecurity had had a cumulative impact on women's emotional well-being. Rukia's narrative highlights the complex social impact of the marine park on local residents—especially on women and single mothers, who have the primary responsibility of feeding and taking care of their children.

The idiom "no peace of mind" (*hatuna raha*) was a common refrain in women's narratives of distress. Women called attention to the marine park's impact not only on their physical well-being but also on their emotional health. Sixty-four-year-old Mwema, for example, expressed her frustration with the marine park by emphasizing that she did not trust the project and that it should be discontinued. "Then," she said, "everything will be alright as before. Because of them, we don't get what we want from the ocean; they have constricted us [*wametubana*], they have held us in a tight grip, squeezed our ribs and left us breathless. They should allow us to go back to our normal way of life . . . they should not continue to constrict us till we are completely breathless."

Mwema's narrative reveals women's lack of trust in the marine park's style of governance and the women's desperation, emotional burdens, and psychosocial distress. Women in the affected villages described the hurt they associated with the marine park staff—who they believed had deprived them of their emotional well-being, their peace of mind. Moreover, they believed that the marine park had intensified their immiseration, marginalization, disempowerment, and vulnerability. The park held them, metaphorically, in a vicelike grip that left them breathless—without access to their farmlands, ocean, and alternative livelihoods. For these women, the marine park had at once revealed the women's structural vulnerability and epitomized their individual depression, anxiety, and suffering.

Women repeatedly expressed their feelings of betrayal of trust by park officials and the effects on their self-esteem, dignity, and, more broadly, mental health. Zainabu explained: "They have hurt us. Their impositions have led to oppression and hurt [*kupandikiza zulma*]. Our life is just like that. If they keep confiscating our nets, firewood, land, and coconut and cashew trees, it will increase our marginalization [*kudidimia*]. They are very cruel to us [*Wanatunyasa sana*]."[14]

Shabia, a fifty-six-year-old mother of eight children, went so far as to blame the marine park and its policies for turning the village children into hooligans. While some men had expressed similar concerns to me, women spoke far more forcefully about concerns regarding their children, who they feared were becoming wayward. Shabia said that much to the dismay of their parents, young children and young men in the village had started wearing "hip-hop pants" well below their waists. She continued: "They look like hooligans and they have become hooligans. They have become thieves [*Wamekuwa wahuni, wamekua wezi*] and they have become unreliable [*hawaaminiki*] and they don't listen to us [*hatuwaelewi*]. It's the marine park that has contributed to this."

Shabia justified her allegation by saying that before the marine park was implemented, when children between the ages of ten and twenty were unemployed, they would go to the ocean to hunt for fish and octopus. Now, however, they were unable to hunt on the beaches. If caught, Shabia said, the park rangers would beat them up. Shabia continued:

> And so . . . really, the marine park has created a bad environment here, especially for our youth. Now if you go to the main road, you'll see our children hanging around the pool table [*poolu*], betting and gambling, because they don't have any work and they cannot go to the ocean to catch fish and to earn some money. The only "work" that they are doing is betting at the pool table because they have no real work to do, and when they run out of money, they go to someone's coconut farm, steal the coconuts and sell them so that they can bet and play pool. Now what can the youth do if they go to the ocean and the marine park rangers constantly threaten them? As mothers, all we can do is sit at home and just be grateful to God that our children haven't got into trouble with the marine park rangers.

Shabia's allegation that the restrictions imposed by the park had led to the village youth becoming hooligans may seem farfetched, and perhaps comical at first. However, such sentiments among parents (both mothers and fathers) were not uncommon in the park villages. In all the main fishing villages where I conducted fieldwork, pool tables were a common sight. Msimbati had a pool table at the main entrance to the village, complete with a thatched structure. Between eight and ten youths could be seen betting and playing pool—with a few young children and hangers-on watching or hovering aimlessly. Stealing coconuts from other people's farms is clearly an anathema in the local cultural context and an act of desperation that is frowned on. Mothers' allegations, however—that their children engage in such acts of desperation to place bets at the pool table—reflects their own despondency. They directly attribute hooliganism in the village to the marine park authorities. The park's restrictions, according to these mothers, have led their children and youth to resort to unethical behaviors—such as stealing coconuts and wasting their time gambling at the pool table.

Relatedly, women often referred to their experiences of food insecurity to express distress in relation to the marine park. One woman described the disruption to her livelihood by stating: "If we go to the ocean, the marine park people shoo us away. If our men go to fish in the ocean, they confiscate their nets. Our food is in the ocean and we are not allowed to access it." Another woman's response in relation to food security was imbued with ethical and moral concerns: "This project has come to humiliate [*kudhalilisha*] us and to rob us of our dignity. It has embarrassed us with regard to food, and it has made us feel like we are thieves [stealing fish from the ocean].... We are people of the coast!" As noted in this and previous chapters, narrators—women in particular—used food insecurity as a metaphor or idiom to express their sense of disempowerment and humiliation resulting from the marine park's restrictions on their access to the ocean for food. For these women, the ocean was their main source of cheap animal protein—as well as their cultural identity.

CONCLUSION

This chapter focused on the micropolitics of marine conservation and on the narratives of despair and powerlessness that reflect the underlying power politics in marine parks. It addressed the community-level hierarchies of power as revealed by those who had benefited from the project, and by those who had not. Furthermore, this chapter explored the coercion and corruption associated with the marine park's governance, as well as the villagers' trust and mistrust of the project.

This chapter also shed light on the historical factors that influence people's disposition toward MPAs. For example, Jamali's support for the marine park (and the gas project) emanated from his deep faith in the government. Jamali believed that the government had implemented these projects with the best intentions: to bring development to the people of Tanzania. However, people's perspectives had changed and evolved over the years. Residents' understandings of the marine park were continuously changing in response to new experiences, including the expansion of the gas project that had dispossessed and displaced more people in the park villages. Many Msimbati residents, for example, had initially supported the marine park—believing that the project would bring them multiple benefits, but they changed their minds once they found the governance style unacceptable and the regulations antithetical to their well-being. By contrast, Nalingu residents who had vehemently opposed the marine park for several years eventually suspended their opposition—as will be explored in more detail in chapter 6.

Moreover, this chapter revealed that the marine park's impact has not been uniformly felt by people living in the catchment villages. Those who continued to support the marine park after more than a decade substantiated their position with examples of how they had personally benefited from the project. More importantly, they highlighted why supporting the project—discontinuing destructive fishing practices and conserving the environment—was in everyone's interest. Others emphasized the project's national significance, the government's foresight, and the project's good intentions. By contrast, those who resented the marine park's presence in their villages highlighted how the project had hurt them personally. For these narrators, the park posed a threat to their very survival because of its restrictions on fishing, fishing gear, access to the mangroves, and, critically, the sale of their ancestral farmlands.

The varied perceptions among villagers—and their diverse responses toward the marine park—underscore the limitations inherent in treating communities as homogeneous entities when examining perceptions, interests, and actions pertaining to marine conservation. As Ferse et al. (2010, 3) have noted, "People are embedded in dependencies and hierarchies, holding different positions and views, and therefore also respond differently to policies and incentives." In the present case, a small minority of the villagers inside the park's catchment area, both men and women, were supportive of the project and lauded the good intentions behind its implementation. A few others, who were not dependent on the ocean for their livelihood, were indifferent to the project or supported it because it did not affect them directly or undermine their livelihoods (see also Robinson, Albers, and Kirima 2014). Those who strongly and vocally opposed the marine park included artisanal fishers, those who were directly or indirectly dependent on the ocean for their livelihood, and those who were prevented from selling their plots of land inside the park's boundaries.

As discussed in chapter 2, and also in this chapter, the lack of support for the marine park could be traced to the lack of transparency and clear communication during the project's initial stages. From the villagers' perspective, the marine park's presence in their area was akin to what scholars have described as blue grabbing or ocean grabbing—the "dispossession or appropriation of use, control or access to ocean spaces or resources from prior resource users, rights holders or inhabitants" (Bennett, Govan, and Satterfield 2015). The scenario described in this chapter suggests that the process of state-mediated dispossession (i.e., divesting properties and traditional means of livelihood) began soon after the marine park was implemented in 2000. Restrictions were swiftly enforced starting in 2002, resulting in the confiscation of fishing gears and in beatings, amid anger and confusion from local residents. Some Msimbati residents' characterization of the marine park as a pretext—a ploy to cover the government's intention to give their farmlands to the gas company—is also at the core of villagers' mistrust. From the residents' perspective, the marine park acted as a secured spatial enclave—a production site protected for the benefit of the gas company, so that it could continue its drilling operations unhindered. Consequently, people's narratives were embedded with feelings of disempowerment and betrayal by the marine park and the government.

In the study villages, dispossession was visible in the form of "no-fishing zones, limitations on utilization of invertebrate and mangrove resources, restrictions on fishing gear, confiscation of fishing gear, appropriation of near-shore areas, fencing of beaches, and lack of benefit-sharing of official fees collected" (Benjaminsen and Bryceson 2012, 350). It was also visible in the changing socio-spatial landscape—caused by the uprooting of thousands of intergenerational coconut trees and cashew trees to make way for the gas pipeline project. In their narratives, locals revealed their feelings of angst, disempowerment, and vulnerability emanating from their awareness of the state-led dispossession they had experienced. Their relationship with the marine park exposed their structural vulnerability; they had little or no power to influence the marine park's presence in their villages. Most had resigned themselves to being silenced through state-led violence.

Finally, this chapter highlights the significance of gendered issues in marine conservation. In their narratives, women affected by the marine park described the project's impact on their emotional well-being. Many women blamed the park for depriving them of their peace of mind. They explained that they were troubled by the constant harassment from the park rangers, who prevented them from fishing in their traditional waters and collecting firewood from their farms.

Overall, most people across the fishing villages vehemently disowned the marine park. They were keen to distance themselves from the project, rejecting the marine park's rhetoric that the project was collaborative. The assertion that local communities did not voluntarily accept the project but rather were "forced" to accept it indicates that while the MPA in question may become a biological success, it was an immediate social failure (Christie 2004). As Chuenpagdee et al. (2013, 234) have rightly cautioned: "When MPAs do not deliver what they intend to do, the damage may already be beyond repair.... Stakeholders may then have lost faith in the MPA and stopped supporting it." Statements from some of my interlocutors, such as "They should have educated us better about the project," point to the importance of incremental environmental education preceding the MPA's actual implementation. Programs aimed at educating local residents on a range of issues related to marine conservation and the general ethos of an MPA—including restrictions and obligations—must be implemented proactively and on an ongoing basis.

Ultimately, good governance is key to the successful management of any MPA—and it does not come easily or cheaply (McClanahan, Allison, and Cinner 2015). Replacing the long-standing mistrust with trust, transparency, and inclusiveness is an important step in ameliorating the tensions associated with the marine park in Mtwara. As will be discussed in chapters 5 and 6, people's attitudes toward the gas project vis-à-vis the marine park had begun to change noticeably over the years. Numerous factors had contributed to this shift, including people's agency. People were beginning to speak more favorably about the gas project, even emphasizing the need for it to be scaled-up even further, while lauding its potential to bring economic and social benefits to the people of

Tanzania. They were also beginning to engage in a discourse about the importance of conserving their environment, while emphasizing that they now understood the important work that the marine park was doing in the region. Significantly, however, people did not see the copresence of the two projects as something that is inherently incompatible in terms of their environmental sensibilities. The next chapter examines this topic in more detail.

PART II
REPROACHMENT

5

"THE GOVERNMENT KNOWS BEST"

Conservation, Extraction, and Environmental Justice

ON THE DAY I arrived in Mtwara to conduct follow-up fieldwork in July 2016, Salum Mnova, my field assistant, invited me to hop on the back seat of the motorcycle he had borrowed from his neighbor in Sinde village. Salum wanted to take me to his cashew farm near Mkubiru village, which he had inherited after his father's passing. As we rode on the sandy, dusty dirt road that ran along the coast, Salum gestured to the right side of the road, to a large stretch of bush scattered with patches of coconut and cashew trees.

"If you come here after a few years," he said, "all this will be gone. Instead of trees, you'll see only shipping containers. That's what the Mtwara Port people have told us."

These changes would come as part of the port's expansion plans. "But there is also another plan," Salum continued. I could barely hear him, his voice muffled by the wind. When we finally arrived at his twenty-eight-acre cashew farm, we stopped in the open field that was close to Mkubiru village.

Salum said, "Actually, this entire area may be gone. An investor from Germany wants to build a fertilizer factory here. He needs more than 400 hectares of land to build the factory, but the government has told him that only 360 hectares of land is available in this area. So we don't know what's going to happen."

"But do you really want a 'fertilizer factory' in this area?" I asked.

"Yes, definitely yes," Salum replied.

"But a fertilizer factory will cause so much pollution in this area," I said. I found the idea of a fertilizer factory inside an MPA to be an unpalatable proposition.

"Yes," Salum replied, "but we'll get jobs, we'll get employment. We'll get development [*Tutapata ajira, tutapata maendeleo*]. I don't care about the pollution," he said, with a broad grin.

I shook my head in disapproval, not knowing what to say. "But this is a marine park, isn't it? *Mazingira itaharibika* [The environment will get spoiled]," I muttered.

"*Ndio* [yes]," Salum said, and continued to grin at me as if to say, "So what?"

This vignette highlights how and why economic concerns often tend to dominate environmental concerns—especially in communities that have been dispossessed and marginalized and are desperately poor and insecure. In Salum's case, it was not that he was unconcerned about how the proposed fertilizer factory would result in air and water pollution in the region, but that he was more concerned about (and interested in) the potential improvements to local residents' economic well-being. On a global scale, leaders of countries such as China and India, for example, have echoed similar arguments regarding the importance of economic development, while downplaying the cost of environmental pollution, at least in the immediate term.

In recent years, scholars have focused their attention on the social and political complexities—and the perceived incommensurability—of industrial extraction in protected areas (Büscher and Davidov 2013; Holterman 2022). As discussed in the introduction, this interest stems from the conviction, particularly among Western scholars and environmentalists, that conservation interventions and ecotourism projects are "spaces that are fundamentally incompatible and opposed to extractive industry" (Stinson 2014, 88). At the same time, resource extraction is seen as an economic necessity, though one that inevitably leads to irreversible environmental degradation (Gilberthorpe and Rajak 2017; Willow 2019). For this and other reasons, scholars who are predominantly from the West have determined that the presence of an extractive project in a protected area is ideologically incompatible with Western ideals of biodiversity conservation.

Put simply, from the point of view of Western scholars and environmentalists, extractive projects should not be implemented in protected areas like national parks and marine parks. Despite their advocacy and advice, however, there is growing realization that the presence of extractive projects in protected areas is far more common than typically assumed (see introduction). Indeed, numerous scholars have begun to grapple with this phenomenon, acknowledging and arguing that these projects are in fact similar in their underlying logic—i.e., the logic of extraction, both of nature and of natural resources. Nature is extracted from protected areas in the form of ecotourism, generating revenue. In other words, nature is commodified, financialized, and extracted—a process that some scholars have subsumed under what they describe as "the neoliberalization of environmental arenas of governance" (Fairhead, Leach, and Scoones 2012, 240) or the "neoliberalization of biodiversity conservation" (Brockington, Duffy, and Igoe 2008; Büscher 2013; Enns, Bersaglio, and Sneyd 2019; Green and Adams 2015; Holmes, Sandbrook, and Fisher 2016).

Similarly, natural resources such as oil, gas, and minerals are extracted from protected areas to generate capital and profit in an uncorrected feedback loop—as profit is reinvested to generate and accumulate more capital, and so on. Notably, researchers have also argued that in situ populations may not necessarily find the copresence of an extractive project and a conservation project within the same geographical space to be as troubling or unacceptable as it might be to environmental activists. This is because in many cases local people see and experience the logic of extraction in both types of projects (Davidov and Büscher 2013, 2; MacKenzie et al. 2017). Echoing Davidov and Büscher's thesis, Robert Fletcher (2013, 70) specifically points out that rather than viewing industrial extraction and postindustrial ecotourism as antithetical to each other, they can be better understood as "two sides of the same neoliberal coin," i.e., both are extractive, capitalist interventions underscored by profit making.

Further, in what he describes as the Janus face of the ecotourism-extraction nexus, Fletcher asserts that it is often the state that plays a key role in encouraging the copresence of ecotourism and extraction at once. As Fletcher (2014, 82) puts it: "[The state] also acts directly to preserve natural resources from the forces of extraction when ecotourism fails to accomplish this aim, employing both neoliberal and command-and-control mechanisms to do so. In the process, the state supports market-based ecotourism, industrial extraction, and fortress conservation simultaneously." Effectively, in doing so, the state can maximize its revenue through both the extraction and strategic protection of its natural resources. As this chapter will demonstrate, the copresence of the natural gas project and the marine park in rural Mtwara is representative of the Tanzanian state's support for a market-based ecotourism project, an industrial extraction project, and a fortress conservation model to ensure the control and protection of its resources.

In this chapter, I focus on rural Mtwara residents' understandings of the notion of incommensurability (*kutowezekana*), or incompatibility (*kutokubaliana*), in relation to the gas project's presence inside the marine park. I also elaborate on people's understandings of and responses to perceptions of environmental (in)justice and social (in)justice in relation to the copresence of the gas project and the marine park.

The chapter begins with a brief review of the literature pertaining to the ecotourism-extraction nexus (Büscher and Davidov 2013) and a review of the key features of environmental and social justice. I go on to detail key research questions concerning the copresence of the gas project and the marine park, which I sought to seek answers to during my fieldwork. Subsequently, this chapter examines narrative segments that reflect people's views on the copresence of the two projects in the same place. These narratives also reflect their concerns regarding land ownership and access to marine resources. Next, I highlight inter- and intra-village differences in people's views regarding the copresence of the gas project and the marine park and whether they considered these two projects to be incommensurable or inconsistent with their own environmental sensibilities. These opinions ranged from justification of the implementation of the gas project inside the marine park, to belief that the marine park had been designed and implemented as an enclave to allow the gas project to take full control over local resources, to faith in the government's good intentions, to condemnation of the state's unjustified violence against local residents. The ethnographic data illuminate how individuals within and across the study villages have reacted to the copresence of the marine park and the gas project in their locale.

I interviewed and held group discussions with men and women who were living in the marine park's core zone—i.e., in Ruvula / Mnazi Bay—and who were living near three of the five gas wells. I also interviewed and held group discussions with people who were living in marine park villages, such as Nalingu and Mkubiru, that were fifteen to twenty-five kilometers away from the gas project's main infrastructure. Many of these residents had never seen the gas project's technological zone because it was inside a security fence and monitored by armed security guards. Nor had they witnessed the nature and extent of the damage caused to the coastal landscape, particularly in Ruvula and Msimbati.[1] But they were all aware of the gas project's presence in the region. These spatial and temporal factors influenced the residents' varied opinions.

Local understandings of the gas project and its impact on the environment varied significantly depending on the person's geographical home base. For example, none of the Mkubiru and Nalingu residents were able to speak to the damage the gas project had caused in Msimbati, like the uprooting of thousands of trees. Others (incorrectly) believed that people in Msimbati and Madimba had in fact prospered because of the presence of the gas project's major infrastructure in their villages—that they were enjoying the employment opportunities generated by the project. "*Wamepata maendeleo.* Look," they would say, "all their houses have corrugated tin roofs [*mabati*] now." A few of them, on the other hand, spoke of the dangers of living close to a gas pipeline and the possibility of an explosion, resulting in loss of life and property.

Others spoke of the gas itself as something that was hot and inflammable and was extracted from deep below the surface—instead of the gas project, its infrastructure, or its activities. They spoke of the flares they had seen or heard of and cooking gas cylinders as proof that the gas was hot and inflammable. Residents explained that crops were failing, that coconuts were falling down on their own—dry, without flesh or water inside. This, they said, was because of the heat the gas project was generating. Similarly, they believed the gas wells and the pipeline were not conducive for fish and turtles to thrive.

During my fieldwork, I sought answers to a few key questions through interviews and focus group discussions. These questions included: What forms of discourse are used to question, criticize, or rationalize the copresence of the marine park and gas project? Why do local people acquiesce, contest, or remain indifferent to such external interventions? What do local people make of the gas project's potential or actual risk of causing environmental damage in their locale? And finally, to what extent do local concepts (or understandings) of social and environmental justice feature in everyday discourse and elicited narratives?

My goal in this chapter is to answer these four main questions and more. As I show in the following pages, people's answers to these questions varied substantially between and across different communities and villages. Ultimately, I will demonstrate that there was no single conceptualization of incommensurability, as is often assumed in the scholarly literature. What people thought about the copresence of the two projects was mediated by spatiotemporal factors, and their dispositions varied depending on their geographical location on the rural Mtwara peninsula and their lived experiences with the two projects over the years. Moreover, their opinions changed over time, often in significant ways.

INCOMMENSURABILITY, SOCIAL JUSTICE, AND ENVIRONMENTAL JUSTICE

Embedded in discussions about the incommensurability of ecotourism and extractive projects are questions pertaining to local understandings of justice (*kinyume na haki*) or fairness—concerns that pertain to social, environmental (or ecological), distributive, and procedural justice. Were the people of Msimbati, for example, thoroughly consulted regarding environmental, social, and economic risk before the government made the decision to implement the gas projects on the rural Mtwara peninsula? Were local people made aware in advance of the potential or real damage that the extractive project would be causing to their landscapes—their farmlands, trees, crops—and livelihoods? Were the local people given sufficient information in advance regarding the compensation (*fidia*) they would be paid if they were to lose their land, trees, and crops to the project? Moreover, did residents have the freedom to opt out of being included inside the marine park's boundaries? Could they decline to "let go" their crops and farmlands to the gas project, refusing the cash compensation they were offered—which they considered inadequate and unfair? Were local people made aware of the detrimental effects the project could have on their livelihoods? Equally, were they made aware of the potential physical dangers and risks they could face, in the immediate and long term, regarding the extractive project?

It is generally acknowledged among conservation scholars that justice needs "to be explicitly addressed for integrated conservation and development projects to achieve sustainability" (Kopnina 2016, 91). The concept of justice is complex and deeply contextual and is approached and interpreted from different angles (Martin 2017). *Social justice* is "fundamentally concerned with equalizing relations between those who have power and those who do not" (Shoreman-Ouimet and Kopnina 2015, 321; Powers and Freedman 2012). *Environmental justice* concerns "the belief that the burden of environmental damage should be equally distributed so that underprivileged communities are not unfairly saddled by exposure to environmental risks or the necessity for environmental repair" (Shoreman-Ouimet and Kopnina 2015, 322; see also Schlosberg 2013; Walker 2012). "*Distributive justice* refers to more equitable distribution of the benefits deriving from the exploitation of natural resources" and procedural justice "refers to greater participation and transparency in decisions over the management of natural resources" (Perreault 2006, 154).

An anthropological perspective on justice enables us to understand how local communities (different groups and individuals) articulate, make sense of, and respond to perceived injustices and threats to their livelihoods, dignity, and self-determination caused by the imposition of top-down policies and interventions.[2] As Adrian Martin (2017, 37) has argued in his book *Just Conservation*, "Perceptions of justice are powerful motives and . . . responses to conservation interventions are very much dependent on how fair and legitimate they are seen to be." He goes on to elaborate, with empirical examples, how "justice is a social construct . . . that it means different things to different people, and that claims about justice and injustice can only really be understood through reference to the particular circumstances that surround it" (Martin 2017, 54).

Scholars who have examined the justice concept's relevance in different domains and communities have acknowledged "the significance of discursive, as well as material forms of power, the complex networks of knowledge and power that connect different actors in conservation landscapes, and associated mechanisms that produce injustices" (Martin, Akol, and Gross-Camp 2015, 167). In other words, representations, narratives, and discourses have a determining influence on how people perceive and behave in relation to changes in their environment (Fabinyi, Evans, and Foale 2014).[3] From an anthropological perspective, examining local understandings of conservation and extraction-related injustices requires situating them in the wider sociopolitical and economic context for a more thorough analysis (Martin, Akol, and Gross-Camp 2015, 167; Fabinyi, Knudsen, and Segi 2010, 620).

In this case, the local response to the copresence of the gas project and the marine park in rural Mtwara must be analyzed not only in terms of people's lived experiences but also in the context of Tanzania's history of conservation and extractive projects, of the historical neglect of the Mtwara region in Tanzania's colonial and postcolonial context (see introduction), of the changes in the country's political leadership and styles of governance, of the ruling Chama Cha Mapinduzi party's overwhelming influence and the state's domination of its citizens over the years (see chapter 1).

WHEN ENVIRONMENTAL DEGRADATION IS BEARABLE

As noted in chapter 3, in June 2012, the noise and flare of the newly drilled gas well MS-1X—near the oceanfront and the marine park's gate office—had prompted some residents of Msimbati and Mtandi to express concern regarding the health effects of the perceptible noise pollution and flaring in their midst. Residents also complained about the damage that the drilling operations and the shooting of seismic lines had done to their farmlands and trees.[4] In August 2014, the oceanfront landscape had been transformed by visible environmental damage, as thousands of planted coconut and cashew trees that once lined the coast had been uprooted. Two years later, in August 2016, the fifty-foot-wide wayleave where the pipeline had been buried looked flat and bald. Signs in English and Kiswahili had been installed along the wayleave, warning people of a buried high-pressure gas pipeline. I was surprised that the widespread uprooting and felling of coconut and cashew trees along the Msimbati oceanfront had not generated serious discussions, let alone protests, among local villagers.

In July 2016, I asked several people who were living in the vicinity of the gas project's infrastructure what they thought about the transformation of their environment (*mabadiliko ya mazingira*) and whether they had seen any significant changes. I expected Msimbati and Ruvula residents to express concern about the damage the gas project was causing to their environment. To my surprise, however, most people—including older men and women I had been interviewing since 2011, who constituted my key interlocutors—were either reticent about the gas project's visible impact on the landscape or would respond with a casual "*ni sawa tu*" (it's okay). They had little to say explicitly in terms of environmental justice—i.e., whether the siting of the gas project on their agricultural lands and fishing grounds was problematic. They were also reticent about the damage the gas project had done to the environment—the ecology—which would disproportionately affect them in terms of their livelihoods in the long term. This is not to suggest that their casual response to the gas project's presence was an indication of disregard for their environment—or that they were completely oblivious of the environmental damage. The questions I asked of them were specifically related to eliciting *local* understandings of environmental justice and the potential incommensurability, or incompatibility, of the two projects. Despite this superficial apathy or ostensible indifference, conversations behind closed doors (sometimes in lowered voices) during in-depth interviews and group discussions revealed people's specific concerns and complaints about the gas project's impact on the environment—as well as its impact on their livelihoods, food security, and economic security.

People gave more direct and impassioned responses when asked about social justice. This was particularly true in discussions of whether compensation for their assets was fair or unfair. Equally, people gave energetic answers when asked about their experiences related to dispossession and displacement. As I explain below, numerous factors influenced the often reticent or casual responses of interlocutors when asked what they really thought about the copresence of the two projects—whether, according to their sensibilities, they considered it problematic or not.

A CONFUSING COPRESENCE

Bi Mkubwa was sixty-two years old when I interviewed her in August 2016. She had been volunteering as a turtle conservation officer with the marine park right from the start, even as most people in her village had avoided offering support to the marine park. When I asked her what she thought about the gas project's presence inside the marine park, her immediate response was that she was confused (*mchanganue*, puzzled). "It makes my head spin [*ina chemsha bongo*—literally, boils my brain]," Bi Mkubwa said, "when I think, how has the government allowed the gas project to dig wells inside the marine park? I am puzzled, but I think the government has allowed this to happen because the gas project is huge." For Bi Mkubwa, the implementation of the gas project inside the marine park was antithetical to what she had learned about conservation in the WWF-sponsored workshops she had attended over the years. She was acutely aware that the gas project's activities were detrimental to the marine environment in Msimbati. "We are living in a wounded land," she had lamented to me in July 2012 (see chapter 3).

After reflecting on the subject, however, she justified the gas project's presence through the benefits it would bring to the local community, the people of Mtwara, and the entire country. Although the gas project had damaged the environment (using chemicals during seismic tests, drilling wells, and uprooting thousands of trees for the pipeline), Bi Mkubwa was not against the project per se; on the contrary, she was supportive of the project and wanted it to expand further. Simultaneously though, she clarified, she wanted the marine park to remain in the area to continue protecting the marine environment—and to circumscribe the gas project's potential excesses. Otherwise, as she said with a mix of apprehension and exaggerated humor, "They'll dig for gas till your porch. . . . If the marine park goes away, then absolutely yes, they'll dig for gas all the way till your toilet or even under your bed!"

Bi Mkubwa elaborated on her confusion surrounding the government's decision to implement a gas project inside the marine park. On the one hand, she wanted the gas project to drill more gas wells but not cause any harm to local biodiversity. On the other hand, she wanted the marine park to stay on and help the local people with their earnings, economic interests, and livelihoods. As Bi Mkubwa said: "So here I am asking myself, how is it that we have a gas project in the same place where we have the marine park? Really, I have failed to make sense of this, it has left me confused because the gas wells are sitting in the middle of the marine park. Maybe they have reached an understanding. I don't know."

Bi Mkubwa's response must be contextualized in relation to her own life history. Her difficulty in making sense of the copresence of the gas project and the marine park was complicated by the fact that all three of her sons had found low-skill jobs on the gas project. Moreover, as one of the original supporters of the marine park, she had benefited from the training that the WWF had provided a group of women from Msimbati village in fish preservation and roasting techniques during the park's early years. For this and other reasons, she was grateful to the marine park and did not want to see it ended or sidelined by the gas project. Overall, while Bi Mkubwa had personally benefited from the gas project and the marine park, the copresence did not make sense to her in terms of her environmental sensibilities. This left her, as she put it, confused and befuddled; she did not see both projects as following the same logic of extraction.

LAND RIGHTS

My questions about whether it was appropriate for the government to implement a gas project inside the marine park—and whether local residents had had any say in the matter—prompted a discussion on land ownership and land rights. To put this into context, as noted in chapter 3, legally, all land in Tanzania is public land. It belongs to the state, and the country's president is constitutionally designated as its trustee on behalf of all Tanzanian citizens (Bluwstein et al. 2018, 810). The Tanzanian state also owns the subsoil and is known to prioritize extraction over the protection of surface land rights. As a result, "land rights-holders are typically little involved in petroleum operations, and procedural rights related to information, participation and compensation in processes of the compulsory acquisition of land are often limited" (Pedersen and Kweka 2017, 218–19). Moreover, under Tanzanian law, a person or a company may be permitted to prospect for oil, gas, or uranium in protected areas (for example, in the Selous Game Reserve—a UNESCO heritage site) provided the activity is initiated by the government, an environmental assessment is carried out, and the necessary fees have been paid (Tanzanian Wildlife Management Authority Act 2013: Section 34[3]; Holterman 2020, 2022; MacKenzie et al. 2017, 324).

The following excerpts from a women's focus group is illustrative of the kinds of challenges local residents face when confronted with questions about land ownership, subsoil versus surface land rights, and related issues. These excerpts also highlight the difficulties they face when asked to distinguish between private land (with customary rights) and government land or public land.

During one women's focus group discussion in Msimbati in August 2016—which I video recorded—Habiba, a relatively well-to-do fifty-four-year-old resident, expressed her understanding of the copresence of the gas project and the marine park as follows: "I don't think the gas project has dug wells in areas that have been protected by the marine park. I think they have drilled wells on private property, on farmlands that belonged to private individuals. And they drilled wells following an agreement they made with the landowners—and they paid them compensation, that's what I know, or that's how I understand it." For Habiba, the fact that the gas project had compensated those whose land was used for seismic tests, drilling, or laying the pipeline meant that the gas project was developing its infrastructure on land that belonged to private citizens—not to the marine park or the government. Put differently, if the land belonged to the marine park and was government land, then the gas project would not be paying compensation to the local people. For Habiba, this itself was proof that the gas project was drilling wells on private property/land or farmlands that belonged to private individuals—landowners—not government entities. Habiba had interpreted the incommensurability question differently—as in whether, in her perspective, the gas project had the right to drill wells and conduct seismic tests on the land that is circumscribed by the marine park. She did not interpret the question as whether it was acceptable, from an environmental standpoint, for the two projects to be implemented in the same geographical area.[5]

After a brief silence, participants looked to Bi Mkubwa—one of the women present. She had been smiling, head lowered, while Habiba articulated her understanding of the gas project and the marine park. As someone who was relatively well versed in questions of land ownership and rights within the marine park's catchment area, Bi Mkubwa broke the silence and explained:

> The sites where the gas wells have been drilled are inside the marine park. They are on private land, yes, but still, they're inside the protected area. Even if it's private land, it is still inside the marine park, that is how the law has been made. There are big laws and there are small laws. The gas project has broken the small law [by damaging the environment]. That is, the people from the gas project who are drilling new wells have broken the small laws, but you cannot restrict them because the income that the gas project generates for the government is huge. They say you cannot enter this area because they have conserved it, but because it's a large project, they have damaged the environment and brought in a law [so] even if you are unhappy with what they've done, they've gone ahead and damaged the environment anyway.

Bi Mkubwa acknowledged that the gas project had drilled wells on land owned by local individuals with customary rights—therefore, they were given compensation. The compensation was not for the land per se but, according to the law, for the "improvements" they had made on their land and perhaps for the crops that were present at the time of acquisition. However, Bi Mkubwa clarified that those private lands were inside the MPA. In other words, the marine park or the government had jurisdiction over the land that was designated as protected. In providing this explanation, Bi Mkubwa elaborated on why the gas project can drill wells and build its infrastructure inside the marine park, even though it was a protected area. In her view, this is because the gas project is a huge [economic] project compared with the marine park. Accordingly, the gas project was able to continue with its operations because it had broken only the "small law" (damaging the environment). Because of the scale of the project and the substantial benefits it had generated in the form of income, it was allowed to continue.[6]

Following her explanation, which was directed at Habiba as a corrective to her (mis)understanding, Bi Mkubwa looked at the other group members and then to my research assistant and me. She said, her voice raised a little:

It is difficult to talk about conservation with someone who has not been educated on the topic, because they find it difficult to understand what conservation means. When you tell people that this area has been restricted for conservation purposes, people will say, "But I have my farm there." For people here, a protected area means an area where humans do not live or where humans are not permitted to enter. That's their understanding of a protected area. So, they cannot understand why this area is called a protected area when humans are already living inside it. They are fine with the idea of their farmland being inside the conservation area, but they would still like to continue to grow crops on their land. Some may decide to sell it, but they wouldn't know why they won't be able to do it because they're not aware of how conservation is conducted. They don't know that our entire village, and many other villages, have been declared as a conservation area. The entire community is living in what is called a marine protected area.[7]

In Bi Mkubwa's view, the lack of education on the subject, and not ignorance on the part of the residents, has resulted in confusion regarding who owns the land inside the marine park. As she put it, people who have not been educated on the matter find it difficult and confusing to hear that their land is in a protected area. Not surprisingly, they tend to ask: "How can an area be protected when people are still farming on their plots of land inside it?"[8] Moreover, people fail to understand why, if they own and are allowed to grow crops on the land (or plots of land) inside the protected area, they are not allowed to sell their land to potential buyers.

Zainabu, who listened intently to Bi Mkubwa's explanation, approvingly acknowledged that the problem was not ignorance among the local people but lack of education on the topic. Zainabu elaborated: "They should have educated us all about this—but they have ignored us." Residents frequently complained that they "should have been educated better" on matters related to marine conservation, the purpose of establishing the marine park, compensation, land issues, and so on.

These excerpts from the women's focus group discussion reveal the complexities that underscore local understandings of the copresence of an extractive project in an MPA. Habiba was one of many local residents who believed that the gas project had the right to drill wells and extract gas from below the surface land because it had paid cash compensation to a private individual who was the landowner under customary law. Habiba expressed that the copresence of the gas project and the protected area is not incommensurable with villagers' understanding of government rights to the land. The concern, if any, is between the gas company and the landowner. Fair compensation, if it is provided, should enable the gas project to operate on "purchased" private land and carry out its extractive activities—even though the gas project was inside an MPA.

Bi Mkubwa's reference to residents' poor understanding of MPAs is also a commentary on the local residents' limited engagement with environmental justice issues as they relate to the gas project. Some residents found the logistics of living inside a protected area difficult to accept or understand. Critically, Zainabu's comment highlights that it is incumbent on the marine park authorities and representatives from the gas project to educate the local residents on matters related to land ownership, extraction, and environmental issues continuingly.

Rehema, a vocal critic of the marine park and the gas project at the time, expressed similar sentiments regarding the land question concerning the projects' copresence. For her, the gas project and the marine park represented a single entity—they were indistinguishable because they were both government projects or institutions. "*Panguo ni moja* [They're from the same cloth]" she said. Bringing up a personal concern that she had expressed to me repeatedly, Rehema said, her frustration visible, "The government can do what it wants, but if I want to sell my own farmland to someone who wants to build a hotel here, then it becomes a big problem. The marine park people will not allow me to sell my land."

Rehema was not particularly concerned that a gas project had been implemented inside an MPA, nor was she focused on the potential environmental damage and injustice that could ensue. She was more concerned about her inability to sell her plot of farmland because of the restrictions that park authorities had placed on the sale of land and property inside the marine park's boundaries. She saw a contradiction in the marine park's decision to allow the gas project to damage the environment (by drilling wells, digging trenches, uprooting trees to lay the pipeline, etc.), while disallowing residents from selling their farmlands to support themselves.

EXPLAINING INDIFFERENCE OR LACK OF CONCERN

People's apparent indifference to the gas project's environmental impact on their farmlands and fishing grounds was influenced by a number of factors. In-depth interviews and focus group discussion revealed at least seven distinct factors underlying residents' ostensible lack of concern for the gas project's detrimental impact on the environment.

"No Big Deal"

In August 2016, Makanzu, a loquacious thirty-nine-year-old former fisher from Msimbati, was working as a bus conductor on one of the dala dala buses that ran between Msimbati and Mtwara town. I asked him what he thought of the environmental damage the gas project had caused near the oceanfront. He responded by saying: "It's not a big deal." His pat response struck me. During an extended conversation, Makanzu downplayed the problem, saying that the damage was neither permanent nor irreversible. "If the people from the gas project cut the mangrove trees to bury the gas pipeline inside a trench [*mtaro*]," he said, "I don't think it will affect us much because we can plant new mangrove trees. It's not a big problem." Makanzu went on to say that he and other volunteers from his village could always be called on to plant new mangrove trees or saplings. He had done this before, he said; he had volunteered with other villagers to plant mangrove saplings and coconut palms in places where they had been cut. For Makanzu and others who responded similarly, the damage caused by the gas project to the mangroves was "not a big deal" because it could be reversed by planting new saplings.

I asked the same question of Mzimba, who was in his late forties and lived very close to the gas wells and gas processing plant in Ruvula. He also said that he did not think the gas project was damaging the environment—but if it was, he said it was unavoidable (*hakizuiliki*) because they had to drill wells to get the gas out. "This is a big project," Mzimba said, "and it'll bring huge benefits to the people of Tanzania." And—as he emphasized—because this was a "big project," the benefits of extracting gas outweighed the losses (environmental damage). Furthermore, Mzimba asserted that those in charge of the gas project were being deliberate, in that they were not drilling unnecessary wells or damaging the landscape without any concern for the environment. He maintained that damage was caused only when necessary.

Several people in Msimbati, Ruvula, and other marine park villages gave similar answers, saying that the environmental damage caused by the gas project was not a big deal. In their eyes, it was something that could be reversed by volunteers from the community who would plant new tree saplings along the oceanfront. "To get something, you will spoil something," they said, matter-of-factly.

"The Government Knows Best"

Local residents' deference to the Tanzanian government's authority was another reason for their lack of concern for the gas project's negative environmental impact. They also felt that they did not have any authority, compared with government officials, regarding the decision to implement the gas project. People repeatedly stated that the gas project and the marine park were both government projects, and it was the government's responsibility to take care of the environment. "We ordinary citizens need not, and should not, intervene," they said.

Haki, who was the chairman of Ruvula village at the time, was not openly opposed to the marine park or the gas project. As an astute politician and activist (who had previously worked for Frontier, an environmental NGO, and Tanganyika Film and Safari Outfitters), he was well versed in the politics behind the gas project–marine park nexus. He was actively involved in making a case for better compensation for those who had lost their farmlands and cashew and coconut trees. In September 2016, Haki said that people from the local communities could not oppose the marine park or the gas project, as both were government projects that had the backing of international stakeholders. "When people ask me why we should not oppose these projects," Haki said, "I remind them that this land belongs to the government, and that there's really no difference between the marine park and the gas project. Both projects belong to the government. They both consult with each other and cooperate with each other. The gas project, once they dig the trenches and bury the pipeline, they leave that place alone. They don't dig again or destroy anything else." Perhaps Haki felt that he needed to make such statements of deference—about his trust in the government and the two projects. For one, he was unwilling to jeopardize his own position as the village chairman. For another, he was aware that if he were to take a confrontational stance against the gas project or the marine park, the district government would move quickly to quash his attempts. As with several of my interlocutors, Haki had flashbacks of the state-directed violence that the people of Msimbati had experienced in May 2013. Ultimately, this deference implies resignation and an acceptance of disempowerment.

"It's Best Left to the Experts"

Katundu, a forty-nine-year-old resident of Msimbati, had actively participated in the planning and implementing of the marine park in 1998 and 2000. In August 2014, Katundu expressed his deep disappointment with the gas project for two reasons: first, its failure to employ "hundreds" of individuals from Mtwara as was initially promised, and second, the poor compensation paid to those who had lost their farmlands and trees to the project. He summed up his feelings by stating that the gas project had brought the people of Msimbati to tears.

Two years later, when I interviewed him on the question of the copresence of the gas project and the marine park, he took a more deferential position, saying: "That's a problem that's best left to the experts to deal with." Katundu said he was confident that the experts must have consulted with marine park officials before drilling the wells, knowing that they would be damaging the environment. "They must have sat down together to discuss it," he said. "From what I see, they've drilled wells and damaged the environment. However, the project has brought us many benefits—it has produced energy for electricity."[9] Katundu's response— "that it's best left to the experts"—was representative of the responses I recorded from dozens of men and women in the marine park villages.

As with several other Msimbati residents, Katundu also believed that the environmental damage caused by the gas project was negated by the benefits the project brought to the people of Tanzania—energy (i.e., cooking gas), electricity, and jobs. He himself had found temporary employment on the gas project for a total of six months. Katundu's response was one I commonly encountered during my fieldwork, indicating a sense of resignation and feelings of disempowerment within constrained circumstances: that ordinary people had very little influence in the matter. In this prevalent view, the decision to site the gas project inside an MPA—and the resulting problem of environmental damage—was best left to the experts. These experts included state representatives, marine conservation experts, and experts from the extractive industry. Katundu's conviction is noteworthy. He believed that despite the gas project's inability to generate the expected wage labor for the in situ population, it was still a worthwhile project that had brought many benefits—particularly electricity—to the local people.

"We Thought We Would Be Stakeholders"

In August 2014, the pipeline had been buried, and President Kikwete had inaugurated the gas processing plant in Madimba amid much fanfare and media attention. At the time, most people in Msimbati and Mtandi were hopeful that the gas project would eventually result in infrastructure development and jobs in the Mtwara Region—as Kikwete had promised. They had been led to believe that as part of its corporate social responsibility, Wentworth (formerly Artumas), the gas company, would provide them with free electricity and build a tarmac road from Ruvula to Msimbati. Local residents believed they could travel faster without the encumbrance of an unpaved dirt road, particularly during the rainy season. Villagers also hoped the gas company would significantly upgrade the village dispensary and the secondary school. More importantly, parents anticipated that there would be job opportunities for their children, either on the gas project or at the factories that would be built in their region. For these reasons, residents did not openly oppose or question the project's potential to degrade the environment.

Two years later, however, in September 2016, Lichumbu, from Msimbati, expressed his sadness as he recalled all the good things that Artumas had originally promised to the local people. Artumas had promised to treat the residents as stakeholders and to provide them with a range of benefits, allowing them to enjoy the fruits of the gas extracted from their lands. As Lichumbu recalled, these promises included an asphalt road from Ruvula to Msimbati, improvements to the village dispensary, and, importantly, free electricity. In reality, people had to pay normal charges to TANESCO for the electricity, "just like everyone else in Tanzania."

What's more, the electricity that was supplied to them came from the Mtwara power plant, not from the twelve-megawatt power plant in Mnazi Bay that Artumas operated. As Lichumbu put it: "They would use chemicals to penetrate deeper and deeper into the sand and rocks. And then they would install their drill to extract the gas. And here we continue living in our huts along with big snakes and insects." In other words, the gas project had not ushered in any development or tangible benefits to the local residents, as most people continued to live in poverty just as they had before the project entered the region.

Msimbati villagers were very concerned that their original trees had been uprooted and that the quality of the soil on their agricultural land had diminished because of the gas project's seismic and drilling activities. Still, most people in the study villages continued to believe that the benefits the gas project would one day bring to local communities would far outweigh the cost of the damage to their landscape. People were so hopeful for infrastructure development and jobs that they disregarded the gas project's environmental impacts. Even when the promises of development failed to materialize, people were still hopeful—or felt helpless.

"We're Helpless"

Most of the local residents were aware that the gas project was owned and implemented by the state/government, in collaboration with international companies such as Artumas (Canada), Maurel & Prom (France), and China Petroleum Technology and Development Corporation (CPTDC) (China). They acknowledged that it was a huge project of national and international importance. They were also convinced that the government had decided to implement and expand the gas project regardless of protest or opposition by the local people; they believed they were powerless against the government.

As described in chapter 3, in May 2013, the government had authorized its security forces to use violence and terror to subdue the people of Msimbati during the Mtwara-wide protests against the Mtwara–Dar es Salaam gas pipeline. At the time, people criticized the gas project not because it had caused "environmental injustice" (e.g., pollution from the gas project that was affecting their health) but because of "social and distributive injustice." The opposition was directed not toward the gas project itself but toward the gas pipeline that was designed to transport the gas from Msimbati to Dar es Salaam. In all of this, environmental justice played a minimal role relative to social and distributive justice in people's everyday discourse. In my conversations with people in Mtwara town who were living farther away from the rural Mtwara peninsula, I found that they were not aware that the gas project's technological zone was inside a marine park, and this was not due to willful ignorance. What's more, there is no mention of the marine park in the scholarly literature on the 2013 "gas riots." Critically, except for a cursory mention, the scholarly literature on the marine park ignores the fact that there is a large gas project in the core area of the marine park—that the gas project has overshadowed the everyday discourse regarding the marine park on the Mtwara peninsula.

The following excerpt from an interview with Rukia, from Mtandi village, in August 2016, is an example of people's feelings of powerlessness against the government and the gas project.

> They paid me 1,700,000 shillings [about $1,000 USD] in 2012 as compensation for my farmland and the trees I had lost to the project. When I protested, saying that they had paid me too little for what I had lost, they said to me, "Whether you give us your consent or not, we will implement this project here, no matter what." It's a great loss for me because when they passed through my farmland [to conduct the seismic survey], they destroyed it by using explosives. They passed through my farm three times, and each time they destroyed it by using explosives. Well Number Three is on my farmland. Then they passed through my land again to erect electricity poles. Then they did it again to widen the roads to bury the pipeline.... When they passed through my farm the first day, I wanted them to compensate me for the crops they had destroyed. I stood there waiting for them to call me and give me the compensation money.... They said, "If we have to cut through more of your land, we will do so. If we have to drill on your farmland, we will do so." I protested: "You're planting those explosives, but my crops are still there!" When they passed through my farm for the third time, they uprooted the coconut trees and cashew trees. They took so much of my land. They widened the road so much that trucks could pass through it. They said I should be okay with it because they've already paid me 1,700,000 shillings, but I said that the area they've compensated me for is much larger than the value of that compensation.

Rukia was clearly distressed about the damage the gas project had done to her farmland and trees. She was also disappointed with the compensation the gas project had paid her for her losses, feeling that the gas project had significantly undervalued the agricultural land and trees that she had lost to the project's expanding infrastructure. Additionally, Rukia took umbrage at the gas project people's "arrogance" toward her [and toward her fellow villagers] in telling her that they would do whatever was necessary to implement the project—regardless of what she or other residents said or did to protest their activities. In sum, Rukia felt helpless and was left ruminating over the loss of her farmland and trees in return for compensation she thought was meager. As Pedersen and Kweka (2017, 219) point out, "The Land Acquisition Act of 1967 only grants compensation for 'improvements' of the land . . . not for the land itself. This has, over the years, disadvantaged customary rights-holders, who have found it difficult to prove that they had improved the land value."

Like Rukia, many people who had lost their farmlands to the project claimed they had not been adequately compensated. They had limited information on the procedural rights related to compulsory land acquisition by the Tanzania government for national projects. Their narratives of loss and perceived injustice were well developed; they expressed them fluently. In addition, they had told their stories and expressed their sentiments multiple times to friends, neighbors, relatives, family members, and their local leaders.

"They Do What They Want. They Don't Care for Us."

The gas company had compensated residents for their assets according to the assessment made by government bureaucrats. However, while no one in the study villages claimed that they had not been paid their compensation, nearly everyone expressed a deep sense of injustice regarding the compensation amount—either for themselves or on behalf of a family member. They lamented the unfairness of the amount paid out to individuals who had lost their trees and crops to the project and the overall disregard shown by gas project personnel to locals. Compensation had become a contentious issue, especially in Msimbati. Over the years, through the labor and investment of several generations, almost the entire area (which had once been forested) had been converted into farmland. The people of Msimbati had transformed the landscape with mango trees, cashew trees, coconut trees, sorghum, rice, and cassava farms.

Habiba, from Msimbati village, described the situation, saying that since Msimbati is a small island, no matter where the gas people "pass through," they were passing through someone's subsistence farm or a cash crop plantation. Habiba lamented that gas project personnel had cut through farms, showing disregard for the owners' sentiments. This was a pervasive complaint among those who had lost their assets to the gas project. In several interviews conducted with the people of Msimbati and Mtandi, I heard the common refrain: "They do what they want. They just dig wherever they want. . . . They don't care for us [*hawatujali*]." People acknowledged that they were promptly given compensation—in cash—for the loss of their trees and crops; however, like Habiba, people complained that the amount they were given was a fraction of their own estimate of the value of the farmland, crops, or trees that were destroyed in the process of seismic surveying and well drilling. Additionally, like Habiba, people complained that their farmlands were no longer fertile because of the chemicals and explosives that were used during the seismic surveys. In other words, while those who had lost their farms and trees to the gas project were being compensated, from the local peoples' perspective they had incurred a loss that was enough to push them toward hunger and even destitution or penury (*ufukara*).

In sum, the discrepancy between the value of land lost to the gas project and the compensation money provided caused significant distress to the local people. As a result, though they acknowledged the gas project's role in damaging their environment, individuals were significantly more concerned with issues of inadequate compensation. Many were not entirely opposed to the gas project itself, but they wanted it to provide local residents with training and employment. Moreover, people were troubled by how rudely the personnel working on the gas project (most of whom were outsiders—*wageni*) related to the local residents.

On a similar note, Yusuf from Msimbati pointed out that local people were powerless against the government—which held all the decision-making powers. "If it wasn't for the government's permission," Yusuf said, "the gas companies would not have been allowed to drill wells in this area to extract the gas. The government gave these companies the license to drill wells inside the marine park, and that's why they are here." As Yusuf implied: If the government does not see a problem with the gas project being located inside an MPA, why should the local people take issue with it? In other words, Yusuf emphasized his powerlessness in the matter. He said: "I don't know if the marine park people see any negative effects of the gas project on the environment. Now if I see that they are damaging the environment, and I were to go there and tell those gas project people not to do this or that, do you think they'll listen to me?"

In raising this rhetorical question, Yusuf expressed his skepticism regarding the government's willingness to pay heed to citizens' concerns. He believed it would be futile for him to be concerned with the damage the gas project might be causing to the environment. Unlike Haki's position on the two projects discussed earlier, Yusuf's comment underscores the overbearing influence of foreign fossil capital on the Tanzania government in an era of neoliberalization of the economy—in complete contrast to the ujamaa years during which the Tanzania government emphasized self-reliance (*kujitegemea*) and nondependence on foreign capital or intervention.

Fear of State-Directed Violence

As discussed in chapter 3, for the people of Msimbati in particular, the physical violence and terror that the government security forces unleashed on their community on May 23, 2013, was still fresh in their minds and bodies. They had no desire to confront the government agents or the staff working on the gas project about environmental degradation for fear of further repercussions—physical violence and oppression. Bi Mkubwa, who always spoke in favor of the marine park and the gas project, recalled her own traumatic experience: "I had seen war on TV, and I had heard so much about it on the radio, but really, that day I got to see and experience firsthand what a war looks like and feels like. It was depressing.... One of my sons called me from Mtwara town saying that the riot police had beaten him with the butt of a gun and that he had fallen and lost consciousness.... The violence continued for two days. We were buried in the violence for two days." Even three years later, some people in Msimbati expressed their deep disbelief and revulsion at the violence while recalling their traumatic experience with the security forces in May 2013. Rehema, who had fallen on a rock while running away from the soldiers, said, "I'm still hurting, my chest is still hurting." Zainabu, pregnant at the time and hiding in her house with her two children, said, "We were all shocked by the violence that our soldiers unleashed on us.... They beat up people very badly, it was very bad, they beat them, they beat them, they beat them a lot." A few people expressed their regret and disappointment with whomever had firebombed the marine park's gate office, which had triggered the state violence. They did not blame the gas project but emphasized that the security forces had been excessively violent. "To punish the entire community," they said, "was unjustified." For the most part, however, most of my interlocutors in Msimbati were reticent about the events that took place in May 2013.

CONSERVATION AS RESOURCE ENCLAVING

As discussed in this chapter's introductory paragraphs, there is a substantial body of scholarly anthropological literature on the presence of extractive projects in protected areas. Anthropologists such as Appel (2019), Ferguson (2005, 2006), Rogers (2015), Willow and Wylie (2014), and Ackah-Baidoo (2012) have used detailed case studies to illustrate and theorize the extractive enclaving process that is a characteristic feature of modern-day extractive practices. In August 2016, Hassani elaborated on a point he had made to me two years earlier: "I don't believe that the marine park people came here to protect marine life, mangroves, or to stop destructive fishing practices. They came here to control the land for the gas company. They knew that there was a lot of gas here. They were aware that companies would soon come to extract gas from the Mnazi Bay area.... They say that the marine park covers 650 square kilometers. Then why do they keep their eyes on about 8 kilometers of the coast where the gas company has drilled wells?"

Hassani's allegation was not baseless.[10] The marine park rangers rarely ventured out into other parts of the marine park on a regular basis to monitor and implement the regulations.[11] The reason for this, however, was said to be economic—a shortage of regular staff to monitor the park's catchment area. Hassani further alleged that ever since the marine park was established, the number of tourists who come to visit the area had gone down to a trickle: "In Mafia there are hotels, employment. Tourists come to enjoy for many days, but here, nothing. Hardly any tourists come to this place." He alleged that the marine park had not promoted tourism (as was originally planned and promised) because it didn't need to; it relied on receiving substantial revenue from the gas company in the form of rent and compensation for environmental damage. Hassani further alleged: "The marine park wants people to stop engaging in dynamite fishing because it damages the environment, but they have allowed the gas company to use explosives during seismic surveys. That's because the marine park profits from the gas company. They knew in advance that 'profit would rain down on them' [*manufa inayesha*] so they established a marine park before the gas project was implemented." In sum, Hassani and others were suspicious of the government's motivation for implementing a marine park on the Mtwara peninsula. Hassani believed the park's real goal was to control the land and other assets in the area so that gas companies could conduct their exploration and extraction activities unhindered and eventually generate income for the government.

Mabruki, a man in his midfifties from Msimbati, was equally cynical about the marine park. He expressed his support for the gas project, stating that he did not see what harm the project has done to the environment, and that if the gas project employees did damage the environment, they did so because they had no other option. However, Mabruki stated, "The marine park people do nothing to conserve the environment. They have decided to remain idle. They are really not conserving anything. They do not have any work. They do not catch those who use bombs [when fishing] and so what are they even conserving?"

In other words, the marine park personnel were neglecting their duties—the prevention of dynamite fishing and other destructive fishing practices in the park's catchment area. In Mabruki's view, if the MPA authorities were serious about conserving the marine environment, they would apprehend and punish the dynamite fishers. From his perspective, the marine park was an ineffective project. By contrast, the gas project was doing what it was supposed to do: drill, explore, and extract gas to generate revenue for the government, jobs for the local people, and electricity. Consequently, Mabruki supported the gas project's presence.

THE FRAILTY OF MARINE CONSERVATION

The marine park authorities had placed restrictions on local residents, preventing them from accessing their farmlands and resources. Over time, people felt alienated from their traditional lands and fishing grounds, i.e., their subsistence and culturally significant landscapes, leading to a lack of concern for the inevitable damage the gas project had caused these areas. Those who were unable to earn their livelihoods from their traditional farmlands were hopeful that the gas project would provide them with alternative economic opportunities. Moreover, residents had a long history of opposition to the marine park prior to resisting the gas pipeline project. For many people, the gas project was damaging the landscape they had been displaced and alienated from. People felt less connected to their farmlands because of the marine park's previous actions—farmlands that were now the gas project's domain. Much of their unwillingness to engage with the environmental damage caused by the gas project was tied to their long history of opposition to the marine park.

This was particularly true for long-term fishers like fifty-nine-year-old Abubakar, a Nalingu village resident who had strongly opposed the marine park from its inception. Abubakar firmly believed that the marine park had not brought any benefits to the people of Nalingu, or to any of the marine park villages. Contrastingly, in speaking about the gas project, Abubakar indicated he would be happy for the project to continue drilling "as many wells as they want, in the entire ocean if they want." Abubakar saw value in supporting the gas project because it would bring concrete, tangible benefits to the people of Mtwara.[12] At the time, Abubakar (mistakenly) believed that the gas project's expansion would mean more job opportunities for the local people. This was clearly not the case; the gas project had not provided employment opportunities to even a fraction of the local people who were vying for jobs on the gas project. Moreover, the people of Msimbati and Ruvula were concerned that they might someday be asked to vacate their villages and resettle elsewhere. None of my interlocutors expressed their willingness to leave their ancestral villages. As sixty-four-year-old Mwema, from Mtandi village, put it: "Yes, we are afraid that one day there might be a gas explosion here or the government will tell us to vacate our village and start our life somewhere else. But where will we go? Namidondi village? It's all dry land there. What will we grow? What will we eat?"

A few others (particularly those in Ruvula, Msimbati, and Mtandi) expressed their fear that they would be the first to die or suffer from injuries if there was a gas explosion. For them, the gas pipeline itself posed a health and safety hazard. As Hassani put it: "We live close to the gas pipeline. It could explode at any time, and we could lose our lives. Our village doesn't even have a fire station [*wazima moto*]."

As with Abubakar, residents of marine park villages located farther away from the gas project's infrastructure were either ambivalent or generally supportive of the project, in contrast with their negative perceptions of the marine park. In July 2017, Abubakar expressed his support for the gas project and its expansion while downplaying the importance of the marine park. He asserted that the marine park should drill more wells, adding that it might be even better if the marine park were to leave Mtwara altogether, so that the gas project could continue unhindered. Abubakar justified his stance by emphasizing that people in the coastal villages were against the marine park because they had not seen any benefits. In the case of the gas project, they had seen real benefits, like electricity. "So," he concluded, "I would like to make a humble request to the marine park people that they should leave this place and go elsewhere."

Abubakar had reframed the question of incommensurability in the context of the gas project and the marine park by arguing that these two projects were indeed incommensurable—incompatible, even—and that the question of incommensurability could be resolved if the marine park (and not the gas project) were to be discontinued. In this scenario, the gas project would be free "to drill as many wells as it wants, in the entire ocean if it wants."

Mwabadi, in his early fifties, who was a resident of Msangamkuu village, echoed Abubakar's sentiments. Mwabadi explained that while he was aware of the need to protect the environment, he also believed that it was imperative to drill more wells and extract more gas to benefit a larger number of people. He asserted: "The conservation efforts and the gas project are both being done for our benefit. The ocean is huge, there'll always be fish, but you can find gas only in certain places, so might as well dig, dig, dig [to get it all out]!" Like Abubakar, Mwabadi resided in a village several kilometers away from the gas project's infrastructure and had not been negatively affected. Therefore, he was enjoying only the benefits of the gas project—mainly electricity. While he and some of his fellow villagers had lost their farmlands and trees to the Mtwara Port Authority (MDC project), they had not suffered dispossession on the scale experienced by the people of Msimbati. Those who had lost their land and trees to the Mtwara Port Authority and the MDC were allowed to continue to cultivate food crops on their farmlands, though a minister had advised them that they should not plant new cashew or coconut trees. By contrast, people in Msimbati, especially those who had lost their land and trees to the gas project, had permanently lost their assets, and those whose farmlands were inside the marine park's gated section were not allowed to collect even firewood from their own plots of land. Mpojola, from Mkubiru village, held a similar view and suggested that it would be better if the gas project continued to expand—and, at the same time, that the marine park be dismantled. Mpojola was not convinced that the marine park was implemented to protect the marine environment. He had neither heard of nor seen the benefits of the conservation work. In his view, marine park staff did nothing to promote ecotourism in the region; very few foreign tourists came to the marine park. He explained: "Yes, it's true that the gas project has spoiled the environment while it is carrying out its activities, and so it's better if the marine park leaves this place. This gas project brings benefits to the entire country. . . . But the marine park people just collect fees from the tourists. And if it wasn't for the marine park, investors would have come here to set up factories [because of the availability of electricity], and we would have got jobs. They are not coming to invest in our villages because we are inside a marine protected area." Mpojola's criticism of the marine park versus the gas project was broadsided. He opposed the marine park right from its inception because it had effectively ended his livelihood as a fisher. In addition, he was not convinced that the marine park was established to protect the environment—because of the incompetence of its staff in preventing destructive fishing practices in the catchment area.

By contrast, he was strongly in favor of the gas project. While he acknowledged that the gas project destroyed the environment through the exploration and extraction process, he justified the damage by claiming that the benefits to the people—not only of Mtwara but of the entire country—far outweighed the cost of environmental damage. As he put it, "The gas project generates revenue that benefits and strengthens the entire country. The marine park collects revenue that benefits only a few people locally." More importantly, Mpojola believed that if the government had not declared this region as a protected area, rural Mtwara would have seen an influx of industrial development because of the gas discoveries; investors would have flocked to the area for its access to reliable electricity. However, Mpojola argued that the marine park was thwarting potential investors—factories could not be established inside a protected area. While this was true concerning the gated section of the marine park in Msimbati, the government was open to allowing investors to set up factories, including a large fertilizer factory (mentioned in this chapter's opening vignette) and a sugar factory inside the protected area.[13] As a resident of Mkubiru village, Mpojola was not directly affected by the gas project regarding displacement or dispossession of livelihood assets. Unlike the people of Msimbati, Mtandi, and Ruvula—many of whom had been dispossessed of their farmland by the gas project—Mpojola had not lost any of his assets to its operations. As a fisher, his grievance was against the marine park and its governance strategy. Many people who opposed the marine park but supported the gas project echoed his insistence that it should leave the peninsula and establish itself elsewhere.

CONCLUSION

The marine park and the gas project in rural Mtwara are both state-directed projects. In the case of both, residents have needed more say in the projects' siting and governance. Moreover, these projects involve multiple stakeholders at the international, including south-south cooperation between Tanzania and China, national, regional, and local levels. From a legal perspective, the Tanzania government's decision to implement an extractive project inside a protected area gazetted by the state itself is not against Tanzanian laws pertaining to extractive activities in protected areas. The Tanzania government has the power to degazette the park if it wants to.[14] In other words, from the Tanzanian state's perspective, the implementation of a gas project inside the boundaries of a marine park is not incommensurable. This is a particularly veritable fact considering that the state has a huge stake in the gas project—as was the case for the 540-kilometer gas pipeline out of Mtwara. Additionally, the decision was supported by the full environmental impact assessment (EIA) conducted (albeit hurriedly) in 2014 before the dramatic expansion of the gas project.

This is not to say that the local situation does not raise questions of environmental justice—nor that there was no environmental damage from the gas project inside the marine park. On the contrary, the environmental damage—particularly the felling of thousands of trees to drill wells and bury the pipeline—was highly visible in Ruvula and Msimbati and all along the pipeline that cut through forested areas between Mtwara and Dar es Salaam. Moreover, unpublished data from the marine park authorities suggested that the significant decrease in turtle hatchlings from as many as 2,122 in 2004 to as few as 514 in 2006 was associated with gas exploration activities (see Machumu and Yakupitiyage 2013, 376). An audit report submitted in 2018 reveals that the gas project was known to engage in the "improper discharge of effluents to the sea without proper treatments and procedures as per regulations" (URT 2018b). As Appel (2019, 29) has argued in her book, oil companies make an infrastructural *choice* to explore and extract oil offshore rather than onshore and near human populations, precisely because they want to minimize the political and reputational risks of visible accessible production (of oil in particular).

The focus of this chapter, however, is on the perceptions of local residents regarding the two projects and their copresence, to find out not only whether the copresence troubles people who live in the vicinity of the gas infrastructure but also how these two projects have affected the peoples' everyday lives, positively (e.g., electricity) and negatively (dispossession and loss of land and livelihood). Most people in the six marine park villages did not consider the two projects incommensurate or paradoxical. They commonly saw both projects as symbols of state power (*serikali*, or government)—projects that the government had initiated and implemented with "good intentions" but with poor governance characterized by an absence of consultation with or involvement of the local communities. People summed up their thoughts with statements such as: "The marine park is the government. The gas project is also the government. We are just ordinary citizens. The government knows what it's doing. We can't tell the government what to do."

Many residents justified the gas project's presence by emphasizing its potential to bring economic and social benefits to the people of Tanzania. Some even asserted that the presence of the marine park was hindering the gas project's expansion and the local people's access to marine resources—implying that they would rather the marine park be decommissioned and the gas project expanded. They saw the park as "a form of resource extraction that has cut villagers off from land and resources they previously used" (Stinson 2014, 102). Parallels can be found between the situation in Mtwara and the situation Stinson (2014) has described in his case study among rural Belizian villagers. Stinson's study revealed that for many Indigenous people in southern Belize, "ecotourism is not seen as fundamentally distinct from and incompatible with resource extraction such as oil development [oil exploration inside a national park], but is itself a form of resource extraction that has served to restrict local access to and use of natural resources" (2014, 88). For Stinson's informants, ecotourism and oil are similar. They extract resources from local control, structuring local livelihoods through low-paid wage labor (Davidov and Büscher 2013, 10; see also MacKenzie et al. 2017).

Residents of Mtwara acknowledged that the gas extraction in the marine park was possible only because the government had given the project environmental clearance. A few people also argued that the marine park was a tactical ploy; the government's intention had been to usurp the land it knew had substantial gas reserves that were first discovered in 1982 in Mnazi Bay to facilitate extraction. In this view, the marine park was a pretext under which the government could set up a socio-spatial enclave or enclosure—where the gas project would be free to conduct its extraction activities without hindrance from local communities. In other words, the government had engaged in "top-down territorialization"—the "territorialization of property relations and resource control" (Bluwstein 2017, 101; see also Muralidharan and Rai 2020).

Furthermore, several residents who argued for the gas project downplayed the resulting environmental damage, pointing to its impermanence. They asserted that removing coconut, cashew, and mango trees in the region was not irreversible; the trees could easily be replaced with new saplings. Advocating for the gas project, they asserted that once the pipeline was buried, gas personnel were unlikely to dig up the area again—and that what they were doing was necessary for the region's development. By contrast, many people emphasized that the marine park was unnecessary, unlike the gas project. People in Msimbati, unhappy with the gas project and how it had unfolded between 2012 and 2014, were now beginning to speak in favor of the gas project vis-à-vis the marine park. They argued that the gas project had at least made it possible to generate electricity in Mtwara—while the marine park had done nothing to improve the lives of local people.

Most people in the coastal villages had long opposed the marine park for various reasons and held a widely shared conviction that it had not delivered on the benefits it had promised. They said it had done little or nothing to generate income from its activities and had not improved the lives or livelihoods of locals. On the contrary, it had hindered the livelihoods of many individuals and households whose identities were closely tied to the ocean. A few people, however, expressed support for the continuation of the marine park. They applauded its commendable work in promoting environmental awareness among the people of the rural Mtwara peninsula and argued that if the marine park were to be degazetted, destructive fishing practices that were banned would likely return to the region. People living in Msimbati, Mtandi, and Ruvula—villages closer to the gas wells and the gas project's infrastructure—were more engaged and entangled with the complex dynamics of state intervention, international capital, and sociopolitical struggles. Unsurprisingly, they had more complex and divergent views regarding the gas project's presence inside the marine park because of their experiences of dispossession and displacement by both initiatives.

Overall, for the majority of people living in marine park villages, the presence of a gas project inside an MPA was not cause for serious concern in terms of its potential for environmental damage or environmental injustice. In the context of poverty, unemployment, very limited alternative livelihood options, and years of marginalization and underdevelopment—for the people of rural Mtwara, damage to their environment was something they were willing to overlook in return for economic opportunities. These included jobs and infrastructure development, such as electricity. Indeed, from an outsider's perspective, a lack of overt concern and advocacy against the gas project's potential to damage the environment could be interpreted as a matter of environmental and social injustice. In the long run, it disadvantages local communities in terms of their livelihoods and food security.

The discourses and narratives I have analyzed in this chapter do not suggest that the people of Msimbati and other villages were overly concerned about the environmental damage the gas project was causing to their environment. Perhaps they had concerns, but they downplayed them, stating that the government knew what it was doing or that these issues were a matter best left to the experts. No organized protest or advocacy action group in the region focused on environmental justice as it related to the gas project. A study conducted by Oxfam on the topic emphasized issues of human rights and land rights but not environmental justice. Again, this does not mean that the local people did not care about their environment. In this case, however, they had not organized themselves into a protest movement or advocacy group, which would have kept an eye on gas project–related environmental damage in the region.

However, people were united in their concerns about the gas project's social justice impact at the local level. This was largely because of the poor compensation villagers had received for assets lost to the project. People were far more divided in their opinion regarding the marine park's benefits in relation to the gas project. While many residents would instead prefer that the marine park be relocated, those who were supportive argued that it played a key role in protecting the environment and the livelihoods of local villagers. This it did by preventing outside investors from purchasing land inside the protected area to build factories or hotels. These differing views have important policy implications for government bureaucrats and technocrats, who are at the helm of the decision-making process regarding the siting of conservation and extractive projects. Critically, residents across the study villages were insufficiently informed about land rights and ownership. The data examined in this chapter underscore the need to increase awareness within marine park villages regarding land issues. Important information—such as which land is government land and which land is village or private land—is needed to mitigate misunderstandings and conflicts over the sale of land. Several residents found it difficult to articulate their thoughts on the incommensurability of the gas project and the marine park. Some did not know what environmental damage the gas project might be causing.

To conclude, over the past two decades, residents of the rural Mtwara peninsula have witnessed significant transformations in the region's physical and social landscape. People's lives and livelihoods have been affected by two projects, both implemented by the government in a top-down manner: the marine park and the gas project. These projects have collectively affected local residents' overall perspectives on infrastructure development, environmental justice, social justice, and distributive justice (transporting the gas to distant places rather than using it to generate electricity within Mtwara and supplying it to local residents at discounted rates), procedural justice (consultation and involvement of local people in decisions related to the siting and governance of the projects), and hope (the promise of jobs and participation in development projects). I argue that local social justice concerns were so overpowering for people that it was difficult for them to focus on abstract issues like the incommensurability of the two projects.

Nearly everyone (particularly in Msimbati) had a story to tell about the social injustice that they, their family members, or relatives had experienced because of the two projects. Examples such as unfair compensation for assets, failed promises of jobs and free electricity, and prohibitions from selling their land even during a financial emergency were widespread. People saw these social injustices as challenges to their well-being, resulting in them "going backward" (*tunarudi nyuma*) or experiencing further impoverishment. Their preoccupation with social justice (fairness, dignity) concerns at the local level had arguably eclipsed their environmental justice concerns—and, by extension, their concern regarding the incommensurability of the two projects.

Ultimately, this chapter has shown that the people of Mtwara yearn for development. They crave better roads, hospitals, schools, and colleges—better electricity supply and jobs—than initiatives like the marine park and the gas project offer. As Salum Mnovo expressed in the opening vignette, he did not care if the proposed fertilizer factory would result in serious air pollution on the Mtwara peninsula—so long as it would generate jobs for local people and bring development to the region. His response was reflective of the kinds of tangible benefits that local residents anticipated from the gas project.

However, residents were unhappy with how these projects were implemented—particularly the nonconsultation and noninvolvement of local people in key decisions. The next chapter discusses the discursive shifts that occurred in the marine park villages, and the factors that prompted locals to become increasingly supportive of the marine park—which they came to appreciate as a "check" on the gas project's potential excesses.

6

"NOW WE ARE ALL EDUCATED"

Rethinking Environmental Subjectivities

ONE EARLY MORNING in July 2016, my field assistant Mama Razak casually mentioned that dynamite fishing in the area had stopped. We were walking from Sinde to Mkubiru village. Mama Razak said, "Now it's quiet here. I have not heard any explosions for five or six months now. . . . They've stopped. Otherwise, I would hear at least five or six explosions in the ocean every morning. Those bombs have stopped." Like Mama Razak, residents of the key fishing villages inside the marine park had, over the years, grown used to hearing explosions in the fishing grounds, as fishers routinely tossed dynamite sticks or homemade bottle bombs into the sea to kill or stun fish before capturing them. Village leaders and local government officials had long recognized the problem but had failed to stop the use of destructive fishing gear and practices amid allegations of corruption. They lacked support from the police and government authorities. But fishing practices were beginning to change in these villages, as was the everyday discourse regarding the environment (*mazingira*). In September 2018, Bi Lulanje, a forty-year-old single mother of two teenage boys, corroborated what several of my interlocutors had told me about the end of illegal fishing practices on the Mtwara peninsula:

I thank God . . . people have stopped using bombs to do their fishing. Otherwise, every morning when the youth [*vijana*] would start tossing their dynamites [*mabomu*] in the shallow waters, we would say, "Oh, here they go!" But now, we don't hear those explosions anymore. People would be very surprised if they hear an explosion in the ocean. They'll start asking, "Hmmm . . . where is that sound [of an explosion] coming from?" We were scared to go to the ocean to catch octopus or glean other sea creatures [crustaceans]. Those explosions would really scare us, we would get startled, but now we don't hear them, so people are able to go into the ocean and do their fishing in peace. Now people are able to catch a lot of fish. I'm really thankful.

Why did fishers in the marine park villages stop engaging in destructive fishing practices after several decades? Why now? What changed? As mentioned in the introduction, dynamite fishing has been a characteristic feature of fishing along Tanzania's coastline since the 1960s. The government's previous attempts to put an end to the practice and the use of destructive fishing gear—including beach seines and small mesh nets such as kokoro and tandilo—were met with only sporadic success. Beginning sometime in mid-2016, however, when I asked residents of seafront villages whether people were continuing to engage in dynamite fishing or the use of kokoro, tandilo, or poison to catch reef fish, villagers emphatically stated: "No, it's all over, absolutely! Illegal fishing, especially dynamite fishing, has reduced significantly or it has stopped completely." These assertions were significant because until 2015 or 2016, dynamite fishing and other destructive fishing practices in the marine park's catchment area were common. Illegal fishing practices continued despite the restrictive enforcement and patrolling undertaken by the marine park in the catchment villages.

I was skeptical of such statements at first; there was a historical precedent to the temporary cessation of dynamite fishing in Mtwara. Consultants who had written evaluation reports following the marine park's implementation had alluded to the cessation of dynamite fishing in the Mtwara Region, particularly in 1997, following Operation Pono (parrotfish). With help from donor countries, the Tanzania government initiated an aggressive campaign to stop dynamite fishing in Tanzanian waters. The campaign involved the Tanzania Naval Command, the Maritime Police, and the prime minister's office. The interventions were temporarily effective; however, the problem soon resurfaced and even worsened. Multiple studies conducted between 2012 and 2015 reported a significant reemergence of dynamite fishing and other illegal destructive fishing practices in the Mtwara coastal region.[1] Nonetheless, I wanted to find out what lay behind the emphatic statements that many of my interlocutors made regarding the cessation of destructive fishing practices in their villages—in other words, what lay behind "the emergence of new subjectivities in relation to the environment" (Agrawal 2005a, 163). I framed my questions in the context of the broader literature on "environmentality" and environmental subjectivities, as I discuss below.

This chapter examines how everyday discourses and practices surrounding marine conservation in the coastal villages of rural Mtwara changed and shifted following the implementation of the marine park in rural Mtwara in 2000. As noted in chapters 2 and 4, the project's initial period was marked by uncertainties and delays. Residents in some villages had high expectations regarding the park's potential to facilitate conservation and economic development through ecotourism. In other affected villages, particularly Nalingu, there was fierce opposition to the marine park. Over the years there were violent protests, overt and covert resistance, indifference, and subsequent acquiescence to the restrictions initiated and enforced by the marine park authorities—at least in some of the key fishing villages. Until 2016, the majority of the park villagers perpetuated a discourse of resentment toward the marine park and its regulatory practices. Beginning sometime in mid-2016, however, I noticed that attitudes were beginning to shift, albeit gradually, to one of two positions. The first was general indifference or apathy toward the marine park (i.e., no overt resistance); the second was support for the project. The latter was marked by a common catchphrase: "Now we are all educated," or "Now we have understood the importance of marine conservation and recognize the benefits of caring for the environment."

In this chapter, I analyze the underlying significance of these expressions and shed light on the factors that prompted this noticeable shift in discourse and practice surrounding the marine park.[2] More specifically, I address the questions: What factors might have contributed to the discontinuation of destructive and unsustainable fishing practices in the fishing villages inside the marine park? Was it the fear of being apprehended and fined for violating the regulations—fear that was generated by the increased presence of naval patrol boats monitoring the coast? Or had people's awareness of the regulations and restrictions increased, leading to a greater awareness of the need to protect the marine environment? What other factors or interventions might have persuaded people to rethink their relationship with their environment? And, critically, why did it take so long (more than fifteen years) for this environmental awareness to build among local inhabitants to the point of action?

My goal in this chapter is to answer these questions by drawing on the ethnographic data I gathered in the marine park villages over a four-year period—from 2016 to 2019. I examine whether people in the catchment villages had indeed become what Arun Agrawal (2005a, b) and others have called "environmental subjects" (or environmentalized subjects)—defined as people who care about the environment and act in conservation-friendly ways on a long-term basis. I sought to find out whether residents had in fact started to care for their environment and whether this change in "mentality" (defined as mindset, attitudes, and behaviors—as captured in talk) is an enduring disposition or a tentative pause in their unsustainable fishing and marine resource harvesting practices, as was documented in the mid-1990s during Operation Pono.

In the following section, I briefly review the literature on the concept of "environmentality." This includes the concepts of environmentalities and multiple environmentalities and is followed by an analysis of the empirical data I gathered in the marine park villages pertaining to people's disposition toward the marine park and, more broadly, the environment. I follow this with reflections on the usefulness and limitations of the concept of environmentality in making sense of people's claims about the "end of destructive fishing practices" in their villages. Finally, I conclude this chapter by emphasizing the need to pay attention to the multiplicity of factors that underlie the question: What does it take for people to change their ideas and practices regarding their environment? I will argue that there is more to environmentality than persuading people to participate in "institutional regimes of environmental protection," such as village liaison committees, environment committees, or beach management units. I assert that people's agency and aspirations to change their behaviors and practices—to improve their environment—cannot be ignored or downplayed with the right conditions.

FRAMEWORKS: RETHINKING ENVIRONMENTALITY AND THE EMERGENCE OF ENVIRONMENTAL SUBJECTS

Over the past few decades, conservationists have sought to answer a fundamental and compelling question: What is necessary to persuade individuals and communities whose livelihoods are significantly dependent on the extraction of marine and terrestrial natural resources to refrain from unsustainable and ecologically destructive extraction practices? Alternatively put, in the conservation debate there are different and often competing models of conservation strategies (Büscher and Fletcher 2020). The ongoing debate relates to the question: Which of these models can be most successfully implemented to achieve the most desirable outcomes when it comes to biodiversity conservation? In other words, what does it take for individuals to become environmental subjects, to become sensitive to environmental issues, and to change their behaviors to protect and manage their environment—in accordance with the Western model of conservation, where nature and culture are discursively separated?

Political scientist Arun Agrawal (2005b, 226), who is credited with articulating and popularizing the concept of environmentality, a union of environment and the Foucauldian concept of "governmentality," defines it as "the knowledges, politics, institutions, and subjectivities that come to be linked together with the emergence of the environment as a domain that requires regulation and protection."[3] He uses the related concept of environmental subjects to refer to "people who have come to think and act in new ways in relation to the environmental domain being governed" (2005b, 7). Agrawal (2005b, 16) also notes that "environmental subjects are those for whom the environment constitutes a critical domain of thought and action." Drawing on his empirical research on forest conservation in North India, he argues that one way to persuade individuals to start caring for their environment (i.e., the creation of environmental subjects) is to bring about a change in people's mentalities (mindset, attitudes, and behaviors) about the environment.

This, he proposes, can be done by facilitating new ways of understanding the environment—enabling individuals "to arrive at subject positions that are quite different from those held earlier" (2005a, 163). Encouraging people's involvement in institutional regimes of environmental regulation—socioecological practices that are geared toward protecting the environment—through monitoring and enforcement is seen as a key strategy in the creation of new environmental subjects. Agrawal further argues that "increased participation in environmental regulation and enforcement produces environmental subjectivities" and that "caring about, acting in relation to, and thinking of one's own actions in terms of environmental protection is directly connected to taking part in the regulatory apparatus of conservation policies. In other words, certain regimes of participatory conservation governance create the conditions for the development of environmental subjectivities, whereby people use the environment as a category that structures their thinking and their actions" (Cortes-Vazquez and Ruiz-Ballesteros 2018, 240).

Agrawal acknowledges that not all people in a given community are likely to become environmental subjects—neither are they likely to reveal significant changes in their subjectivities simply because they have been persuaded to do so by external agencies and institutions. Nonetheless, he emphasizes what might be possible through external interventions and people's participation in institutional regimes. Thus, he asks: "When and for what reasons do socially situated actors come to care about, act in relation to, and think about their actions in terms of something they identify as 'the environment'?" (2005a, 162). What is it that distinguishes these actors from those who continue not to care about or act in relation to the environment?

Numerous scholars have criticized Agrawal's initial propositions regarding environmentality—and the cultivation of environmental subjects—for their simplistic representation of on-the-ground realities. In particular, scholars noted the eliding of human agency and aspirations in matters related to environmental protection and management—"the ways that local people could self-mobilize to exercise relatively autonomous and locally-directed forms of environmental governance" (Fletcher 2017, 313). Scholars have tested, questioned the analytical and political utility, modified, elaborated on, and reworked Agrawal's concepts to examine their relevance to environmental conservation (projects) in different real-world geographical and political settings (see Bluwstein 2017; Cepek 2011; Pandya 2023). Segi (2013), for example, employed Agrawal's concept of environmentality to an MPA in the Philippines and found that "although marine harvesters were sympathetic to the conservation value of MPAs, this resulted less from their appreciation of the value of conservation itself than from the perceived economic advantages they would derive [cf. Pollnac, Crawford, and Gorospe 2001]. The spillover effect from the MPA was the main anticipated benefit" (Segi 2013, 341). Segi (2013, 343) concludes by arguing that "focusing on the level of resource users' adherence to regulations as a sole indicator for subjectivity formation is not helpful for identifying varieties of environmental subjectivity. Rather, more attention needs to be paid to the specific regulations the resource users subjectively choose to follow and/or discard, as well as to how these actions are understood and expressed within the local context." In other words, just because people start adhering to the regulations does not necessarily mean they have accepted the rationale behind the regulations—that is, to protect the environment. People could be adhering to the regulations and restrictions simply out of fear of repercussion—of fines or other forms of punishment, including physical beatings.

In an influential article, Robert Fletcher (2010) draws on a poststructuralist political ecology perspective (Peet and Watts 1996)—coupled with Foucault's analysis of "governmentality" and the application of the concept of environmentality (Luke 2011; Agrawal 2005a, 2005b)—to make an argument that there are in fact "multiple governmentalities" at work in environmental politics. These consist of sovereign, disciplinary, neoliberal, and truth environmentalities, which may operate separately or in tandem to "conduct the conducts" of citizens-subjects with the ultimate goal of protecting the environment (see Bluwstein 2017, 102). As Youdelis (2013, 166) points out, in a neoliberal context, "monitoring community members' activity requires time and resources, [therefore] producing subjects who will conduct themselves in adherence with park conservation goals through the governmentalizing practices of ecotourism is a far more efficient and effective way of reforming community members' behaviors." Notably, sovereign environmentality is akin to the fortress conservation model, in which the nation-state uses its power (law, security forces, etc.) to preserve natural resources through the creation and patrol of protected areas and the use of barriers or "fences and fines" strategies.

Disciplinary environmentality (or governmentality) seeks to "conduct the conducts" (Foucault 1991) of citizen-subjects through the internalization of certain discourses and ethical norms—a particular vision of the environment—with the intention that citizen-subjects will behave in conservation-friendly ways. Neoliberal environmentality, in contrast, seeks to motivate subjects through incentives and monetary rewards for pro-conservation behavior. However, in the real world, "these various environmentalities may be mixed and matched in particular positions within the conservation debate" (Fletcher 2010, 177; see also Youdelis 2019, 2). Accordingly, Fletcher (2010, 172) has encouraged social scientists "to productively explore the interplay among different environmentalities operating within the conservation debate in order to analyse how conservation discourse and practice manifest within particular locales" and determine whether the complex model that he has proposed "is indeed capable of parsing the various strands of conservation practice in concrete situations" (180).

NARRATIVES OF CHANGE: DISCURSIVE SHIFTS IN MSIMBATI, NALINGU, AND MKUBIRU

Between 2011 and 2014, Mtwara peninsula residents frequently complained about the persistence of dynamite fishing in their fishing grounds despite the marine park's presence. Some of them accused the marine park rangers of corruption—of deliberately ignoring the destructive fishing practices that were going on "in front of their own eyes." They blamed park personnel for shirking their responsibilities.

In addition to interviewing people in Msimbati, Nalingu, Mkubiru, and Msangamkuu, I recorded my observations during my interactions with the fishers and fish vendors on the beaches and landing sites over the four-year period. Over time, my field observations and my interactions with fishers and fish vendors on the beaches corroborated residents' broad claims that destructive and unsustainable fishing practices on the peninsula had reduced significantly or had completely stopped in their respective fishing villages. In 2018, I asked my key interlocutors if they could explain why residents of some of the key fishing villages inside the marine park's catchment area had stopped engaging in destructive (*haram*) fishing practices *now*, after so many years. Their most common response was, "Now we are all educated," suggesting that they had started to care for their environment. In other words, viewed from a Foucauldian perspective, and as Agrawal (2005a, 2005b) would suggest, their subject positions had changed; they had now become "environmental subjects" or "environmentalized."

"We Have Always Cared for Our Environment"

A small minority of residents insisted that they had *always* cared about their environment—that they had *always* had deep respect for it (*watu wanaheshima sana*)—even before the marine park was implemented in their region in 2000. Issa, the former chairman of Nalingu village, asserted with pride that the government had indeed chosen the Mtwara peninsula as the site for the marine park precisely because it was a pristine coastal region—and that the locals themselves had cared for it and kept it beautiful. At the same time, people acknowledged that they were unsure of how to curb their harmful practices or those of their fellow villagers. For one, they needed to cut down trees to clear the land for their cashew farms, to make charcoal for cooking, and to get firewood. They needed to cut trees from the mangroves to build their huts and pit latrines. They needed to extract and burn coral to make chalk (*choka*) to paint the walls of their homes. And they needed to use kokoro and tandilo to catch small fish like dagaa—a staple used to make relish. As Bi Amri, a single mother of five from Mkubiru who was in her midforties, ruefully said to me: "There are no trees or mangroves left in Mkubiru. Our elders finished them all a long time ago. Now if we need a wooden pole or a plank, we must buy it from people who bring them here from Mozambique." Similarly, Habiba, from Msimbati, said: "There are no trees left in Msimbati. No matter where you go on this island, you'll be trespassing on someone's farm, cashew nut farm, or coconut farm."

Ndembo, a sixty-six-year-old opinion leader in Msimbati who had participated in my research since 2012, assuredly said that the people of

Msimbati have a lot of respect for the ocean and marine resources. He claimed that they do not destroy the corals and that the fishers do not use illegal fishing gear. Even on the dry land, he said, people do not cut down trees "just like that [*hivyo hivyo*]," especially the mangroves. "I myself have gone to plant tree saplings in the mangroves," Ndembo said. "They [marine park people/Tanzania Social Action Fund (TASAF)] told us to protect the mangrove trees and not to indiscriminately cut down trees. They told us to plant more mangrove trees, to increase the mangroves, so we did that job, of protecting the environment, from the ocean to the dry land and the mangroves. No, no one cuts down trees to make charcoal. They told us to protect the environment and not to let our village become a desert." Ruvula residents were prohibited from cutting down trees to make charcoal. This was mainly because the burning of trees would pose a fire hazard to the gas project's infrastructure, particularly the gas pipeline.

Ndembo spoke with conviction, asserting that the people of Msimbati were doing everything possible to protect the environment—both the ocean and the land. He added that if there were occasional reports of dynamite fishing or other destructive fishing practices, the perpetrators were invariably from some of the other villages, not from Msimbati itself. He followed by shifting his narrative, as was his habit, and accused the marine park officials of failing to apprehend dynamite fishers under the pretext that they did not have enough fuel in their speedboats to chase and apprehend them. In making these allegations, Ndembo implied that the people of Msimbati were far more concerned about the environment than were the marine park rangers themselves. He stated, "People care for the environment, but the marine park does not help us.... The marine park rangers are just salaried government employees. They are not local people. But for us, protecting the ocean and our environment—it's our life and our livelihood."

Ndembo was an outlier in his claims that Msimbati residents had *always* cared for their environment. Most of my interlocutors acknowledged that people were destroying the environment—they were not caring for it because of poverty, overdependence on marine resources for their livelihoods, population increase, energy needs, and lack of education and awareness on the topic. Mpojola, from Mkubiru village, was candid and forthcoming with his views. As a matter of fact, he explained almost defiantly, "Yes, we degrade our environment because we have no other option. We are dependent on the ocean and the land for our livelihoods. We can't buy a big net or a big motorized boat to go fishing in the deep waters, so yes, we spoil the environment. Our environment became degraded over the years because there were no restrictions on the kinds of gear or methods we were using to do our fishing.... The government is telling us that we are destroying our environment, yes, that's true, but we are helpless." The sentiment underlying Mpojola's well-rehearsed statement was that given the poverty and structural constraints, the government should not expect poor fishers to refrain from unsustainable fishing practices in pursuit of their livelihoods without providing them with alternative fishing gear and financial support. In Mpojola's view, people were aware that their coastal environment was deteriorating in part because of their overreliance on it for their livelihoods. However, they were also aware that they did not have a workable alternative. In other words, Mpojola and others were laying the blame squarely on the government, specifically on the marine park authorities for not providing them with the legal fishing gear they were initially promised. While they acknowledged that they were damaging their environment, none of my interlocutors invoked climate change or even changes in the weather patterns as critical factors in their explanations for why they were "forced" to "destroy" their environment or why the fish sizes and catches in their fishing grounds had gone down (cf. Bunce, Brown, and Rosendo 2010; Liwenga et al. 2019).

Nearly all my interlocutors asserted that they now understood the importance of protecting the environment and were doing something about it. As I will illustrate, the individual histories of each of the study villages affected how residents in each village articulated their explanations for how and why fishers were no longer engaging in destructive fishing practices. I probed the ostensible shift in people's "mentalities" and practices by posing specific questions about the environment in the spatiotemporal context to individuals in six marine park villages. I interviewed some of the older residents (both men and women) in the marine park villages—particularly those who had participated in the marine park's initial planning and implementation stage, to get a long-term perspective. Participation included serving as members of the Village Environment Committee, the Village Liaison Committee, and Beach

Management Units and/or as volunteers offering support to the marine park's initiatives, such as turtle conservation. Subsequently, I interviewed some of the younger village residents. While some were full-time fishers, others had taken to farming (mainly cashews), construction work, and driving motorcycle taxis. Others were simply unemployed.

"NOW WE ARE ALL EDUCATED": ENVIRONMENTALITY IN MSIMBATI

In August 2018, I asked Bi Mkubwa whether the residents of Msimbati village had genuinely started caring (*kujali*) for their environment, as many of my interlocutors had claimed. Given her extensive involvement with the marine park's conservation efforts since the park's inception, Bi Mkubwa was able to provide a longitudinal, temporal perspective on the shifts in Msimbati residents' environmentality. Bi Mkubwa responded with an emphatic "*Kabisa!*" (Absolutely!) and said that she had seen a significant change in the environment because of people's increased awareness. As an illustrative example, she said that many people from Msimbati had recently volunteered to plant mangrove saplings along the coast. Bi Mkubwa explained: "People have stopped using bombs to capture fish, they are not using illegal fishing gear, especially kokoro, to catch small fish. At least in Msimbati, I haven't seen it. I see that things are going on fine regarding environmental change. Our environment has improved." When I asked her to elaborate on the changes she had witnessed, Bi Mkubwa said that people were protecting the environment because they had a better understanding (*watu wengi wameelewa*; *hamasa na elimu*, motivation and education, *kuhamamisha mazingira*, encouragement, motivate) of the importance of environmental protection. "These days," she said, "if you tell someone that they need to protect the environment—if you tell people that they should not use illegal fishing gears or dynamites—they don't get angry at you. They don't accuse you of being strict with them, they understand." She added that even young schoolchildren know to protect the environment. Bi Mkubwa emphasized that from what she had seen, people had accepted the idea that they must protect their environment. There was no resistance. "You see," she averred, "now we are all educated about the environment."

Bi Mkubwa's assertions were consistent with statements made by other Msimbati residents. As mentioned in previous chapters, Msimbati was the main village in the marine park's catchment area. It was a "showcase village" where the marine park's main office and ticketing office were located. For this reason, the marine park's warden, staff, and local volunteers in particular were more likely to engage with local villagers to promote environmental protection/conservation and persuade people to refrain from engaging in destructive fishing practices. In addition to these contextual factors, representatives from big NGOs (BINGOs) such as the World Wildlife Fund (WWF) and funding agencies such as SwissAid-Tanzania and TASAF had initiated projects designed to increase awareness among the local people, including schoolchildren, regarding the benefits of marine conservation. All these factors had contributed to a change in people's "mentality" regarding the environment over time. As Bi Mkubwa put it, "People have accepted the idea... there's no resistance [against the marine park]."

However, Bi Mkubwa's assertion that "things are going on fine" (*mambo yana enda vizuri*) does not shed light on why things had only started going on fine in 2015–16—and not earlier. There was significant opposition to the marine park from its implementation in 2000 into 2016. Why did it take so long for the people of Msimbati to start caring for their marine environment—the way the marine park authorities wanted them to?

This was not the first time I had heard the expression "now we are all educated" during my fieldwork. In reviewing my field notes and the transcriptions of my audio-recorded interviews and group discussions from 2016 and 2017, I found that several of my interlocutors had used this expression to assert that there was no evidence of dynamite fishing or other destructive fishing practices in their villages. They used different expressions such as "Tumeshaelewa" (We have understood); "Tumepata uelewa" (We have received understanding or awareness); "Hakuna matatizo" (There's no hassle); "Maeneo tunatunza vizuri" (We are protecting the environment very well); "Simamizi mazuri" (Restrictions/regulations have been managed well); "Sasa hazipo kabisa" (Now it [destructive fishing] is not there at all); and "Watu wamekumbatia mazingira" (People have embraced [the idea of protecting] the environment) to emphasize that people had begun to care seriously (*tunajali*) for their environment.

However, what I had *not* heard before was the absolute confidence with which Bi Mkubwa asserted that even young children were well informed and well educated about the need to protect and conserve the environment—particularly the marine environment. If this were the case, what factors or conditions had turned the residents of Msimbati and other coastal villages into environmental subjects in 2016? I asked several of my interlocutors for their thoughts.

"We Are Doing Well, Because We Understand"

Kachakacha, a young and energetic thirty-year-old Ruvula resident, was volunteering with the marine park at the time I interviewed him in August 2019. He gave a detailed response, saying: "The environment is good, we are doing well, and we are at peace." Kachakacha continued: "Now everyone knows what environment means and how a human being lives with the environment. . . . Now we are doing well, not only in the ocean, but also on dry land . . . self-awareness has increased. People are not recklessly cutting down trees and mangroves." That same day, in a focus group I held with six men in Ruvula who were in their late twenties and early thirties, Kachakacha had more to say: "The environment has changed so much that right now, people have become smarter [*waelevu*], they understand well, and if they understand you, it is possible that if you give them any advice regarding the environment, they will understand. It's not that you give education [teaching about valuing their resources and protecting the environment] to a relative or a fellow villager today and he will accept it immediately. It must be something you have to follow up on. . . . We are doing well, because we understand." As someone who was living in Ruvula, where the marine park's administrative office is located, and as a volunteer with the marine park, Kachakacha was able to present a positive view of the changes he had witnessed in the physical environment and in the ideas and practices of the people who lived in Ruvula and Msimbati. Importantly, Kachakacha was clear in emphasizing that people's ideas and practices regarding the environment do not change overnight or immediately following their participation in educational programs. As he put it, "It's something you have to follow up on." The creation or emergence of environmental subjects requires patience on the part of the protagonists; the provision of environmental education is only a first step.

Young women in Ruvula expressed similar sentiments regarding the changes they had witnessed regarding their environment. For example, Bi Punjawadi, in her midthirties and a mother of two young children, asserted: "Now we have awareness. A lot of education has come. So I can only say that the marine park has brought a great deal of support, regarding the disadvantages of not protecting the ocean and what is illegal fishing and what is legal fishing. Right now, I think we are very good." Bi Punjawadi was echoing Kachakacha's words, a key educator in the village who had taken his role as a volunteer with the marine park seriously.

"Now People Are Really Afraid"

In September 2018, Haki, the chairman of Ruvula village, gave a matter-of-fact explanation as to why people in the marine park villages had given up on destructive fishing practices. It was not so much that people had become more educated about conservation, Haki said, but that they were more afraid of the current government's oversight and diligence in implementing park restrictions. Haki's assertions regarding the shift in people's behavior aligned with changes in Tanzania's recent sociopolitical history. John Magufuli, who was elected president in October 2015, ran on an anticorruption platform. His administration had begun to streamline bureaucracy and governance using hardline tactics (see chapter 1). As in all sectors of the economy, there was fear among the people of Mtwara peninsula that they would be punished for breaking rules. "It's mainly because of enforcement," Haki said, "the 'big power of the government,' that people have given up destructive fishing. People are afraid [*hofu*] of being apprehended and punished by government agents/police, not because of the marine park's efforts to educate the people about protecting the environment." Haki emphasized that it was the current government's oversight (*usimamizi*) that personnel were showing more "accountability" to their unit or departments—resulting in the stricter enforcement of regulations.

In short, from Haki's perspective, local residents had given up their destructive fishing practices not because they had become environmental subjects but because they were now afraid of being apprehended and punished by government agents/police. This was because the new government, under President Magufuli, had tightened up restrictions and patrolling activities in the coastal area. Haki described a scenario that was emblematic of the kind of environmentality that Fletcher (2010) has labeled as sovereign—enacted by way of implementing laws, using (or threatening) force, and exacting fines to ensure citizens' compliance with certain behaviors. His narrative was also an example of disciplinary environmentality, which seeks to influence citizen-subjects through the "internalization of certain discourses and ethical norms" about caring for the environment.

As noted earlier, Sadala, from Msimbati village, was one of the original members of the village committee involved in planning and implementing the marine park. He explained the changes he had observed in the discourse and practice surrounding destructive fishing practices in Msimbati. Rather than attributing the shift to a sudden fear of government action, Sadala cited long-term changes in the village in the background. He asserted that there was no illegal fishing going on in Msimbati. Three or four people continued to use illegal fishing gear, but after they were "educated" about the problems their fishing practices were causing, they stopped altogether. He said those who were using explosives to do their fishing had also stopped (*wamethibitisha*).

Sadala attributed the shift to several factors, First, people had realized that dynamite fishing was a dangerous practice, as some dynamite fishers had lost their limbs and others their lives while using dynamite. Second, there were few fish left in the areas where people had been using dynamite. The coral reefs that served as *nyumba ya samaki* had been destroyed over the last several decades, and fishers were going into the ocean and coming back without fish. Third, most of the wooden boats and dugout canoes previously used were old—many were broken or had been destroyed by the marine park rangers. Fourth, people were afraid of the government, which had begun implementing laws around illegal fishing more seriously. Many people in Msimbati realized that engaging in illegal fishing practices was impossible because of the risk of arrest, imprisonment, fines, or even being beaten by the police. "Now people are really afraid," Sadala said. Fifth, and finally, those who could no longer count on the ocean for their livelihoods had turned to farming. As Sadala said: "That's what many people have done, they have taken to farming, they are growing rice and millet." For these reasons, illegal fishing had diminished significantly in the area.

According to Sadala, it was not only the fear of being arrested, imprisoned, or fined that acted as a deterrent to fishers who would have otherwise engaged in illegal activities, but the fact that people were becoming less dependent on the ocean and marine resources for their livelihoods. This perspective differs from Haki's, who exemplified a pure form of sovereign or disciplinary environmentality. Sadala emphasized multiple factors—including long-term shifts in land use—that contributed to behavior changes.

"The Marine Park Is Our Brother-in-Law"

Women in Msimbati believed that residents had stopped engaging in destructive fishing practices because they were better educated about the need to protect the environment. Significantly, those who had painted a very negative picture of the marine park up until 2014 and 2015 (see chapter 4) spoke very positively about the marine park in 2018 and 2019. Several of my key interlocutors in Msimbati/Mtandi, particularly Rehema and Zainabu, who had had harsh words for the marine park and its staff until around 2015 (see chapters 3 and 4), had changed their opinions. Now they spoke about the marine park in positive terms. Bi Mkubwa described this shift eloquently:

> The marine park became very toxic to the villagers. . . . We were used to cutting our mangroves, eating our turtles, doing what we wanted to do ourselves. Those who came to teach us, they started telling us, "You cannot do this, you cannot do that." So they became poison to us [*wale wakawa sumu kwetu*]. Why are they forbidding us from doing our things? Why? Those people [working for the marine park] are coming from [mainland] Mbeya, Musoma, and elsewhere to tell us [coastal people] what we can and cannot do. They came to stop us from doing things here in Msimbati, they were telling us not eat our turtles, not to cut our mangroves, why? [But] they started teaching us little by little. They insulted us, we insulted them, we pushed each other [tug of war], until we reached some understanding and that's when we started saying aah well!! Protecting the environment is something important for us. Now we all know that the marine park is not toxic to us. Now it is up to us to treat the marine park as our own protected area and support it with our hearts.

Bi Mkubwa's positionality as someone who was involved in the planning and early implementation of the marine park was critical in this statement. Her main message here is that a host of miscommunications and misunderstandings had strained the relationship between the marine park representatives and the local people. Locals felt insulted because "experts" who were not from the coast were telling them how to behave in a marine environment and blaming them for being recalcitrant and irresponsible fishers who engaged in destructive fishing practices. Locals in turn insulted the marine park personnel by characterizing them as corrupt and incompetent. Eventually, people "understood," but that understanding took a long time to materialize. People had indeed become environmental subjects. Their subjectivities had changed, they had started caring for their environment "with their hearts," but the process was long drawn out.

During a focus group discussion, Zuhura, a twenty-nine-year-old woman from Msimbati, emphasized that things had changed a lot over the years regarding people's disposition toward the environment. She credited the marine park for creating awareness regarding environmental degradation and the need to protect the environment. Zuhura explained: "Now there is increased education [*upeo wa elimu*]. In the past, a fisher would use dynamites for fishing, without knowing what damage it was doing [to the coral reefs]. All that the fisher knew was that if he blasts a bomb in the water, he gets lots of fish. He did not know what harm he was doing to the ocean. But things have changed since the marine park has arrived and provided adequate education to local fishers. Now everyone [in the village] has become a security guard [i.e., as guardians who have taken it on themselves to protect the environment]." Zuhura's fellow discussants shared her conviction regarding fishers' previous lack of education and their current awareness regarding the destructive impacts of dynamite fishing in particular. Importantly, others in the group agreed with Zuhura's statement that the marine park had been instrumental in increasing people's awareness regarding the dangers of illegal and unsustainable fishing practices. This was a significant shift in the discourse coming from Msimbati residents, who a few years earlier blamed the marine park authorities for making their lives difficult by implementing restrictions and disallowing them from selling their land inside the gated section the park. As forty-seven-year-old Somoye, an engaging single mother of two children who was participating in the discussion, concluded: "The marine park is our security guard [*Marine park ni walinzi wetu*]." And laughingly added, "The marine park is now our brother-in-law [*Marine park ni shemeji zetu*]."

Somoye and others invoked fictive kinship with the marine park to indicate that they had decided to put their differences and enmities aside and had indeed taken on the task of protecting the environment as one unit. In such a system, everyone is a "security guard" who deters potential perpetrators from engaging in unsustainable fishing and mangrove harvesting practices and is not at loggerheads with the marine park authorities. Phrased differently, people had reconciled with the reality that they were unlikely to successfully "drive the marine park away" because it was a government project. They had also acknowledged the fact that the authorities were going to continue with their restrictive practices. At the same time, people had come to recognize their role in protecting the environment, captured in the stock phrase "Now we are all educated. Now we have understood."

"THE OCEAN IS CALM": MULTIPLE ENVIRONMENTALITIES IN NALINGU

Elsewhere on the peninsula, Nalingu residents also stated that they had discontinued all forms of illegal (*haram*) fishing and marine resource harvesting practices. The shift in Nalingu residents' disposition is particularly significant given Nalingu's sustained opposition to the marine park since its inception—opposition that was marked by threats of violence, even (as mentioned in chapter 1) leading consultants for the marine park to describe Nalingu as a "violent village" in their reports. Issa, who was the chairman of Nalingu for several years, asserted: "No, it wasn't the marine park that brought an end to dynamite fishing and illegal nets in this region. People were continuing to use them here even after the marine park was established. Dynamite fishers were coming here from Msangamkuu, and even from Mtwara town, but the people of Nalingu were being blamed for using illegal fishing methods. It was the district commissioner and his security committee that stopped dynamite fishing and illegal nets here. They came to talk to us, and because we are people of the ocean, we understood what they were telling us." Issa had attended a series of seminars and workshops focusing on conservation organized by local NGOs. He had shared what he learned from the experts with his fellow villagers during village meetings. As he put it: "People themselves said that they understood.... They saw the need to obey orders without coercion, and people began to accept, and that's how illegal fishing nets and dynamite fishing ended here."

Since I first interviewed Issa in 2011 (see chapter 2), he was clear that the people of Nalingu did not lack agency or self-awareness in deciding whether they should or should not participate in the marine park's mandate. His statement that people were continuing to engage in unsustainable fishing practices for several years after the marine park was established was meant to underscore the fact that the marine park was ineffective in ending illegal fishing practices in the region. Ultimately, as people whose lives are closely tied to the ocean, to nature, their cognitive congruence—their appreciation of the district commissioner's and the experts' advice—led to a change in people's behaviors. Thus, Issa wanted to retain agency by emphasizing that the marine park personnel's' expert intervention had been unsuccessful in stamping out destructive fishing practices in Nalingu and Mnazi. The practices had ended only when the people of Nalingu had decided to end destructive fishing practices.

Ali, who was in his midforties, contextualized the significance of the shift in Nalingu residents' attitudes more broadly, first recalling the tense relationship between the marine park representatives and the villagers, followed by words of praise for the marine park for its role in changing Nalingu residents' ideas about protecting their environment. Ali explained: "Initially, it was like a war, the situation was not good, there were serious clashes between the marine park and the people of this area.... But now people have understood that this marine park is, in fact, protecting the environment. Initially, we thought they would even kill anyone stepping on the beach.... But really, they are the protectors of our environment. Now people are living their normal lives." Ali gave his comprehensive explanation in one breath—as though he had previously rehearsed what he wanted to say about the marine park and its role in changing people's ideas and practices related to the environment. His key points in the above segment were widely shared and repeated by nearly all my interlocutors in Nalingu. Residents echoed Ali's reference to years of misunderstanding and tension between the Nalingu residents and the marine park, their realization that the marine park was there to protect the marine environment and not restrict people from entering their fishing grounds, and the changes people had undergone in terms of their fishing practices and attitudes. Importantly, it had taken many years for people to become environmental subjects—or at least to acknowledge that the marine park was here to stay and that there was very little local residents could do to discontinue it in their region.

Now It's All Very Quiet

Women in Nalingu expressed their relief at the cessation of dynamite fishing and using kokoro in their fishing grounds. They explained that these practices had had a direct impact on their gleaning and food security. Jinaya, a loquacious fifty-nine-year-old woman from Nalingu, explained her views on the changes she had witnessed. In 2019, Jinaya asserted that she had not heard any blasts for a long time and confirmed that people were not using illegal fishing nets. "Thank God," she said, "the soldiers came and ended dynamite fishing." The village secretary and the councillor (Diwani) had confiscated all the illegal nets in the village. They had piled the nets near a baobab tree at the Mnazi landing site and set them on fire. "So there is absolutely nothing," Jinaya said. "The sea is calm. Now it's all very quiet. In the past, when we used to go to the beach to glean for shellfish, octopus, and small fish, we would find mostly dead fish. But if you go there now, you can find shellfish, plugs, and other crustaceans that are alive—they are adults, not small [babies or juveniles]. You can prepare your *mboga* [relish or curry] with them and serve it with *ugali*, cassava [*muhogo*], and your children are full. In the evening they can go and play or listen to music." Jinaya attributed this shift to the intervention from the soldiers (navy patrol), the village secretary, and the councillor. For Jinaya, the use of force and the threat of punishment had effected the shift, not the increased awareness regarding conservation among fishers. Jinaya was more inclined to accept these top-down interventions because of the direct impact she observed in relation to her access to gleaning on the beach and on well-being. In her view, the improved food security in the village had contributed to the village children's ability to spend their time playing with one another and listening to music, activities that were important for their well-being.

Abubakar, from Nalingu village, was among those who had strongly opposed the marine park for several years. Over time, however, he had accepted the park's restrictions and joined a group of twenty fishers. The marine park had given this group a motorized fishing boat and a large fishing net. Abubakar and his group members were now earning their livelihoods by fishing in the ocean using legal fishing gear. Abubakar expressed that people in his village were now better educated about conserving the environment. "Overall, illegal fishing has reduced, especially kokoro. Because of education, and that's after people took a close look at the harm that kokoro nets were doing to the environment, they've stopped using them. We ourselves monitor the use of kokoro here in this village."

In other words, not only had Nalingu residents become better informed about the importance of protecting the environment, but they also were taking the initiative and responsibility (i.e., demonstrating their agency) to monitor and prevent the use of destructive fishing gear in their waters. As a fisher who was using legal gear and adhering to the marine park's restrictions, Abubakar was himself invested in protecting the marine environment. As he explained: "So if we have protected the ocean, it's because of the education [understanding] that *we* have provided to the people, by telling them that kokoro will not be allowed and that they will also not be allowed to cut the mangrove trees just like that [*ovyo ovyo*]. . . . It's because of the education that *we* provided to the people. . . . Today if you tell people to stop using illegal fishing gear, they'll understand, they believe you, they accept it, they respect your word. In the past, people would simply retort by saying, '*Mimi nitakula nini*?!' [And what will I eat?!]." Abubakar repeatedly emphasized that destructive and unsustainable fishing practices in Nalingu, Mnete, and the Mnazi area had stopped because people had started to care for their environment. He also reiterated that environmental education had played a key role in this shift. He attributed this shift not just to increased awareness and education but to a combination of other factors as well—restrictions, regulations, and local political leaders' initiative, leaders who were under pressure from government bureaucrats to show that they had taken concrete steps to put an end to illegal and unsustainable fishing practices in their villages. Abubakar also acknowledged that while residents understood the importance of protecting the environment, there was no guarantee that the government and local leaders had successfully put an end to unsustainable fishing practices.

Abubakar reflected on a common experience among residents of Nalingu and other fishing villages inside the park: initially, when representatives from the marine park had said they needed to conserve the environment, people thought they wanted to stop all fishing activities and marine resource extraction. However, once marine park staff had explained to the villagers that this was not the case—that certain areas (no-take zones) like fish nurseries (*mazalia ya samaki*) were not to be touched, while others would remain accessible to fishers with legal nets (specified-use zones)—people began to understand the meaning and importance of protecting the marine environment. Like Ali's statements, Abubakar said that it was because of miscommunication and misunderstanding that opposition to the marine park had continued for several years. Once people understood the real goals of the marine park, he said, and the importance of protecting the marine environment, they started to care for it.

"Why We Destroy Our Environment"

Most people in Nalingu acknowledged that after they had been informed or made aware of what it means to preserve the marine environment, residents protected their local waters. At the same time, they lamented the fact that people were cutting down trees for firewood and cooking charcoal. "But we are still cutting down trees just like that to make charcoal" was a common lament. Mtopwa, a forty-eight-year-old prosperous cashew and coconut farmer, affirmed that people in Nalingu had stopped engaging in destructive fishing activities. He remarked that he could confidently say that in the last three or four years, he had not heard a single explosion in the ocean—which he believed was a good indication that the "environment was getting better" and that people had given up on using dynamite. Simultaneously, however, he expressed regret that on dry land, people were continuing to cut down trees, carelessly, to meet their energy needs. Mtopwa explained that what was once a wooded area now looks like a desert—people had cut down all the trees to make charcoal. He continued: "But if we look at the ocean, the marine environment, from how it was about five years ago and now, I see that the situation is calm because dynamite fishing has stopped." While Mtopwa was confident that the people of Nalingu had become environmentally conscious with regard to their marine environment, he believed that environmental awareness had not transferred into practice in their treatment of the terrestrial environment. He did not blame his fellow villagers for cutting down trees: "They were doing this to meet their energy needs," he said, and elaborated that unless people had ready and affordable access to cooking gas (TSh18,000, or $7 USD, at the time for one 7.5-kilogram tank), they were likely to continue to cut down trees to make charcoal for their cooking needs. Villagers had indeed become environmental subjects—they were concerned about their environment and were taking steps to protect it. But the everyday realities of life and the lack of affordable alternatives had accentuated their reliance on charcoal for cooking and had pushed residents to continue clearing the forest for farming. In all, this shift had increased pressure on land and contributed to the increasing levels of deforestation taking place in and around the fishing villages.

"Now We Are Cutting Down Trees Carelessly"

Emphasizing this "disconnect" between how people were relating to the marine environment and how they were relating to the terrestrial environment, Bi Karuma, from Nalingu, affirmed that she had seen things improve regarding the marine environment but not regarding the dry land and trees. "I'm saying all this because I have seen it myself," she stated. "Both men and women are carelessly [*ovyo ovyo*] cutting down trees to make charcoal. Our village is on a hill. There have been no improvements here, but on the coast, people have completely stopped using destructive fishing gears and practices." In short, people were protecting the marine environment but not the terrestrial one.

As Mtopwa's and Bi Karuma's statements reveal, while Nalingu residents had started to care for their marine environment, they were not demonstrating the same level of care toward protecting and conserving their trees and forests. People were cutting down trees ovyo ovyo—carelessly. This begged the question of whether Nalingu residents had become environmentally conscious if they were not demonstrating the same level of care for the land as for the sea. Because of the absence of cooking gas and other technologies (such as electric ovens), residents of Nalingu relied on firewood and charcoal as cooking fuel. For this reason, while residents were aware of the need to protect their terrestrial environment, they could not demonstrate this awareness in practice. On the one hand, this "discrepancy," or "disjuncture," in how people relate to their marine and terrestrial environment reveals the local complexity and heterogeneity of what environmentality stands for. On the other hand, the growing environmental awareness in the park villages enables residents like Mtopwa and Bi Karuma to see the inconsistencies in the park's implementation and messaging and at the same time express their concern about the unrestrained manner in which their fellow villagers were destroying the trees and forests around the village.

ENVIRONMENTALITIES IN MKUBIRU

Mkubiru (described in detail in chapter 2) is a relatively small seafront village with a population of approximately 450 households (*kaya*). For administrative reasons, Mkubiru is divided into four subsections. The settlements located close to the beach are known as Pwani and Juu. The settlements located about a kilometer away from the beach, closer to the main dirt road that connects Msangamkuu and Mtwara town, are known as Mwinje and Nangurukuru. The village primary school is located in Nangurukuru.

Mwanaidi, a thirty-seven-year-old fast-talking, enthusiastic member of the "village environment committee" in Mkubiru, asserted that illegal fishing in Mkubiru had been significantly reduced: "One hundred percent because of our *own* participation in the monitoring activities," she emphasized. Mwanaidi continued: "Those who were using legal nets had also taken the initiative because they were frustrated with those who were using dynamites and illegal fishing nets to catch their fish. Those who were using legal fishing gear were coming back empty-handed or with dead fish." Emphasizing people's agency in bringing an end to destructive fishing practices in her villages, Mwanaidi explained: "No, the marine park on its own would not have been able to stop these illegal fishing practices. The marine park, local citizens, and the government have worked together to put an end to these illegal fishing practices. Yes, the beatings [from soldiers and police officers] had some effect, and the regular patrolling was also effective because they confiscated the illegal nets and burned them. They also destroyed the boats. If they've destroyed your nets and boats, it's a big loss. Your family also hurts. . . . Fishers worry about it, that's why they have stopped engaging in illegal fishing practices."

Mwanaidi was acutely aware of the interventions that were going on in her village related to the protection and management of the marine environment. She made it clear that while destructive fishing practices had stopped in Mkubiru, she did not attribute their cessation to the marine park's intervention. Rather, she credited the local residents' agency and initiative in bringing an end to destructive fishing practices. Mwanaidi also alludes to self-realization among fishers—of the danger not only to themselves but also to their family members should they continue their illegal fishing practices. As Mwanaidi's commentary shows, it was a combination of factors—not just the marine park's interventions—that had brought destructive fishing practices to an end in Mkubiru. Taken together, as with many of my interlocutors, Mwanaidi emphasized people's agency in caring for their environment, their own realization and willingness to give up on unsustainable fishing practices, and not just out of fear in response to high-handed interventions and enforcement from the marine park authorities or the security forces who were patrolling the waters more diligently.

The situation regarding illegal fishing practices had clearly changed on the rural Mtwara peninsula over the years. Since the inauguration of a new government (Magufuli's administration) in 2015, people had dramatically stopped engaging in destructive and unsustainable fishing practices. Fish vendors at the Kivonkoni fish market told me they were being especially cautious about buying from fishers they suspected engaged in illegal fishing practices. Vendors feared they would be caught and fined for buying and selling fish that was caught through illegal fishing methods, particularly dynamite fishing. Women in particular were thankful for the reduction in illegal fishing practices because it positively affected their food security. In September 2019, when I brought up this topic with Salum, my field assistant from Sinde, he told me that following a six-month ban on dynamite fishing and the use of illegal nets in 2019, fishers were catching such large numbers of fish that they did not know what to do with them. "*Wapo wengi, wengi, wengi*" [There are lots and lots of fish], he said, with a characteristic hand gesture to emphasize the dramatic impact the ban on destructive fishing had on fish abundance in coastal Mtwara.

Haki, a licensed fisher, corroborated the increased abundance of fish in the Msimbati-Mnazi Bay area. "If you go there to catch fish," he said, "you'll find them in plenty." But others, such as Mwanaidi in Mkubiru, said: "Illegal fishing in the ocean is over but the ocean itself does not have fish [there are no fish left in the ocean]. That's because the fish have just finished on their own. People are complaining that the government has implemented a marine park here, there are still no fish in the ocean, so what's the point of this marine park? What are the benefits of the marine park? But people don't know that since the marine park came here, illegal fishing like dynamite fishing has been banned." Years of dynamite fishing and using kokoro nets did have a destructive impact on the local fishing grounds in Mkubiru—but the discourse and practice in the marine park villages in relation to the environment had indeed changed.

CONCLUSION

After over a decade of overt opposition to and resentment toward the marine park and its regulations, people living in the park villages began engaging in everyday discourses and practices that were increasingly pro-conservation. They spoke favorably about the marine park, and about changing their fishing practices—particularly the cessation of dynamite fishing and the use of illegal fishing nets—in a bid to protect their environment. This shift in people's discourse and practice, however, occurred over a long period. Starting in mid-2016, people began to use the phrase "Now we are all educated" to explain why they had stopped their destructive fishing practices and had become more environmentally conscious.

It is important to understand how and why people in the marine park villages changed their behaviors to follow the park regulations and protect their marine resources. Understanding the shifting discourses and practices "will show that local populations subjected to the regulations, environmental knowledges, and narratives of conservation can actively appropriate these and recreate them in a new way" (Cortes-Vazquez and Ruiz-Ballesteros 2018, 233). The chapter, however, does not provide a clear answer to the overarching research question raised at the beginning: whether a significant number of rural Mtwara peninsula residents had become environmental subjects because of the marine park's interventions. Instead, a combination of factors contributed to the discursive shift in people's disposition toward their environment and the marine park. This shift was *not* mainly due to "people's greater involvement in institutional regimes of environmental regulation" as a pathway to creating new environmental subjects (Agarwal 2005a, 2005b). The shift had occurred *despite* the absence of people's participation in environment committees, beach management units, or even marine conservation workshops organized by NGOs in the region. As discussed in the previous chapters, increased environmental regulations had, in fact, angered most local residents, prompting them to remain opposed to the park's presence in their villages for several years. A key complaint from local community members was that—although they had been promised the role of stakeholders in the park's mandate—they were neither substantially involved in setting its goals nor in designing its regulations. Moreover, they had not been sufficiently educated about the importance of protecting their environment.

If villagers were not actively participating in any of the village-level environment committees, how did this discursive shift occur in the villages? What factors could have contributed to the cessation of destructive fishing practices? What factors could have contributed to "a greater willingness to abide by regulations" (Agrawal 2005a, 170) among Nalingu residents in particular, and how permanent was this willingness? There were several political, cultural, and contextual factors that facilitated the shift in outlook in the marine park villages from mid-2016 onward.

For one, in 2015, the Tanzanian government recommitted itself to eliminating dynamite fishing from its territorial waters. To that end, through the international initiative of the Indian Ocean Commission's Smartfish program, the Tanzanian government implemented the Multi-Agency Task Team (MATT) to stop destructive, illegal, and criminal activities in the fisheries sector. In short, necessary funds and resources were made available to the enforcement authorities. Second, there was a change in the country's leadership and styles of governance. John Magufuli, elected as Tanzania's new president in October 2015, quickly moved to implement his new work ethic mandate (*hapa kazi tu*), which was applicable to government functionaries and ordinary citizens. This resulted in stricter enforcement of the restrictions, fines for infractions by villagers, regular naval patrols, and the direct involvement of the district commissioner and local leaders—elected officials and government officials, such as the VEO and the village chairman—in confiscating and destroying illegal fishing gear at the village level. While the people of Mtwara had become increasingly aware of the importance of caring for their environment, government intervention and the threat of punishment contributed significantly to their shift in mentality.

Third, while a small number of people from Msimbati, Nalingu, and Mkubiru may have participated superficially in VECs and VLCs, coordinated efforts in Nalingu and Mnazi to confiscate and destroy illegal fishing gear and apprehend those who engaged in dynamite fishing had a significant influence on the dispositions and "mentalities" of the people living in the catchment villages. Thus, there are multiple readings of the testimonial "Now we are educated"—from "Now we really understand the importance of protecting the (marine) environment and want to do something about it" to "Now we are terrified of the power of the government to punish us/those who violate the restrictions and regulations that the marine park has put in place, and therefore we want to adhere to those restrictions."

Fourth, because of the marine park's restrictive practices, an increasing number of people (hitherto fishers or would-be fishers) in the coastal villages had taken to farming. This had lessened residents' dependence on the ocean but had created problems of its own, resulting in further deforestation in the region, as seen in Msimbati and Nalingu. Fifth, implementing the gas project in rural Mtwara shifted the discourse away from the marine park and toward the gas project and its resultant inequities (see chapter 5).

Finally, as noted in the introduction, many young men had found alternative employment opportunities, particularly working as boda boda drivers as motorcycles from India and China were readily available, relatively cheap, and omnipresent on the roads. As a corollary, the motorized ferry (which could carry large numbers of people and goods between Msemo and Kivonkoni) directly affected the increased saliency of motorcycle taxis on the Mtwara peninsula—making it much easier for young men to become boda boda drivers.

To be sure, multiple factors came together to explain why residents of the Mtwara peninsula had become more concerned with caring for their marine environment. This chapter illustrates how contextual and cultural explanations can answer the important question: What does it take for individuals to become environmental subjects—defined as people who care about the environment and act in conservation-friendly ways on a long-term basis?

The concept of environmentality, as originally articulated by Arun Agrawal, may have lost its luster and has been discredited about its claims regarding "how to create new environmental subjects." Nonetheless, its usefulness in gaining insights into the multiplicity of factors that underpin why some individuals become environmentally friendly subjects while others do not cannot be discounted. As Pandya (2023, 7) has recently observed, "An environmentality framework remains useful for this analysis due to its capacity to illuminate the particular ways in which forms of environmental governance aim to 'conduct the conduct' in pursuit of specific forms of subjectivity, even if these are not necessarily achieved in practice." The empirical data examined in this chapter have shown "the limitations of treating environmentality as a top-down form of subject creation and not taking seriously the agency and aspirations of subjects themselves" (Youdelis 2019, 2). The data clearly show that residents of key fishing villages inside the marine park—Ruvula, Msimbati, Nalingu, and Mkubiru—had become environmental subjects even without actively participating in "institutional regimes of environment regulation and enforcement." Exceptions, in this case, were Bi Mkubwa, Kachakacha, Maukilo, and a few others who had volunteered with the marine park. These people were guiding or conducting the conduct of others in their respective villages. In most cases, multiple environmentalities were at play—including sovereign (restrictions against fishing in the core areas), disciplinary (fines for using illegal nets), and neoliberal environmentality (incentivized through the distribution of legal nets and a few fishing boats with outboard motors). In sum, neoliberal environmentality was not the only reason people had become environmental subjects.

Notwithstanding these shifts, however, there is no guarantee that the changes in the marine park villages in favor of environmental protection—this "fragile environmentality" (Segi 2013, 344)—will endure. It is quite possible that a change in the political leadership or decreased funding for the marine park's monitoring activities could lead at least some villagers to return to their previous fishing practices. This was a fear that several of my interlocutors expressed—that if the marine park were to be dismantled, illegal fishing practices would once again become commonplace in their villages (see chapter 5).

7

"WHAT REALLY MATTERS"

Conservation and Well-Being

ONE HOT AFTERNOON in September 2019, I entered a restaurant (*mghawa*) in Msimbati, along with my research assistants, to get lunch. Mama Samia had converted her house on the main road in Msimbati into a restaurant with no name. Outside the fenced perimeter made of sticks, a large display board listed the available dishes. As we sat on plastic chairs around a table, Mama Samia came to tell us that she had no food in her restaurant—only chai. The tea, which was in a large vacuum flask, was stale, so I decided not to order it. "There are no customers... people don't have money. So I make only black chai [*chai kavu*]," she said, looking disheartened. Acknowledging Mama Samia's difficulties, my research assistants and I settled into a corner of her shaded veranda. We stayed there in the shade for a while before going to another section of the village, to facilitate a men's group discussion on well-being, which we had scheduled for that afternoon.

In the meantime, Mama Samia's sister had converted the veranda into a temporary kitchen—peeling and chopping vegetables and raw mango and cleaning small blue crabs to make curry for three of her young children, who were hovering around her in anticipation of their late lunch. Two ducks were sifting through the wet mud in the front yard, searching for food in vain. The main road was deserted. On the other side, a few

FIGURE 11 A restaurant in Msimbati

young men were seated on the bench under a neem tree, which served as an important baraza, where men of all ages would meet every day to socialize. They were staring blankly, with glum faces. Later in the evening, I went to join them. One of the men told me, looking dejected: "Life has become bad [hard]. It's become very difficult to get money. Life has gone backward. Money is not circulating [*pesa haizunguki*]." I had heard versions of this statement throughout my fieldwork in Mtwara, but the emphasis on the "noncirculation of money" as the cause of suffering was relatively new.

Expressions of "life is hard" (maisha magumu, hali tete sana) were a staple of everyday conversation in the marine park villages and across Mtwara District, eliciting the description of the phrase as "a national anthem that everyone is singing." I also noticed that people were greeting each other with "*Habari ya pirika pirika?*" (How are your struggles going on?) more commonly than the customary "Habari?," or "Hujambo?" Significantly, however, in everyday conversations, people did not invoke the marine park as the main source of their hardships. The general sentiment was that everyone in Tanzania was leading a hard life, not just those living in Mtwara or the marine park villages. People frequently attributed their difficulty in accessing money (cash—*pesa* or *fedha*) to the hardline measures that the Magufuli government had taken to stamp out corruption in the country. These measures had particularly affected the cash poor, who rely on daily wage work (*kibarua*) and hawking food or selling used clothes as a source of livelihood.

Amid the different conservation debates, there is growing acknowledgement among conservation scholars and practitioners that, in addition to taking measures to protect nonhumans in protected areas, ensuring the well-being of in situ human populations is also crucial for sustainable biodiversity conservation. Indeed, one of the marine park's stated virtuous goals is to promote biodiversity conservation in Mtwara's coastal region while also being attentive to the well-being of the people living inside the park's boundaries. The marine park's General Management Plan (URT 2005; revised in 2011) explicitly states that the warden-in-charge must be cognizant of the livelihoods and well-being of the thousands of people living inside the park's boundaries—whom its implementation will directly affect. The park's ultimate goal, as outlined in the General Management Plan, is to consolidate a win-win situation where sustainable marine conservation supports human well-being. This goal underscores a key policy issue that has emerged in conservation: "how to reconcile conservation with human development" (Woodhouse et al. 2015, 1).

What role has the marine park played in improving people's lives, and specifically their well-being? Do villagers associate their well-being positively or negatively with the marine park? And importantly, how can we ascertain and evaluate the park's impacts on well-being when the on-the-ground situation is rapidly changing and is further complicated by the expansion of a large natural gas extraction project inside the marine park? As Woodhouse et al. (2015, 7) note: "Well-being is not a discrete outcome, but an ongoing dynamic process, changing through the course of an intervention and beyond."

As detailed in previous chapters, most people in the marine park villages did not believe that the marine park authorities had done anything significant to help them improve their livelihoods and well-being. On the contrary, people commonly used the stock phrase: "We have not seen the fruits of the marine park yet [*hatujaona matunda ya marine park, bado*]."

Only a handful of fishers and non-fishers in the park villages had received legal fishing gear and boats. A few others, such as Bi Mkubwa and her best friend, Siwema, had benefited from the training that the WWF had offered to women in Msimbati in modern fish roasting techniques. Most people, however, saw the marine park as a bulwark against their freedoms and way of life—against their cultural identity, livelihoods, and life goals, including educating their children through secondary school and beyond. Villagers described the marine park as a source of emotional distress and misery (see chapters 2 and 4). They viewed the restrictions and regulations implemented by the park authorities as antithetical to local residents' material and social well-being. Unsurprisingly, they remained vocally opposed to the marine park for more than a decade.

Over the years, however, their resistance and apathy had given way to acquiescence and support for the marine park and its mandate—reflected in statements such as: "Now we have understood," or "Now we are all educated and understand the importance of protecting our environment." In the context of the ongoing social transformation and attitudinal changes I documented in the marine park villages (see chapter 6), this chapter seeks to address some fundamental questions pertaining to human well-being, including: How do people who live in the marine park villages define well-being? What do they believe is important for them to live the life they want? What role do they think the marine park has played in contributing to, or inhibiting, their pursuit of well-being? And what are their hopes and aspirations for the future?

The growing literature on human well-being, ecosystem services, and conservation interventions suggests that the ideas, policies, and practices for achieving win-win biodiversity conservation and human development outcomes have shifted significantly in recent years.[1] The conceptual and policy shift—from the traditional top-down model of environmental governance to a more locally managed, community-based model, in which ecosystem services and human well-being are seen as intimately connected, has further prompted academic interest in human well-being as it relates to conservation.

An example of this new, locally focused approach is the linguistic shift in conservation initiative master plans. As Fry et al. (2015, 70) point out, the emergent "use of the term well-being rather than the term poverty represents a conceptual shift towards a more positive approach to development, focusing on what is good and improves people's lives rather than primarily what is bad or lacking." There is a general consensus among academics, practitioners, and policy makers that "interventions that support local well-being can increase environmentally desirable behavior, and lead to positive local perceptions and engagement" (Woodhouse et al. 2015, 2; see also Ban et al. 2019). However, questions surrounding what exactly constitutes well-being, how it can be measured, and what is needed to promote it continue to be debated (Abunge, Coulthard, and Daw 2013; Agarwala et al. 2014). As Beauchamp et al. (2018, 28) note, "Despite the term's popularity, well-being is rarely defined or carefully examined in an empirical context by those concerned with conservation."

This chapter provides an overview of the concept of well-being, its brief history in the academic literature, and some of the frameworks that have been associated with the measurement of objective and subjective components of well-being. This is followed by a review of the theoretical literature on well-being and the ethnographic component of the chapter—which includes a discussion and analysis of the empirical data related to well-being (emic perspective) gathered in the marine park villages.[2] Through individual narratives, this chapter explores local residents' understanding of the idea of well-being—what they believe constitutes well-being and what they consider important for their own well-being.[3] In addition, I outline the marine park's perceived and real effects using local frameworks of well-being. In conclusion, I emphasize the challenges involved in studying well-being in the context of marine conservation and also validate the importance of human well-being for the success of marine conservation interventions and human development.

WELL-BEING IN THREE DIMENSIONS

Early discussions on the importance of human well-being in relation to development interventions in poor and developing countries can be traced to the work of Nobel Prize laureate Amartya Sen. In his work, Sen put forward the idea that poverty is not just about what you have, or do not have, but what you can claim (entitlements) and what you can do (capabilities). He viewed development as being about having the freedom to live a life you have reason to value (Sen 1999; Woodhouse et al. 2017,

100; see also Stiglitz, Sen, and Fitoussi 2009, 12). Over the years, scholars have offered numerous definitions and theories of human well-being, as well as frameworks for its study (see Edwards, Reid, and Hunter 2016; Palmer et al. 2017). Ian Gough and Allister McGregor's (2007) framework remains the most well known. They define well-being as "a state of being with others, where human needs are met, where one can act meaningfully to pursue one's goals, and where one enjoys a satisfactory quality of life" (2007, 34; see also Sen 1985; Stiglitz, Sen, and Fitoussi 2009).

Drawing on Sen's work on *capabilities* in particular, Gough, McGregor, and Camfield pioneered their three-dimensional framework as part of the Wellbeing in Developing (WeD) Countries Research group, located at the University of Bath (Gough, McGregor, and Camfield 2007, xxii).[4] This group emphasized that well-being is best understood as a multidimensional, context-dependent concept. It can be best operationalized and measured by examining the "three interacting dimensions: (i) the objective material circumstances of a person; (ii) subjective evaluation of one's own life, and the meanings and values ascribed to the processes one engages in and the outcomes of those processes; (iii) a relational component focusing on how people engage with others to meet their needs and achieve goals" (McGregor and Sumner 2010). As Mahajan and Daw (2016, 109–10) explain, "In this definition, material well-being refers to what people have and whether or not their needs are met; relational well-being considers how social relationships enable an individual to pursue well-being; and subjective well-being refers to how individuals feel about what they have." This last dimension acknowledges that individual well-being is pursued in relation to other people—that social connectedness is a human need and that definitions of a good life are socially constructed (Coulthard, McGregor, and White 2018, 243–44; Deneulin and McGregor 2010; Fisher 2014; Milner-Gulland et al. 2014, 1162). In other words, there is more to well-being than the fulfilment of basic needs; there are human social and psychological needs that must also be fulfilled (see Fry et al. 2015).

Woodhouse et al. (2017, 99) point out that well-being "focuses on what is good and positive in people's lives. . . . It prioritizes the views and perspectives of those people whom interventions and development changes will impact." In addition to offering definitions and frameworks, scholars who have examined human well-being in real-world situations have acknowledged the difficulties associated with operationalizing and measuring the concept because of its lack of specificity and context.[5] As I show later in this chapter, I operationalized the concept of well-being in interviews with Mtwara residents through a list of questions that covered the material, subjective, and relational aspects of well-being.[6] All interviews began with questions about the interviewee's socioeconomic background and material assets (farmland, fishing gear, type of house, and household assets),[7] followed by three basic questions: Could you tell me the meaning of *ustawi*, or good life (*maisha mazuri*), as you understand it? What does a good life mean to you? And finally, what does ordinary life mean to you, or how is good life different from ordinary life?

GOOD LIFE, ORDINARY LIFE, HARD LIFE

During informal conversations on the topic of well-being, I learned from my key interlocutors that the closest match to the notion of well-being in Kiswahili is *ustawi*. Ustawi, as in *ustawi wa maisha*, or good life (*maisha mazuri*), could be contrasted with ordinary life (*maisha ya kawaida*) and difficult life (*maisha magumu*).[8] In subsequent interviews and group discussions in the study villages, my interlocutors articulated their understanding of what ustawi or maisha mazuri meant by using examples and vignettes from their own life experiences. They gave elaborate responses and often used their present situations, as compared with the past, to illustrate their understanding of ustawi.

Good Life Shows on Your Face

In September 2019, I interviewed Sadala on the subject of ustawi. He was in his late sixties at the time. I spoke with him on the porch outside his house, where he sat with one of his grandchildren on his lap. Given his extensive experience in local and regional politics, I often consulted with him and took his advice on the research I was doing in rural Mtwara. Sadala had served as the village chairman for over ten years; he was also elected as a councillor (*diwani*) to the Mtwara District Council for two terms, lasting a total of ten years. Moreover, as the village chairman, he had been actively involved in the planning and implementation of the marine park. He was therefore able to provide crucial insights into how the marine park and the gas project had affected the people of Msimbati over time.

Sadala had led a fairly good life compared with several of his contemporaries in Msimbati village, who were struggling with their livelihoods at the time. However, many others in Msimbati village were far better off than Salada was in economic terms. When I asked him about his understanding of the term ustawi and what it signified to him and the people of Msimbati, he said: "A good life [*maisha mazuri*] is when a person has the ability [*uwezo*] and the resilience [*kujikumu*] to lead his life the way he wants to for as long as he wants. It means being able to get food for yourself and your family without worry, and if you have to buy other necessities, you should have no problem. You know all the time that you can get those necessities." His statements reflect what Sen and others have conceptualized as "capabilities"—the ability to choose what one is and does. His emphasis on the fulfilment of material needs—to be able to buy everyday necessities without anticipatory anxiety—calls attention to two important and interrelated components of well-being: food security and income security.

Furthermore, Sadala's interpretation of well-being prized good health and income security. As he said: "If I am able to get the things that I want, without having to struggle all the time to get them, then I can say that I have a good life. But when I cannot do that, my life is difficult." When asked to contrast his understanding of a good life with that of an ordinary life, Sadala thought the question through. After a moment, he said: "Ordinary life is when you get food, even though it may not be enough, it's good, you do not go hungry for three days, you may not have enough food, but you are satisfied. . . . So, ordinary life is very stressful and we have to struggle a lot." For most people living in the park villages, a life that involved everyday struggles and uncertainties—particularly with regard to food—was tantamount to an ordinary or "normal" life. As Sadala explained, those who lead an ordinary life are not food secure. They often have limited access to the resources and the capabilities that would enable them to lead a good life. Sadala said that just by looking at a fellow villager, he could confidently tell whether they had a good life. "You don't have to study a person in detail," he explained, "or to know everything about that person. It shows on his face, that he has a good life, that he is a healthy person who is aware of the future [existential certainty]."

In Sadala's perspective, there are three crucial components to well-being: first, food security—i.e., guaranteed access to sufficient food and two to three meals (*mlo*) a day; second, good health, which often means access to good health care and money to cover the cost of prescriptions; and third, a reliable source of income. These three components are deeply interconnected. Sadala's ability to identify a fellow villager as having a good life (or otherwise) just by looking at them—that it, as he put it, "shows on his face"—has important implications. It points to the fact that in the coastal villages, the cultural model of well-being is well recognized and shared—food and income security are crucial in this model, followed by other components. Put differently, being able to see one's well-being on one's face points to a social and relational understanding of well-being.

Several of my key interlocutors, including Bi Mkubwa, confirmed that one could determine just by looking at a person whether he or she has a good life or not. I had interviewed Bi Mkubwa numerous times and was aware that she had struggled to lead an economically secure life until her late forties. Starting in 2002, however, she had demonstrated her enterprising attitude by getting involved in the marine park's mandate. Bi Mkubwa had benefited significantly from the alternative income-generating projects that the marine park had implemented in Msimbati with the WWF's help. She owned nine acres of land, which she used for different income-generating activities. In 2019, she had used three acres of her farmland to grow watermelons (*tikiti maji*), but her crop had failed. She had also invested in a fishpond (*mabwawa*) to farm milk fish, but she was not happy with the outcome. "I don't know why, but the fish in my pond are small. Other people (men) are able to harvest big fish in their ponds," she lamented.

Moreover, three of her sons had found employment on the gas project. For Bi Mkubwa, this was far more important for her well-being than her own income. When asked how she would describe someone as "doing well" or having a "good life," she gave a detailed response. Bi Mkubwa described a good life as one that is fulfilling (*kutimiza*). "It's when someone has the ability [*uwezo*, freedom] to live the life he or she wants to live," she said. As with Sadala, Bi Mkubwa's representation of ustawi also reflects what Sen and others have conceptualized as "capabilities."

She emphasized the visible material components of a good life that are recognizable at the community level—income security and a good house to sleep in—one made of cement bricks (*matofali*), with a roof made of corrugated metal sheets (*mabati*). She also specified having enough food to eat and a car for travel [means of transport]. A means of transportation was particularly important for Msimbati residents, given the village's distance from, and reliance on, Mtwara town. She explained: "You have all the things that you need and you don't even have to say, Ha! Where can I get this thing that I want?"

For Bi Mkubwa, a good life is one where a person's needs have been fulfilled [*kutimiliwa*], where one can get what one wants, and as much of it as possible. Bi Mkubwa added that having good health insurance is also key to well-being. As she put it, "If you are sick, and if you don't have health insurance, then it means that you don't have a good life because your life goals have not been fulfilled [*haujatimiliwa*]."[9] Bi Mkubwa emphasized the material components of well-being. She addressed relational components only when specifically asked.

This is not to suggest that relational components are not as important as material components of well-being; they are, however, less discussed in interview contexts. For example, during survey interviews in Beauchamp et al.'s (2018) study in Cambodia, people mentioned a house, agricultural material, water availability, the road, family and love, and solidarity in the village, but they did not mention freedom of choice and autonomy as components of well-being. In the marine park villages, people did discuss some of these relational aspects of well-being, but only after they were asked specific questions that were meant to elicit such commentary. This could be regarded as a methodological limitation of using interviews and focus group discussions to elicit people's understandings of the notion of well-being. It could be an artifact of how questions aimed at eliciting people's understandings of well-being are categorized into material, subjective, and relational components. Or it could be that in contexts of poverty and marginalization, people do prioritize material components of well-being over other components—including subjective and relational components.

When asked to contrast a good life with an ordinary life—and whether she could tell what kind of life a fellow villager was leading—Bi Mkubwa responded with this illustrative example:

> In this village, for example, you can look at someone and say: "That person there . . . ha! He's got life—a good life! [*Huyu, ana maisha!*]" Yes, absolutely,

you can look at some people and say they are leading a very good life, but then you look back and you also see people who are leading ordinary lives. You see that some people have a [good] life [*wana maisha*], that they can live well, but on other days, they don't have a good life, so they have an average life, because on some days they have problems, on other days, they are able to achieve their goals [*mambo yanakuta*]. People who lead an ordinary life are able to get food for four days, but they struggle to get food for the next two days [*unayumba yumba*], and there are people who struggle to get food for even up to five or six days.[10]

Bi Mkubwa acknowledges the inequalities within her village, where some people have access to things that enhance their well-being, while others live a life of uncertainty and insecurity—sometimes unable to get food for up to a week. Bi Mkubwa emphasized that one's well-being is evident through one's material assets; in other words, it is first and foremost defined by access to material needs. Material assets refer to the kind of house one lives in: a thatched hut (*mbanda*) versus a concrete house; one with electricity or one without; one with a TV and a refrigerator or one without; a well-furnished living room versus one that is barely furnished, and so on. During one women's focus group discussion in Msimbati, we were seated inside a well-furnished living room. Bihaya, who was one of the participants, gestured to the TV, fan, and large couches and said, "This is good life! You see? This is good life!" All other participants spontaneously said, "*Ndio! Ndio! Ndio!*" (Yes! Yes! Yes!) in unison.

Not everyone agreed on this point. For example, sixty-year-old Abdallah, from Nalingu, interjected during a group discussion to emphasize that people's material possessions may be deceptive. Material possessions, he said, may hide the difficulties—the unfreedoms—that an individual or a family may be experiencing. Looking at me, he elaborated: "As an outsider, you might think that people's lives have really improved because you see that many people are now living in houses made of cement bricks [*matofali*]. You'll see that someone has built a house that is fit for an ambassador [*nyumba ya kifahari*]. But if you go inside his house and see how he eats with his wife and children, you'll see that he may not have enough food for himself and his family. In the past, even if we were living in a hut [*nyumba ya nyasi*], we were living a good life, because we had food security." As noted in chapter 1, most people in Nalingu spoke of the past, i.e., during Julius Nyerere's administration and the ujamaa era, as a time when they lived a peaceful coexistence in their village and were food secure. The marine park's entrée in the region had sown discord and insecurity among the local residents and resulted in substantial violence and disdain (*chuki*), especially toward the MPA personnel. This repeated theme—that "what you see is not always what is real"—was particularly common in Msimbati and Mngoji, where a significant number of people had lost their farms and trees to the gas project. People repeatedly told me that those who had received cash compensation for their farmlands and trees had quickly invested a portion of the money in upgrading their houses—spending the remainder on household goods, furniture, and daily necessities such as food, or even squandering the money. In the long term, many of these people had become deeply food insecure, despite living in new concrete houses (see chapters 3, 4, and 5).

While conducting a household survey of the gas project (see Kamat et al. 2019) in August 2016, I asked the chairman of Mngoji village whether the concrete house across from his office, with its shiny tin roof and satellite dish, belonged to a wealthy resident. The chairman shook his head and ruefully said: "No, that's all he has. He has built that house with the money he received from the gas project as compensation for the land he lost.... He lost all his land to the gas project, nine acres in total." Many people in Mngoji had lost their land to the sprawling gas processing plant that was built in October 2015. In 2017, when I asked my interlocutors whether the cash compensation that some people had received for their assets had increased inequalities and jealousies in their villages, they vehemently denied that cash compensation correlated with fortune. On the contrary, nearly everyone said that they felt sorry for those who had lost their land, as many had become poorer and food insecure in the process; some had even become paupers (*fukara*).

Good Life Has Temporality

Hassani was well known in Msimbati as a vocal critic of the marine park and the gas project (see chapters 4 and 5). He believed that both projects had disrupted people's lives in Msimbati and other villages. In August 2019, when I interviewed him on his understanding of the idea of ustawi, he explained: "A normal life is one where a person wants something he desires or intends to get. He gets it, but not in time. A good life is when you can get something at the intended time. You get everything you have intended to get, in time, you get it because you have the means [*uwezo*, ability] to get it." For Hassani, being able to access material needs "when one really needs them—in time, and not when it's too late" was key to leading a good life. Several other people who participated in my research echoed this sentiment, emphasizing temporality as an important component of one's well-being—whether one is able to get what one wants, or needs, in time. These needs might range from having the capacity (ability) to eat two or three meals a day, to having access to the capital necessary to start a new business, to expanding an existing business, to being able to fix the roof in time before the rainy season, to having the resources to visit friends and family elsewhere in Mtwara, and to having the ability to pay for health care and medical treatment as well. Cumulatively, age, ability, gender, education, skills, social capital, and the size of one's social network, social relations, interdependency, and freedoms are critical factors in determining whether one gets what one wants in time. In sum, temporality, or whether one gets what one wants in time, does matter for one's well-being.

Good Life Has Certainty

Zainabu had been participating in my research since 2012, when I first recorded her life history. As with several of my key interlocutors, I had recorded Zainabu's life history in detail during previous interviews and made a note of how her life had changed over seven or eight years. Zainabu echoed some of the key components of well-being that other participants had raised before contrasting a "good life" with what she described as the life that she and most of her fellow villagers lead. For Zainabu, normal life, or maisha ya kawaida, was one of subsistence (*kujikumu*) or self-sufficiency (*kujitosheleza*). As she put it: "You wake up in the morning and get just tea and bread, and then you get another meal during the daytime. On another day, you miss getting lunch, and you get to eat only dinner—at night before you go to bed. Normal life is when you can plan for just today, but you don't have plans for tomorrow. That is, you're just waiting till tomorrow to find out what God has planned for you—or what God will do for you. That is a normal life, with no plans for the future [no long-term plans]." In Zainabu's view, a normal life is one of uncertainty, especially in terms of food security. As she put it, people like her, who lead ordinary lives, can plan only for today; they are uncertain about what life has in store for them the next day, or in the near future. These uncertainties stem from everyday insecurities, particularly concerning food and income. What really matters for well-being is certainty.

Bi Malombe, who was in her early sixties, had been married twice and was living as a single mother in Msimbati with her three children and several grandchildren. She described a good life as one that is closely tied to one's ability to eat well and according to desire. By contrast, normal life is being able to drink just tea in the morning without any snack to go with it, porridge (*uji* or *ugali*) for lunch in the afternoon, and in the evening, perhaps plain cooked rice. A good life is being able to eat three meals a day. Bi Malombe reflected that she had once had a good life, when she would wake up in the morning, drink tea or soup and eat a snack with it. She said: "I used to plan with my children and grandchildren, and ask them what they wanted me to cook for them in the afternoon, and in the evening for dinner—should we cook rice or ugali, I would ask them, and we used to drink tea, and my grandchildren would say 'Bibi, we are all full so we would like to go to sleep and wake up in the morning to drink tea.' So, my normal life was good life, but now my circumstances have changed and constricted my life." For older women like Bi Malombe, well-being revolved around food security (and variety). In her narrative, she emphasized that she had known a good life—in her case, access to more diverse foods. When her circumstances changed though, she was no longer as food secure as she had been. In her own assessment, then, she was currently *not* leading a good life. Her inability to cook the food that she would like, for herself and her family, epitomized this.

Kusum, a thirty-two-year-old single mother, was recently divorced and living with her young son in a hut that belonged to her maternal grandmother. Her brother had given her a small plot of land on which she had planted rice. For Kusum, someone with a good life has an abundance of material or valuable things. Someone who is leading a normal life, like herself, lives in a mud house with a thatched grass roof and eats ordinary meals. "That's normal life," she said. "You work on your own farm and you grow food and you eat what you grow." She continued, "Sometimes you feel like eating chicken and fries (*kuku na chipsi*), but you end up eating only cassava porridge, yes, that's how the days go by." In the same breath, however, Kusum emphasized that she considered herself lucky, especially when it came to food security, because her parents owned a substantial amount of farmland in Msimbati. As she explained: "We have enough food in the house, like rice for this year. God has given that to us, he gives us sustenance. We have rice and my parents have coconut plantations. When we go to harvest coconuts and sell them, we buy fish with the money, we dry our rice, we grind, and we eat, life goes on. So even if I have to spend two or three days without even a hundred shillings (5¢) in hand, I don't worry because I know there is enough food inside the house." Kusum was reminiscing a time when marriage safeguarded her ability to eat a variety of food, including chicken and fries. As a result of her status as a divorced single mother, however, she could afford to eat only cassava porridge and *not* the food she really desired.

Kusum described that she was unhappy with her life. Her husband had left her to marry another woman. She did not have electricity in her hut and relied on a wick lamp. She said that she had good relations with her neighbors, and they exchanged everyday greetings, but she did not rely on them for help. Instead, she relied on her parents and her brother, and because of them, was food secure. While this was an important component of well-being, it did not translate into Kusum's sense of happiness and fulfilment in life. Ideally, for Kusum, being married, living with a husband who earned a regular income, and being food secure at the same time were crucial for well-being. In other words, for Kusum, food security alone did not produce well-being. In sum, for Kusum, what really mattered was not just food security but also emotional and social connectedness.[11]

Good Life Means Being Absolutely Satisfied

Shakila, an energetic twenty-five-year-old resident of Ruvula, was volunteering with the marine park when I first met her in 2019. She was living with her husband, a subsistence farmer. A year earlier, Shakila and her husband had endured a personal tragedy when both of their newborn twins had died within the first two weeks of their birth. Consequently, Shakila spent time helping her identical twin sister, Zaituni, who lived in the same neighborhood in Ruvula, with her two children. For Shakila, those who are well have all the good things that they need and are content with those things. They eat well, they have a video player at home, a nice couch, a radio, and electricity. As Shakila put it, "A person who has a good life will have sufficient food to eat until the end of his life. That is what comes to mind when I think of a person who has a good life." In describing what ordinary life is, she summarized: "It's the kind of life we live here. We live in an ordinary place, we live in a mud house with a thatched roof, and we just have a small wooden bed to sleep on, and some furniture, buckets, pots, and pans, so we can't compare ourselves with a person who claims to have a good life. You get to eat something only after you have struggled to get it by working on the farm, and when you come back from your farm, you are tired, and you get something to eat. That is the normal life." In other words, someone who leads a "normal life" does not have desirable things like video players, solar panels, or electricity. "You have only one stove to cook your food," Shakila said, "until the room is filled with smoke from the firewood." Additionally, for Shakila, a person with a good life has a guaranteed job—ideally with a salary. Shakila alluded to a young man living in Ruvula, whom she described as someone she would consider leading a good life. He was living in a cement house, owned a motorcycle, and ran a small grocery store. More importantly, he was the "go-to" person when someone in the village needed urgent help with cash. Other interlocutors in Ruvula corroborated Shakila's impression of the man as someone who was an exemplar of a good life, someone who not only had valuable assets and a business but also had cash in hand to help others.

Good Life Means Money

Men more than women emphasized the importance of money (*pesa*) in their discussions about well-being. Their emphasis on money, with its multiple meanings, was striking. In Msimbati, for example, Shaibu, who was participating in a focus group discussion said: "Here, we are leading a life of uncertainty—a life of 'maybe, maybe not, unsure.' . . . A life of uncertainty is an ordinary life, one where there is no guarantee or certainty about anything [*tunaolabdia*]. If you have money in your pocket, everything becomes easy. Life becomes good. Money is the soap of human beings. It's the soap of the soul [*Maisha ni mazuri—fedha ni sabuni ya binadamu. Sabuni ya roho*]. Money is everything. There is nothing that is more important than money because money makes it possible for me to have everything. I can spend it on everything, make sure my children go to school. If I have money, then I see that there is nothing more important than money."

Mzura, a fellow discussant, agreed, saying, "If you have a substantial coconut farm, and if you have a large cashew farm, then you'll be respected in the village. In you have a house in the town or city, if you have a nice house, tenants will respond. Respect comes, you are counted, you are known, you are respected. And if you have relatives in the city, then you'll be even more respected." In other words, money and material assets are important to one's well-being because they provide economic security and food security. Additionally, social connections in urban centers are equally important to one's well-being because they bring respect and status to individuals.

In Kilambo, men reiterated the importance of money and material components of well-being. Mfaume, who was in his midfifties, summed up his thoughts: "A good life is to have money, it's the most important thing in life. When you have money, you have a good life, not a life where you are just wandering around aimlessly or fluttering like a sail." Swalehe, who participated in a men's focus group in Kilambo, put it succinctly: "What we value most is having a good income. Even if people don't value you or your family, if you have money, you should be able to make a living. . . . People value money so much because if you have money, you don't ask, What shall we eat today?" In sum, money is more than just "cash"—what it materially signifies but also what it brings: reassurance, status, and freedom from everyday anxieties regarding food for one's family.

In a context of increasingly neoliberal economic rationalities, with social safety nets nearly nonexistent for the poor, a rapidly increasing cost of living, and very low levels of employment, money (economic security) was critical. Men in particular spoke frankly about their worries and constraints, emphasizing the materiality of cash and its importance for one's survival and well-being. Here, money, with its multiple meanings, offered people freedom, choice, and autonomy (see Beauchamp et al. 2018). Money provides a gateway to more freedoms and choices, even when other avenues such as education and migration are limited.

Good Life Is Living in Peace

While the vast majority of people living in the marine park villages highlighted material components of well-being, this did not preclude the importance of subjective and relational components of well-being. Jamila, a fifty-six-year-old mother of three children, had spent her entire life in Kilambo. Her father, she said, was very protective of his children and did not want any of them to leave Kilambo. As a discussant in a women's focus group in Kilambo, Jamila explained: "If I have a job, peace, and security, I will lead a good life, but if there is a war going on, then I will feel insecure. For example, if you are working on your farm, and if you suddenly hear gunfire, you'll have to run away from the field as people on the Mozambican side do." The talk of gunfire in Jamila's response is a reference to the ongoing insurgency and the threat of al-Shabaab attacks on the Mozambican side of the Ruvuma River. Kilambo, which is located on Tanzania's border with Mozambique, has a shared history of war and insurgency. During discussions on the subject of well-being, the people of Kilambo often added a tag sentence to statements about their own well-being, saying: "Thankfully, we are not in a situation like our colleagues on the Mozambican side, where they are constantly under the threat of war and violence." As I discuss in the epilogue, in October 2020, insurgents calling themselves "al-Shabaab" crossed the Ruvuma River to attack Kilambo and Kitaya, setting houses on fire and leaving many people dead.

Good Life Is Doing What Other People Do

Most people in the park villages described their lives as "normal" or "ordinary"—to indicate that they lived a life of uncertainty, but not one of extreme poverty. Ashula a thirty-five-year-old woman from Msimbati, specifically explained why she was leading a hard life. Ashula had lived her entire life in Msimbati. Her husband had divorced her three years earlier and she was living as a single mother with her two young children in the house she had inherited from her father. She owned just one acre of land, on which she had planted cashew trees. Ashula said: "Most people here lead a normal life or ordinary life. But in my case, I don't have a normal life. I lead a very difficult life." She ran a small business, selling tomatoes and *mandazi* (half cake) to earn a living. Importantly, she said that she did not have anyone in Msimbati who could help her in times of trouble—not even a neighbor or a family member in the community. I was struck by Ashula's narrative because an overwhelmingly majority of my interlocutors emphasized that even though they were poor and had to deal with their daily struggles, they knew they had a family or a neighbor or a friend whom they could count on for help during an emergency. "Thankfully," she said, "so far I have not experienced an illness that would have required me to be hospitalized for a few days. I am grateful to God for that." The deepening poverty and worsening economic situation in Tanzania, where "money was no longer circulating," had worsened Ashula's life even further. Yet, she was thankful to God that her life had not taken a turn for the worse because of a serious illness. Her precarity, however, manifested in her statement that she was not able to do what other people do.

In summary, most people emphasized the material components of well-being until they were specifically asked about other elements. For many villagers (across different age groups), income and food security were key constituents of well-being. Additionally, nearly everyone mentioned the desire for a nice house made of cement blocks—with a corrugated tin roof rather than one of thatched palm fronds or grass. Furthermore, good health (and access to good health care) was important for one's well-being. Finally, people asserted that they would like to have family, friends, and neighbors they could rely on for support. While material components of well-being were considered important for one's well-being, relational components were also vital.

FREEDOM, UNITY, AND WELL-BEING

To reiterate, the Capabilities Approach focuses on a key question: What is each person able to do and to be? It focuses on the opportunities available to each person; it is *focused on choice or freedom*—opportunities, or what Sen calls "substantial freedoms" (Nussbaum 2011, 18–20). "Capability is thus a kind of freedom: the substantive freedom to achieve alternative functioning combinations. . . . [Capabilities] are not just abilities residing inside a person but also the freedoms or opportunities created by a combination of personal abilities and the political, social, and economic environment" (Nussbaum 2011, 20).[12] In asking: How do you feel about what you have—and what you can do with what you have?, I sought to gauge whether people felt they had the freedom to do what they wanted with their lives. In response, a vast majority of my interlocutors described their lives as "ordinary," characterized by everyday insecurities and uncertainties. Strikingly, however, the majority of men and women confidently asserted that they had the freedom to do what they wanted with their lives despite their poverty and food insecurities. They described their freedoms in terms of movement, assembly, religion, customs, traditions, cultural practices, and free speech on political matters. A few of them clarified that fishers had suffered from a loss of their freedoms because of the restrictions imposed by the marine park, but this was not an important component in conversations about freedoms and well-being.

Bi Mkubwa emphasized the importance of education to one's well-being. She said: "Education is everything. If you have a little bit of education, then things 'sit well' for you because first, you have a vision and you know what to do. You can do these things because of your education." For Bi Mkubwa, education was an important aspect of well-being because it provided opportunities and a sense of purpose that superseded "ordinary life" in the village. In this sense, education increases a person's freedom in effective and meaningful ways.

Bi Mkubwa also focused on other components of well-being: freedom and unity. She said: "Work, freedom, and unity, these three things are important for people. They enable one to lead a better life. Freedom is about doing everything you want to do without being pushed or coaxed." In other words, freedom to do something is as important as freedom from something.

Zainabu, who often lamented the hardships she had to endure, emphasized that she nevertheless had the freedom to do what she wanted with what she had. In my previous interviews with Zainabu, she had spoken repeatedly about being suppressed and exploited by the government, the marine park, and the gas project (see chapter 3). Still, she said, "I have the freedom to do what I want because here in our village, we live without conflict. So everyone here lives the way they can, as much as they can. No one here tells you that you should live your life this way or that way—you have the freedom to live the way you want." Whether Zainabu's response is truly indicative of residents' "freedom to live" the kinds of lives they want—and whether it reflects gender equality in the village—is moot. Nonetheless, her perspective on freedom is important. According to Zainabu, even though people in her village did not have the freedom from feelings of everyday insecurity surrounding food, they did have some kinds of freedoms—of religion, movement, and speech, which they cherished.

For Zainabu, peace and security were important components of well-being. She emphasized that there was indeed peace and unity in Msimbati and that people cooperated and worked together. As she put it: "There's unity and social cohesion in the community. We don't have divisions. If there was any political conflict in the village, they surface during the elections. But after that, people came together to demonstrate their unity, particularly during the Maulidi and Eid al-Fitr." In other words, people's religiosity, religious commitment to Islam, and *ummah* (Islamic community) trumped other potential social and political divisions. Furthermore, residents engaged in social functions, events, and activities such as funerals and weddings—all of which were good for social cohesion and people's well-being. Zainabu's reflections on unity, peace, and security in her village are notable because, at the time, Msimbati village was overwhelmingly represented by the opposition party (CUF) and there were persistent fears among villagers that the ruling CCM party would suppress any form of dissent.

Kusum (introduced earlier) emphasized that in addition to being food secure because of her parents, she was free to live as she wanted. She said: "Freedom—absolutely, without a doubt, I have freedom, I am not tied to anyone [in her case, a husband] and if I need to travel, I just plan and I just leave and say goodbye at home so that they know that I have left, and I will come back tomorrow or the day after tomorrow. I will go somewhere just to walk or roam around for two or three days, and then I come back. Yes, that's the freedom I have seen." In a region where divorce is extremely common and women are often left financially and socially vulnerable, women such as Kusum emphasize the positive side of divorce—having the freedom to move around, to travel and be mobile without being tied to anyone. This freedom was important for Kusum's sense of well-being. She was able to do this because she was living on her own with her child. Because she was divorced, there was no husband to restrict her movements.

Bi Malombe echoed similar sentiments. Having been previously married twice and now living as a single mother, she said that she had gained freedom by being unmarried. While her life was not as good as it had been, she emphatically stated that she had the freedom to do what she wanted. Moreover, she stated that she herself was the root of this freedom. Bi Malombe explained: "I stand by myself, since no one can tell me what to do. I don't know if it's God's wish that I am destined to be in this situation, but I have the freedom to do what I want. I say that because I am alone, and in that sense, if I decide that I want to do something, I will do it, then there is no one to blame me or stop me." The phrase "standing by myself" refers to self-reliance, or *kujitegemea*. Freedom to do what one wants may come with income insecurity. In this case, Bi Malombe does not have a husband, but she has older children who live with her and are there to support her in the context of income insecurity.

Jamila, from Kilambo, similarly asserted her sense of freedom by emphatically stating: "I have the freedom to do what I want. For example, I have a farm, I have the freedom to grow food on my own farm. I have enough resources to achieve my life goals. For example, I get enough food from my farm. I can educate my children or grandchildren [send them to school] by depending on the farm. If I want to sell it, I have the ability to do so, and I can also sell my house if I want to. I am free and can use my possessions the way I want to. . . . Yes, I can go to the beach with my bucket and get some fish (crustaceans) and I can sell the fish." As someone who had spent her entire life in Kilambo, Jamila had built her own assets, in that they belonged to her and therefore she had the freedom to do what she wanted with them.

Mfaume, a participant in the men's focus group in Kilambo, emphasized the importance of freedom from oppression to his well-being. He said, "The most important thing to lead a good life is freedom to do what I want to do without being oppressed by anyone. If I do what I want for peace, and even society does things peacefully, and the country is also at peace, then you can do your things in peace and with freedom." When asked about unity, Mfaume elaborated: "Yes, we have unity in this village. We cooperate and do not discriminate against anyone. We have cooperated with each other for decades without discrimination [*bila ubaguzi*]. Our unity has allowed us to lead the kind of life we want. For example, we can go out and work on our farms. We can also go to the sea to catch fish. That's the kind of freedom and unity we have seen here."

SUBJECTIVE CHANGES IN WELL-BEING

Interlocutors were asked to reflect on the last ten years of their lives. They were then asked whether they felt their lives had improved, remained the same, or worsened over this period. Interlocutors gave varied responses. Out of the 140 people I interviewed, the vast majority 95 (68 percent) described their life as ordinary (*wastani*, average) and unchanged; 27 (19 percent) said that they were currently leading a "good life" (*maisha mazuri*); 11 (8 percent) specifically said that their life was "okay" (*njema tu*), i.e., it was neither good nor bad, and it had neither improved nor worsened over the years; and the remaining 10 (7 percent) said that their life had indeed become hard over the years.

Sadala, for example, said that in comparing his situation now with how he had lived in the past (specified as ten years ago), it was evident that he was not currently leading a good life. "*Mazingira sio rafiki*," he said—a colloquial expression that literally translates as "The environment is not a friend" or "Conditions are not good or friendly." Even though he seemed relatively healthy, Sadala's life was not what it used to be. "I cannot do the kind of hard work I used to do in the past," he explained. "I don't have the ability to do that now." For Sadala, the ability to work hard—to be productive and provide for one's family—was an important aspect of one's well-being—and he was not able to live up to that because of his age.

By contrast, Jamila said: "If I compare my life as it is today with the life I led ten years ago, I will say that in the past I led a difficult life. Today, I don't have to ask myself, what am I going to eat today? Now I have a TV in my house. My life has changed—I used to live in a thatched house, but now I live in a house with a tin roof. I had one farm then, but now I have two farms. Right now, we grow modern agricultural produce. For example, we grow modern tomatoes. My life has improved, but not a lot. I am grateful to God for that."

For others, their lives had remained the same. For example, Mozza, a participant in a women's focus group in Kilambo, said: "I find that my life today is similar to the life I led before. . . . Now, we have access to electricity. It has made a difference in my life, but not a lot. Now we have gas stoves, electric stoves, we have benefited from that, but life is just normal." Mozza's response regarding electricity is significant because contrary to what development planners advocating for rural electrification would have believed—that people would be delighted with the electricity in their villages, most people were worried about the associated expenses. People were pleased about the arrival of electricity but regarded a regular salaried job a truly meaningful change in local residents' lives; they could obtain other things through hard work. That these jobs never materialized explains why Mozza and others said their lives had not really improved—despite having new things like a fridge, a TV, and other material assets.

Still others gave mixed messages in their responses. Zainabu, for example, responded by saying: "My life is very hard. It's largely from despair. In fact, the past was very difficult because of the challenges of life. . . . But now, even though I don't have a motorcycle, I own the house where I live, and I have my business, I struggle for myself. . . . I'm not dependent on anyone. Even though I have only a small capital, I thank God for the things that I have." Zainabu's life was hard in the past, and it had remained so over the last ten years. She continued to struggle and to raise her children on her own. Zainabu's response is about existential insecurity. People have money and food today but do not know if they can be assured of those same things next week. In Zainabu's case, when I interviewed her about well-being, she had been recently divorced. She was not the normal, smiling, happy-looking woman I had come to know. She looked worried and did not want to share her story—especially surrounding her divorce. Nonetheless, she said that she was grateful to God for the things that she had.

Others, such as Bi Mkubwa, had seen both ups and downs over time. In my previous interviews with her in 2012, 2014, 2016, and 2017, she had repeatedly told me how well her business of supplying roasted fish to banks and other offices in Mtwara town was doing. However, in September 2019, when asked about her life in the context of her well-being, she said that her life had become difficult and that she was facing financial difficulties. "If you talk to anyone here, they'll say 'Life is difficult.' It has become like a national anthem, you listen to others and you too start singing the anthem 'Life is difficult,'" she said.

Other interlocutors used this same metaphor to highlight the scale of hardship that people were facing in Tanzania. Using her own example, Zainabu explained: "I would say that at least ninety percent of the people who live in this region resemble me in terms of the changes I have experienced in my life. In fact, whenever I make a phone call to people who live in other regions, our relatives and friends, the first thing they start narrating is the same thing—that life is hard, that their conditions are bad, that life has become very difficult . . . it has become a national song." Bihaya, who was participating in a women's focus group discussion in Msimbati, gave her perspective on how she and the people in her village were coping with a life that had become increasingly difficult. She said: "Life is constricted, we are still just struggling, we are just exasperated, we have no other option, life is hard, really. The heart is going bad. . . . But we are grateful to God (*Mwenyezi Mungu*, Allah) for protecting us, and we get satisfaction from what little we get to eat and we are alive and have a life. We are thankful to God for whatever He gives, we are grateful."

HOPES AND ASPIRATIONS FOR THE (UNCERTAIN) FUTURE

Interlocutors were asked whether they believed their lives will improve, remain the same, or worsen in the next ten to fifteen years and to elaborate on why they felt optimistic or pessimistic about their futures. They were also asked whether, in the future, they believed they would be able to fulfill their hopes and aspirations. Most interviewees gave qualified responses. Zainabu, for example, believed that "life will continue to be challenging because 'life is life,' it goes on, so you cannot say that life in the future will not be a challenge, because it is a future issue." In qualifying her thoughts, she gave an illustrative example. Her former brother-in-law had owned a coconut and cashew farm in Msimbati. She said he had been doing well. However, after a survey, the gas company had drilled a gas well on his farm—giving him compensation in return. He had gone through the compensation money quickly and was ultimately left with nowhere to harvest coconuts or cashews. "He has become a pauper [*fukara*]," Zainabu concluded.

People from Ruvula, where three of the five gas wells are located, expressed their concern that, as the gas project expanded, they would be forced to vacate the village and relocate. Kachakacha voiced his fear: "Yes, that's the fear I have and that's what I have been telling my fellow villagers, 'Let's be ready, we may be asked to leave this village anytime and go to another village and do other activities.' ... We live close to the gas wells. We live in danger zones. So I strongly believe that in the near future, we will be leaving this place [village] and going elsewhere because it is unsafe for us to continue to live in this village." Residents of Ruvula were aware of potential future threats of living in a "danger zone" (gas explosion); however, only a few interviewees specifically stated that they were concerned about having to relocate. They did not feel that evacuation was an imminent threat to their livelihoods or way of life.

Finally, when participants were asked whether they had the resources to achieve their immediate and future life goals, most of them said they did not. However, Omari concluded on an optimistic note: "If a country is as peaceful as ours—not like our neighbors, Mozambique, where there is no peace—I will be able to achieve my goals in life."

CONCLUSION

This chapter examined local conceptualizations of well-being in the marine park villages. Through their articulations, interlocuters revealed what really matters to them when they think of their well-being: money, food security, health, social relations, and so on. These constitutive elements were positioned to improve their well-being at a time when their lives are closely tied to the marine park and the gas project. As Beauchamp et al. (2018, 28) assert, "Grounded knowledge, rather than generalizations, about which well-being dimensions are prioritized and how that varies across a landscape is required when it comes to designing realistic project goals and incentives and understanding intervention impacts." By engaging with the questions of what really matters to people who live in an MPA and how the goal of biodiversity conservation levels up with people's ideas about their well-being through in-depth interviews and focus group discussions, this chapter provides crucial ethnographic insights into the limitations of Tanzania's current marine conservation policy and governance of MPAs. The marine park's dual mandate—to protect the region's marine biodiversity and to support the livelihoods and well-being of people living inside the park's boundaries—has clearly not been achieved. As documented in previous chapters, most people living in the marine park villages had been in fierce opposition to the park in its early years. They had not, they said, experienced any improvements in their livelihoods and well-being attributable to the park. Instead, they had experienced negative well-being outcomes in the form of displacement and dispossession. Men and women of all ages believed that there was no point in implementing a conservation project to protect marine biodiversity if human beings have to go hungry in the process. Women, in particular, expressed their distress, explaining that the marine park authorities' high-handedness resulted in the loss of food security and, consequently, their peace of mind. In all, men and women who were already marginalized, impoverished, and food insecure were experiencing increased social suffering as a result of the park's restrictions.

How does one reconcile the marine park's mandate to promote residents' well-being with residents' experiences of negative impacts to their well-being? What factors are most important to the people of rural coastal Mtwara to be able to lead the lives they want? As shown in this chapter, cultural interpretations and experiences of well-being among the residents of the marine park villages were heterogeneous, shifting, and complex. There were some similarities across the villages in terms of the key components of well-being—including food security and income security. There were, however, important differences across village contexts—and even within communities, households, gender, occupations (e.g., fishers versus farmers), and age groups. Beauchamp et al. (2018, 28), in their study of well-being in a conservation context in Cambodia, found "geographical location or village context to be a more important factor than gender or wealth in explaining variation in conceptualization of well-being, with generational variation being an important secondary line of variations." My findings corroborate their study in terms of the importance of geographical location compared with gender or occupation in how people conceptualize well-being. Ruvula and Msimbati residents, for example, emphasized unity and social cohesion (*umoja*) as an important component of their well-being. People in

Kilambo, on the other hand, spoke of the improved infrastructure they had seen in their village as a contributor to a good life, and also "peace" (absence of war) as vital to their well-being.

More broadly, however, participants shared a common understanding of well-being. People generally agreed that food, cash income, health, a solid house, good relationships with neighbors, peace, unity, and so on were indicators of well-being. There were patterns in discussions of well-being across different villages and generations, as well as within communities. However, there were differences and complexities across the different park villages as well. As Coulthard, McGregor, and White (2018, 247) have emphasized, "Different people have different ideas about what is important for their wellbeing and about how they should seek to achieve wellbeing; they also have different dependencies upon ecosystem services."

Older women in park villages, and especially those living with young children, emphasized food security as the most important component of their well-being. By contrast, men across all age groups emphasized the importance of money. With money, they asserted, they could buy "everything" they needed. People spoke of money in concrete terms as in the materiality of cash—to buy food, pay children's school fees—and also as a metaphor for security and freedom from everyday anxiety as well as the ability to travel when necessary.

As noted in the introduction and chapter 2, many people in the park villages, including those who were primarily subsistence farmers, relied significantly on store-bought food grains, pulses, flour, cooking oils, and sundries. People's well-being was therefore tied to their income security. Most people believed that employment—specifically a long-term salaried job with a regular monthly salary—was vital to one's well-being, as a stable income allowed villagers to purchase everyday necessities without anticipatory anxiety or stress (*dhiki*). Additionally, people frequently mentioned physical safety and comfort—a "nice house" to live in, with a proper corrugated tin roof—as basic necessities for one's well-being. Thus, interventions that aim to improve people's livelihoods through conservation are more likely to be successful, compared with those that focus on conservation without giving equal importance to the economic well-being of in situ populations. This is, of course, a well-trodden argument.

Beyond material needs, older interviewees in particular mentioned subjective aspects of well-being when specifically asked. This raises an important methodological question in the study of well-being. As Abunge, Coulthard, and Daw (2013, 1015) have pointed out, "A methodological limitation of asking an entirely open question on well-being is that some aspects of well-being might not be raised within the discussions." Like Beauchamp et al.'s (2018) study, my research revealed that well-being is contextual and, critically, that eliciting local responses to understandings of well-being without prompting has its limitations. This suggests that prompting may be a useful technique in eliciting responses about subjective and relational aspects of well-being (see also Fischer 2014).

A small number of people mentioned the ability to work hard—to be productive and provide for one's family—as an important aspect of well-being. For others, having good neighbors, family, or friends in the community who they could rely on for help during an emergency was important to their well-being. This was especially important in an increasingly neoliberal context where social safety nets offered through government programs had dwindled significantly. A majority of interlocutors described the lives as ordinary—maisha ya kawaida. For these people, a normal life was one where people struggled to meet their daily subsistence or self-sufficiency needs and faced daily struggles to ensure food and income security. In short, a normal life is one of uncertainty—especially in terms of food security. Strikingly, however, despite narratives of poverty and food insecurity, nearly all my interlocutors emphasized that they enjoyed their personal freedoms: freedom of movement and speech, freedom to pursue their occupations, freedom of religion, and the freedom to cherish and practice their traditional customs.

As this chapter shows, the meaning of well-being, and its constituent elements, varies according to, but also within, contexts. In this regard, my research confirms that understanding "local conceptions of well-being can provide insights into livelihood decisions and suggest routes toward more locally legitimate and socially just management strategies" (Woodhouse and McCabe 2018, 43). For people living in the marine park villages, their primary concern is their material well-being: a reliable source of income, food security, a privately owned form of transportation, health security, a secure house to live in, and the ability to pay school fees for their children. Other aspects of life, such as strong relationships with their neighbors and peace in their communities, were significant—but did not trump the material conditions. Initially, residents saw the marine park as a bulwark against their livelihoods and material well-being. They disregarded it as an unnecessary intervention. However, as the previous chapter explored, villagers' opinions about the marine park were beginning to change. They had started to see the park's role in improving their environment, their ecosystem, and their lives more positively.

The marine park's success is closely tied to the well-being of the in situ people. As Woodhouse et al. (2015, 6) point out, "People's current well-being takes place in the context of past experiences, as well as expectations, fears and aspirations about the future. . . . Conservation may increase feelings of insecurity, even if implemented in the hope of improving environmental security in the longer term." People living on the rural Mtwara peninsula were indeed concerned about their well-being. They were far more forthcoming when discussing their material and subjective well-being (Do I have enough food for the family? Do I have enough money? A reliable source of income to buy food? Is my life better compared with five or ten years ago?), as compared with their relational well-being (Do I live peacefully with my neighbors? Can I trust and rely on my friends and neighbors in times of need?).

As of this writing, the marine park has not been successful in creating alternative opportunities that are commensurate with the hopes, expectations, and aspirations of the local people. People decried the governance mechanisms that the park authorities had put in place, which did not resonate with local conceptions of justice. The promised income-earning opportunities from ecotourism in the region have not materialized. Livelihoods were upended because of the park's restrictions—more importantly, no alternatives were given. Regardless of the government's good intentions in implementing the marine park, contributions to the well-being of most coastal residents have been negligible.

In recent years, residents of the park villagers had begun to acknowledge the marine park's role in protecting their ecosystem, in putting an end to dynamite fishing in the area, and in urging people to protect their environment. In doing so, it indirectly contributed to local well-being. Importantly, however, a significant number of people spoke more favorably about the gas project than about the marine park, despite the gas project's role in the dispossession of their farmlands and their unforgettable experiences of state-directed violence and humiliation.[13]

Some even argued that the marine park was restricting the gas project's expansion—expansion they believed would bring them economic benefits. Residents felt that by restricting the gas project's activities, the park was hindering their employment opportunities—and by extension, their well-being. The copresence of the gas project and the marine park on the Mtwara peninsula thus complicated people's understandings of their well-being, largely along lines of materiality. For one, people living in some of the coastal villages initially believed, or were led to believe, that the marine park would contribute to their well-being through earnings from tourism and from fish abundance that would result from the *tengefu* measures. Those promises did not come to fruition. *Hamna faida* (no benefit or profit) were the two words that, for the most part, summarized the sentiments of the local people regarding the marine park. For another, the implementation of the gas project had also heightened people's expectations surrounding economic well-being, mainly through job opportunities. While a handful of people were able to secure regular employment through the gas project, it had not contributed to most people's overall well-being. In fact, it had dispossessed many local residents of their farmlands and pushed them toward food and income insecurity. Unsurprisingly, in conversations and interviews regarding well-being, most people did not mention either of the two projects. The few who did stated that if the two projects had created jobs, sustainable, alternative livelihoods, and income-earning opportunities, then people would have been able to achieve their goals and aspirations. Ultimately, in contexts of persistent and worsening poverty, money matters to meet people's immediate and aspirational goals. People yearn for a guaranteed source of monthly income to improve their economic stability and status and to contribute to a sense of empowerment and self-worth.

CONCLUSION

Conservation, Extraction, and Just Governance

IN THIS BOOK, I have traced how an ecotourism project—the Mnazi Bay-Ruvuma Estuary Marine Park—and an extractive project—the Mnazi Bay gas project—unfolded in tandem over a decade in Tanzania's southeastern coastal region. By drawing on interdisciplinary literature and ethnographic data gathered through fieldwork in Mtwara over several years, I analyzed the social complexities underlying the siting of these projects in the same geographical space. Case studies, vignettes, excerpts from life histories, and narratives form the basis of an ethnographic representation of how villagers living inside the marine park's boundaries related to the marine park and the gas project—and experienced their impacts over time. Through fieldwork, I sought to answer the following empirical questions: How did people relate to the projects in their midst? What were their perceptions of how these projects affected their everyday lives and well-being? How did these perceptions vary within and across villages, and how did they change over time?

As described in the substantive chapters, the marine park's impacts varied significantly across and within villages and among fishing and farming households. Moreover, the marine park covered a much larger geographical area compared with the gas project and its infrastructure. Therefore, residents of the marine park villages did not uniformly experience the gas project's impacts. Some villages, such as Ruvula, Msimbati, and Mngoji, abutted the gas project's infrastructure. People from these villages were dispossessed of their farmlands and trees. Other villages inside the marine park, such as Msangamkuu, Nalingu, and Kilambo, located several kilometers away, experienced the gas project mostly positively, particularly regarding access to electricity.

What lessons can be learned from the local response to these two projects, particularly regarding marine biodiversity conservation, gas extraction, human well-being, environmental justice, and social justice? How relevant and generalizable are the main findings and arguments made in this book to other MPAs in Tanzania, East Africa, and beyond? My cultural analysis of the local response to the marine park and the gas project has illustrated rural residents' profoundly complicated local dynamics and the heterogeneous, shifting responses toward state-directed conservation and extraction projects. These dynamics and responses are less tangible and measurable. They are often omitted or oversimplified in scholarly texts about environmentality or incommensurability and are only rhetorically mentioned in master plans prepared for MPAs, which tend to focus more on the biological and technical aspects and less on the social aspects of marine conservation.

As I show in this book, the response toward the marine park and the gas project varied across the region and changed over time because of a combination of factors. These factors included a realization among residents that they were powerless against the government, while they also believed that they were now better educated about the well-meaning goals of the marine park in particular. This observation regarding variation and change is crucial because it shows that change is possible, although it is contingent on serious consideration of and respect for people's agency. However, the process can take years, especially if strategic mistakes made at the MPA's planning and implementation stage must be undone. The paragraphs that follow revisit some of the key issues emerging from the substantive chapters and discuss important considerations in making marine ecosystem conservation interventions and extractive projects sensitive and responsive to environmental and social justice concerns.

REITERATING THE IMPORTANCE OF HUMAN DIMENSIONS

Scholars and advocates of marine biodiversity conservation have repeatedly emphasized that the success of MPAs depends on how much importance planners give to the biological components versus the social and cultural dimensions (see Bennett 2022; Giakoumi et al. 2018; Gill et al. 2019). They have also underscored that ensuring the well-being of local communities whose livelihoods depend on extracting marine resources is indispensable for the long-term sustainability of biodiversity conservation interventions (Palmer et al. 2017). The interconnectedness of the biological and sociocultural dimensions of MPAs has been increasingly reflected in scholarly publications, conservation forums, and master plans (Bennett et al. 2019; Charles and Wilson 2009; Mwaipopo 2008).

Despite utilizing the popular rhetoric around "people first" and community-based participatory conservation projects, empirical evidence has repeatedly revealed that conservation interventions are implemented in a top-down manner. Local stakeholders are minimally involved or remain as bystanders—with serious consequences. As Agardy, di Sciara, and Christie (2011, 227) have cautioned, "A far-too-common phenomenon that dooms many an MPA to failure is insufficient involvement of stakeholders in the planning process—either because too few stakeholders were engaged with underrepresentation of certain stakeholder groups, or because the stakeholders were brought in too late in the planning process. User groups have demonstrated a vociferous opposition to MPAs when they have no buy-in; stakeholder engagement can generate that buy-in, as can transparent, participatory planning processes."

Similarly, marine conservationists with a background in social sciences, political ecology, and anthropology, in particular, have observed that marine conservation interventions fail to achieve their intended goals when "the fine grained marine human-environmental interactions at the local scale" (Aswani 2019, 223) are downplayed. Furthermore, "international and global conservation strategies are often in complete disjuncture with resident understandings and what occurs or needs to occur locally" (Aswani 2019, 224). Situations like the ones described in this book are emblematic of the problems associated with the top-down implementation of conservation interventions. Many anthropologically grounded scholars have documented similar pitfalls in MPA interventions in East Africa (Moshy, Bryceson, and Mwaipopo 2015; Walley 2004) and other parts of the world (Eder 2005; Fabinyi, Evans, and Foale 2014; Hoffman 2014). To that end, rigorous ethnographic research into local realities provides essential insights into the impact of social complexities, interpersonal dynamics, and community-level micropolitics on MPA implementation and outcomes. With these insights, measures can be taken to prevent costly financial, social, cultural, and environmental mistakes.

EDUCATION AT "STEP ZERO"

Given growing calls to take marine biodiversity conservation more seriously and to increase the number, scope, and size of MPAs to achieve global targets, it is critical to ensure that the human dimensions of MPAs are integrated into planning and implementation from the start. While this is not a novel argument, it reaffirms what many anthropologists and social scientists have emphasized over the years regarding the problems associated with inattention to the human dimensions of MPAs.[1] It bears repeating that serious gaps exist between the rhetoric of stakeholder engagement in marine conservation and the on-the-ground realities of MPAs—despite claims to the contrary (see Bennet et al. 2021; Mascia et al. 2017).

Through examples, I have explored how failure on the part of the marine park authorities to earn the trust of its catchment population during the initial phase resulted in prolonged and often bitter resentment toward the marine park. At the same time, I have shown how people came to acknowledge the park's role in protecting their environment, despite previous determined opposition to its top-down style of governance. People explained the shift in their disposition by asserting that they had now "understood" and "appreciated" the importance of conservation, indicating that during the marine park's first phase of implementation, the proponents had failed to effectively communicate the marine park's mandate and goals—including the benefits of conserving the environment—to the local people.

This lack of "relevant education" about "institutionalized environmental conservation" (West 2016, 113) or mainstream conservation had, in turn, resulted in considerable confusion and anger toward the park by locals. Bi Mkubwa, for example, characterized the marine park's top-down interventions as "poison" (see chapter 6). Over time, however, people came to appreciate the marine park's role in helping them end destructive and unsustainable fishing practices in their region. Clearly, strategic mistakes were made from the start, despite the fact that the planners had substantial experience dealing with the social dynamics, the interpersonal wrangling, the "social drama," and acts of resistance on the Mafia Island Marine Park (see Walley 2004). Although efforts were made subsequently to mitigate the situation through educational interventions, mangrove replanting, and the district commissioner's involvement in persuading village-level leaders to confiscate and destroy illegal fishing nets, the process of reconciliation with the local communities was delayed and incurred economic and social costs. These costs could have been avoided or minimized with greater consultation and involvement of residents during implementation. As the locals repeatedly emphasized, while they appreciated the idea of the marine park as protecting the marine environment and promoting ecotourism in the region, they felt that the top-down way the marine park representatives went about implementing the project was antithetical to the very essence of the project—community engagement.

UNTANGLING THE NEXUS

Following the implementation of a gas project inside its core zone, the marine park in rural Mtwara became emblematic of the ecotourism-extraction nexus. Chapter 1 explored the broader political and historical context in which these two projects were conceived and implemented. By focusing on Msimbati and Nalingu—two large villages with divergent social and political histories—I highlighted people's diverse experiences during the various ideological shifts in Tanzania's political and social history. Tanzania had transitioned from being a socialist state to a neoliberal state. However, the vestiges of its socialist past were still intact, particularly regarding the continuation of a centralized, top-down style of governance and the de facto state ownership of all land in the country. As it turned out, the state ownership of land worked in favor of the nexus and in opposition to organized resistance from local inhabitants in the Mtwara Region. By asserting that all natural resources in the country belong to the state, the Tanzania government (Chama Cha Mapinduzi, the ruling party) had "othered" the people of Mtwara and used violence as a means to repress any form of opposition to the marine park and the gas project (chapters 3 and 4). The government justified the violence as necessary to achieve the country's developmental goals. As Andreucci and Kallis (2017, 100) have shown in their case study of Peru, governments use violence against those who oppose extractive activities or policies, particularly marginalized communities who live in extractive frontiers, by "othering" Indigenous people, by depicting them as "enemies of the people" and justifying the use of violence that sustains extraction "as a necessary condition of possibility of the country's development." More broadly, the people of Nalingu, Msimbati, and Mtwara had experienced firsthand the lengths the government would go to achieve its "developmental goals," including the use of extreme violence.

Chapter 5 focused on local perceptions of the ontological (in)commensurability of the marine park and the gas project and the project's environmental and social justice impacts on local communities. Local people's understandings and responses to the copresence of these projects varied across social hierarchies (local elites versus ordinary citizens), gender (men versus women), age (older citizens versus the youth), and geographical locations (villages near the gas project's assemblages versus those farther away). In other words, there were spatiotemporal differences in residents' narratives and intra- and inter-village variations in how people articulated their sense of environmental and social justice—and how their viewpoints shifted over time. Most Mtwara residents were not opposed to the gas project, despite its damaging effects on people's livelihoods and the environment. Some residents wanted the gas project scaled up, believing this would contribute to socioeconomic development in Mtwara by strengthening infrastructure and generating employment opportunities.

More broadly, given that the gas project, and particularly the gas pipeline, was predominantly state-owned (TPDC), the nature of the ecotourism-extraction nexus was different from what it would have been—in terms of corporate social responsibility, claims of biodiversity conservation, greening or greenwashing, and also exclusionary practices, for example—had it been owned and operated by a multinational oil and gas company (cf. Adams 2017; Enns, Bersaglio, and Sneyd 2019; Le Billon 2021; Osti et al. 2011; Pedersen and Jacob 2017; Pedersen and Kweka 2017). Since all land in Tanzania is "public land" vested in the president, the nature of the nexus and territorialization was considerably less complicated in terms of land acquisition, compensation, environmental and social impact assessment, and clearance. Some residents alleged that the government had implemented the marine park primarily to seize the land, fence it, and convert it into an enclosure to protect gas exploration and extraction activities. Others argued that it was a good thing the marine park was present, as it provided oversight of the gas project's potential excesses and prevented potential vandalism of the gas project's infrastructure. Such differences between the marine park communities' interpretations underscore the need to appreciate the complexities and nuances in studies of the ecotourism-extraction nexus.

Implementing a gas project in the same geographical space as the marine park was not as disconcerting for most people living on the rural Mtwara peninsula as I had initially expected. Awareness of the gas project's potential environmental damage was minimal, even among those who lived near the gas project's infrastructure. The project's promise of infrastructure development, electricity, and job opportunities had eclipsed the promises that the marine park representatives had made during the early years of its implementation—of better income-earning opportunities, alternative livelihoods through ecotourism, fish abundance, and so on.

In all this, there was significant variation in how people perceived and responded to the copresence of the gas project and the marine park in the same area—within and between villages. People living farther from the gas project's infrastructure were less concerned about environmental impacts. Most people could not clearly articulate what damage the gas project might be doing other than to say the gas was "too hot" and unsuitable for the fish. Even people living only a few meters from the gas project's infrastructure downplayed the project's environmental impact—although some acknowledged that they were living in a danger zone where a deadly gas explosion was looming.

Despite these differences, the ethnographic data highlighted that people in Mtwara were optimistic about development opportunities and largely unconcerned with the ideological or ontological incompatibility of the marine park and the gas project. They justified any discrepancy in their understanding by emphasizing that these were both government projects and that "the government knew what it was doing." This euphemism acknowledged their powerlessness against the government, which they had learned through lived experience, particularly during the state-directed violence unleashed on them in May 2013 (see chapter 4).

POWERLESSNESS

Notwithstanding people's experiences of dispossession, displacement, and unfair compensation, there was no organized protest in the marine park villages against the government or the gas company (see chapters 3 and 4). There was no discussion, either in everyday conversations or in the media, about how the gas project and its expansion might damage the very space that the government had territorialized as an MPA. When the Tanzanian state demonstrated its willingness to use deadly force against its citizens to suppress protests or dissent against the gas project in 2013 (chapter 3), very few people in Mtwara town were aware that the gas project was located inside an MPA. Additionally, awareness regarding land ownership and land rights in the marine park villages was generally low (chapter 4). As Ruth Hall et al. (2015, 471) have observed: "Social groups that [are] expelled or threatened with expulsion by land deals, or whose livelihoods are threatened more generally, do not automatically get organized and mount resistance.... Classic literature on agrarian politics [suggests] that there are triggers of and conditions for the emergence of these kinds of politics, and that the presence or absence of allies may be key to the kind of reaction that emerges 'from below.' Probably most of those who suffer from 'unjust land deals' do not openly resist." Despite deep feelings of injustice, residents who had lost their farmlands and trees did not pursue organized protest because of feelings of powerlessness and fear of violent state-led repression. Moreover, dispossession, displacement, and the potential for forced relocation were embedded in people's collective historical memory—particularly from the ujamaa era (see chapter 1).

Remembered violence featured prominently in people's cultural memory of both projects. Msimbati residents experienced terror in 2013 at the hands of security forces in connection with the gas project. Nalingu residents also experienced significant physical violence and harassment from security forces during the early stages of the marine park. Yet, people had taken a more pragmatic view of the situation over several years. They discontinued engaging in illegal and unsustainable fishing practices. Local leaders publicly condemned these practices and demonstrated their resolve by burning illegal nets in their respective villages and levying fines on those who violated the marine park's regulations.

Throughout this book, I have suggested that people living in the park villages had initially understood the marine park's ability to bring economic benefits in the form of tourism-related jobs and income-earning opportunities—not so much in terms of biodiversity conservation. When these economic benefits failed to materialize, people were disappointed; they began to see the marine park as a barrier in their lives. They wanted it to go away (*utoweke, uhamishwe*) but could not do anything to persuade the government to discontinue the marine park. Recall Athumani's statement (chapter 4) that if the marine park were a private company, the villagers would have driven it away a long time ago—but because it was a government project, they felt powerless in taking such drastic action. Other scholars have recorded similar sentiments of powerlessness amid resentment in the Mafia Island Marine Park (see Moshy, Bryceson, and Mwaipopo 2015; Walley 2004). Indeed, Holmes (2013) has argued that conservation projects can be successful even without the support of local communities.[2] It could be argued that the marine park was "successful" in that it could continue its mandate without support from local residents.

Put differently, the Tanzanian state had succeeded in wearing down the people living in park villages to the point that they felt utterly powerless in opposing park authorities or resisting the restrictions that were put in place. People rationalized their acquiescence by saying that the government had implemented the project with good intentions and that they were now educated about the importance of the park's role in protecting their environment. Arguably, the residents' preoccupation with their daily struggles surrounding food and income security further deterred them from organized protests against the marine park or the gas project. Their powerlessness underscored their rationale for refraining from organizing protests against these interventions.

WHEN CHANGE TAKES TIME

After over a decade of persistent opposition, residents began to accept the marine park and its regulatory practices. By mid-2016, overt opposition to the marine park had largely faded from the region. This attitudinal shift was noticeable in people's everyday discourse and practice. Destructive and unsustainable fishing practices, such as dynamite fishing and illegal fishing nets like beach seines and small mesh nets (kokoro), had mostly stopped. This transition—from overt opposition to a reluctant but general acceptance of the marine park and its activities—occurred over several years. While the shift became noticeable in 2016, triangulated data revealed that individuals' perspectives had been shifting for over a decade in the park's key villages. If residents had indeed become environmental subjects in relation to marine conservation, their subjectivities had changed gradually because of multiple factors.

Human agency was important, i.e., people's initiative and desire to cooperate. Recall, for example, statements from my interlocutors in Mkubiru, who asserted that destructive fishing practices had stopped not only because of patrolling and police interventions but also because of their participation in the monitoring activities. Mwanaidi, a "village environment committee member," asserted that the park authorities would not have been able to end unsustainable fishing practices independently; they needed the villagers' active cooperation (see chapter 6). In other words, people's agency and desire to change their behaviors and practices—their "will to improve" (Li 2007) their environment—was integral to understanding why people do or do not become environmental subjects in the context of multiple environmentalities (see Youdelis 2019, 2).

Chapter 6 focused on the concepts of environmentality, environmental subjects, and multiple environmentalities to analyze the environmental narratives and discourses that varied across different villages. I demonstrated "how conservation discourse and practice manifest within particular locales" (Fletcher 2010, 172) and change over time. Additionally, I argued that there is more to environmentality than persuading people to participate in "institutional regimes of environmental protection"—such as environment committees or beach management units. I illustrated that "environmentality" and "environmental subjects" are produced over long periods, in that it often takes several years for people's disposition toward the environment to change. Moreover, agentive aspects (i.e., people deciding to protect their environment) play a vital role in this change. Even then, not everyone in even the most environmentally engaged village (in this case, Msimbati) was concerned about caring for the environment. Recall, for example, Kachakacha (chapter 6), who was volunteering at the marine park, emphasizing the need to demonstrate patience in changing people's ideas and practices regarding the environment. As he put it, "It is something you must follow up on." The creation or emergence of environmental subjects requires patience and consistency—and environmental education is only a first step.

WELL-BEING MATTERS

The book's last ethnographic chapter (chapter 7) explored whether the marine park and the gas project had any perceived impacts on the well-being of local residents. Detailing how people in the study villages understood and explained human well-being (ustawi), with its material, relational, and subjective components, I examined how they perceived their well-being in relation to the marine park and the gas project's activities. The overwhelming response among those directly affected by the projects was that both projects had undermined key components of their well-being: food and income security. Moreover, these projects had not contributed toward improving their capabilities—their livelihoods, food security, freedoms, and hope. In essence, most people on the Mtwara peninsula did not associate the marine park or the gas project with their well-being. Advocates had sought to convince the local people that the marine park and its regulatory practices would improve the peninsula's coastal ecosystem. In their view, this would, in turn, contribute to the well-being of the local people, who rely on ecosystem services for their livelihoods and well-being. In short, a healthy, well-functioning, biodiverse ecosystem would improve food security, health, livelihoods, and well-being for the local populations. Overall, both projects' perceived positive impacts were marginal and limited to only a few individuals (see chapter 4). The benefits, if any, were negated by the losses they had incurred through the dispossession and displacement of their livelihood assets. Except in Kilambo, interlocutors argued that the quality of the infrastructure and services had worsened over the years—the quality of health care at the local clinics had stagnated, the roads had not been repaired or covered with asphalt as was originally promised, plentiful jobs never materialized, and the promise of free electricity was not fulfilled (see also Barlow 2022). Even those with access to electricity complained that they were paying their bills (tariff) at the same rate as Tanzanians elsewhere in the country; they had not received any discounts or privileges in exchange for losing their farmlands. As for the marine park, people repeatedly stated that they had not benefited from its activities. The promise that fishers would be given modern and legal nets and fishing boats was fulfilled minimally in some select villages. Those affected by the two projects explained that their lives and livelihoods had been disrupted as they were further pushed into poverty and insecurity that they had not experienced before.

To conclude, successful win-win biological and social outcomes through MPAs are at once aspirational and challenging to realize. Therefore, social and political complexities must be continuously negotiated to ensure human well-being in conjunction with sustainable marine biodiversity conservation. Despite the rhetoric in the marine park's General Management Plan around sustainability and community involvement, few policy statements were implemented in practice. Village committees were barely active. Indeed, for the most part, the marine park was implemented using the "fortress conservation" model, with fences and fines, leading to prolonged bitterness and disillusionment among local resource users. The scenario described in this book clearly shows that developing and implementing a governance strategy that is just and responsive to peoples' food security concerns, gender relations, social hierarchies, aspirations, and well-being is indispensable for sustainable marine biodiversity conservation. Moreover, in contexts where the implementation of a marine conservation project is accompanied by an extractive project in the same geographical space, a just governance strategy becomes even more important in ensuring environmental *and* social justice (Bennett et al. 2019; Bennett et al. 2021; Martin 2017).

The extraction of oil, gas, and minerals in protected areas is legal in Tanzania, provided certain conditions are met (Holterman 2020; Jacob et al. 2016; MacKenzie et al. 2017; Pedersen et al. 2016). However, environmental degradation, dispossession, and displacement of local people and land alienation have immediate and long-term impacts that cannot be downplayed. Nor can these effects be justified on the grounds that national interests precede human well-being in project-affected communities. Instead, undesirable environmental and social impacts should be anticipated, problematized, documented, and mitigated to ensure that those directly affected by the gas project are rendered the environmental and social justice they deserve. These justice-affirming interventions should include recognition, dignity, fair compensation, employment opportunities, alternative livelihood opportunities, food security, freedoms, and hope.

Studying perceptions of incommensurability and experiences of dispossession in Mtwara demonstrates that notions of environmental and social justice are local. They also vary within and across communities—which outsiders often perceive as homogenous. Therefore, it is important to consider local contexts and justice concerns when planning and implementing conservation and extractive projects. Put differently, social science and ethnographic studies should be a proactive aspect of the MPA planning process rather than an exercise to "mop up the problems" (see Aswani 2019; Blount and Pitchon 2007). Moreover, as Martin (2017, 54) has emphasized, "Justice is a social construct [in] that it means different things to different people, and ... claims about justice and injustice can only really be understood through reference to the particular circumstances that surround it." As this book demonstrates, ideas about justice and what is fair and unfair are spaciotemporal. They change in light of new experiences and reflections.

Regarding the ecotourism-extraction nexus, most people on the Mtwara peninsula did not see the two projects as incommensurate; they did not see the presence of the two projects in the same geographical space as paradoxical or as a source of anxiety. Instead, they saw both projects as emblematic of state power and domination that had resulted in their dispossession. They acknowledged that both projects belonged to the government and deferred to the "experts," thus acknowledging their powerlessness in standing up to the government. Tanzania's long history of a one-party state, top-down interventions, centralized governance as well as state violence and domination had buttressed attitudes of deference toward the government (see chapter 1). When viewed in terms of the government's unbridled power to control and extract resources from land and sea in the name of national interest, the two projects were indistinguishable to residents.

Inattention to the human dimensions of conservation can result in high social and economic costs. These costs affect not only the conservation initiatives but also local populations. With this in mind, this book provides important insights into what *not* to do when planning and implementing MPAs. It also illustrates how on-the-ground situations can be complicated by implementing extractive projects inside MPAs—leading to confusion and unrealistic expectations among local residents. Finally, this book demonstrates the importance and usefulness of ethnographic insights for developing conservation interventions and extractive projects that are cognizant of human well-being through just governance. The extractive industry's economic and social impact on local communities has reemerged as a critical component of corporate social responsibility and national policy documents. Accordingly, the government of Tanzania must adhere to some of the provisions it has made in its policies to increase transparency and engage with local-level actors in a meaningful manner. The aim should be to mitigate the harms that the gas development activities have brought to the people of Mtwara. In this regard, accountability mechanisms must be instituted to ensure equitable compensation for those who have lost their farmlands and other livelihood assets to the gas project, deepening their poverty. Those at the helm of policymaking and governing actions must act in response to people's concerns regarding dispossession, violence, compensation, and employment of those who have lost their land and livelihoods to the gas project. Crucially, on the marine conservation front, at a time when global commitments have been made to protect at least 30 percent of the world's oceans from human interventions by 2030, the number of MPAs around the world will certainly increase. The hope is that in pursuit of this global conservation effort, human health and well-being will be given the same level of importance as the health of the oceans and marine life.

EPILOGUE

Insurgency and Counterinsurgency

TWO WEEKS BEFORE my departure from Tanzania in September 2019, I traveled to Mkubiru to take photos of the different types of houses in the village and to schedule another round of interviews with my interlocutors. The baraza, near the entrance to the village, served as a place for me to chat with the men who had gathered there. It was a simple shaded structure made of wooden poles and palm fronds. Six logs from a dead coconut tree functioned as seats; two boda boda drivers had parked their motorcycles inside the baraza for shade.

As I showed the photos I had taken that day with my phone to the men resting under the baraza, Yusuf Amri took the phone out of my hand and started flipping through the photos on his own. I knew he was just being inquisitive, but the ease with which he had taken the phone out of my hand made me uncomfortable. After swiping through a few more photos, Yusuf asked me, "Why do you come here all the way from Canada?"

"To do research. I like it here," I said and asked for my phone back.

The conversation drifted to China. Some men wondered how far Mtwara was from Beijing. "So many people from Mtwara are going to China these days," one of them said.

"It is very far, yes, very far," I said.

FIGURE 12 The baraza in Mkubiru village

While we were speaking, to my pleasant surprise, Ali Mfaume had rushed home and returned with an old paperback *Oxford School Atlas*. Soon, everyone was poring over maps—asking me to check on my phone the distance in kilometers from Mtwara to Beijing, from Mtwara to Vancouver, and so on.

"Now you can leave that iPhone for me," Yusuf quipped, and we all laughed. None of them were interested in discussing marine conservation with me that day. They were far more interested in finding out from me what life was like in *ulaya*, or Canada. They knew that Artumas, the company that had started extracting natural gas in the Mnazi Bay area, was Canadian. They also knew that a Chinese state-owned company had built the Mtwara–Dar es Salaam gas pipeline. "But we still don't have electricity and running water in Mkubiru," one of them complained.

I had made plans to return to the field the following year to study how the cessation of destructive and unsustainable fishing practices in Mtwara had affected the food security situation in the marine park villages. The COVID-19 pandemic–related restrictions on travel and doing in-person interviews for ethical and health reasons delayed my plans to return to Tanzania to do additional research. Nonetheless, I remained in regular contact with my research assistants, who provided me with news and updates—and, occasionally, photographs from the field. I found it difficult to discuss my research in Mtwara without referring to the pandemic's looming presence, which was unfolding with devastating intensity across the globe.

I traveled to Mtwara in August 2022 after a three-year hiatus. I wanted to reconnect with some of my key interlocutors and do follow-up research. When I arrived on the main road connecting Mtwara town and Nalingu village, my destination that day, I was surprised to see a group of men, women, and teenagers managing a roadblock. One of them approached me with a serious face and asked for my *kitambulisho* (ID—passport and research permit), which I had left in the guesthouse in Mtwara town, where I was staying. I soon found out that villagers had set up similar roadblocks and checkpoints at the entrance to every village I entered. The Tanzania army had instructed villagers to set up these checkpoints and to check every vehicle for potential terrorists (*magaidi*) to prevent cross-border attacks on local villages and villagers by "al-Shabaab terrorists" from the Mozambican side of the border. Every village office had a list of names prominently displayed on a board of local villagers assigned duties to manage the roadblocks and take turns, day and night, surveilling and monitoring the roads. People were told to remain vigilant and to keep an eye out for suspicious individuals and activities.

One midafternoon in August 2022, as I stepped out of the village government office in Msimbati, a convoy of heavily armed commandos in their balaclavas sped through the village in their 4x4 military vehicles at high speed toward the marine park's gate office, raising clouds of dust. I was overwhelmed by the sight. However, the newly appointed female village executive officer (VEO), in her midtwenties, and some of my key interlocutors with whom I had just finished a meeting were nonchalant. "They are going to the camp," the VEO told me calmly and matter-of-factly. Ruvula, the site of the gas wells and the marine park's prime beach, had become an army camp as part of the counterinsurgency measures following the terrorist attacks on the gas project in the gas-rich Cabo Delgado Province on the Mozambican side, operated by France's TotalEnergies. Somoye, one of my interlocutors, resentfully said: "We managed to save ourselves from *korona* [COVID-19], but now we have this new *janga* [disaster]—terrorists. The army has closed our beach. Our fishers have been told to use ring nets and to catch fish in the deep waters. However, the security forces have advised them not to venture too far into the ocean, or near the Ruvuma River, for fear of being attacked or kidnapped by terrorists from the Mozambican side. Maisha imekua magumu, magumu sana (Life has become hard, very hard)."

That same week, I spent time chatting up local residents—men, women, and children—in Mnazi, inside the marine park, and making notes on my observation on the beach. I had befriended several young fishers in the village while conducting research focused on how the marine park residents were dealing with the compounding effects of COVID-19 and the war in Ukraine on food security (price of wheat and cooking oil had doubled) and with the threat of cross-border terrorism (*ugaidi*) and terrorist attacks (*shambulizi*). As I watched the fishers repair the large ring nets and asked them questions related to their fishing trips, they would often ask me for a *buku* (TSh1000/50 cents) to buy food, reiterating that life had become difficult and that fishing had become an unworthy occupation—that there were too little fish in the ocean and too many people who were going out to catch fish in the same area.

Young women would wander around near the village center with empty buckets (*ndoo*, small plastic cooking oil drums) in their hands or on their heads. Close to the beach a raised concrete platform served as a fish market—a place for fishers to auction their catch. The platform also served as a spot for the village chairman to make some announcements. Young women with their plastic buckets would sit along the platform, for three or four hours, chatting with one another while waiting for the fishing boats to return as the tide came close to the shore. As I sat under the awning of one of the small thatched huts on the beach, watching the ocean tide at a distance, some young women came and sat next to me, using their empty upturned buckets as seats. I engaged in a casual conversation with them, asking whether they were living in Mnazi or Nalingu and whether they were fish vendors (*wachuuzi*). To my surprise, only one or two women I conversed with described themselves as fish vendors—they were in Mnazi to buy fish and sell it for profit elsewhere in Mtwara. Most of the young women who came to the beach with the buckets were there to earn a buku. One such young woman had returned from her trip to Dar es Salaam the previous evening and joined her friend with a bucket to earn a buku or two that day to buy food for herself and her four-year-old daughter. They would sit there for hours, patiently waiting for the fishing boats to arrive with their catch. On each boat, there were between twelve and fifteen fishers, each with their ring net, buoys, and fishing sticks. Between twenty and twenty-five women would wade through the hip-deep water, toward the boat(s) and carry back a bucketload of fish on their head, most commonly dagaa. Once on shore, the women took the fish to the central marketplace or straight to the flat grounds behind the village to sundry. Fishers or their agents auctioned the catch on the beach as well as in the central marketplace—for double the prices I had recorded in 2019. A pile of small barracuda fish now sold for TSh19,000 ($8 USD). A bucket of dagaa sold for TSh22,000 ($9 USD). And a bucket of sundried dagaa sold for Tsh40,000 ($16.50 USD). Other reef fish, including a medium-size parrot fish, sold for Tsh2,500 ($1.50 USD) each. The process was quick, and all the fish were sold in a matter of minutes. The busy central market platform would quickly empty of people. Women would trail the shoppers, offering to clean the fish on the beach before selling it back to the buyer.

Amid these significant changes in the Mtwara Region, a brand-new signage welcoming visitors to the marine park had been installed at the intersection in Madimba. A new dirt road connecting Madimba and Msimbati had been cut through the fields and forests, bypassing the sprawling gas processing plant in Madimba. This was done for regional security concerns but also to keep it "out of sight" of people and potential tourists who travel between Madimba and Msimbati. The new bypass road and community-managed checkpoints and roadblocks in every village were part of the Tanzania government's counterinsurgency measures following the cross-border attacks by insurgents, claiming to be al-Shabaab, from the Mozambican side. These incidents had resulted in several deaths and destruction of property in some of the border villages, particularly Kitaya. Effectively, the marine park had been militarized.

NOTES

INTRODUCTION

1. There is a rich body of scholarship on the complicated history and politics of terrestrial conservation in East Africa, particularly in Tanzania (see Adams and Hutton 2007; Adams and McShane 1992; Benjaminsen et al. 2013; Bluwstein 2017; Brockington, Duffy, and Igoe 2008; Brockington, Sachedina, and Scholfield 2008; Gardner 2016; Kideghesho et al. 2013; MacKenzie 1988; Neumann 1998; Nelson 2012; Sirima and Backman 2013; Weldemichel 2020).
2. A protected area refers to "a clearly defined geographical space, recognised, dedicated and managed, through legal or other effective means, to achieve the long term conservation of nature with associated ecosystem services and cultural values" (Dudley 2008, 8). A marine reserve is a type of marine protected area, usually small in size, where fishing, harvest of marine animals, and development are legally prohibited. Marine parks are usually larger in terms of their boundaries. IUCN defines a marine protected area (marine park) as "any area of intertidal or subtidal terrain, together with its overlying water and associated flora, fauna, historical and cultural features, which has been reserved by law or other effective means to protect part or all of the enclosed environment" (Kelleher 1999, xviii; see also Laffoley 2008). See Laffoley et al. (2019) and Wells et al. (2016) for an insightful early and contemporary history of MPAs around the world.
3. Ethnographic research and theorizing on aspects of *marine* conservation on East Africa's coast is relatively sparse (Kamat 2014; Moshy and Bryceson 2016; Mwaipopo 2008; Walley 2004). The dominance of biological and economic approaches in the study of marine conservation may partly explain the dearth

of studies on its social dimensions (Coulthard, Johnson, and McGregor 2011, 455; see also Aswani 2019).

4. See Chaigneau and Brown (2016) for a detailed discussion on the problems associated with win-win discourses in conservation and development, with a focus on MPAs.

5. Despite historical conflicts, scholars have emphasized that MPAs can be valuable management tools in maintaining marine biodiversity and supporting the well-being of coastal populations concurrently (Aswani and Furusawa 2007; Bennett and Dearden 2014; Fox et al. 2012; Mascia et al. 2017). At the same time, scholars have also provided empirical evidence demonstrating substantial challenges and difficulties in the successful implementation of MPAs in different parts of the world (Agardy et al. 2011; Eder 2005; McClanahan and Abunge 2015; McClanahan et al. 2009). Over the years, social scientists—particularly anthropologists—have made repeated calls to researchers and policymakers to pay equal attention to the social impacts of MPAs as they do to their biological impacts. This is vital to actualize so-called win-win scenarios in marine conservation (Aswani 2019; Blount and Pitchon 2007; Broad and Sanchirico 2008; Charles and Wilson 2009; Christie 2004; Fabinyi, Evans, and Foale 2014; Ferse et al. 2010; Mascia, Claus, and Naidoo 2010; Sowman and Sunde 2018).

6. See Arsel and Büscher (2012), Büscher et al. (2012), Büscher, Dressler, and Fletcher (2014), Fletcher, Dressler, and Büscher (2014), Gardner (2016), Hill, Byrne, and de Vasconcellos Pegas (2016), Neumann (1998).

7. See also Büscher and Fletcher (2020) for a discussion on "the great conservation debate" in the Anthropocene, or Capitalocene, and the relationship between neoliberalism and neoprotectionism.

8. Anthropologists Blount and Pitchon (2007, 106) have argued that although MPAs are created principally to manage human behavior, the selection criteria are geared primarily toward biological and ecological factors in the protection of marine life and habitat. Consequently, the place and role of people in relation to the MPA tends to become secondary.

9. See Enns, Bersaglio, and Sneyd (2019) and Holterman (2020). Moreover, there is growing concern that protected areas across Africa are being downgraded, downsized, degazetted (PADDD) to accommodate natural resource extraction (Albrecht et al. 2021; Edwards et al. 2014; Mascia et al. 2014).

10. See for details Gardner (2016). From a political ecology perspective, these areas have been "territorialized through conservation" (see Bluwstein and Lund 2018; Neumann 2001; Vandergeest and Peluso 1995; see also Fletcher Chmara-Huff 2014 for territorialization in relation to MPAs).

11. Following independence, the Land Acquisition Act of 1967 was introduced; it provided the legal basis for acquiring land for "public purpose." This included the extractive sectors, large-scale agricultural investments, urban development, industrial sites, and housing. In 1999, the Land Act No. 4 and Village Land Act No. 5 were introduced. The 1999 land acts, which came into force on May 1,

2000, divided all land in Tanzania into three categories: general land, reserved land, and village land. "Reserved land refers to lands set aside for special purposes such as forest reserves and game reserves and are governed by nine different laws. Village land refers to that land managed by each village council. General land is all land that is neither reserved land nor village land" (Gardner 2016, 73). As Pedersen et al. note, the 1999 Land Act marks an improvement in procedural rights—that is, people's right to information, participation, and compensation when compulsory acquisition of land takes place. This act is significantly different from the wide-ranging discretionary power granted to the state by the 1923 colonial land ordinance and the 1967 Land Acquisition Act (Pedersen et al. 2016; see also Gardner 2016). I return to a discussion of the relevance of these land acts in the book's later chapters.

12. See Aswani et al. (2018); Bauer and Ellis (2018), Büscher and Fletcher (2020), Dewan (2021), Mathews (2020), Moore (2019), and Vaughn (2022).

13. The success of MPAs as optimal tools to conserve marine biodiversity and human well-being is predicated on numerous factors, such as the MPA's age, size, location, style of governance, funding, and a host of sociopolitical, cultural, and contextual factors determining access to resources and their usage (Bennett and Dearden 2014; Bennett et al. 2019; Christie 2004; Mascia et al. 2017; Sowman and Sunde 2018).

14. See for example, Agardy et al. (2011), Benjaminsen and Bryceson (2012), Bennett and Dearden (2014), Bennett et al. (2016), Charles et al. (2016), Christie (2004), Christie et al. (2009), Christie et al. (2017), Chuenpagdee et al. (2013), Eder (2005), Jentoft, Cheunpagdee, and Fernandez (2011), Moshy, Bryceson, and Mwaipopo (2015), and Sowman and Sunde (2018).

15. Numerous researchers have demonstrated that "conflict is often at the heart of protected-area establishment and maintenance"—both terrestrial and marine (West, Igoe, and Brockington 2006; see also Anderson and Berglund 2003; Anderson and Grove 1987; Brockington 2008; Butt 2012; Garland 2008; Hoffman 2014; Holmes 2007; Levine 2007; McClanahan et al. 2009; Sanchirico, Cochran, and Emerson 2002; Sesabo, Lang, and Tol 2006; Upton et al. 2008). In the marine park's context, researchers have indicated how violent conflicts between the park managers and the locals—the purported beneficiaries of the marine park—threatened the project's long-term sustainability (Gawler and Muhando 2004; Robinson, Albers, and Kirima 2014).

16. See, for example, Aswani (2019), Bennett and Dearden (2014), Blount and Pitchon (2007), Charles and Wilson (2009), Christie (2004), Christie et al. (2003), Chuenpagdee et al. (2013), Ferse et al. (2010), Levine (2004), Rosendo et al. (2011), Singleton (2009), and Voyer, Gladstone, and Goodall (2013).

17. See Bennett and Dearden (2014), Chaigneau and Brown (2016), Christie et al. (2017), and Rees et al. (2013).

18. Buffer zones are created to reduce fishing pressure within the marine ecosystems and promote sustainable development.

19. See Guard and Masaiganah (1997), UNDP/GEF (2004), Guard and Mgaya (2002), Machumu and Yakupitiyage (2013), Malleret-King (2004, 10), and Mwaipopo and Ngazy (1998).
20. These consultations led to the adoption of the Mtwara Resolution on Mnazi Bay-Ruvuma Estuary Marine Park in April 1999 (see Tortell and Ngatunga 2008, 29).
21. In September 2010, Artumas Group Inc. changed its name to Wentworth Resources Limited as a result of a business combination transaction between the two companies. In November 2018, Wentworth Resources Limited reregistered as Wentworth Resources Plc. (RPS Energy Consultants Ltd. 2019, 1–2).
22. The gas-to-electricity power plant in Ruvula generated first electricity on December 24, 2006. Commissioning of the Mnazi Bay gas processing facility and tie-in connection to the Mtwara area power generating facility was completed on March 5, 2007 (See for details RPS Energy Consultants Ltd. 2019, 1, 3, 4).
23. Drawing on Büscher and Davidov's (2013) "ecotourism-extraction nexus" thesis, Fletcher (2013, 70) has also argued that "far from the aggressively antagonistic adversaries they are commonly considered, (industrial) extraction and (postindustrial) ecotourism can be understood as two sides of the same neoliberal coin." The need to problematize the analytical opposition between ecotourism and extraction is to dispel the popular belief that these two interventions are somehow adversarial and that their coexistence is unacceptable or inexplicable. I will be returning to this point repeatedly in various chapters of this book.
24. See Lal (2015), Liebenow (1971), and Seppälä and Koda (1998, 56).
25. See Kamat (2013).
26. The Mtwara Development Corridor (MDC) was inaugurated in 2004 as a Spatial Development Initiative (SDI), comprising the contiguous areas of southern Tanzania, northern Mozambique, northern and central Malawi, and eastern and northern Zambia (Lal 2015).
27. See Cinner (2010), Grilo, Chircop, and Guerreiro (2012), and Wells et al. (2009).
28. See Braulik et al. (2017), Guard and Masaiganah (1997), Fox and Caldwell (2006), Katikiro and Mahenge (2016), Slade and Kalangahe (2015), Samoilys and Kanyange (2008), and Tobey and Torell (2006).
29. A wide range of gear is used in the marine park villages, including set nets of various mesh sizes, *kokoro, kavogo, juya* (beach seine nets), hand lines, long lines, spears, spear guns, *tandilo* (mosquito) nets, traps, and tidal weirs.
30. See Green (2014, 104) for a discussion on the symbolic and practical significance of the village visitors' book in Tanzania.
31. My initial research into the social and economic impact of the MDC on project-affected people in Mtwara led me to examine the marine park's social impact—particularly in villages that were inside the park's boundaries.
32. The anthropological literature on "infrastructure" has burgeoned in the last few years, spurring new theoretical engagement and numerous empirical studies

focusing on built infrastructural networks, pipelines, oil rigs, roads, bridges, city water supply, and so on (see, for example, Hetherington 2019).

33. There is a growing body of literature on China's involvement in Africa and its influence in the region (see Kinyondo 2019; Ross 2013). In Tanzania's case, Chinese involvement dates back to the 1970s, epitomized most materially by the Tanzania-Zambia Railway (TAZARA), also called Africa's Freedom Railway (Monson 2009).

34. See Jacka (2018, 68) on why the environment may not be the primary point of contention for locals in contexts of mining operations.

35. The concept of "good life" has found a footing in mainstream anthropology (Fischer 2014), but to my knowledge, social scientists focused on biodiversity conservation have so far centered their attention on the concept of well-being. In some cases, they have used it interchangeably with good life.

36. The latest census was conducted from August 23 to September 5, 2022.

37. Liebenow (1971) and Wembah-Rashid, (1998) have provided insights into the origins of the Makonde people in the Mtwara Region. Factors such as natural disasters, the villagization program that was implemented on the Tanzanian side in the late 1960s and early 1970s, and the Mozambican War of Liberation from Portugal in the early 1970s, where the nationalist party Frente de Libertação de Mocambique (Frelimo) had begun a long and bloody liberation struggle against Portuguese rule, also contributed to the Makonde people's migration (officially refugees) from Mozambique to Tanzania (Lal 2015, 22–23; Sætersdal 1999, 126).

38. Of the 140 individuals who participated in my research between 2016 and 2019, 104 (74 percent) described their primary source of livelihood as farming (*mkulima*), and only 2 (1.4 percent) individuals relied exclusively on fishing. Moreover, 75 (53.5 percent) of the households were neither raising chickens nor livestock.

39. While Islam allows for polygyny, very few men I interviewed were actively living polygamously. Divorce was extremely common. Of all the people I interviewed on the subject in 2014, only two women in their early fifties said that they had never been divorced. Twenty-two of the eighty (27.5 percent) women I spoke with between 2014 and 2015 were not married at the time of their interviews. Most had either been divorced or were living with someone to whom they were not yet married (*sijaolewa, bado*, "not married, not yet," as against *nina mume*, i.e., "I have a husband," which was a common expression). Some of my older interlocutors—men and women—had married and divorced five or six times in their lives. While divorce itself was not frowned on, divorced women experienced a range of hardships, particularly financial insecurity in their lives. I elaborate on the intense distress experienced by these women in the substantive chapters, which focus on social suffering and well-being. Divorces were generally initiated by men, though some women did demand divorce on various grounds. Incompatibility and "unacceptable behavior" (philandering, disobey-

ing) were the two most common explanations for divorce. In a small number of cases, divorced couples later remarried.

40. The issues underlying social complexities are occasionally acknowledged in policy documents and master plans, such as the marine park's master plan, but they are not acted on in top-down approaches to conservation and extractive interventions. As a result, the gap between the stated objectives of marine conservation and the on-the-ground reality remains wide—a fact that must be acknowledged, addressed, and narrowed through attention to local context and consideration of local issues by scholars, policymakers, and conservation interventionists.

CHAPTER 1

1. On Tanzania's early political history, see Askew (2002), Coulson (1982), Keshodkar (2013), and Shivji (2012).
2. John Magufuli died on March 17, 2021. Vice President Samia Suluhu was sworn in as Tanzania's sixth and current president.
3. See Askew (2002, 180), Coulson (1982, 235), McHenry (1994, 16), and Walley (2004, 109).
4. Until 1977, TANU was the only legal political party on the mainland (McHenry 1979, 61). TANU, which became the CCM party, continues to dominate the political landscape well into 2023 and rules the republic against a weak opposition that has limited resources and no unifying message (cf. Katundu 2018; Cheeseman, Matfess, and Amani 2021).
5. See Askew (2002, 237) and Kikula (1997).
6. See Snyder (2001, 135), Coulson (1982), Barkan (1994), McHenry (1994), and Tripp (1997).
7. See Baregu (1994) and World Bank (1993).
8. See Brockington, Duffy, and Igoe (2008), Brockington, Sachedina, and Scholfield (2008), Gardner (2016), Nelson, Nshala, and Rodgers (2007), Nelson (2012), and Walley (2004).
9. Mwinyi's rule (1985–95) is remembered as a period of *ruksa*, a Kiswahili word perhaps best translated as "full permission to do your own thing."
10. See Baregu (1994) and Weiss (2002).
11. See Issa Shivji (2012, 112) for a critique of Mkapa's ten years in power (1995–2005).
12. See Cooksey (2017), Gratwick, Ghanadan, and Eberhard (2006), and Gray (2015) for details on the Richmond scandal and the Independent Power Tanzania Limited (IPTL) scandal.
13. Over the next nine years (2010–19), I returned to these six villages to conduct fieldwork. I held group discussions and interviewed people—many of whom I had interviewed before while documenting their life histories. This strategy of returning to conduct in-depth interviews with the same individuals from previous rounds of fieldwork was initially done out of convenience, but it soon

proved to be very useful in ensuring continuity in the narratives that I elicited. It also allowed me to return to the same individuals to verify information I had recorded during previous interviews and informal conversations and, in some cases, learn about the significant changes that had taken place in their lives from one year to another.

14. See Nordstrom (1997) for a detailed ethnographic analysis of the brutal war between Frelimo and the Portuguese colonial forces beginning in the 1960s till independence was achieved in 1975. Thereafter, the then white-majority Rhodesian government (now Zimbabwe), and later the South African government, created and trained an anti-Frelimo rebel group called Renamo (Resistencia Nacional Mozambiqueña—Mozambican National Resistance) to destabilize the Frelimo-led Mozambican government.
15. See Lal (2015) on rural Mtwara residents' nostalgic representations of the past.
16. Thousands of Chinese nationals lived in Tanzania in the 1970s, when the Chinese-funded Tanzania-Zambia (TAZARA) railway was being constructed over a period of eleven years (see Monson 2009).

CHAPTER 2

1. The United Nations identifies four components of food security: (1) availability of food (e.g., fish); (2) access; (3) utilization, i.e., the ability to prepare and consume the food; and (4) the stability of the food base (UNDG 2011; see also Charles et al. 2016, 170).
2. The chapter is based on the data I gathered over four years—2010, 2011, 2012, and 2013—in six coastal villages on the rural Mtwara peninsula.
3. See Aswani and Furusawa (2007), Aswani and Weiant (2004), Cinner et al. (2014), Darling (2014), Fabinyi, Dressler, and Pido (2017), Foale et al. (2013), McClanahan, Allison, and Cinner (2015), Moshy, Masenge, and Bryceson (2013), Moshy, Bryceson, and Mwaipopo (2015), and Walley (2004).
4. See Rosendo et al. (2011) for a discussion on the importance of community participation in MPAs.
5. At the time, I interviewed mainly older men and women—including leaders, village chairpersons, and village executive officers. I did not interview the youth or young fishers until 2013, when I focused attention on youth perceptions of dynamite fishing.
6. The early experiences of the people on Mafia Island with the MIMP had caused some villagers in the coastal villages on the Mtwara peninsula to be skeptical of the claims made by those promoting the marine park. Several researchers have documented the general unpopularity of the MIMP among local fishing households during its formative years (Walley 2004; Benjaminsen and Bryceson 2012; Moshy, Bryceson, and Mwaipopo 2015; Mwaipopo 2008).
7. The subject of gear exchange remained contentious (see Katikiro 2016; Robinson, Albers, and Kirima 2014).

8. Rehema's allegations regarding the mooring buoys were not unfounded. The Audit Report (URT 2018, 20–21) reveals that the marine park authorities had not installed any mooring buoys for all three years under audit.
9. See Walley (2004) and Levine (2007) for similar discursive dissonance in the contexts of the Mafia Island Marine Park and Zanzibar's MPAs.
10. See Aswani and Furusawa (2007), Darling (2014), Mascia, Claus, and Naidoo (2010), Moshy, Bryceson, and Mwaipopo (2015), Moshy, Masenge, and Bryceson (2013), Mwaipopo (2008), Weiant and Aswani (2006), and Walley (2004).
11. See Mangora, Shalli, and Msangameno (2014), Moshy, Masenge, and Bryceson (2013), Moshy, Bryceson, and Mwaipopo (2015), Mwanjela (2011), and Walley (2004).
12. The question of whether MPAs increase, decrease, or have no impact on people's overall food security remains contextual and debatable.
13. See Aswani and Furusawa (2007), Eder (2005), Moshy, Masenge, and Bryceson (2013), Moshy, Bryceson, and Mwaipopo (2015), Moshy and Bryceson (2016), and Walley (2004).
14. According to the Mtwara Region Socio-economic Profile, published by the government of Tanzania (URT 2018, 30), 37 percent of the households in Mtwara Rural were eating three meals a day, 58 percent were eating two meals a day, and 5 percent were eating only one meal a day—indicating food insufficiency in the region—based on data collected in 2007/8.
15. During one Maulidi festival in Sinde, a group of twelve women gathered early in the morning under a mango tree to prepare about 100 kilos (220 pounds) of rice. Prior to the celebration, the rice had been stored in twenty-liter plastic buckets and tubs, which were more commonly used for washing clothes. The women used large winnowing sieves to clean the rice for *pilau*, the main course for the occasion. In a makeshift outdoor kitchen a few meters away, another group of women were cooking meat with aromatic spices while chatting loudly with one another. By midafternoon, male volunteers had transformed the area by putting dark blue plastic tarpaulin and plaited mattresses (*mkeka*) around the tree. Eight village elders in their white *kanzus* and embroidered *kofias* (caps) had taken a distinguished place under the tree. A public address system was set up under the tree in preparation of the upcoming celebration. Shortly after, fifty young boys between the ages of six and fourteen arrived, wearing their colorful madrasa (Qur'an school) uniforms. The boys sat opposite one another, each carrying either a drum (*duf*) or a tambourine. At the same time, a group of fifty young girls wearing golden hijabs and colorful printed skirts arrived. They were seated at a distance from the boys. Guided by the village elders and the *shehe* (priest), the children began to sing while rhythmically swaying. Alongside the boys, adult men began to sing and sway. Soon, adult women gathered behind the girls and joined the celebration. The joyous singing and dancing lasted for half an hour. The shehe then used the microphone to give a sermon while helpers lit the aromatic *uudi* (incense) and incense sticks that were placed

under the tree. This was followed by two older boys playing the flute. By then, a different group of young girls and boys in the colorful uniforms of another village's madrasa had arrived for the celebration. Later in the afternoon, the shehe delivered a second sermon, and upon its conclusion, all those present enjoyed a feast of the pilau and soda.

16. Ivers and Cullen (2011) and Moreno-Black and Guerron-Montero (2006). See also Baker-Médard (2016) and Walker and Robinson (2009).
17. Baseline studies on the socioeconomic and occupational structure of the communities slated to be included in the marine park's boundaries were conducted prior to the park's actual implementation in 2000. Additional studies were conducted in 2004 (Malleret-King 2004; Malleret-King and Simbua 2004), but these baseline studies did not focus on food security in quantitative terms.
18. See Weaver and Hadley (2009) and Pike and Patil (2006) for a discussion on the association between food insecurity and maternal anxiety, mental health, depression, and distress.

CHAPTER 3

1. At the time, my research permit was limited to conducting research on food security in the marine park villages. I did not have permission to gather data specifically related to the gas project, which was one of the reasons I decided to stay away from the rig.
2. See Anyimadu (2016), Green (2014), Lokina and Leiman (2014), and Shanghvi and Jingu (2013).
3. See Ahearne and Childs (2018), Appel (2019), Barlow (2022), Calignano and Vaaland (2018), Kinyondo and Villanger (2017), Jacob and Pedersen (2018), Lange and Kinyondo (2016), Lange and Wyndam (2021), Moshi (2014), Must (2018), and Must and Rustad (2019).
4. The development of gas finds in the Mnazi Bay concession area was pursued through Artumas Group (Artumas), a small Canadian-based independent energy company. Artumas became Wentworth-Resources in 2008 and was sold to Maurel & Prom (M & P) in 2009. Between 2009 and 2012, when additional offshore gas deposits were discovered, the "gas rush" involved about twenty oil and gas companies—including major international oil companies, such as BP, ExxonMobil, Ophir, Petrobras, Shell, and Statoil (now Equinor). However, only after the Chinese government became involved in the project (offering a $1.2 billion soft loan to the government of Tanzania to build a pipeline from Mnazi Bay to Dar es Salaam) that the gas project took on a new meaning and was greatly expanded. Artumas had initially taken on this project with the aim of generating electricity and supplying it directly to potential customers; in reality, it ended up supplying gas to the state-owned TANESCO. TANESCO in turn took control of the gas-generated electricity (see Pedersen and Bofin 2019, 413 and 417).

5. Artumas had proposed a plan in 2004 to develop the Mnazi Bay gas fields to supply liquefied natural gas (LNG) and compressed natural gas (CNG), especially to Kenya (Artumas 2004, 3).
6. As of this writing, despite media reports of the Tanzania government's keen desire to kickstart the ambitious LNG project, progress on the project has been slow, with few potential investors.
7. The violent protests that took place in the Mtwara Region in May 2013 were preceded by nonviolent protests in December 2012, and in the Lindi Region in May 2012 (Poncian 2019).
8. This chapter draws on the data I gathered in the rural Mtwara Region in July and August of 2013, and from August to December of 2014.
9. In David Harvey's (2005) analysis of Marx's classic theory of primitive or original accumulation—which he reinterpreted as "accumulation by dispossession" for modern-day social analysis—incorporates some of Marx's fundamental tenets without the temporal assumption found in primitive accumulation (Hall 2013; West 2016, 19). While some scholars use primitive accumulation and accumulation by dispossession interchangeably, others make a conceptual distinction between the two (Hall 2013, 1585).
10. The Songo Songo gas project, which was initiated in the 1990s and designed to supply gas to the power plant in Ubongo, Dar es Salaam, was several years behind schedule. It became operational only in 2004 (Pedersen and Bofin 2019, 416).
11. The long delay between the initial gas discoveries in the Mnazi Bay area in 1982 and the impetus to develop the gas fields starting in 2003 was due to many factors (see for details Bofin, Pederson, and Jacob 2020, 9–10).
12. In the interim years, Tanzania's energy sector was sullied by numerous grand corruption scandals. Gray (2015) has detailed some of the well-known grand corruption scandals under the presidencies of Benjamin Mkapa and Jakaya Kikwete (see also Anyimadu 2016; Bofin, Pederson, and Jacob 2020; Cooksey and Kelsall 2011; Cooksey 2017).
13. See Appel (2019, 200–21) for an explanation of a "Dutch Disease."
14. See Lokina and Leiman (2014), Moshi (2014), Poncian (2014), and Shanghvi and Jingu (2013).
15. See Lee and Dupuy (2018), Melyoki (2017), Mwanyoka, Mdemu, and Wernstedt (2021), Pedersen and Bofin (2015), Pedersen and Bofin (2019), Pedersen and Kweka (2017), Poncian (2018), and Poncian (2019).
16. See Ahearne (2016), Lal (2015), Ndimbwa (2014), Must and Rustad (2019), Poncian (2018), and Poncian (2019).
17. See Pedersen and Bofin (2019), for details about the pipeline.
18. Artumas acknowledged the environmental sensitivity of the project site in Mnazi Bay—that it was an MPA. Accordingly, it conducted an environmental impact assessment (EIA) in accordance with the World Bank Group's Category "A" requirements (Artumas 2004, 23).

19. Land acquisition has been a particular focus of attention as well, especially given Tanzania's statist land tenure regime and the "re-emergence of state-owned enterprises as direct investors in operations and as holders of key infrastructure" (Pedersen and Kweka 2017, 916). In Tanzania, the right to own property is guaranteed by the Constitution of the United Republic of Tanzania (1977) (Oxfam 2017, 19–20). The Land Acquisition Act, 1967; the National Land Policy, 1995; the Land Act, 1999; and the Village Land Act, 1999, call for fair and prompt compensation if land is appropriated for public use (Nuhu et al. 2020, 986).
20. As Pedersen and Bofin (2019, 413–14) point out, although Artumas was keen to generate and supply electricity by itself, it ended up handing over the responsibility to TANESCO because of the Tanzanian authorities' dislike of a fully private solution.
21. See Moshi (2014); Pedersen and Bofin (2015); Shanghvi and Jingu (2013).
22. See Levien (2013, 383) for similar analysis in the Indian context.
23. Distributive justice refers to more equitable distribution of the benefits deriving from the exploitation of natural resources (see Horowitz 2011, 1380; see also Abuya 2015).

CHAPTER 4

1. One reviewer of the manuscript asked as a rhetorical question: "How many anthropologists would approach communities as spatially bound, homogenous, or static structures?" The obvious answer is none. The truism in anthropology is that communities are by definition dynamic, heterogeneous, and multivocal. And yet, in master plans and policy documents, including those calling for community-based conservation (CBC) interventions, proceed on the assumption that somehow communities are homogenous and coherent and that providing education to "the community" about matters related to conservation will result in jubilant win-win outcomes. For criticism of this flawed approach, see Büscher (2013) and Bennett (2019).
2. See Agrawal and Gibson (1999), Baker-Médard (2016), Eder (2005), and Horowitz (2011).
3. See Charles et al. (2016), Gruby et al. (2016), and Fox et al. (2012).
4. See Baker-Médard (2016) for an ethnographic perspective on gender bias, gender inequalities, and underrepresentation of women in marine conservation in Madagascar.
5. See Benjaminsen and Bryceson (2012), Bennett and Dearden (2014), Bunce, Brown, and Rosendo (2010), Christie (2004), Chuenpagdee et al. (2013), Katikiro (2016), Katikiro, Macusi, and Deepananda (2015), Levine (2004), McClanahan et al. (2009), Moshy, Bryceson, and Mwaipopo (2015), Voyer, Gladstone, and Goodall (2013), and Walley (2004).
6. See Chaigneau and Brown (2016), Fabinyi, Evans, and Foale (2014), Fabinyi, Faole, and Macintyre (2015), McShane et al. (2011), and Benjaminsen and Bryceson (2012).

7. Inspired by Bangladesh's Grameen Bank, VICOBAs are small savings banks that member villagers manage.
8. Here, Jamali complicates oft-told narratives about how individuals in peripheral regions such as Mtwara are consistently economically oppressed and subjugated by state apparatus. Jamali instead shows that these individuals have agency and the desire to support and strengthen their government. I thank Jan Lim for reminding me about this point.
9. Sadala spoke about climate change and sea level rise in a different interview I conducted with him in 2016.
10. As the former chairman of Msimbati and a protagonist of the marine park, Sadala had most likely internalized the negative narratives about the in situ resource users' role in damaging the ecosystem by engaging in destructive extractive practices. Accordingly, he focused on his own and his community's responsibility in the rising sea level, as opposed to considering the global factors that had contributed to climate change. I thank Olivia Brophy for calling my attention to this interpretation.
11. See Manjela and Lokina (2016, 149) for similar findings regarding the "disconnect" between how the marine park authorities perceive land inside the park's boundaries and how "local communities view land as property with which they can decide to do whatever they want."
12. Here, Makonde acknowledges that all land in Tanzania is public land, vested in the president on behalf of all citizens.
13. The Southern Zone Confederation for Conservation of the marine environment (SOZOC) and community-based organization (CBO) most commonly known as SHIRIKISHO had taken the initiative in 1996 to end dynamite fishing in Kilwa, Lindi, and Mtwara Districts.
14. During my fieldwork and through a detailed analysis of the narratives that I had elicited, I found that men in general did not use certain locally meaningful words and expressions like *wametunyenga nyenga* or *wametudhoofika*. These were more commonly used by women to express their distress. Instead, I found that men would use the word *kutulaghai*, as in cheating, hoodwinked, or being betrayed, to express their disappointment with the marine park.

CHAPTER 5

1. Many people in the park villages had not actually visited the gas project's infrastructure in Ruvula, but they had seen the vast, highly visible TPDC gas-processing plant sited along the main road connecting Madimba and Msimbati.
2. See Brockington, Igoe, and Schmidt-Soltau (2006), Coumans (2010), (2011), Escobar (1998), Fabinyi, Evans, and Foale (2014), Gilberthorpe and Rajak (2017), Martin, Akol, and Gross-Camp (2015), Martin et al. (2016), Twinamatsiko et al. (2014), Willow (2014), Willow and Wylie (2014), West (2016), and West, Igoe, and Brockington (2006).

3. See also Agrawal (2005a, 2005b), Tsing (2005), and Li (2007).
4. Doing seismic surveys involves carving one-meter-wide trains in a grid across the entire exploration zone, setting explosive charges at intervals of several hundred meters, and detonating these charges to generate an echogram of the underground in pursuit of geological signs that might mean gas or oil is present (Gustafson 2020, 206).
5. The significance of Habiba's comment lies in the fact that local residents were not sufficiently informed or educated on matters related to their land rights. They were in a disadvantaged situation, which made negotiation and advocacy work difficult. At the same time, it showed that people were genuinely concerned with these legal and economic matters.
6. This anecdote also shows that knowledge of land tenure is varied but does exist in the community (cf. Habiba's comments with Bi Mkubwa's response). Bi Mkubwa had been significantly involved in conservation work with the marine park authorities and the WWF. This experience had informed her response. I thank Chung Liu for calling my attention to this point.
7. Rather than being condescending toward Habiba or other participants in the discussion, Bi Mkubwa came across as someone who was worried about the lack of education and information regarding the legality of the two projects prevalent in her community.
8. Interlocutors demonstrated that they did understand a protected area in the Western sense, where entry is restricted and, in some cases, completely prohibited. Outside of the Western context, there are sacred forests, sacred groves, etc., where entry is either completely prohibited or restricted to certain individuals from the community.
9. Although electricity was first generated in Msimbati from Artumas's twelve-megawatt gas-fired power plant in Ruvula in December 2006, it took more than ten years for electricity to reach villages on the Mtwara peninsula where I conducted fieldwork. These included villages like Msangamkuu and Nalingu. Mkubiru did not have electricity when I visited the village in August 2022.
10. Hassani's assertion that the marine park was established solely as an enclave or an enclosure to "control the land" was not widely shared among the people of Msimbati. Perhaps several other people in Msimbati and Ruvula held the same view, but they did not express it in interviews or informal conversations, or it was not the most important concern on their minds when talking about the two projects.
11. These missteps and incompetence, including inadequate patrols to prevent illegal activities inside the park's boundaries, have been documented in the Controller and Auditor General's report (2018) on the marine park.
12. As a resident of Nalingu, Abubakar was not directly affected by the gas project's infrastructure, including the pipeline. Moreover, his lack of support for the marine park hinged on his belief that it had not brought any tangible benefits to the people who lived inside its catchment area.

13. In September 2019, I found out that the government had leased three thousand acres of agricultural land to SJ Sugar Distillery and Power Private Company (through the Tanzania Investment Centre), an Indian investment company which planned to grow sugarcane and start a sugar factory in Kilambo. The factory would double as an energy-producing (electricity) installation as part of the Southern Agricultural Growth Corridor of Tanzania (SAGCOT) (Kilimo Kwanza) policy initiative. During a chance meeting in Kilambo, the project coordinator of SJ Sugar delved into a description of his proposed sugar factory and fifteen-megawatt power plant. He said, "If you come here after two years, you won't recognize this place—it'll be fully developed, with electricity." He went on to say that 70 to 80 percent of the employees on his project would be Tanzanian citizens. I interjected, "I'm here to do research on marine conservation. You know that this is a marine park." He looked at me with a blank expression, as if to say he did not understand what I told him. Perhaps he was not aware that the three thousand hectares of land he had been allotted by the government, on which he planned to grow sugarcane and set up a sugar factory, was inside the marine park. In March 2020, SJ Sugar had planted sugarcane seedlings on five hundred acres of land near Kilambo. Heavy rains, however, had swelled the Ruvuma River, which had flooded the plantation and destroyed the entire farm. With the Kilambo project scuttled, the government had offered the investor alternative farmland of up to ten thousand acres in Mahurunga and Kihimika—villages that were inside the marine park, but the project never really took off, in part because of the threat of terrorist attacks from the Mozambican side in October 2020 (see epilogue).
14. On the Mozambican side of the Ruvuma River, the government of Mozambique has refrained from declaring an MPA in Cabo Delgado Province because of the vast quantity of natural gas that was discovered off the coast in 2010. The multibillion-dollar LNG project is managed by the French energy giant TotalEnergies.

CHAPTER 6

1. See Kamat (2019), Katikiro and Mahenge (2016), Katikiro, Macusi, and Deepananda (2013), and Slade and Kalangahe (2015).
2. Discursive shifts in relation to the environment are to be expected. Walley (2004), for example, reports that while she was on Mafia Island doing her doctoral dissertation–related fieldwork, the people of Chole in particular were very supportive of the marine park and applauded its role in stamping out dynamite fishing on their island. Three years later, however, when she returned to Mafia Island to do some follow-up fieldwork, she noted that the people who were once supportive of the marine park were now angry and resentful of it, blaming it for making their lives miserable—for exploiting them and pushing them to the brink of hunger and death. As noted in chapters 2 and 4 of this

book, I recorded similar sentiments expressed by the inhabitants of Msimbati, Nalingu, and Mkubiru—where most people were vehemently opposed to the marine park's presence in their villages. In this chapter, however, I document quite the opposite scenario: how and why the discourse of opposition shifted to one of general support for the marine park and its activities, after years of active opposition.

3. Governmentality, or "conduct of conduct," refers to how we rationalize the use of power to create subjects from the level of the state down through smaller institutions and eventually to how we discipline ourselves (Peterson et al. 2017, 403; see also Andreucci and Kallis 2017, 96–97).

CHAPTER 7

1. See Abunge, Coulthard, and Daw (2013), Breslow et al. (2016), Coulthard, Johnson, and McGregor (2011), Coulthard, McGregor, and White (2018), Gill et al. (2019), Martin (2017), Woodhouse et al. (2015), Woodhouse et al. (2017), and Woodhouse and McCabe (2018).
2. In 2019, I extended the geographical scope of my research to include Kilambo as one of the study villages, given its significance and location inside the marine park's catchment area (see chapter 2).
3. Fischer (2014, 207) reminds us that a well-rounded understanding of well-being cannot be founded on numerical analysis alone. Instead, it must integrate, as anthropologists would argue, "a subjective understanding of what people value, what their view of the good life is and could be, the pathways they see for realizing their aspirations." In other words, while material considerations such as money do matter to a person's sense of well-being, they cannot singularly convey the intricate details of one's worldview.
4. The Capability, or Capabilities, Approach focuses not only on the *end* goals of increased well-being but also on the *means* to achieve these goals, conceptualized in people's *capabilities* to function—what people are able to choose to do and to be. Sen (1999) argues that it is people's freedoms and choices to live the lives they want to lead that are ultimately important. Capability, therefore, speaks directly to the overarching "freedoms and choices" component of well-being and is at the heart of the MA framework (Abunge, Coulthard, and Daw 2013, 1012; see also Nussbaum 2011, 28).
5. See for example, Agarwala et al. (2014), Ban et al. (2019), de Lange, Woodhouse, and Milner-Gulland (2016), and Woodhouse et al. (2015).
6. The specific questions were drawn and adapted from different sources (Abunge, Coulthard, and Daw 2013; Buzinde, Kalavar and Melubo 2014; Coulthard, McGregor, and White 2018; Gross-Camp 2017; Woodhouse et al. 2015; Woodhouse et al. 2017; Woodhouse and McCabe 2018) and modified to reflect the local context and the research focus. I interviewed seventy adult women and seventy adult men in August and September of 2019—with the help of my

research assistants. I also conducted fourteen focus group discussions in the marine park villages.

7. Of the 140 interviewees, 84 percent were living in their own homes; the remaining 16 percent lived in rented houses. Two-thirds (66 percent) were living in an *udongo* (mud and wattle) house; 15 percent in a *matofali* (cement bricks) house, and the remaining 19 percent were living in a house made of mud, dead coral, and cement. As much as 82 percent of the interviewees owned agricultural land ranging from one acre to ten or more acres. Of the interviewees, 45 percent owned less than three acres of land, and 18 percent (five men, twenty women) did not own any agricultural land. Of the interviewees, 90 percent did not own any fishing gear—neither nets nor boats.

8. These terms or phrases—good life, ordinary life, difficult life—do not easily translate directly into English and have culturally specific meanings related to temporal and subjective changes in people's lives (see Baker et al. 2021).

9. As with several of the older participants, Bi Mkubwa prioritized food and income security but also listed good health care as an important component of one's well-being.

10. The reference to a good life here is to the visible assets: the quality of one's house, a concrete house with a tin roof, a motorcycle, a TV with a satellite dish, clothes worn by family members, etc. Goals often refer to owning a successful farm, engaging in a business venture, replacing a thatched roof with a tin roof, having electricity in the house, and paying children's school fees so they can receive their education.

11. Relational aspects of a good life may be more important for women for securing material resources. Women may be engaged in caretaking for dependents, including sharing material resources with their children. They may also be more heavily reliant on male family members to receive an income. As a result, women may present themselves as having more multifaceted lived experiences of well-being. Equally, subjective forms of well-being are also more relational, i.e., ability to be free from abusive relationships, ability to care for children. I thank Jan Lim and Olivia Brophy for calling my attention to this interpretation.

12. As Nussbaum (2011, 28) clarifies, the "Capabilities Approach is not a theory of what human nature is, and it does not read norms off from innate human nature. Instead, it is evaluative and ethical from the start: it asks, among the many things that human beings might develop the capacity to do, which ones are the really valuable ones, which are the ones that a minimally just society will endeavor to nurture and support? An account of human nature tells us what resources and possibilities we have and what our difficulties may be. It does not tell us what to value."

13. Many people believed that the gas project had provided the people of Mtwara with at least one tangible benefit—electricity, although many found it difficult to pay the bills. By contrast, they had not yet seen the fruits of the marine park.

These responses, however, varied across different villages and across other factors, including socioeconomic differences and occupational status.

CONCLUSION

1. See Aswani (2019), Bennett (2022), Bennett and Dearden (2014), Bennett et al. (2017), Bunce, Brown, and Rosendo (2010), Blount and Pitchon (2007), Charles and Wilson (2009), Charles et al. (2016), Christie (2004), De Santo (2013), Gruby et al. (2016), Mascia (2003), McGregor, Salagrama, and Bahadur (2014), Pomeroy, Parks, and Watson (2004), and Walley (2004).
2. In his case study of the Ebano Verde Scientific Reserve in the Dominican Republic, Holmes (2013, 80) has argued that conservation organizations are far more powerful and resourceful than they present themselves to be. Consequently, their projects do not need support from the local people to be successful in achieving their goals. Holmes notes that the people living inside the reserve were all too keen for it to be declassified so that they could reclaim their traditional forest resources. However, the villagers were forced to bide their time, in recognition that "they were largely prevented from challenging the reserve and altering its policies by memories of state violence, lack of time and opportunities to coordinate action against the reserve, social links to guards and cultural norms of behaviour, and the inability to reach important decision-making arenas."

REFERENCES

Ablo, Austin, and Vincent Asamoah. 2018. "Local Participation, Institutions and Land Acquisition for Energy Infrastructure: The Case of the Atuabo Gas Project in Ghana." *Energy Research and Social Science* 41:191–98.

Abunge, Caroline, Sarah Coulthard, and Tim Daw. 2013. "Connecting Marine Ecosystem Services to Human Well-Being: Insights from Participatory Well-Being Assessment in Kenya." *Ambio* 42 (8): 1010–21.

Abuya, Willice. 2013. "What Is in a Coconut? An Ethnoecological Analysis of Mining, Social Displacement, Vulnerability, and Development in Rural Kenya." *African Studies Quarterly* 14 (1–2): 1–21.

Abuya, Willice. 2015. "Mining Conflicts and Corporate Social Responsibility: Titanium Mining in Kwale, Kenya." *Extractive Industries and Society* 3 (2): 485–93.

Ackah-Baidoo, Abigail. 2012. "Enclave Development and 'Offshore Corporate Social Responsibility': Implications for Oil-Rich Sub-Saharan Africa." *Resource Policy* 37 (2): 152–59.

Adams, Jonathan, and Thomas McShane. 1992. *The Myth of Wild Africa*. Berkeley: University of California Press.

Adams, William. 2017. "Sleeping with the Enemy? Biodiversity Conservation, Corporations and the Green Economy." *Journal of Political Ecology* 24 (1): 243–57.

Adams, William, and Jon Hutton. 2007. "People, Parks and Poverty: Political Ecology and Biodiversity Conservation." *Conservation and Society* 5 (2): 147–83.

Agardy, Tundi, Giuseppe Notarbartolo di Sciara, and Patrick Christie. 2011. "Mind the Gap: Addressing the Shortcomings of Marine Protected Areas Through Large Scale Marine Spatial Planning." *Marine Policy* 35 (2): 226–32.

Agarwala, Matthew, Giles Atkinson, Benjamin Fry, Katherine Homewood, Susana Mourato, J. Rowcliffe, et al. 2014. "Assessing the Relationship Between Human

Well-Being and Ecosystem Services: A Review of Frameworks." *Conservation and Society* 12 (4): 437–49.

Agrawal, Arun. 2005a. "Environmentality, Community, Intimate Government, and the Making of Environmental Subjects in Kumaon, India." *Current Anthropology* 46 (2): 161–90.

Agrawal, Arun. 2005b. *Environmentality: Technologies of Government and the Making of Subjects*. Durham: Duke University Press.

Agrawal, Arun, and Clark Gibson. 1999. "Enchantment and Disenchantment: The Role of Community in Natural Resource Conservation." *World Development* 27 (4): 626–49.

Agrawal, Arun, and Kent Redford. 2009. "Conservation and Displacement: An Overview." *Conservation and Society* 7 (1): 1–10.

Ahearne, Robert. 2016. "Development and Progress as Historical Phenomena in Tanzania: 'Maendeleo? We Had that in the Past.'" *African Studies Review* 59 (1): 77–96.

Ahearne, Robert, and John Childs. 2018. "'National Resources? The Fragmented Citizenship of Gas Extraction in Tanzania." *Journal of Eastern African Studies* 12 (4): 696–715.

Albrecht, Renee, Carly Cook, Olive Andrews, Kelsey Roberts, Martin Taylor, Michael Mascia, and Rachel Kroner. 2021. "Protected Area Downgrading, Downsizing, and Degazettement (PADDD) in Marine Protected Areas." *Marine Policy* 129: 104437.

Anderson, David, and Eeva Berglund. 2003. *Ethnographies of Conservation: Environmentalism and the Distribution of Privilege*: New York: Berghahn Books.

Anderson, David, and Richard Grove. 1987. "Introduction: The Scramble for Eden: Past, Present and Future in African Conservation." In *Conservation in Africa: Peoples, Policies and Practice*, edited by David Anderson and Richard Grove, 1–12. Cambridge: Cambridge University Press.

Andreucci, Diego, and Giorgos Kallis. 2017. "Governmentality, Development and the Violence of Natural Resource Extraction in Peru." *Ecological Economics* 134:95–103.

Andrews, Greg. 1998. "Mafia Island Marine Park, Tanzania: Implications of Applying a Marine Park Paradigm in a Developing Country." *ITTMES Case Studies: Destructive Fishing Practices and Collecting Methods.*

Anyimadu, Adjoa. 2016. "Politics and Development in Tanzania: Shifting the Status Quo." Chatham House, March 18, 2016.

Appel, Hannah. 2019. *The Licit Life of Capitalism*. Durham: Duke University Press.

Araghi, Farshad. 2009. "Accumulation by Displacement: Global Enclosures, Food Crisis, and the Ecological Contradictions of Capitalism." *Review (Fernand Braudel Center)* 32 (1): 113–46.

Arsel, Murat, and Bram Büscher. 2012. "Nature™ Inc.: Changes and Continuities in Neoliberal Conservation and Market-Based Environmental Policy." *Development and Change* 43 (1): 53–78.

Artumas. 2004. *Annual Report*. http://www.ageorg.ca/Reports/Artumas-Annual-Report_2004.pdf.

Artumas. 2005. *Annual Report*. http://www.ageorg.ca/Reports/Artumas-Annual-Report_2005.pdf.
Artumas. 2006. *Annual Report*. http://hugin.info/136496/R/1120508/206026.pdf.
Askew, Kelly. 2002. *Performing the Nation: Swahili Music and Cultural Politics in Tanzania*. Chicago: University of Chicago Press.
Aswani, Shankar. 2019. "Perspectives in Coastal Human Ecology (CHE) for Marine Conservation." *Biological Conservation* 236:223–35.
Aswani, Shankar, Xavier Basurto, Sebastian Ferse, Marion Glaser, Lisa Campbell, Joshua Cinner, et al. 2018. "Marine Resource Management and Conservation in the Anthropocene." *Environmental Conservation* 45 (2):192–202.
Aswani, Shankar, and Takuro Furusawa. 2007. "Do Marine Protected Areas Affect Human Nutrition and Health? A Comparison Between Villages in Roviana, Solomon Islands." *Coastal Management* 35 (5): 545–65.
Aswani, Shankar, and Pamela Weiant. 2004. "Scientific Evaluation in Women's Participatory Management: Monitoring Marine Invertebrate Refugia in the Solomon Islands." *Human Organization* 63 (3): 301–19.
Avery, R. 2003. "Marine and Terrestrial Conservation Planning: How Different Are They?" In *Conserving Marine Environments: Out of Sight, Out of Mind*, edited by Pat Hutchings and Daniel Lunney, 18–40. Mosman, Australia: Royal Zoological Society of New South Wales.
Baker, Dana, Grant Murray, Jackson Kaijage, Arielle Levine, David Gill, and Makupa Enock. 2021. "Relationships Matter: Assessing the Impacts of a Marine Protected Area on Human Wellbeing and Relational Values in Southern Tanzania." *Frontiers in Marine Science* 8:1–14.
Baker-Médard, Merrill. 2016. "Gendering Marine Conservation: The Politics of Marine Protected Areas and Fisheries Access." *Society and Natural Resources* 30 (6): 723–37.
Ban, Natalie, Georgina Gurney, Nadine Marshall, Charlotte Whitney, Morena Mills, Stefan Gelcich, et al. 2019. "Well-Being Outcomes of Marine Protected Areas." *Nature Sustainability* 2:524.
Baregu, Mwesiga. 1994. "The Rise and Fall of the One-Party State in Tanzania." In *Economic Change and Political Liberalization in Sub-Saharan Africa*, edited by J. A. Widner, 158–81. Baltimore: Johns Hopkins University Press.
Barkan, Joel, ed. 1994. *Beyond Capitalism versus Socialism in Kenya and Tanzania*. Boulder, Colo.: Lynne Rienner.
Barker, Jonathan. 1979. "The Debate on Rural Socialism in Tanzania." In *Towards Socialism in Tanzania*, edited by Bismarck Mwansasu and Cranford Pratt, 95–124. Toronto: University of Toronto Press.
Barlow, Aidan. 2022. "Piping Away Development: The Material Evolution of Resource Nationalism in Mtwara, Tanzania." *Journal of Southern African Studies* (2022):1–19.
Barlow, Aidan. 2023. "The Temporalities of Extractive Frontiers: The Promises of Booms and Going Bust in the Tanzanian Gas Sector." *Geoforum* 138 (2023):103664.

Barry, Andrew. 2006. "Technological Zones." *European Journal of Social Theory* 9 (2): 239–53.
Bauer, Andrew, and Erle Ellis. 2018. "The Anthropocene Divide: Obscuring Understanding of Social-Environmental Change." *Current Anthropology* 59 (2): 209–27.
BBC. "Tanzania Mtwara Gas Riots: 'Pregnant Woman Killed.'" May 24, 2013. https://www.bbc.com/news/world-africa-22652809.
Beauchamp, Emilie, Emily Woodhouse, Tom Clements, and Eleanor Milner-Gulland. 2018. "'Living a Good Life': Conceptualizations of Well-Being in a Conservation Context in Cambodia." *Ecology and Society* 23 (2): 28.
Becker, Felicitas. 2019. *The Politics of Poverty: Policy-Making and Development in Rural Tanzania* Cambridge: Cambridge University Press.
Benjaminsen, Tor, and Ian Bryceson. 2012. "Conservation, Green/Blue Grabbing and Accumulation by Dispossession in Tanzania." *Journal of Peasant Studies* 39 (2): 335–55.
Benjaminsen, Tor, Mara Goldman, Maya Minwary, and Faustin Maganga. 2013. "Wildlife Management in Tanzania: State Control, Rent Seeking and Community Resistance." *Development and Change* 44 (5): 1087–1109.
Bennett, Nathan. 2019. "Marine Social Science for the Peopled Seas." *Coastal Management* 47 (2): 244–52.
Bennett, Nathan. 2022. "Mainstreaming Equity and Justice in the Ocean." *Frontiers in Marine Science* 9 (2022): 1–6.
Bennett, Nathan, and Philip Dearden. 2014. "Why Local People Do Not Support Conservation: Community Perceptions of Marine Protected Area Livelihood Impacts, Governance and Management in Thailand." *Marine Policy* 44 (February): 107–16.
Bennett, Nathan, Antonio Di Franco, Antonio Calò, Elizabeth Nethery, Federico Niccolini, Marco Milazzo, and Paolo Guidetti. 2019. "Local Support for Conservation Is Associated with Perceptions of Good Governance, Social Impacts, and Ecological Effectiveness." *Conservation Letters* 12 (4): e12640.
Bennett, Nathan, Hugh Govan, and Terre Satterfield. 2015. "Ocean Grabbing." *Marine Policy* 57 (July): 61–68.
Bennett, Nathan, Laure Katz, Whitney Yadao-Evans, Gabby Ahmadia, Scott Atkinson, Natalie Ban, et al. 2021. "Advancing Social Equity in and Through Marine Conservation." *Frontiers in Marine Science* 8 (2021): 711538.
Bennett, Nathan, Robin Roth, Sarah Klain, Kai Chan, Patrick Christie, Douglas Clark, et al. 2017. "Conservation Social Science: Understanding and Integrating Human Dimensions to Improve Conservation." *Biological Conservation* 205:93–108.
Blommaert, Jan. 2014. *State Ideology and Language in Tanzania*. 2nd ed. Edinburgh: Edinburgh University Press.
Blount, Ben, and Ariana Pitchon. 2007. "An Anthropological Research Protocol for Marine Protected Areas: Creating a Niche in a Multidisciplinary Cultural Hierarchy." *Human Organization* 66 (2): 103–11.
Bluwstein, Jevgeniy. 2017. "Creating Ecotourism Territories: Environmentalities in Tanzania's Community-Based Conservation." *Geoforum* 83:101–13.

Bluwstein, Jevgeniy, and Jens Lund. 2018. "Territoriality by Conservation in the Selous–Niassa Corridor in Tanzania." *World Development* 101:453–65.

Bluwstein, Jevgeniy, Jens Lund, Kelly Askew, Howard Stein, Christine Noe, Rie Odgaard, et al. 2018. "Between Dependence and Deprivation: The Interlocking Nature of Land Alienation in Tanzania." *Journal of Agrarian Change* 18 (4): 806–30.

Bofin, Peter, and Rasmus Pedersen. 2017. *Tanzania's Oil and Gas Contract Regime, Investments and Markets DIIS Working Paper 2017: 1.* Copenhagen, Denmark: Danish Institute for International Studies.

Bofin, Peter, Rasmus Pedersen, and Thabit Jacob. 2020. "The Politics of Power and Natural Gas in Tanzania: How Political Settlement Dynamics Shapes Deals in a 'New Oil Country.'" ESID Working Paper No. 149. Manchester: Effective States and Inclusive Development Research Centre, University of Manchester.

Braulik, Gill, Anja Wittich, Jamie Macaulay, Magreth Kasuga, Jonathan Gordon, Tim Davenport, and Douglas Gillespie. 2017. "Acoustic Monitoring to Document the Spatial Distribution and Hotspots of Blast Fishing in Tanzania." *Marine Pollution Bulletin* 125 (1): 360–66.

Breslow, Sara, Brit Sojka, Raz Barnea, Xavier Basurto, Courtney Carothers, Susan Charnley, et al. 2016. "Conceptualizing and Operationalizing Human Wellbeing for Ecosystem Assessment and Management." *Environmental Science and Policy* 66:250–59.

Broad, Kenneth, and James Sanchirico. 2008. "Local Perspectives on Marine Reserve Creation in the Bahamas." *Ocean and Coastal Management* 51 (11): 763–71.

Brockington, Dan. 2006. "The Politics and Ethnography of Environmentalism in Tanzania." *African Affairs* 105 (418): 97–116.

Brockington, Dan. 2008. "Corruption, Taxation and Natural Resource Management in Tanzania." *The Journal of Development Studies* 44 (1): 103–26.

Brockington, Dan, Rosaleen Duffy, and Jim Igoe, ed. 2008. *Nature Unbound: Conservation, Capitalism and the Future of Protected Areas.* London: Earthscan.

Brockington, Dan, James Igoe, and Kai Schmidt-Soltau. 2006. "Conservation, Human Rights, and Poverty Reduction." *Conservation Biology* 20 (1): 250–52.

Brockington, Dan, Hassan Sachedina, and Katherine Scholfield. 2008. "Preserving the New Tanzania: Conservation and Land Use Change." *International Journal of African Historical Studies* 41 (3): 557–79.

Bunce, Matthew, Katrina Brown, and Sergio Rosendo. 2010. "Policy Misfits, Climate Change, and Cross-Scale Vulnerability in Coastal Africa. How Development Projects Undermine Resilience." *Environmental Science and Policy* 13 (6): 485–97.

Bunce, Matthew, Sergio Rosendo, and Katrina Brown. 2010. "Perceptions of Climate Change, Multiple Stressors, and Livelihoods on Marginal African Coasts." *Environment Development and Sustainability* 12 (3): 407–40.

Burchell, Graham, Colin Gordon, and Peter Miller, eds. 1991. *The Foucault Effect: Studies in Governmentality: With Two Lectures by and an Interview with Michel Foucault.* Chicago: University of Chicago Press.

Büscher, Bram. 2013. *Transforming the Frontier: Peace Parks and the Politics of Neoliberal Conservation in Southern Africa*. Durham: Duke University Press.

Büscher, Bram, and Veronica Davidov. 2013. "Conceptualizing Lived Experiences Within the Political Economy of the Ecotourism-Extraction Nexus." In *The Ecotourism-Extraction Nexus: Political Economies and Rural Realities of (Un)comfortable Bedfellows*, edited by Bram Büscher and Veronica Davidov, 17–34. New York: Routledge.

Büscher, Bram, and Veronica Davidov. 2016. "Environmentally Induced Displacements in the Ecotourism–Extraction Nexus." *Area* 48:1–7.

Büscher, Bram, Wolfram Dressler, and Robert Fletcher. 2014. *Nature Inc.: Environmental Conservation in the Neoliberal Age*. Critical Green Engagements. Tucson: University of Arizona Press.

Büscher, Bram, and Robert Fletcher. 2020. *The Conservation Revolution: Radical Ideas for Saving Nature Beyond the Anthropocene*. New York: Verso.

Büscher, Bram, Sian Sullivan, Katja Neves, Jim Igoe, and Dan Brockington. 2012. "Towards a Synthesized Critique of Neoliberal Biodiversity Conservation." *Capitalism Nature Socialism* 23 (2): 4–30.

Butt, Bilal. 2012. "Commoditizing the Safari and Making Space for Conflict: Place, Identity and Parks in East Africa." *Political Geography* 31:104–13.

Buzinde, Christine N., Jyotsna Kalavar, and Kokel Melubo. 2014. "Tourism and Community Well-Being: The Case of the Maasai in Tanzania." *Annals of Tourism Research* 44:20–35.

Calignano, Giuseppe, and Terje Vaaland. 2018. "Local Content in Tanzania: Are Local Suppliers Motivated to Improve?" *Extractive Industries and Society* 5 (1): 104–13.

Caplan, Patricia. 2007. "'But the Coast, of Course, is Quite Different': Academic and Local Ideas About the East African Littoral." *Journal of Eastern African Studies* 1 (2): 305–20.

Carr, Mark, Joseph Neigel, James Estes, Sandy Andelman, Robert Warner, and John Largier. 2003. "Comparing Marine and Terrestrial Ecosystems: Implications for the Design of Coastal Marine Reserves." *Ecological Applications* 13 (sp1): 90–107.

Cepek, Michael. 2011. "Foucault in the Forest: Questioning Environmentality in Amazonia." *American Ethnologist* 38 (3): 501–15.

Chaigneau, Tomas, and Katrina Brown. 2016. "Challenging the Win-Win Discourse on Conservation and Development: Analyzing Support for Marine Protected Areas." *Ecology and Society* 21 (1): 36.

Charles, Anthony, Lena Westlund, Devin Bartley, Warrick Fletcher, Serge Garcia, Hugh Govan, and Jessica Sanders. 2016. "Fishing Livelihoods as Key to Marine Protected Areas: Insights from the World Parks Congress." *Aquatic Conservation, Marine and Freshwater Ecosystems* 26 (Suppl.2):165–84.

Charles, Anthony, and Lisette Wilson. 2009. "Human Dimensions of Marine Protected Areas." *ICES Journal of Marine Science* 66 (1): 6–15.

Cheeseman, Nic, Hillary Matfess, and Alitalali Amani. 2021. "Tanzania: The Roots of Repression." *Journal of Democracy* 32 (2): 77–89.

Christie, Patrick. 2004. "Marine Protected Areas as Biological Successes and Social Failures in Southeast Asia." *American Fisheries Society Symposium* 42:155–164.

Christie, Patrick, Nathan Bennett, Noella Gray, T. 'Aulani Wilhelm, Nai'a Lewis, John Parks, et al. 2017. "Why People Matter in Ocean Governance: Incorporating Human Dimensions into Large-scale Marine Protected Areas." *Marine Policy* 84:273–84.

Christie, Patrick, Bonnie McCay, Marc Miller, C. Lowe, Alan White, Richard Stoffle, et al. 2003. "Toward Developing a Complete Understanding: A Social Science Research Agenda for Marine Protected Areas." *Fisheries* 28 (12): 22–25.

Christie, Patrick, Richard Pollnac, Enrique Oraciion, Agnes Sabonsolin, Rixie Diaz and Diana Pietri. 2009. "Back to Basics: An Empirical Study Demonstrating the Importance of Local-level Dynamics for the Success of Tropical Marine Ecosystem-Based Management." *Coastal Management* 37 (3): 349–73.

Chuenpagdee, Ratana, Jose Pascual-Fernandez, Emese Szelinszky, Juan Alegret, Julia Fraga, and Svein Jentoft. 2013. "Marine Protected Areas: Rethinking Their Inception." *Marine Policy* 39:197–211.

Cinner, Joshua. 2010. "Poverty and the Use of Destructive Fishing Gear near East African Marine Protected Areas." *Environmental conservation* 36 (4): 321–26.

Cinner, Joshua, Tim Daw, Cindy Huchery, Pascal Thoya, Andrew Wamukota, Maria Cedras, and Caroline Abunge. 2014. "Winners and Losers in Marine Conservation: Fishers' Displacement and Livelihood Benefits from Marine Reserves." *Society and Natural Resources: An International Journal* 27 (9): 994–1005.

Cooksey, Brian. 2017. *ITPL, Richmond and Escrow: The Price of Private Procurement in Tanzania*. London: African Research Institute.

Cooksey, Brian, and Tim Kelsall. 2011. *The Political Economy of the Investment Climate in Tanzania*. African Power and Politics Programme. Research Report. London: Overseas Development Institute.

Cortes-Vazquez, Jose, and Esteban Ruiz-Ballesteros. 2018. "Practicing Nature: A Phenomenological Rethinking of Environmentality in Natural Protected Areas in Ecuador and Spain." *Conservation and Society* 16 (3): 232–42.

Coulson, Andrew. 1982. *Tanzania: A Political Economy*. Oxford: Oxford University Press.

Coulthard, Sarah, Derek Johnson, and Allister McGregor. 2011. "Poverty, Sustainability and Human Wellbeing. A Social Wellbeing Approach to the Global Fisheries Crisis." *Global Environmental Change* 21 (2): 453–63.

Coulthard, Sarah, Allister McGregor and Carole White. 2018. "Multiple Dimensions of Well-Being in Practice." In *Ecosystem Services and Poverty Alleviation: Trade Offs and Governance*, edited by Georgina Mace, Kate Schreckenberg, and Mahesh Poudyal, 243–56. Abingdon: Routledge.

Coumans, Catherine. 2010. "Alternative Accountability Mechanisms and Mining: The Problems of Effective Impunity, Human Rights, and Agency." *Canadian Journal of Development Studies* 30 (1–2): 27–48.

Darling, Emily. 2014. "Assessing the Effect of Marine Reserves on Household Food Security in Kenyan Coral Reef Fishing Communities." *PLOS|one* 9.

Davidov, Veronica, and Bram Büscher. 2013. "Introduction: The Ecotourism-Extraction Nexus." In *The Ecotourism-Extraction Nexus: Political Economies and Rural Realities of (Un)comfortable Bedfellows*, edited by Bram Büscher and Veronica Davidov, 1–16. London and New York: Routledge.

de Lange, Emiel, Emily Woodhouse, and Eleanor Milner-Gulland. 2016. "Approaches Used to Evaluate the Social Impacts of Protected Areas." *Conservation Letters* 9 (5): 327–33.

Dempsey, Jessica, and Daniel Suarez. 2016. "Arrested Development? The Promises and Paradoxes of 'Selling Nature to Save It.'" *Annals of the American Association of Geographers* 106 (3): 653–71.

Deneulin, Séverine, and Allister McGregor. 2010. "The Capability Approach and the Politics of a Social Conception of Wellbeing." *European Journal of Social Theory* 13 (4): 501–19.

De Santo, Elizabeth. 2013. "Missing Marine Protected Areas (MPA) Targets: How the Push for Quantity over Quality Undermines Sustainability and Social Justice." *Journal of Environmental Management* 124 (July 30): 137–46.

Dewan, Camelia. 2021. *Misreading the Bengal Delta: Climate Change, Development, and Livelihoods in Coastal Bangladesh*. Seattle: University of Washington Press.

Dudley, Nigel, ed. 2008. *Guidelines for Applying Protected Area Management Categories*. Gland, Switzerland: International Union for Conservation of Nature.

Duffy, Rosaleen. 2014. "Waging a War to Save Biodiversity: The Rise of Militarized Conservation." *International Affairs* 90 (4): 819–34.

Eastman, Carol. 1994. "Swahili Ethnicity: A Myth Becomes Reality in Kenya. Continuity and Autonomy." In *Swahili Communities: Inland Influences and Strategies of Self-Determination*, edited by David Parkin, 83–97. London: School of Oriental and African Studies.

Eastmond, Marita. 2007. "Stories as Lived Experience: Narratives in Forced Migration Research." *Journal of Refugee Studies* 20 (2): 248–64.

Eder, James. 2005. "Coastal Resource Management and Social Differences in Philippine Fishing Communities." *Human Ecology* 33 (2):147–69.

Edwards, David, Sean Sloan, Lingfei Weng, Paul Dirks, Jeffrey Sayer, and William Laurance. 2014. "Mining and the African Environment." *Conservation Letters* 7 (3): 302–11.

Edwards, Gareth, Louise Reid, and Colin Hunter. 2016. "Environmental Justice, Capabilities, and the Theorization of Well-Being." *Progress in Human Geography* 40 (6): 754–69.

Elbin, Rachel. 2021. "Tumeshaulika. Performing Development in Post-conflict Mtwara." PhD dissertation, Department of Anthropology, Michigan State University.

Enns, Charis, Brock Bersaglio, and Adam Sneyd. 2019. "Fixing Extraction Through Conservation: On Crises, Fixes and the Production of Shared Value and Threat." *Environment and Planning E: Nature and Space* 2 (4): 967–88.

Escobar, Arturo. 1998. "Whose Knowledge, Whose Nature? Biodiversity, Conservation, and the Political Ecology of Social Movements." *Journal of Political Ecology* 5 (1): 53–82.

Fabinyi, Michael, Wolfram Dressler, and Michael Pido. 2017. "Fish, Trade and Food Security: Moving Beyond 'Availability' Discourse in Marine Conservation." *Human Ecology* 45 (2): 177–88.

Fabinyi, Michael, Louisa Evans, and Simon Foale. 2014. "Socio-ecological Systems, Social Diversity, and Power: Insights from Anthropology and Political Ecology." *Ecology and Society* 19 (4): 28.

Fabinyi, Michael, Simon Faole, and Martha Macintyre. 2015. "Managing Inequality or Managing Stocks? An Ethnographic Perspective on the Governance of Small-Scale Fisheries." *Fish and Fisheries* 16 (3): 471–85.

Fabinyi, Michael, Magne Knudsen, and Shio Segi. 2010. "Social Complexity, Ethnography and Coastal Resource Management in the Philippines." *Coastal Management* 38 (6): 617–32.

Fairhead, James, Melissa Leach, and Ian Scoones. 2012. "Green Grabbing: A New Appropriation of Nature?" *Journal of Peasant Studies* 39 (2): 237–61.

Farmer, Paul. 2004. "The Anthropology of Structural Violence." *Current Anthropology* 45 (3): 305–25.

Ferguson, James. 2005. "Seeing Like an Oil Company: Space, Security, and Global Capital in Neoliberal Africa." *American Anthropologist* 107 (3):377–382.

Ferguson, James. 2006. *Global Shadows: Africa in the Neoliberal World Order.* Durham, N.C.: Duke University Press.

Ferse, Sabastian, Maria Costa, Kathleen Manez, Dedi Adhuri, and Marion Glaser. 2010. "Allies, Not Aliens: Increasing the Role of Local Communities in Marine Protected Area Implementation." *Environmental Conservation* 37 (1): 23–34.

Fischer, Edward. 2014. *The Good Life: Aspiration, Dignity, and the Anthropology of Wellbeing.* Stanford: Stanford University Press.

Fletcher, Chmara-Huff. 2014. "Marine Protected Areas: Territorializing Objects and Subjectivities." *EchoGeo* 29 (1): 1–19.

Fletcher, Robert. 2010. "Neoliberal Environmentality: Towards a Poststructuralist Political Ecology of the Conservation Debate." *Conservation and Society* 8 (3): 171–81.

Fletcher, Robert. 2013. "Between the Cattle and the Deep Blue Sea: The Janus Face of the Ecotourism Extraction Nexus in Costa Rica." In *The Ecotourism-Extraction Nexus: Political Economies and Rural Realities of (Un)comfortable Bedfellows,* edited by Bram Büscher and Veronica Davidov, 69–87. London and New York: Routledge.

Fletcher, Robert. 2017. "Environmentality Unbound: Multiple Governmentalities in Environmental Politics." *Geoforum* 85: 311–15.

Fletcher, Robert, Wolfram Dressler, and Bram Büscher. 2014. "Introduction to Nature Inc.: The New Frontiers of Environmental Conservation." In *Nature Inc. Environ-*

mental Conservation in the Neoliberal Age, edited by Wolfram Dressler, Robert Fletcher, and Bram Büscher, 3–21. Tucson: University of Arizona Press.

Foale, Simon, Dedi Adhuri, Porfiro Allin, Edward Allison, Neil Andrew, Philippa Cohen, Louisa Evans, Michael Fabinyi, et al. 2013. "Food Security in the Coral Triangle Initiative." *Marine Policy* 38: 174–83.

Fouéré, Marie-Aude. 2014. "Julius Nyerere, Ujamaa, and Political Morality in Contemporary Tanzania." *African Studies Review* 57 (1): 1–24.

Fouéré, Marie-Aude. 2015. *Remembering Julius Nyerere in Tanzania: History, Memory, Legacy*. Oxford: African Books Collective.

Fox, Helen, and Roy Caldwell. 2006. "Recovery from Blast Fishing on Coral Reefs: A Tale of Two Scales." *Ecological Applications* 16 (5): 1631–35.

Fox, Helen, Jed Holtzman, Kelly Haisfield, Catherine McNally, Gonzalo Cid, et al. 2014. "How Are Our MPAs Doing? Challenges in Assessing Global Patterns in Marine Protected Area Performance." *Coastal Management* 42 (3): 207–26.

Fox, Helen, Michael Mascia, Xavier Basurto, Alice Costa, Louis Glew, et al. 2012. "Reexamining the Science of Marine Protected Areas: Linking Knowledge to Action." *Conservation Letters* 5 (1): 1–10.

Fox, Helen, Carrie Soltanoff, Michael Mascia, Kelly Haisfield, Alfonso Lombana, Christopher Pyke, and Louisa Wood. 2012. "Explaining Global Patterns and Trends in Marine Protected Area (MPA) Development." *Marine Policy* 36 (5): 1131–38.

Fry, Palmer, Matthew Agarwala, Giles Atkinson, Tom Clements, Katherine Homewood, Susana Mourato, et al. 2015. "Monitoring Local Well-Being in Environmental Interventions: A Consideration of Practical Trade-offs." *Oryx* 51 (1): 68–76.

Gardner, Benjamin. 2016. *Selling the Serengeti: The Cultural Politics of Safari Tourism*. Atlanta: University of Georgia Press.

Garland, Elizabeth. 2008. "The Elephant in the Room: Confronting the Colonial Character of Wildlife Conservation in Africa." *African Studies Review* 51 (3): 51–74.

Gawler, Meg, and Christopher Muhando. 2004. *Development of the Mnazi Bay-Ruvuma Estuary Marine Park: Mid-term Evaluation*. Final Report. Nairobi: United Nations Development Programme.

Giakoumi, Sylvaine, Jennifer McGowan, Morena Mills, Maria Beger, Rodrigo Bustamante, Anthony Charles, et al. 2018. "Revisiting 'Success' and 'Failure' of Marine Protected Areas: A Conservation Scientist Perspective." *Frontiers in Marine Science* 5.

Gilberthorpe, Emma, and Dinah Rajak. 2017. "The Anthropology of Extraction: Critical Perspectives on the Resource Curse." *Journal of Development Studies* 53 (2): 186–204.

Gill, David, Samantha Cheng, Louise Glew, Ernest Aigner, Nathan Bennett, and Michael Mascia. 2019. "Social Synergies, Tradeoffs, and Equity in Marine Conservation Impacts." *Annual Review of Environment and Resources* 44 (1): 347–72.

Gjertsen, Heidi. 2005. "Can Habitat Protection Lead to Improvements in Human Wellbeing? Evidence from Marine Protected Areas in the Philippines." *World Development* 33 (2): 199–217.

Glassman, Jim. 2006. "Primitive Accumulation, Accumulation by Dispossession, Accumulation by 'Extra-economic' Means." *Progress in Human Geography* 30 (5): 608–25.
Gough, Ian, and Allister McGregor. 2007. *Wellbeing in Developing Countries: From Theory to Research.* Cambridge: Cambridge University Press.
Gough, Ian, Allister McGregor, and Laura Camfield. 2007. "Theorizing Wellbeing in International Development." In *Wellbeing in Developing Countries: From Theory to Research,* edited by Ian Gough and J. Allister McGregor, 3–44. Cambridge: Cambridge University Press.
Gratwick, Katharine, Rebecca Ghanadan, and Anton Eberhard. 2006. "Generating Power and Controversy: Understanding Tanzania's Independent Power Projects." *Journal of Energy in Southern Africa* 17 (4): 39–56.
Gray, Hazel. 2015. "The Political Economy of Grand Corruption in Tanzania." *African Affairs* 114 (456): 382–403.
Gray, Noella. 2010. "Sea Change: Exploring the International Efforts to Promote Marine Protected Areas." *Conservation and Society* 8 (4): 331–38.
Greco, Elisa. 2016. "Village Land Politics and the Legacy of Ujamaa." *Review of African Political Economy* 43 (sup1): 22–40.
Green, Kathryn, and William Adams. 2015. "Green Grabbing and the Dynamics of Local-Level Engagement with Neoliberalization in Tanzania's Wildlife Management Areas." *Journal of Peasant Studies* 42 (1): 97–117.
Green, Maia. 2014. *The Development State: Aid, Culture and Civil Society in Tanzania.* Suffolk: James Currey.
Grilo, Catarina, Aldo Chircop, and Jose Guerreiro. 2012. "Prospects for Transboundary Marine Protected Areas in East Africa." *Ocean Development and International Law* 43 (3): 243–66.
Gross-Camp, Nicole. 2017. "Tanzania's Community Forests: Their Impact on Human Well-Being and Persistence in Spite of the Lack of Benefit." *Ecology and Society* 22 (1): 37.
Gruby, Rebecca, Noella Gray, Lisa Campbell, and Leslie Acton. 2016. "Toward a Social Science Research Agenda for Large Marine Protected Areas." *Conservation Letters* 9 (3): 153–63.
Guard, Martin, and Mwajuma Masaiganah. 1997. "Dynamite Fishing in Southern Tanzania, Geographical Variation, Intensity of Use and Possible Solutions." *Marine Pollution Bulletin* 34 (10): 758–62.
Guard, Martin, and Yunus Mgaya. 2002. "The Artisanal Fishery for Octopus Cyanea Gray in Tanzania." *Ambio* 31 (7/8): 528–36.
Gustafson, Bret. 2020. *Bolivia in the Age of Gas.* Durham: Duke University Press.
Hall, Derek. 2013. "Primitive Accumulation, Accumulation by Dispossession and the Global Land Grab." *Third World Quarterly* 34 (9): 1582–1604.
Hall, Ruth, Marc Edelman, Saturnino M. Borras, Ian Scoones, Ben White, and Wendy Wolford. 2015. "Resistance, Acquiescence or Incorporation? An Introduction to Land Grabbing and Political Reactions 'From Below.'" *Journal of Peasant Studies* 42 (3–4): 467–88.

Harvey, David. 2003. *The New Imperialism*. New York: Oxford University Press.
Harvey, David. 2004. "The 'New' Imperialism: Accumulation by Dispossession." *Social Register* 40: 63–87.
Harvey, David. 2005. *A Brief History of Neoliberalism*. Oxford and New York: Oxford University Press.
Hemer, Susan. 2016. "Emplacement and Resistance: Social and Political Complexities in Development-Induced Displacement in Papua New Guinea." *Australian Journal of Anthropology* 27 (3): 279–97.
Hetherington, Kregg, ed. 2019. *Infrastructure, Environment, and Life in the Anthropocene*. Durham: Duke University Press.
Hill, Wendy, Jason Byrne, and Fernanda de Vasconcellos Pegas. 2016. "The Ecotourism-Extraction Nexus and Its Implications for the Long-Term Sustainability of Protected Areas: What Is Being Sustained and Who Decides?" *Journal of Political Ecology* 23 (1): 308–27.
Hoffman, David. 2014. "Conch, Cooperatives, and Conflict: Conservation and Resistance in the Banco Chinchorro Biosphere Reserve." *Conservation and Society* 12 (2): 120–32.
Holden, William, Kathleen Nadeau, and Daniel Jacobson. 2011. "Exemplifying Accumulation by Dispossession: Mining and Indigenous Peoples in the Philippines." *Geografiska Annaler Series B-Human Geography* 93B (2): 141–61.
Holmes, George. 2007. "Protection, Politics and Protest: Understanding Resistance to Conservation." *Conservation and Society* 5 (2): 184–201.
Holmes, George. 2012. "Biodiversity for Billionaires: Capitalism, Conservation and the Role of Philanthropy in Saving/Selling Nature." *Development and Change* 43 (1): 185–203.
Holmes, George. 2013. "Exploring the Relationship Between Local Support and the Success of Protected Areas." *Conservation and Society* 11 (1): 72–82.
Holmes, George, and Connor J. Cavanagh. 2016. "A Review of the Social Impacts of Neoliberal Conservation: Formations, Inequalities, Contestations." *Geoforum* 75:199–209.
Holmes, George, Chris Sandbrook, and Janet Fisher. 2016. "Understanding Conservationists' Perspectives on the New-Conservation Debate." *Conservation Biology* 31 (2): 353–63.
Holterman, Devin. 2014a. "The Biopolitical War for Life: Extractivism and the Ugandan Oil State." *The Extractive Industries and Society* 1 (1): 28–37.
Holterman, Devin. 2014b. "Slow Violence, Extraction and Human Rights Defense in Tanzania: Notes from the Field." *Resources Policy* 40 (June): 59–65.
Holterman, Devin. 2020. "Unlikely Allies? The Intersections of Conservation and Extraction in Tanzania." PhD dissertation, York University.
Holterman, Devin. 2022. "Stopping the Slaughter: The Economic Rationale to Antipoaching in Tanzania." *Geoforum* 135:106–17.
Horowitz, Leah. 2008. "'It's Up to the Clan to Protect': Cultural Heritage and the Micropolitical Ecology of Conservation in New Caledonia." *Social Science Journal* 45 (2): 258–78.

Horowitz, Leah. 2011. "Interpreting Industry's Impacts: Micropolitical Ecologies of Divergent Community Responses." *Development and Change* 42 (6): 1379–91.

Horton, Mark, and John Middleton. 2000. *The Swahili: The Social Landscape of a Mercantile Society*. Oxford: Wiley-Blackwell.

Hunter, Emma. 2008. "Revisiting Ujamaa: Political Legitimacy and the Construction of Community in Post-colonial Tanzania." *Journal of Eastern African Studies* 2 (3): 471–85.

Hydén, Göran. 1980. *Beyond Ujamaa in Tanzania: Underdevelopment and an Uncaptured Peasantry*. Oakland: University of California Press.

Hydén, Göran. 1999. "Top-Down Democratization in Tanzania." *Journal of Democracy* 10 (4): 142–55.

Igoe, Jim, and Dan Brockington. 2007. "Neoliberal Conservation: A Brief Introduction." *Conservation and Society* 5 (4): 432–49.

Ivers, Louise, and Kimberley Cullen. 2011. "Food Insecurity: Special Considerations for Women." *American Journal of Clinical Nutrition* 94 (6): 1740S of 1744S.

Jacka, Jerry. 2018. "The Anthropology of Mining: The Social and Environmental Impacts of Resource Extraction in the Mineral Age." *Annual Review of Anthropology* 47 (1): 61–77.

Jackson, Deborah. 2011. "Scents of Place: The Dysplacement of a First Nations Community in Canada." *American Anthropologist* 113 (4): 606–18.

Jacob, Thabit, and Rasmus Pedersen. 2018. "New Resource Nationalism? Continuity and Change in Tanzania's Extractive Industries." *Extractive Industries and Society* 5 (2): 287–92.

Jacob, Thabit, Rasmus Pedersen, Faustin Maganga, and Opportuna Kweka. 2016. *Rights to Land and Extractive Resources in Tanzania (2/2): The Return of the State*. DIIS Working Paper. Denmark: Danish Institute for International Studies.

Jentoft, Svein, Ratana Cheunpagdee, and Jose Pascual Fernandez. 2011. "What Are MPAs for: On Goal Formation and Displacement." *Ocean and Coastal Management* 54 (1): 75–83.

Jentoft, Svein, Jose Pascual-Fernandez, Raquel De la Cruz Modino, Manuel Gonzalez-Ramallal, and Ratana Chuenpagdee. 2012. "What Stakeholders Think About Marine Protected Areas: Case Studies from Spain." *Human Ecology* 40 (2): 185–97.

Kamat, Vinay. 2013. *Silent Violence: Global Health, Malaria, and Child Survival in Tanzania*. Tucson: University of Arizona Press.

Kamat, Vinay. 2014. "'The Ocean Is Our farm': Marine Conservation, Food Insecurity, and Social Suffering in Southeastern Tanzania." *Human Organization* 73 (3): 289–98.

Kamat, Vinay. 2017. "Powering the Nation. Natural Gas Development and Distributive Justice in Tanzania." *Human Organization* 76 (4): 304–14.

Kamat, Vinay. 2018. "Dispossession and Disenchantment: The Micropolitics of Marine Conservation in Southeastern Tanzania." *Marine Policy* 88:261–68.

Kamat, Vinay. 2019. "Dynamite Fishing in a Marine Protected Area in Tanzania: Why Youth Perceptions Matter." *Coastal Management* 47 (4): 387–405.

Kamat, Vinay, Philippe Le Billon, Rosemarie Mwaipopo, and Justin Raycraft. 2019. "Natural Gas Extraction and Community Development in Tanzania: Documenting the Gaps Between Rhetoric and Reality." *Extractive Industries and Society* 6 (3): 968–76.

Katikiro, Robert. 2016. "Improving Alternative Livelihood Interventions in Marine Protected Areas: A Case Study in Tanzania." *Marine Policy* 70:22–29.

Katikiro, Robert, Ashoka Deepananda, and Edison Macusi. 2015. "Interplay Between Perceived Changes in Fishery and Social Structures in Tanzanian Coastal Fishing Communities." *Fisheries Research* 164 (April): 249–53.

Katikiro, Robert, Edison Macusi, and Ashoka Deepananda. 2013. "Changes in Fisheries and Social Dynamics in Tanzanian Coastal Fishing Communities." *Western Indian Ocean Journal of Marine Science* 12 (2): 95–110.

Katikiro, Robert, Edison Macusi, and Ashoka Deepananda. 2015. "Challenges Facing Local Communities in Tanzania in Realising Locally-Managed Marine Areas." *Marine Policy* 51:220–29.

Katikiro, Robert, and Jairos Mahenge. 2016. "Fishers' Perceptions of the Recurrence of Dynamite-fishing Practices on the Coast of Tanzania." *Frontiers in Marine Science* 3 (233): 1–14.

Katundu, Mangasini. 2018. "Why Is Tanzanian Opposition Weak Twenty-Five Years Since its Re-introduction?" *African Journal of Political Science and International Relations* 12:69–84.

Kelleher, Graeme, ed. 1999. *Guidelines for Marine Protected Areas*. Gland, Switzerland: International Union for Conservation of Nature.

Kelly, Alice. 2011. "Conservation Practice as Primitive Accumulation." *Journal of Peasant Studies* 38 (4): 683–701.

Kelsall, Tim. 2002. "Shop Windows and Smoke-Filled Rooms: Governance and the Re-politicisation of Tanzania." *Journal of Modern African Studies* 40 (4): 597–619.

Keshodkar, Akbar. 2010. "Marriage as the Means to Preserve 'Asian-ness': The Postrevolutionary Experience of the Asians of Zanzibar." *Journal of Asian and African Studies* 45 (2): 226–40.

Keshodkar, Akbar. 2013. *Tourism and Social Change in Post-socialist Zanzibar*. Lanham, Maryland: Lexington Books.

Kideghesho, Jafari, Alfan Rija, Kuruthumu Mwamende, and Ismail Selemani. 2013. "Emerging Issues and Challenges in Conservation of Biodiversity in the Rangelands of Tanzania." *Nature Conservation* (6):1–29.

Kikula, Idris. 1997. *Policy Implications on Environment: The Case of Villagisation in Tanzania*. Uppsala: Nordic Africa Institute.

Kinyondo, Abel. 2019. "Is China Recolonizing Africa? Some Views from Tanzania." *World Affairs* 182 (2): 128–64.

Kinyondo, Abel, and Espen Villanger. 2017. "Local Content Requirements in the Petroleum Sector in Tanzania: A Thorny Road from Inception to Implementation?" *Extractive Industries and Society* 4 (2): 371–84.

Kleinman, Arthur, Veena Das, and Margaret Lock, ed. 1997. *Social Suffering*. Berkeley: University of California Press.

Koda, Bertha. 1998. "Changing Land Tenure Systems in the Contemporary Matrilineal Social System. The Gendered Dimension." In *The Making of a Periphery: Economic Development and Cultural Encounters in Southern Tanzania*, edited by Pekka Seppälä and Bertha Koda, 195–221. Uppsala, Sweden: Nordic Africa Institute.

Kopnina, Helen. 2016. "Nobody Likes Dichotomies (But Sometimes You Need Them)." *Anthropological Forum* 26 (4): 415–29.

Krall, Pieter. 2005. "A Grammar of Makonde (Chinnima, Tanzania)." PhD dissertation, Leiden University.

Laffoley, Dan, ed. 2008. *Towards Networks of Marine Protected Areas: The MPA Plan of Action for IUCN's World Commission on Protected Areas*. Gland, Switzerland: IUCN WCPA.

Laffoley, Dan, John Baxter, Jon Day, Lauren Wenzel, Paula Bueno, and Kathy Zischka. 2019. "Marine Protected Areas." In *World Seas: An Environmental Evaluation*, edited by Charles Sheppard, 549–69. London: Academic Press.

Lal, Priya. 2015. *African Socialism in Postcolonial Tanzania: Between the Village and the World*. Cambridge: Cambridge University Press.

Lange, Siri, and Abel Kinyondo. 2016. "Resource Nationalism and Local Content in Tanzania: Experiences from Mining and Consequences for the Petroleum Sector." *Extractive Industries and Society* 3 (4): 1095–1104.

Lange, Siri, and Victoria Wyndham. 2021. "Gender, Regulation, and Corporate Social Responsibility in the Extractive Sector: The Case of Equinor's Social Investments in Tanzania." *Women's Studies International Forum* 84:102434.

Lawi, Yusufu. 2007. "Tanzania's Operation Vijiji and Local Ecological Consciousness: The Case of Eastern Iraqwland, 1974–1976." *Journal of African History* 48 (1): 69–93.

Le Billon, Philippe. 2021. "Crisis Conservation and Green Extraction: Biodiversity Offsets as Spaces of Double Exception." *Journal of Political Ecology* 28 (1): 854–88.

Lee, Bryan, and Kendra Dupuy. 2018. "Understanding the Lie of the Land: An Institutional Analysis of Petro-Governance in Tanzania." *Journal of Energy and Natural Resources Law* 36 (1): 85–101.

Leisher, Craig., P. J. H. Van Beukering, and Lea Scherl. 2007. *Nature's Investment Bank: Marine Protected Areas Contribute to Poverty Reduction*. Arlington, Va.: Nature Conservancy.

Levien, Michael. 2013. "Regimes of Dispossession: From Steel Towns to Special Economic Zones." *Development and Change* 44 (2): 381–407.

Levine, Arielle. 2004. "Local Responses to Marine Conservation in Zanzibar, Tanzania." *Journal of International Wildlife Law and Policy* 7 (3–4): 183–202.

Levine, Arielle. 2007. "Staying Afloat: State Agencies, Local Communities, and International Involvement in Marine Protected Areas Management in Zanzibar, Tanzania." *Conservation and Society* 5 (4): 562–85.

Li, Tania. 2007. *The Will to Improve: Governmentality, Development, and the Practice of Politics*. Durham: Duke University Press.

Li, Tanya. 2009. "To Make Live or Die? Rural Dispossession and the Protection of Surplus Populations." *Antipode* 41 (1): 66–93.

Liebenow, Gus. 1971. *Colonial Rule and Political Development in Tanzania: The Case of the Makonde*. Evanston: Northwestern University Press.

Liwenga, Emma, P. Ndaki, F. Chengula, and R. Kalokola. 2019. "Coastal Communities' Perceptions on Climate Change Impacts and Implications for Adaptation Strategies in Mtwara, Southern Tanzania." In *Climate Change and Coastal Resources in Tanzania*, edited by Ian Bryceson, Yanda Pius Zabhe, Haji Mwevura, and Claude Mung'ong'o, 155–68. Cham: Springer.

Lockhart, Chris. 2008. "The Life and Death of a Street Boy in East Africa: Everyday Violence in the time of AIDS." *Medical Anthropology Quarterly* 22 (1): 94–115.

Lofchie, Michael. 1988. "Tanzania's Economic Recovery." *Current History* 87 (529): 209–12.

Lofchie, Michael. 2014. *The Political Economy of Tanzania: Decline and Recovery*. Philadelphia: University of Pennsylvania Press.

Lokina, Razack, and Anthony Leiman. 2014. *Managing Natural Resources for Sustainable Growth and Human Development in Tanzania: The Case of Extractive Industry*. ESRF Discussion Paper. Dar es Salaam, Tanzania: Economic and Social Research Foundation.

Luke, Timothy. 2011. "Environmentality." In *Oxford Handbook of Climate Change and Society*, edited by John Dryzek, Richard B. Norgaard, and David Schlosberg, 96–110. Oxford: Oxford University Press.

Machumu, Ernest, and Amararatne Yakupitiyage. 2013. "Effectiveness of Marine Protected Areas in Managing the Drivers of Ecosystem Change: A Case of Mnazi Bay-Marine Park, Tanzania." *Ambio* 42 (3): 369–80.

MacKenzie, Catrina, Rebecca Fuda, Sadie Ryan, and Joel Hartter. 2017. "Drilling Through Conservation Policy: Oil Exploration in Murchison Falls Protected Area, Uganda." *Conservation and Society* 15 (3): 322–33.

MacKenzie, John. 1988. *The Empire of Nature: Hunting, Conservation and British Imperialism*. Manchester: Manchester University Press.

Mahajan, Shauna, and Tim Daw. 2016. "Perceptions of Ecosystem Services and Benefits to Human Well-Being from Community-based Marine Protected Areas in Kenya." *Marine Policy* 74:108–19.

Malleret-King, Delphine. 2004. *A Socio-economic Baseline Assessment of the Mnazi Bay-Ruvuma Estuary Marine Park*. Nairobi: International Union for Conservation of Nature East African Regional Office.

Malleret-King, Delphine, and J. Simbua. 2004. *The Occupational Structure of the Mnazi Bay-Ruvuma Estuary Marine Park Communities*. Nairobi: International Union for Conservation of Nature East African Regional Office.

Mangora, Mwita, Mwanahija Shalli, and Daudi Msangameno. 2014. "Livelihoods of Coastal Communities in Mnazi Bay-Ruvuma Estuary Marine Park, Tanzania." In *Vulnerability of Agriculture, Water and Fisheries to Climate Change: Toward Sus-*

tainable Adaptation Strategies, edited by Margaret Muteng'e, Mohamed Behnassi, Gopalchandran Ramchandran, and Kirit Shelat, 271–87. New York: Springer.

Martin, Adrian. 2017. *Just Conservation: Biodiversity, Wellbeing and Sustainability*. London and New York: Routledge.

Martin, Adrian, Anne Akol, and Nicole Gross-Camp. 2015. "Towards an Explicit Justice Framing of the Social Impacts of Conservation." *Conservation and Society* 13 (2): 166–78.

Martin, Adrian, Brendan Coolsaet, Esteve Corbera, Neil Dawson, James Fraser, Ina Lehmann, and Iokiñe Rodriguez. 2016. "Justice and Conservation: The Need to Incorporate Recognition." *Biological Conservation* 197:254–61.

Marx, Karl. (1867) 1975. *Capital*. Vol 1. Translated by Ben Fowkes. New York: Penguin.

Mascarenhas, Adolpho. 1979. "After Villagization, What?" In *Towards Socialism in Tanzania*, edited by Mwansasu Bismarck and Pratt Cranford, 145–66. Toronto: University of Toronto Press.

Mascia, Michael. 2003. "The Human Dimension of Coral Reef Marine Protected Areas: Recent Social Science Research and its Policy Implications." *Conservation Biology* 17 (2): 630–32.

Mascia, Michael, David Burns, Dana Murray, and Shalynn Pack. 2014. "Protected Area Downgrading, Downsizing, and Degazettement (PADDD) in Africa, Asia, and Latin America and the Caribbean, 1900–2010." *Biological Conservation* 169:355–61.

Mascia, Michael, Anne Claus, and Robin Naidoo. 2010. "Impacts of Marine Protected Areas on Fishing Communities." *Conservation Biology* 24 (5): 1424–29.

Mascia, Michael, Helen Fox, Louise Glew, Gabby Ahmadia, Arun Agrawal, Megan Barnes, et al. 2017. "A Novel Framework for Analyzing Conservation Impacts: Evaluation, Theory, and Marine Protected Areas." *Annals of the New York Academy of Science* 1399 (1): 93–115.

Mathews, Andrew. 2020. "Anthropology and the Anthropocene: Criticisms, Experiments, and Collaborations." *Annual Review of Anthropology* 49 (1): 67–82.

McAfee, Kathleen. 1999. "Selling Nature to Save It? Biodiversity and Green Developmentalism." *Environment and Planning D: Society and Space* 17 (2): 133–54.

McClanahan, Timothy. 2010. "Effects of Fisheries Closures and Gear Restrictions on Fishing Income in a Kenyan Coral Reef." *Conservation Biology* 24 (6): 1519–28.

McClanahan, Timothy, and Caroline Abunge. 2015. "Perceptions of Fishing Access Restrictions and the Disparity of Benefits Among Stakeholder Communities and Nations of Southeastern Africa." *Fish and Fisheries* 17 (2): 417–37.

McClanahan, Timothy, Edward Allison, and Joshua Cinner. 2015. "Managing Fisheries for Human and Food Security." *Fish and Fisheries* 16 (1): 78–103.

McClanahan, Timothy, Joshua Cinner, Albogast Kamukuru, Caroline Abunge, and January Ndagala. 2009. "Management Preferences, Perceived Benefits, and Conflicts Among Resource Users and Managers in the Mafia Island Marine Park." *Environment Conservation* 35 (4): 340–50.

McGregor, Allister, Venkatesh Salagrama, and Aditya Bahadur. 2014. "Fisheries in Coastal India: Extraction, Livelihoods and a Way of Life." In *Handbook of Sustainable Development*, edited by Giles Atkinson, Simon Dietz, Eric Neumayer, and Matthew Agarwala, 93–107. Cheltenham, UK: Edward Elgar.

McGregor, Allister, and Andy Sumner. 2010. "Beyond Business as Usual: What Might 3-D Wellbeing Contribute to MDG Momentum?" *IDS Bulletin* 41 (1): 104–112.

McHenry, Dean E. 1979. *Tanzania's Ujamaa Villages*. Berkeley: Institute of International Studies.

McHenry, Dean. 1994. *Limited Choices: The Political Struggle for Socialism in Tanzania*. Boulder, Colo.: Lynne Rienner.

McIntosh, Janet. 2009. *The Edge of Islam: Power, Personhood, and Ethnoreligious Boundaries on the Kenyan Coast*. Durham: Duke University Press.

McShane, Thomas, Paul Hirsh, Tran Chi Trung, Alexander Songorwa, Ann Kinzig, Bruno Monteferri et al. 2011. "Hard Choices: Making Trade-offs Between Diversity Conservation and Human Well-Being." *Biological Conservation* 144 (3): 966–72.

Melyoki, Lemayon. 2017. "The Governance of the Petroleum Sector in Tanzania: Institutional Arrangements and the Role of the National Oil Company." *The Extractive Industries and Society* 4 (1): 180–90.

Middleton, John. 1992. *The World of the Swahili: Mercantile Civilization*. New Haven: Yale University Press.

Milner-Gulland, Eleanor, J. McGregor, M. Agarwala, G. Atkinson, P. Bevan, T. Clements, et al. 2014. "Accounting for the Impact of Conservation on Human Well-Being." *Conservation Biology* 28 (5): 1160–66.

Monson, Jamie. 2009. *Africa's Freedom Railway: How a Chinese Development Project Changed Lives and Livelihoods in Tanzania*. Bloomington: Indian University Press.

Moore, Amelia. 2019. *Destination Anthropocene: Science and Tourism in The Bahamas*. Oakland: University of California Press.

Moreno-Black, Geraldine, and Carla Guerron-Montero. 2006. "Speaking of Hunger and Coping with Food Insecurity: Experiences in the Afro-Ecuadorian Highlands." *Ecology of Food and Nutrition* 44 (5): 391–420.

Moshi, Humphrey. 2014. "Opportunities and Challenges for the Extraction of Natural Gas in Tanzania: The Imperative of Adequate Preparedness." *African Journal of Economic Review* 11 (1): 25–37.

Moshy, Victoria, and Ian Bryceson. 2016. "Seeing Through Fishers' Lenses: Exploring Marine Ecological Changes Within Mafia Island Marine Park, Tanzania." *SAGE Open* 6 (2): 1–18.

Moshy, Victoria, Ian Bryceson, and Rosemarie Mwaipopo. 2015. "Socioecological Changes, Livelihoods and Resilience Among Fishing Communities in Mafia Island Marine Park, Tanzania." *Forum for Development Studies* 42 (3): 529–53.

Moshy, Victoria, Jacob Masenge, and Ian Bryceson. 2013. "Undernutrition Among Under-Five Children in Two Fishing Communities in Mafia Island Marine Park, Tanzania." *Journal of Sustainable Development* 6 (6): 1–14.

Muhando, Christopher, Y. Mndeme, and A. Kamukuru. 1999. *Mnazi Bay-Ruvuma Estuary Proposed Marine Park: Environmental Assessment Report*. IUCN and World Bank.

Muralidharan, Rahul, and Nitin Rai. 2020. "Violent Maritime Spaces: Conservation and Security in Gulf of Mannar Marine National Park, India." *Political Geography* 80:102160.

Must, Elise. 2018. "Structural Inequality, Natural Resources and Mobilization in Southern Tanzania." *African Affairs* 117 (466): 83–108.

Must, Elise, and Siri Rustad. 2019. "'Mtwara Will Be the New Dubai': Dashed Expectations, Grievances, and Civil Unrest in Tanzania." *International Interactions* 45 (3): 500–531.

Mwaipopo, Rosemarie. 2008. "The Social Dimensions of Marine Protected Areas: A Case Study of the Mafia Island Marine Park in Tanzania." In *Samudra Monograph*. Chennai, India: International Collective in Support of Fishworkers.

Mwaipopo, Rosemarie, and Z. Ngazy. 1998. *Mnazi Bay-Ruvuma Estuary Marine Park: Social and Economic Assessment Report*. IUCN and World Bank.

Mwanjela, Geofrey. 2011. "The Myth of Sustainable Livelihoods: A Case Study of the Mnazi Bay-Marine Park in Tanzania." *Tropical Resources. The Bulletin of the Yale Tropical Resources Institute* 30:1–17.

Mwanjela, Geofrey, and Razack Lokina. 2016. "What Does It Take to Be Heard in Managing Marine Protected Areas? Insights from Tanzania Coastal Communities." *African Journal of Economic Review* 4 (1): 143–56.

Mwanyoka, Iddi, Makarius Mdemu, and Kris Wernstedt. 2021. "The Reality of Local Community Participation in the Natural Gas Sector in Southeastern Tanzania." *Extractive Industries and Society* 8 (1): 303–15.

Ndimbwa, Raphael. 2014. "Natural Gas Conflict in Tanzania and the Impacts to the Population of Mtwara Municipality." Master's thesis, Norwegian University of Life Sciences.

Nelson, Fred. 2012. "Blessing or Curse? The Political Economy of Tourism Development in Tanzania." *Journal of Sustainable Tourism* 20 (3): 359–75.

Nelson, Fred, Rugemeleza Nshala, and W. A. Rodgers. 2007. "The Evolution and Reform of Tanzanian Wildlife Management." *Conservation and Society* 5 (2): 232–61.

Neumann, Roderick. 1995. "Local Challenges to Global Agendas. Conservation, Economic Liberalization and the Pastoralists' Rights Movement in Tanzania." *Antipode* 27 (4): 363–82.

Neumann, Roderick P. 1998. *Imposing Wilderness: Struggles over Livelihood and Nature Preservation in Africa*. Berkeley: University of California Press.

Neumann, Roderick P. 2001. "Africa's 'Last Wilderness': Reordering Space for Political and Economic Control in Colonial Tanzania." *Africa* 71 (4): 641–65.

Ngware, Suleman. 2000. "Institutional Capacity Building: Local Self-Governance Under Multiparty System in Tanzania." In *Multipartism and People's Participation*, edited by S. Ngware, L. Dzimbri, and R. Ocharo. Dar es Salaam: TEMA.

Nolan, Callum, Michael Goodman, and Filippo Menga. 2020. "In the Shadows of Power: The Infrastructural Violence of Thermal Power Generation in Ghana's Coastal Commodity Frontier." *Journal of Political Ecology* 27 (1): 775–94.

Nordstrom, Carolyn. 1997. *A Different Kind of War Story*. Philadelphia: University of Pennsylvania Press.

Nowakowski, Justin, Steven Canty, Nathan Bennett, Courtney Cox, Abel Valdivia, Jessica Deichmann, et al. 2023. "Co-benefits of Marine Protected Areas for Nature and People." *Nature Sustainability* 1–9.

Nuhu, Said, Lazaro Mngumi, Matilda Ntiyakunze, and Daniel Msangi. 2020. "Regulatory Framework and Natural Gas Activities: A Curse or Boon to Host Communities in Southern Tanzania?" *The Extractive Industries and Society* 7 (3): 982–93.

Nussbaum, Martha. 2011. *Creating Capabilities: The Human Development Approach*. Cambridge: Harvard University Press.

Nyerere, Julius. 1968. *Freedom and Socialism: A Selection from Writings and Speeches 1965–1967*. London: Oxford University Press.

Nyerere, Julius. 1977. *The Arusha Declaration: Ten Years After*. Dar es Salaam: Government Printer.

Osti, Maeea, Lauren Coad, Joshua Fisher, Bastian Bomhard, and Jonathan Hutton. 2011. "Oil and Gas Development in the World Heritage and Wider Protected Area Network in sub-Saharan Africa." *Biodiversity Conservation* 20 (9): 1863–77.

Oxfam. 2017. *Balancing Infrastructure Development and Community Livelihoods. Lessons from Mtwara-Dar es Salaam Natural Gas Pipeline*. Dar es Salaam: OXFAM.

Paget, Dan. 2017. "Tanzania: Shrinking Space and Opposition Protest." *Journal of Democracy* 28 (3): 153–67.

Paget, Dan. 2020. "Again, Making Tanzania Great: Magufuli's Restorationist Developmental Nationalism." *Democratization* 27 (7): 1240–60.

Painter, Michael, and Oscar Castillo. 2014. "The Impacts of Large-Scale Energy Development: Indigenous People and the Bolivia-Brazil Gas Pipeline." *Human Organization* 73 (2): 116–27.

Pandya, Revati. 2023. "An Intersectional Approach to Neoliberal Environmentality: Women's Engagement with Ecotourism at Corbett Tiger Reserve, India." *Environment and Planning E: Nature and Space* 6 (1): 355–72.

Pedersen, Rasmus. 2014. "The Politics of Oil, Gas Contract Negotiations in sub-Saharan Africa." In *Policies and Finance for Economic Development and Trade*. Copenhagen: Danish Institute for International Studies.

Pedersen, Rasmus, and Peter Bofin. 2015. "The Politics of Gas Contract Negotiations in Tanzania: A Review." In *Danish Institute for International Studies Working Papers*. Copenhagen: Danish Institute for International Studies.

Pedersen, Rasmus, and Peter Bofin. 2019. "Muted Market Signals: Politics, Petroleum Investments and Regulatory Developments in Tanzania." *Journal of Eastern African Studies* 13 (3): 409–27.

Pedersen, Rasmus, and Thabit Jacob. 2017. "Reconfigured State-Community Relations in Africa's Extractive Sectors: Insights from Post-liberalisation Tanzania." *Extractive Industries and Society* 4 (4): 915–22.

Pedersen, Rasmus, Thabit Jacob, Faustin Maganga, and Opportuna Kweka. 2016. "Rights to Land and Extractive Resources in Tanzania (1/2): The History." In *Danish Institute for International Studies Working Papers*. Copenhagen: Danish Institute for International Studies.

Pedersen, Rasmus, and Opportuna Kweka. 2017. "The Political Economy of Petroleum Investments and Land Acquisition Standards in Africa: The Case of Tanzania." *Resources Policy* 52 (June): 217–25.

Peet, Richard, and Michael Watts. 1996. *Liberation Ecologies: Environment, Development, Social Movements*. London: Routledge.

Perreault, Thomas. 2006. "From the Guerra Del Agua to the Guerra Del Gas: Resource Governance, Neoliberalism and Popular Protest in Bolivia." *Antipode* 38 (1): 150–72.

Peterson, Nils, E. von Essen, H. Hansen, and T. Peterson. 2017. "Illegal Fishing and Hunting as Resistance to Neoliberal Colonialism." *Crime, Law, and Social Change* 67 (4): 401–13.

Pike, Ivy, and Crystal Patil. 2006. "Understanding Women's Burdens: Preliminary Findings on Psychological Health Among Datoga and Iraqw Women of Northern Tanzania." *Culture Medicine and Psychiatry* 30 (3): 299–330.

Pollnac, Richard, Brian Crawford, and Maharlina Gorospe. 2001. "Discovering Factors that Influence the Success of Community-Based Marine Protected Areas in the Visayas, Philippines." *Ocean and Coastal Management* 44:683–710.

Poncian, Japhace. 2014. "Embracing Natural Gas Discovery and Extraction as a Blessing for Equitable and Sustainable Benefits to Tanzania." *IOSR Journal of Humanities and Social Sciences* 19 (6): 55–61.

Poncian, Japhace. 2018. "Extractive Resource Ownership and the Subnational Resource Curse: Insights from Tanzania." *Extractive Industries and Society*. 6 (2): 332–42.

Poncian, Japhace. 2019. "When Government Commitment Meets Community Proactiveness: Governing Gas and Community Engagement in Tanzania." *Energy Research and Social Science* 52:78–90.

Poncian, Japhace, and Henry Kigodi. 2018. "Transparency Initiatives and Tanzania's Extractive Industry Governance." *Development Studies Research* 5 (1): 106–21.

Povinelli, Elizabeth. 2001. "Radical Worlds: The Anthropology of Incommensurability and Inconceivability." *Annual Review of Anthropology* 30:319–34.

Powers, Meredith, and Darcey Freedman. 2012. "Applying a Social Justice Framework to Photovoice Research on Environmental Issues. A Comprehensive Literature Review." *Critical Social Work* 13 (2): 80–100.

Rabinow, Paul, and Nikolas Rose. 2006. "Biopower Today." *Biosocieties* 1 (2): 195–217.

Rasheed, Rifaee. 2020. "Marine Protected Areas and Human Well-Being: A Systematic Review and Recommendations." *Ecosystem Services* 41:101048.

Raycraft, Justin. 2019. "'In Search of a Good Life': Perspectives on Village Out-Migration in a Tanzanian Marine Park." *Journal of Rural Studies* 70:36–48.

Raycraft, Justin. 2020. "The (Un)making of Marine Park Subjects: Environmentality and Everyday Resistance in a Coastal Tanzanian Village." *World Development* 126:1–12.

Rees, Sian, Lynda Rodwell, Spike Searle, and Andrew Bell. 2013. "Identifying the Issues and Options for Managing the Social Impacts of Marine Protected Areas on a Small Fishing Community." *Fisheries Research* 146 (September): 51–58.

Robinson, Elizabeth, Heidi Albers, and Stephen Kirima. 2014. "The Role of Incentives for Sustainable Implementation of Marine Protected Areas: An Example from Tanzania (Mnazi Bay-Ruvuma Estuary Marine Park)." *International Journal of Sustainable Society* 6 (1/2): 28–46.

Rogers, Douglas. 2015. "Oil and Anthropology." *Annual Review of Anthropology* 44:365–80.

Rosendo, Sergio, Katrina Brown, Alison Joubert, Narriman Jiddawi, and Micas Mechisso. 2011. "A Clash of Values and Approaches: A Case Study of Marine Protected Area Planning in Mozambique." *Ocean and Coastal Management* 54 (1): 55–65.

Ross, Anthony. 2013. "Infrastructure and Influence: China's Presence on the Coast of East Africa." *Journal of the Indian Ocean Region* 9 (2): 134–49.

RPS Energy Consultants Ltd. 2019. *Mnazi Bay Field. Reserves Assessment at December 31, 2019*. Prepared for Maurel et Prom and Wentworth Resources by RPS Energy Canada Ltd.

Sachedina, Hassanali. 2008. "Wildlife Is Our Oil: Conservation, Livelihoods and NGOs in the Tarangire Ecosystem, Tanzania." PhD dissertation, University of Oxford.

Sætersdal, Tore. 1999. "Symbols of Cultural Identity: A Case Study from Tanzania." *African Archaeological Review* 16 (2): 121–35.

Samoilys, Melita, and W. N. Kanyange. 2008. *Natural Resource Dependence, Livelihoods, and Development. Perceptions from Tanga, Tanzania*. IUCN, ESARO.

Sanchirico, James, Kathryn Cochran, and Peter Emerson. 2002. *Marine Protected Areas: Economic and Social Implications*. Discussion Paper 02–26. Washington, DC: Resources for the Future.

Sanders, Todd. 2001. "Save Our Skins: Structural Adjustment, Morality and the Occult in Tanzania." In *Magical Interpretations, Material Realities: Modernity, Witchcraft and the Occult in Postcolonial Africa*, edited by Henrietta Moore and Tod Sanders, 160–83. London and New York: Routledge.

Sanders, Todd. 2008. *Beyond Bodies: Rain-Making and Sense-Making in Tanzania*. Toronto: University of Toronto Press.

Sarris, Alexander, and Roger Van Den Brink. 1993. *Economic Policy and Household Welfare During Crisis and Adjustment in Tanzania*. New York: New York University Press.

Saul, John. 2012. "Tanzania Fifty Years On (1961–2011): Rethinking Ujamaa, Nyerere and Socialism in Africa." *Review of African Political Economy* 39 (131): 117–25.

Schlosberg, David. 2013. "Theorising Environmental Justice: The Expanding Sphere of a Discourse." *Environmental Politics* 22 (1): 37–55.

Schneider, Leander. 2004. "Freedom and Unfreedom in Rural Development: Julius Nyerere, Ujamaa Vijijini, and Villagization." *Canadian Journal of African Studies* 38 (2): 344–92.

Schneider, Leander. 2006. "Colonial Legacies and Postcolonial Authoritarianism in Tanzania: Connects and Disconnects." *African Studies Review* 49 (1): 93–118.
Scott, C. James. 1998. *Seeing Like a State.* New Haven: Yale University Press.
Segi, Shio. 2013. "The Making of Environmental Subjectivity in Managing Marine Protected Areas: A Case Study from Southeast Cebu." *Human Organization* 72 (4): 336–46.
Sen, Amartya. 1985. *Commodities and Capabilities.* Delhi: Oxford University Press.
Sen, Amartya. 1999. *Development as Freedom.* New York: Anchor Books.
Seppälä, Pekka, and Bertha Koda, eds. 1998. *The Making of a Periphery: Economic Development and Cultural Encounters in Southern Tanzania.* Uppsala: Nordiska Afrikainstitutet.
Sesabo, Jennifer, Hartmut Lang, and Richard Tol. 2006. *Perceived Attitude and Marine Protected Areas (MPAs) Establishment: Why Households' Characteristics Matters in Coastal Resources Conservation Initiatives in Tanzania.* Working Papers FNU-99, Research Unit Sustainability and Global Change, Hamburg University, revised March 2006.
Shanghvi, Ian, and John Kiang'u Jingu. 2013. *Tanzania and the Quest for Sustainable Utilization of Oil and Natural Gas.* ESRF Discussion Paper. Dar es Salaam: Economic and Social Research Foundation.
Shivji, Issa G. 2012. "Nationalism and Pan-Africanism: Decisive Moments in Nyerere's Intellectual and Political Thought." *Review of African Political Economy* 39 (131): 103–16.
Shoreman-Ouimet, Eleanor, and Helen Kopnina. 2015. "Reconciling Ecological and Social Justice to Promote Biodiversity Conservation." *Biological Conservation* 184 (April): 320–26.
Singleton, Sara. 2009. "Native People and Planning for Marine Protected Areas: How Stakeholder Processes Fail to Address Conflicts in Complex, Real-world Environments." *Coastal Management* 37 (5): 421–40.
Sirima, Agnes, and Kenneth Backman. 2013. "Communities' Displacement from National Park and Tourism Development in the Usangu Plains, Tanzania." *Current Issues in Tourism* 16 (7–8): 719–35.
Slade, Lorna, and Baraka Kalangahe. 2015. "Dynamite Fishing in Tanzania." *Marine Pollution Bulletin* 101 (2): 491–96.
Smith, James. 2022. *The Eyes of the World: Mining the Digital Age in the Eastern DR Congo.* Chicago: University of Chicago Press.
Snyder, Katherine. 2001. "Being of 'One Heart': Power and Politics Among the Iraqw of Tanzania." *Africa* 71 (1): 128–48.
Sowman, Merle, and Jackie Sunde. 2018. "Social Impacts of Marine Protected Areas in South Africa on Coastal Fishing Communities." *Ocean and Coastal Management* 157 (May): 168–79.
Stiglitz, Joseph, Amartya Sen, and Jean-Paul Fitoussi. 2009. *Report by the Commission on the Measurement of Economic Performance and Social Progress.*
Stinson, James. 2013. "Mother Nature's Best Kept Secret? Exploring the Discursive Terrain and Lived Experience of the Ecotourism-extraction Nexus in Southern

Belize." In *The Ecotourism-Extraction Nexus: Political Economies and Rural Realities of (Un)comfortable Bedfellows*, edited by Bram Büscher and Veronica Davidov, 88–109. London and New York: Routledge.

Stoger-Eising, Viktoria. 2000. "Ujamaa Revisited: Indigenous and European Influences in Nyerere's Social and Political Thought." *Africa* 70:118–43.

Tobey, James, and Elin Torell. 2006. "Coastal Poverty and MPA Management in Mainland Tanzania and Zanzibar." *Environmental Issues in the Western Indian Ocean* 49 (11): 834–54.

Topan, Farouk. 2008. "Tanzania: The Successful Development of Swahili as a National and Official Language." In *Language and National Identity in Africa*, edited by Andrew Simpson, 253–66. Oxford: Oxford University Press.

Tortell, Philipe, and Benjamin Ngatunga. 2007. *Terminal Evaluation of the Development of the Mnazi Bay-Ruvuma Estuary Marine Park*. New York: United Nations Development Fund.

Townsend, Meta. 1998. *Political-Economy Issues in Tanzania*. New York: Edwin Mellen.

Tripp, Aili Mari. 1997. *Changing the Rules: The Politics of Liberalization and the Urban Informal Economy in Tanzania*. Berkeley: University of California Press.

Tsing, Anna Lowenhaupt. 2005. *Friction: An Ethnography of Global Connection*. Princeton: Princeton University Press.

Twinamatsiko, Medard, Julia Baker, Mariel Harrison, Mahboobeh Shirkhorshidi, Robert Bitariho, Michelle Wieland, et al. 2014. *Linking Conservation, Equity and Poverty Alleviation: Understanding Profiles and Motivations of Resource Users and Local Perceptions of Governance at Bwindi Impenetrable National Park, Uganda*. International Institute for Environment and Development.

UNDG (United Nations Development Group). 2011. *Integrating Food and Nutrition Security into Country Analysis and UNDAF*.

UNDP/GEG (United Nations Development Programme/Global Environment Facility). 2004. *Development of Mnazi Bay-Ruvuma Estuary Marine Park: Mid-term Evaluation*. Final Report, Institute of Marine Sciences, University of Dar es Salaam.

Upton, Caroline, Richard Ladle, David Hulme, Tao Jiang, Dan Brockington, and William Adams. 2008. "Are Poverty and Protected Area Establishment Linked at a National Scale?" *Oryx* 42 (1): 19–25.

URT (United Republic of Tanzania). 2005. *Mnazi Bay Ruvuma-Estuary Marine Park, General Management Plan*. Dar es Salaam: Marine Parks and Reserves Unit.

URT (United Republic of Tanzania). 2011a. *Annual Report (2010/2011) for the Mnazi Bay-Ruvuma Estuary Marine Park*. Dar es Salaam: Marine Parks and Reserves Unit, Ministry of Livestock Development and Fisheries.

URT (United Republic of Tanzania). 2011b. *Mafia Island Marine Park, General Management Plan (Revised)*. Dar es Salaam: Marine Parks and Reserves Unit.

URT (United Republic of Tanzania). 2011c. *Mnazi Bay Ruvuma-Estuary Marine Park, General Management Plan (Revised)*. Dar es Salaam: Marine Parks and Reserves Unit.

URT (United Republic of Tanzania). 2011d. *Tanga Coelacanth Marine Park, General Management Plan.* Dar es Salaam: Marine Parks and Reserves Unit.

URT (United Republic of Tanzania). 2015. Petroleum Act 2015. Dar es Salaam: Government Printer.

URT (United Republic of Tanzania). 2016. *Tanzania in Figures 2016.* Dodoma, Tanzania: National Bureau of Statistics.

URT (United Republic of Tanzania). 2018a. *Mtwara Region: Socio-economic Profile, 2015.* Mtwara: Regional Commissioner's Office, National Bureau of Statistics.

URT (United Republic of Tanzania). 2018b. *National Audit Office. Performance Audit Report on Marine Protected Areas Management: A Report of the Controller and Auditor General.* Dar es Salaam: National Audit Office, Ministry of Livestock and Fisheries Development.

Vandergeest, Peter, and Nancy Peluso. 1995. "Territorialization and State Power in Thailand." *Theory and Society* 24 (3): 385–426.

Vaughn, Sarah. 2022. *Engineering Vulnerability: In Pursuit of Climate Adaptation.* Durham, N.C.: Duke University Press.

Voyer, Michelle, William Gladstone, and Heather Goodall. 2013. "Understanding Marine Park Opposition: The Relationship Between Social Impacts, Environmental Knowledge, and Motivation to Fish." *Aquatic Conservation: Marine and Freshwater Ecosystems* 24 (4): 441–62.

Walker, Barbara, and Michael Robinson. 2009. "Economic Development, Marine Protected Areas and Gendered Access to Fishing Resources in a Polynesian Lagoon." *Gender, Place and Culture* 16 (4): 467–84.

Walker, Gordon. 2012. *Environmental Justice: Concepts, Evidence and Politics.* London: Routledge.

Walley, Christine. 2004. *Rough Waters: Nature and Development in an Eastern African Marine Park.* Princeton: Princeton University Press.

Watts, Michael. 2004 "Resource Curse? Governmentality, Oil and Power in the Niger Delta, Nigeria." *Geopolitics* 9 (1): 50–80.

Weaver, Lesley Jo, and Craig Hadley. 2009. "Moving Beyond Hunger and Nutrition: A Systematic Review of the Evidence Linking Food Insecurity and Mental Health in Developing Countries." *Ecology of Food and Nutrition* 48 (4): 263–84.

Weiant, Pamela, and Shankar Aswani. 2006. "Early Effects of a Community-Based Marine Protected Area on the Food Security of Participating Households." *SPC Traditional Marine Resource Management and Knowledge Information Bulletin* 19:16–31.

Weiss, Brad. 2002. "Thug Realism: Inhabiting Fantasy in Urban Tanzania." *Cultural Anthropology* 17 (1): 93–124.

Weldemichel, Teklehaymanot. 2020. "Othering Pastoralists, State Violence, and the Remaking of Boundaries in Tanzania's Militarised Wildlife Conservation Sector." *Antipode* 52 (5): 1496–1518.

Wells, Sue. 2009. "Dynamite Fishing in Northern Tanzania—Pervasive, Problematic and yet Preventable." *Marine Pollution Bulletin* 58 (1): 20–23.

Wells, Sue, Carleton Ray, Kristina Gjerde, Alan White, Nyawira Muthiga, Juan Bezaury Creel, Billy Causey, Jerry McCormick-Ray, Rod Salm, Sue Gubbay, Graeme Kelleher, and Joe Reti. 2016. "Building the Future of MPAs—Lessons from History." *Aquatic Conservation: Marine and Freshwater Ecosystems* 26 (S2): 101–25.

Wembah-Rashid, J. A. R. 1998. "Is Culture in South-eastern Tanzania Development-Unfriendly?" In *The Making of a Periphery: Economic Development and Cultural Encounters in Southern Tanzania*, edited by Pekka Seppälä and Bertha Koda, 39–57. Uppsala: Nordiska Afrikainstitutet.

West, Paige. 2016. *Dispossession and the Environment: Rhetoric and Inequality in Papua New Guinea*. New York: Columbia University Press.

West, Paige, James Igoe, and Dan Brockington. 2006. "Parks and Peoples: The Social Impact of Protected Areas." *The Annual Review of Anthropology* 35:251–77.

Willow, Anna. 2014. "The New Politics of Environmental Degradation: Un/expected Landscapes of Disempowerment and Vulnerability." *Journal of Political Ecology* 21 (1): 237–57.

Willow, Anna. 2019. *Understanding ExtrActivism. Culture and Power in Natural Resource Disputes*. London and New York: Routledge.

Willow, Anna, and Sara Wylie. 2014. "Politics, Ecology, and the New Anthropology of Energy: Exploring the Emerging Frontiers of Hydraulic Fracking." *Journal of Political Ecology* 21 (1): 222–36.

Woodhouse, Emily, Katherine M. Homewood, Emilie Beauchamp, Tom Clements, Terrence McCabe, David Wilkie, and Eleanor Milner-Gulland. 2015. "Guiding Principles for Evaluating the Impacts of Conservation Interventions on Human Well-Being." *Philosophical Transactions of the Royal Society B* 370 (1681).

Woodhouse, Emily, Katherine Homewood, Emilie Beauchamp, Tom Clements, Terrence McCabe, David Wilkie, and Eleanor Milner-Gulland. 2017. "Understanding Human Well-Being for Conservation: A Locally Driven, Mixed Methods Approach." In *Decision-Making in Conservation and Natural Resource Management: Models for Interdisciplinary Approaches*, edited by Eleanor Milner-Gulland, Emily Nicholson, and Nils Bunnefeld, 97–122. Cambridge: Cambridge University Press.

Woodhouse, Emily, and Terrence McCabe. 2018. "Well-Being and Conservation: Diversity and Change in Visions of a Good Life Among the Maasai of Northern Tanzania." *Ecology and Society* 23 (1): 43.

World Bank. 1993. *World Development Report: Investing in Health*.

Youdelis, Megan. 2013. "The Competitive (Dis)advantages of Ecotourism in Northern Thailand." *Geoforum* 50:161–71.

Youdelis, Megan. 2019. "Multiple Environmentalities and Post-politicization in a Canadian Mountain Park." *Environment and Planning E: Nature and Space* 3 (2): 346–64.

INDEX

Pages in bold indicate direct quotations of interviewees.
Pages in italics indicate maps, illustrations, and photographs.

Abdallah (Nalingu village), 254–55
Abubakar (Nalingu village), **203, 204, 234–35**, 307n12
accumulation by dispossession, 122–23, 304n9. *See also* dispossession
Adamu (Mkubiru village), 156–58
Agardy, di Sciara, Christie, 8
Agip, 123–24
Agip (Azienda Generale Italiana Petroli), 17–18
Aisha (Nalingu village), **71–72**
Ali (Nalingu village), **232–33**
al-Shabaab, 43, 261, 291–93
Amina (Msangamkuu village), **103–4**
Amri (Mkubiru village), **221**
Amri, Yusuf (Mkubiru village), **289–90**
Appel, Hannah, 30–31
Araghi, Farshad, 122
Artumas (later Wentworth Resources), 17–18, 127–28, 132–33, 195–96, 298n21, 303n4, 304n5, 304n18. *See also* Tanzania Petroleum Development Corporation
Arusha Declaration, 51–53, 58. *See also* Nyerere, Julius; *ujamaa*

Asha, **106–7**
Ashula (Msimbati village), **261–62**
Athumani (Msimbati village), **145–46**, 283
Azimio la Arusha. *See* Arusha Declaration

Bibi Malango (Msangamkuu village), 61
Bibi Mtiti, 66
Bihaya (Msimbati village), 254
Bi Karuma (Nalingu village), **236**
Bi Lulanje, **213–14**
Bi Malombe (Msimbati village), **257, 265**
Bi Mkubwa (Msimbati village): activities of, 89, 247, 252, 307n6; on community relations with the marine park, **89–90**, 188–91, 224–25, 229–30, 279; on education, 150–52, 189–91, 224–25, 229–30; experience of state violence, **200**; experience with WWF programs, 150–52, 247, 307n6; on the gas project, **118, 186–87**; on land rights within the marine park, 188–89, 191, 307n6, 307n7; on well-being, 252–54, 263, 267
Bi Musa (Msangamkuu village), **107–8**
biodiversity, xi–xii, 3–39. *See also* conservation

Bi Punjawadi (Ruvula village), **227**
boats, 23, 23, 27, 93, 97, 106–7, 108–9, 228. *See also* fishing gear
boda boda. *See* motorcycle taxis
Büscher, Bram and Veronica Davidov, 21
Bwamkuwa (Msimbati village), **146–47, 162, 163**

Canada, 289–90. *See also* Artumas (later Wentworth Resources)
capability, 248, 262–63, 309n4, 310n12. *See also* well-being, human
cash: access to, 103, 153, 244–45, 265, 292–93; as enabling a good life, 146–47, 259–60; food security and, *98*, 103, 104, 106, 110–13
cashew trees, 9, 12, 24, 36, 37, 104, 108, 142, 159. *See also* deforestation
CCM. *See* Chama Cha Mapinduzi
cell phones, 72, 79, 289–90
CHADEMA, 59–60
Chama Cha Mapinduzi (Party of the Revolution, CCM), 33–34, 48, 58–60, 79–80, 127, 129–30, 134, 154, 280, 300n4
charcoal, 221–22, 235–37
children: activities of, 67, 108, 169–70, 233–34; education of, 36, 62–63, 97, 107, 146, 260; food insecurity and, 99, 100, 103–4, 106–7, 112, 233–34. *See also* youth
China, 31, 75, 125, 152–53, 290, 299n33, 301n16, 303n4
China National Pipeline Corporation (CNPC), 125
China Petroleum Pipeline Bureau (CPPB), 125
China Petroleum Technology and Development Corporation (CPT-DC), 125, 127, 196
Civic United Front (CUF), 129–30, 134, 264
climate change, 76, 97, 155, 223, 306n9, 306n10
clothing, 74, 77, 78–79

CNPC. *See* China National Pipeline Corporation
coconut trees: damaged and uprooted, 9, 24, 118–19, 136; importance of, 12, 36, 37, 119, 136, 159; theft of coconuts, 103–4, 106–7, 169–70
coelacanth, 5, 91, 118
colonialism, 51–52, 73–74, 77, 296n11, 301n14
commodification. *See* ecotourism; extraction
compensation, 24–25, 188, 268, 305n19; inadequacy of, 24–25, 268; as indication of legal status of gas project, 188; legal basis for, 24–25
conservation: approaches to, 7–12, 22, 48–49, 179–80, 277–79, 286, 311n2; ecotourism and (*See* ecotourism); extraction and, 8–9, 20–23, 39–40, 43, 177–84, 296n9; human dimensions of, 7, 147–49, 218–20, 277–79, 295n3, 305n1 (*See also* well-being, human); marine, 3–8, 6, 12–17, 147, 295n3, 300n40, 305n4 (*See also* marine protected areas; Mnazi Bay-Ruvuma Estuary Marine Park)
conservation, terrestrial, 3–4, 7–9, 147, 162, 217, 236–37
coral, 26–27, 64, 155, 221, 228
corruption, 58, 59, 77–78, 114, 124, 126, 162–63, 304n12
COVID-19 pandemic, 43, 59, 290–91, 292
CPPB. *See* China Petroleum Pipeline Bureau
CPT-DC. *See* China Petroleum Technology and Development Corporation
CUF. *See* Civic United Front

dala dala. *See* minivan taxis
Daranga (Msangamkuu village), **25, 87–88, 106**
Dar es Salaam. *See* Mafia Island Marine Park; National Natural Gas Infrastructure Pipeline

Davidov, Veronica and Bram Büscher, 21
Daw, Tim and Shauna Mahajan, 249
deforestation, 9, 33, 172, 184–85, 197–98, 207, 221, 235–36
development: international involvement, 13–14, 18, 66–67, 125, 127, 196, 249; local attitudes regarding, 20, 184–85, 188–89, 192–201, 204–6, 211, 281; state support for, 33–34, 52–53
Dewji, Mohamed, 60
displacement, 24–25, 41, 49, 53–55, 119, 152, 172–73, 203–4, 269. See also villagization
dispossession, 24–25, 41, 49, 141–42, 172–73; accumulation by, 122–23, 304n9; compensation for, 24–25, 132–36, 141–42, 152, 254–55
drought, 56, 102, 115

ecotourism: benefits of, 16–17, 91, 153; conservation and, 8, 16–17, 20–23, 91, 153; as a form of extraction, 179–80, 208, 298n23; lack of infrastructure for, 64, 161
education: of children, 36, 62–63, 97, 107, 146, 260; infrastructure for, 62–63; lack of money for, 146–47, 160, 260; well-being and, 263
electricity: as benefit of gas development, 73, 120, 127, 128, 130, 134, 195–96, 266–67, 307n9; power plants for, 18, 20, 128, 196, 298n22, 304n10, 307n9; state control of, 130, 195–96, 303n4, 305n20
employment: gas project and, 124–25, 127–29, 132–33, 135, 152, 181, 187, 194–95, 202, 203, 252; marine park and, 114, 129, 151; MDC and, 25; well-being and, 110–12, 244–46, 252, 271; of youth, 124, 131–33, 169, 241–42
environmentality, 216–20, 224–37, 239–43, 284–85, 307n8
extraction: ecotourism as a form of, 179–80, 208, 298n23; foreign involvement in, 30, 31, 58, 187–88; in protected areas, 8–9, 20–23, 39–40, 43, 177–84; role of the state in, 79, 142–44, 187–88, 280–82. See also natural gas extraction
Extractive Industries Transparency Initiative, 144

FAO (Food and Agricultural Organization), 13–14
farming, subsistence: environmental effects of (See deforestation); poor crop yields, 76, 93, 103, 104, 115; as practiced in Mtwara, 36, 37–38, 108–10, 150, 159, 161, 199, 258–59, 271; as primary activity, 12, 83, 228–29, 241, 299n38
Fatu (Mkubiru village), 111
fieldwork: format and approach, 30, 61, 87, 109–10, 181, 223–24, 266, 299n39, 300n13, 301n5, 309n6
Finnida. See Finnish International Development Agency
Finnish International Development Agency (Finnida), 66–67
firewood: alternatives to (See electricity; natural gas); as cooking fuel, 235, 236, 257; environmental damage caused by, 221, 235–37; restrictions on collecting, 150, 167, 173, 205; as source of cash, 76
fishing: destructive, 95, 213–17, 228–30, 284–85 (See also fishing, dynamite); fish catch size, 17, 76, 98, 99–100, 102, 104–5, 223, 237, 239; knowledge of, 95–96, 151, 227, 230, 234–35; legal, 16, 91, 156, 157–58, 234, 237, 247; out-migration of fishers, 105; poaching, 152–53, 157; restrictions placed on (See Mnazi Bay-Ruvuma Estuary Marine Park); as source of cash, 103, 116, 292–93; subsistence, 12, 37–38, 83, 106, 108–10, 145, 156
fishing, dynamite, 26–28, 83, 86, 108, 158, 165, 213–17, 220–21, 224, 231, 240, 306n13

fishing gear, 298n29, 310n7; confiscation of, 27, 29, 88, 93–96, 106–9, 153, 162, 214; legal, 91, 97, 109, 114, 157–58
fish vendors, 220–21, 238, 292–93
Fletcher, Robert, 179–80, 219–20
Food and Agricultural Organization (FAO), 13–14
food insecurity: access to store-bought foodstuffs, 98, 103–4, 110; dimensions of, 111, 113, 115–16, 301n1; effects of development projects on, 25, 101, 141–42; effects of marine park restrictions on, 25–26, 40–41, 82–85, 95–96, 99–101, 105–6, 146, 170, 233–34, 238–39; in Mtwara region, 25, 101–13, 302n14; well-being and, 251–52, 255–58, 303n18
fortress conservation. *See* conservation
fossil fuels. *See* natural gas extraction; oil extraction
France, 17–18, 127, 130, 196, 291, 303n4, 308n14
Francisca (Mkubiru village), 111–12
Frelimo (Mozambique Liberation Front), 69, 75, 299n37, 301n14

gas pipeline. *See* National Natural Gas Infrastructure Pipeline
gas project. *See* Tanzania Petroleum Development Corporation
gas wells: exploratory, 9, 17–18; proximity to Ruvula and Msimbati villages, 32, 118–19, 163, 181, 184–85, 192–93, 209, 268–69, 291; sited within marine park, 9, 18, 20, 118–19, 128, 137, 186–87, 189
Gawler, Meg and Christopher Muhando, 29
GEF (Global Environmental Facility), 82
gender. *See* men; women
Germany, 177–78
Gjertsen, Heidi, 99
gleaning, 26, 105, 108, 111, 150, 167, 233–34, 265
Global Environmental Facility (GEF), 82

Gough, Ian and Allister McGregor, 249
governmentality, 217, 219–20, 309n3
Greco, Elisa, 55, 79
Green, Maia, 55
grocery stores, 98, 103, 104, 110, 159

Habiba (Msimbati village), **188–89**, 191, **199, 221**, 307n5, 307n6, 307n7
Hadija (Msimbati village), **139**
Hadija (Nalingu village), **77–78**, 78
Haji (Mtandi village), **136**
Haki (Ruvula/Msimbati village), **32**, 32–33, 64–65, **75, 155–56, 193–94, 227–28, 239**
Halima (Mkubiru village), **110**
Hall, Derek, 123
Hamisi (Mtandi village), **102, 130**
Hassan (Msangamkuu village), **27, 86, 103**
Hassani (Msimbati village), **159–60, 201–2, 204, 255–56**, 307n10
Hawa (Sinde village), **104**
health: access to care, 62, 67–68, 70, 73, 94, 156, 251–52, 253, 256, 262, 271, 286; effects of conservation projects on, 99–100, 114, 168, 272, 285; effects of development projects on, 128, 143, 184, 196, 204; infrastructure, 62, 67–68, 70, 94, 286. *See also* food insecurity
Hela (Mnomo/Msangamkuu village), **25**
Horowitz, Leah, 148
housing, 64, 155, 221, 252–53, 257, 310n7
Hunter, Emma, 52
Hydrotanz Limited, 126

IMF, 13, 56–57
incommensurability, 20–22, 178–80, 182–84
Independent Power Tanzania Limited (IPTL), 126
infrastructure: for ecotourism, 64, 82, 161; for education, 62–63; for gas project, 9, 18, 20, 30–31, 118–19, *120*, 128, 293, 306n1 (*See also* gas wells; National

Natural Gas Infrastructure Pipeline; Tanzania Petroleum Development Corporation); for health care, 62, 67–68, 70, 94, 286; scholarship on, 299n32; for transportation, 24, 130, 195, 291

International Union for Conservation of Nature (IUCN), 14, 16, 18

IPTL (Independent Power Tanzania Limited), 126

Islam, 35, 37–38, 264, 299n39

Issa (Nalingu village), 29–30, **95–96**, 221, **231–32**

IUCN (International Union for Conservation of Nature), 14, 16, 18

Jackson, Deborah Davis, 119
Jamali (Msimbati village), **32–33**, **65–66**, **129–30**, 146, **152–54**, 162, 170–71, 306n8
Jamila (Kilambo village), **261**, **265**, **266**
Jinaya (Nalingu village), **233–34**
jongoo (sea cucumbers), 64, *64*, 74–75, 152–53
justice: distributive, 182–84, 305n23; environmental, 22–23, 41–42, 144, 182–85, 209–10, 286–88; social, 22–23, 41–42, 182–85, 210–12, 286–88
Juu. *See* Mkubiru
Juwazi (Msimbati village), **73–74**

Kachakacha (Ruvula village), **226**, **269**, **285**
Kadude (Msimbati village), **91**
Kagera War, 50, 56
Katundu (Msimbati village), **132**, 194–95
Kenya, 3–4, 14, 47, 50, 56, 100, 143
Kihimika, 83
Kikwete, Jakaya, 30, 31, 59, 119–20, 124, 125, 127, 135–36
Kilambo, 82, 261, 308n13, 309n2
Kilambo villagers: Jamila, **261**, **265**, **266**; Mfaume, **260**, **265–66**; Mozza, **266–67**; Swalehe, **260**
Kiswahili, 30, 47, 52, 53
Kitaya, 261

Kusum (Msimbati village), **257–58**, **264**
Kweka, Opportuna and Rasmus Pedersen, 198

Lal, Priya, 78, 80
Land Acquisition Act (1967), 25, 152, 198, 296n11
Land Act No. 4, 296n11
land rights: held by interviewees, 310n7; lack of knowledge about, 282, 307n5, 307n6, 307n7, 307n8; legal framework governing, 24–25, 187–88, 279–82, 296n11, 305n19, 306n12; marine park restrictions on, 92, 159, 187–91
Lawi, Yusufu, 51–52
Leslie-Moore, Latham, 65, 66
Levien, Michael, 122
Li, Tanya, 142
Lichumbu (Msimbati village), **139–40**, **195–96**
Likong'o, 121
liquified natural gas (LNG), 121. *See also* National Natural Gas Infrastructure Pipeline; natural gas extraction
Litembe, 82
LNG. *See* liquified natural gas
Lofchie, Michael, 47, 59, 60
Lowassa, Edward, 126

Mabruki (Msimbati), **202**
Madimba, 9, 293, 306n1
Mafia Island Marine Park (MIMP), 5, 6, 14, 100–1, 147, 162, 283, 301n6, 308n2
Magufuli, John, 48, 59, 127, 227, 240–41, 246, 300n2
Mahajan, Shauna and Tim Daw, 249
Maharuf (boda boda driver), 24
Makanzu (Msimbati village), **192**
Makonde people, 37–38, 299n37
Malleret-King, Delphine, 29
Mama Razak (Rehema Njowele, Sinde village), **213**
Mama Samia (Msimbati village), **244**, *245*

mango trees, 24, 62, 199, 208
mangroves, 82, 89, 150, 221, 222, 224
Maraba people. *See* Makonde people
Mariam (research assistant), 109
marine park. *See* Mafia Island Marine Park; marine protected areas; Mnazi Bay-Ruvuma Estuary Marine Park
Marine Parks and Reserves Act No. 29, 13
Marine Parks and Reserves Unit (MPRU), 16, 18, 89
marine protected areas (MPAs): in East Africa, 3–7, 6; factors affecting success of, 297n13; human dimensions of, 10–13, 39–40, 42, 83–85, 116–17, 149, 162–63, 170–74, 219, 269–74, 277–79, 285–86, 296n5, 296n8, 298n18, 302n12; international support for, 10, 13–14 (*See also* World Wildlife Fund); multiple-use *versus* no-take, 11, 14–16; resource extraction in, 39–40; scholarship regarding, 5, 10–12, 227–78, 296n5; top-down *versus* community implementation of, 7, 13, 84–85, 162–63, 170–74, 219; types of, 295n2. *See also* Mafia Island Marine Park; Mnazi Bay-Ruvuma Estuary Marine Park
Martin, Adrian, 183, 287
Marx, Karl, 122–23
Masudi (Mkubiru village), **96**
MATT (Multi-Agency Task Team), 240
Maukilo (Nalingu village), 68, **68–69, 165–66**
Maulidi celebrations, 38, 302n15
Mau Mau (Msimbati village), **130**
Maurel & Prom, 17, 127, 130, 196, 303n4
MBREMP. *See* Mnazi Bay-Ruvuma Estuary Marine Park
McGregor, Allister and Ian Gough, 249
MDC. *See* Mtwara Development Corridor
men: occupations of, 111–12, 131–32, 241–42; out-migration of, 105, 114; well-being as defined by, 148–49, 206n14, 259–60, 271; young, 27–28, 76, 87, 97, 124, 129–32, 149–50, 241–42, 301n5

Mfaume (Kilambo village), **260, 265–66**
Mfaume, Ali (Mkubiru village), 290
micropolitics, 147–49
Middleton, John, 35
Mikumi National Park, 153
MIMP. *See* Mafia Island Marine Park
minivan taxis (dala dala), 24, 62
mitumbwi. *See* boats
Mkapa, Benjamin, 58–59
Mkubiru, 83, 108–12, *109*, 181, *209*, 237–39, 289–90
Mkubiru villagers: Adamu, 156–58; Amri, **221**; Amri, Yusuf, **289–90**; Fatu, **111**; Francisca, **111–12**; Halima, **110**; Masudi, **96**; Mfaume, Ali, 290; Mohamed, **135**; Mpojola, **161–62, 205, 222–23**; Mwanaidi, **237–38, 239, 284**
Mnawene, 109. *See also* Mkubiru
Mnazi, 69, 292
Mnazi Bay Production Sharing Agreement, 17
Mnazi Bay-Ruvuma Estuary Marine Park (MBREMP): alternative employment and, 114, 151; buffer zone of, 61, 83; community participation in, 84–86, 89–90, 161–62, 188–91, 223–24; conservation successes of, 96–99; development and extraction within, 308n13 (*See also* Tanzania Petroleum Development Corporation); displacement and dispossession by, 84–85, 113–14, 163, 171–73, 203, 208, 281, 307n10, 308n13; ecotourism and, 16–17, 64, 161, 201–2; education by, 42, 146, 150–51, 154–55, 173, 224–31; effects on women, 100, 105, 148–49, 167–70, 233–34, 238–39, 306n14; enforcement of restrictions, 93–94, 191, 202, 227–29, 233, 238, 241, 281, 283, 307n11; failed promises of, 16–17, 91, 201–2, 209, 310n13; food insecurity and, 25–26, 40–41, 82–85, 95–96, 99–101, 105–6, 113, 115–16, 146, 170, 233–34, 238–39, 303n17; gate

office of, 9, 64, 118–19, 136–40, *138*; hardships caused by, 25–26, 34, 82–85, 92, 96–99, 105–8, 146, 155–56, 161–62, 247, 306n14 (*See also* food insecurity; well-being, human); international involvement in, 225 (*See also* World Wildlife Fund); land rights within, 92, 155–56, 159–61, 167, 188–91, 208, 211, 281, 308n13; malfeasance of park officials, 114, 162–63, 191, 202, 222, 307n11; management plan of, 14–17, *15*, 82, 84, 88, 90, 223–24; militarization of, 291, 293; misunderstandings and miscommunication, 28, 86–87, 89–92, 161–62, 188–91, 229–30, 232–33, 235, 278–79; opposition to, 17, 29, 34, 69–70, 92–95, 114–15, 149–50, 159–66, 201–5 (*See also* Nalingu); overview, 5–6, *6*, 14–16, *15*; relationship to gas project, 9, 18–20, 118–19, 163–64, 172–73, 186–87, 191, 197, 201–3, 208, 281 (*See also* Tanzania Petroleum Development Corporation); shifts in attitudes regarding, 42, 213–17, 239–43, 308n2; as state-directed project, 9, 33–34, 90, 164, 193–94, 206–7, 279–82; support for, 149–58, 239–43, 308n2 (*See also* Bi Mkubwa); top-down implementation of, 28–29, 84–86, 87, 90, 146, 278–79; usage zones of, 15–16, 93, 105, 235; violence associated with, 28–30, 93–94, 136–40, *138*, 164–66, 227–29, 247, 297n15

Mngoji, 9, 255

Mngosi, 65

Mnomo, 27–28

Mnomo villagers: Hela, **25**

Mnova, Salum (research assistant), 29–30, 64, 87, **177–78**, 211, **238–39**

Mnuyo, 63. *See also* Msimbati

Mohamed (Mkubiru village), **135**

motorcycle taxis (boda boda), 24, 62, 241–42

Mozambique: conservation in, 4–5, 14, 308n14; government of, 60; insurgency and, 69, 74–75, 261, 269, 291–93; migration to and from, 37, 61, 70, 89, 105, 299n37; sea cucumber trade and, 74–76

Mozambique Liberation Front (Frelimo), 69, 75, 299n37, 301n14

Mozza (Kilambo village), **266–67**

MPAs. *See* marine protected areas

Mpojola (Mkubiru village), **161–62, 205, 222–23**

MPRU (Marine Parks and Reserves Unit), 16, 18, 89

Msangamkuu, *23*, 23–24, 61, 82–83, 85–88, 115

Msangamkuu villagers: Amina, **103–4**; Bibi Malango, 61; Bi Musa, **107–8**; Daranga, **25**, **87–88**, **106**; Hassan, 27, 86, **103**; Hela (Mnomo/Msangamkuu), **25**; Mwabadi, **204–5**; Rashidi, **86–87**; Waziri, **104–5**

Msemo landing site, 23, *23*

Msimbati: gas project and, 9, 181; marine park and, 9, 32, 83, 88–93, 115, 171; overview, 49, 62–66, *63*, *65*, 73–76; violence and, 32, 291–92. *See also* individual interviewees

Msimbati villagers: Ashula, **261–62**; Athumani, **145–46**, 283; Bihaya, **254**; Bi Malombe, **257**, **265**; Bi Mkubwa, 89, **89–90**, 118, **150–52**, **186–87**, **188–91**, 191, **200**, **224–25**, **229–30**, 247, 252, **252–54**, **263**, **267**, **279**, 307n6, 307n7; Bwamkuwa, **146–47**, **162**, **163**; Habiba, **188–89**, 191, **199**, **221**, 307n5, 307n6, 307n7; Hadija, **139**; Haki (Ruvula/Msimbati), 32, 32–33, 64–65, **75**, **155–56**, **193–94**, **227–28**, **239**; Hassani, **159–60**, **201–2**, 204, **255–56**, 307n10; Jamali, 32–33, **65–66**, **129–30**, 146, **152–54**, 162, **170–71**, 306n8; Juwazi, **73–74**; Kadude, **91**; Katundu, **132**, **194–95**; Kusum, **257–58**, **264**; Lichumbu, **139–40**, **195–96**; Makanzu, **192**;

Mama Samia, **244**, *245*; Mau Mau, **130**; Mwanaidi, **138**; Mwanajuma, 74; Mwema (Mtandi/Msimbati), **133**, **168**; Mzura, **260**; Ndembo, 221–22; Rehema (Mtandi/Msimbati), **92–93**, **160–61**, **191**, **201**, **229**, 302n8; Rukia (Mtandi/Msimbati), **167**, **197–98**; Sadala, **154–55**, **228–29**, **250–51**, **251–52**, **266**, 306n9, 306n10; Shabia, **168–70**; Shaibu, **259–60**; Siwema, **152**, 247; Somoye, **230–31**, **291–92**; Yusuf, **90–91**, **199–200**; Zainabu, 76, **133**, **168**, **190**, **201**, **229**, **256–57**, **263–64**, **267**, **268**; Zuhura, **230**

Mtandi, 63. *See also* Msimbati

Mtandi villagers: Haji, **136**; Hamisi, **102**, 130; Musa, **97**; Mwema, **133**, **168**; Rehema, **92–93**, **160–61**, **191**, **201**, **229**, 302n8; Rukia, **167**, **197–98**

Mtendachi, 83

Mtopwa (Nalingu village), **235–36**

Mtwara-Dar es Salaam gas pipeline. *See* National Natural Gas Infrastructure Pipeline

Mtwara Declaration, 90

Mtwara Development Corridor (MDC), 24–25, 101, 107–8, 114, 205, 298n26, 298n31

Mtwara-Lindi Rural Water Supply Project, 66–67

Mtwara region: administrative divisions of, 36; demographics of, 12, 36, 299n37; economic aspects of, 12, 36–38, 81, 115–16; gas development protests in, 125–26, 304n7; Mtwara Port, 23, 75, 177–78

Muhando, Christopher and Meg Gawler, 29

Muhongo, Sospeter, 125

Multi-Agency Task Team (MATT), 240

Murchison Falls Protected Area, 9, 21

Musa (Mtandi village), **97**

Mussa (Nalingu village), **70–71**, **76–77**

Mwabadi (Msangamkuu village), **204–5**

Mwanaidi (Mkubiru village), **237–38**, **239**, **284**

Mwanaidi (Msimbati village), **138**

Mwanajuma (Msimbati village), 74

Mwema (Mtandi/Msimbati village), **133**, **168**

Mwinje. *See* Mkubiru

Mwinyi, Ali Hassan, 57–59, 74, 76, 77, 300n9

Mzimba (Ruvula village), **192–93**

Mzura (Msimbati village), **260**

Nalingu: gas project and, 181; marine park and, 28–31, 69–70, 83, 93–96, 115, 164–66, 171, 231–37; overview, 49, 66–73, 67, 68–72, 76–79; violent reputation of, 28–31, 69–70, 164–66

Nalingu villagers: Abdallah, **254–55**; Abubakar, **203**, **204**, **234–35**, 307n12; Aisha, **71–72**; Ali, **232–33**; Bi Karuma, **236**; Hadija, **77–78**, 78; Issa, 29–30, **95–96**, 221, **231–32**; Jinaya, **233–34**; Maukilo, 68, **68–69**, **165–66**; Mtopwa, **235–36**; Mussa, **70–71**, **76–77**; Salama, 78, **93–94**; Sofia, **78–79**, 158

Namera, 82–83

Namidondi, 83

Nangurukuru. *See* Mkubiru

National Natural Gas Infrastructure Pipeline (NNGI), 17, *19*, *137*; environmental impact of, 9, 33, 127, 136, 172, 181, 184–85, 197–98, 207; international involvement in, 125, 127, 303n4; protests against, 32, 125–27, 135, 196–97

natural gas: for cooking, 181, 194, 236; discovery of, 17–18, 120, 123–24, 303n4, 304n11, 307n4; extraction of (*See* natural gas extraction); liquified, 291, 304n5, 304n6, 308n14

natural gas extraction: international involvement in, 30–31, 121, 124–25, 303n4, 304n11 (*See also* Agip; Artumas

[later Wentworth Resources]; Maurel & Prom); justifications for, 22, 119–21, 140–44; protected areas and, 3, 7, 8–9; in Tanzania, 17–20, *19*, 124
Ndembo (Msimbati village), **221–22**
Ndonde people. *See* Makonde people
Nelson, Fred, 58
neoliberalism, 7–8, 48–50, 57–60, 78–79
nets, 27, 93, 95, 108–9, 157–58, 214, 221, 224. *See also* fishing gear
Njowele, Abdallah (research assistant), 23–24, 30, 64, 87
Njowele, Rehema (Mama Razak, Sinde village), **213**
NNGI. *See* National Natural Gas Infrastructure Pipeline
Nnima people. *See* Makonde people
Norway, 13
Nyerere, Julius, 48, 50–56, 69, 73–74, 77, 154. *See also ujamaa*

octopus, 26, 88, 111, 169, 214, 233
oil crises, 56
oil extraction, 8–9, 17, 21, 30, 39–40, 121, 124, 187–88, 207–8, 287, 303n4, 307n4
Operation Pono, 214–15
Operation Vijiji, 50, 53–56, 70–71, 80. *See also* Nyerere, Julius; *ujamaa*; villagization

Paget, Dan, 51
Pan African Power Limited, 126
Pedersen, Rasmus and Opportuna Kweka, 198
pipeline, gas. *See* National Natural Gas Infrastructure Pipeline
poaching, 3, 152–53, 157
Poncian, Japhace, 122
pool tables, 169–70
poverty: conservation and, 9, 85, 95–96, 105, 115, 222–23, 286; contrasted with well-being, 247–48, 253, 261–62, 263, 272; effects of development on, 22, 25, 124, 140, 143, 196, 209, 286, 288; of Mtwara region, 36; villagization and, 54. *See also* well-being, human
power plants, 18, 20, 128, 196, 298n22, 304n10, 307n9
privatization, 7–8, 57–61, 80–81. *See also* neoliberalism
protected areas. *See* conservation; marine protected areas
protests, 113, 135, 136, 304n7; disinterest in, 142, 185, 282–84; violent state response to, 29, 32, 121, 125–26, 136–40, 196, 282
Pwani. *See* Mkubiru

Rashidi (Msangamkuu village), **86–87**
reefs, 14, 18, 228, 230
Rehema (Mtandi/Msimbati village), **92–93, 160–61, 191, 201,** 229, 302n8
Renamo (Resistencia Nacional Mozambiqueña), 69, 74–75, 301n14
resource extraction. *See* extraction
Rukia (Mtandi/Msimbati village), **167, 197–98**
Ruvula, 63, 93, 134, 222, 269, 291–92, 298n22. *See also* Msimbati
Ruvula villagers: Bi Punjawadi, **227**; Haki, 32, **32–33**, 64–65, **75, 155–56, 193–94, 227–28, 239**; Kachakacha, **226, 269, 285**; Mzimba, **192–93**; Shakila, **258–59**
Ruvuma River, 14, 36, 37, 68, 83, 261, 292, 308n12, 308n13

Sadala (Msimbati village), **154–55, 228–29,** 250–51, **251–52, 266,** 306n9, 306n10
Salama (Nalingu village), **78, 93–94**
sand dunes, 14
SAP (Structural Adjustment Programs), 50, 56–57
sea cucumbers, 64, *64*, 74–75, 152–53
security personnel: employment as, 129; protection of gas infrastructure by,

30–31, 118–19, 128, 136–37, 181, 291–92; violence and intimidation by, 27, 32, 60, 93–94, 121, 165, 196, 200–1, 238, 283. *See also* violence, state

Segi, Shio, 219

self-reliance, 52–53, 55, 57, 140, 200, 265

Sen, Amartya, 248, 262–63

Serengeti National Park, 3

Shabia (Msimbati village), **168–70**

Shaibu (Msimbati village), **259–60**

Shakila (Ruvula village), **258–59**

Shirikiso Hifadhi ya Mazingira ya Bahari Kanda ya Kusini (SHIRIKISO), 165, 166, 306n13

Shivji, Isaa, 51, 52

Sinde, *23*, 23–24, 82–83

Sinde villagers: Hawa, **104**; Mama Razak (Rehema Njowele), **213**

Siwema (Msimbati village), **152**, 247

socialism, 22, 48–56, 58, 141, 279

social suffering, 84–85, 270, 299n39. *See also* well-being, human

Sofia (Nalingu village), **78–79**, **158**

Somoye (Msimbati village), **230–31**, **291–92**

Songo Songo gas project, 124, 304n10

step zero, 88, 117, 278–79

Stinson, James, 178

Structural Adjustment Programs (SAP), 50, 56–57

subsistence: *versus* environmental sustainability, 202, 221–23; farming, 12, 36, 37–38, 83, 106, 108–10, 150, 159, 161, 199, 228–29, 241, 258–59, 271, 299n38; fishing, 12, 37–38, 83, 106, 108–10, 145, 156; state appropriation of, 123, 199, 202

Swahili Coast, 35–36

Swahili people, 35–36

Swalehe (Kilambo village), **260**

SwissAid-Tanzania, 225

TACMP (Tanga Coelacanth Marine Park), 5, 6

TANESCO. *See* Tanzania Electric Supply Company Limited

Tanga Coelacanth Marine Park (TACMP), 5, 6

TANU (Tanganyika African National Union), 52, 300n4. *See also* Chama Cha Mapinduzi

Tanzania: map of, *4*, *6*; politics and history of, 40, 47–61, 73–74; administrative districts of, 36, 47; international involvement in, 56–57, 58–59, 177–78, 200, 289–90, 303n4; land rights in, 24–25, 187–88, 279–82, 296n11, 305n19, 306n12 (*See also* land rights); natural gas extraction in, 17–20, *19*, 30–31 (*See also* natural gas extraction; specific projects); protected areas in, 5–6, *6*, 9, 12–17 (*See also* marine protected areas; specific protected areas)

Tanzania Electric Supply Company Limited (TANESCO), 126, 130–31, 195–96, 303n4, 305n20

Tanzania Petroleum Development Corporation (TPDC), 17, 125; broken promises of, 33, 34, 131–36, 195–96, 255, 269; dangers from, 203–4, 269; displacement due to, 203–4, 269; dispossession by, 73, 131–34, 152, 188–89, 197–200, 209, 255, 269; economic promise of, 18–20, 62–63, 127–28, 131–34, 195–96, 209; electricity as benefit of, 73, 127–28, 194–96, 305n20, 310n13 (*See also* electricity); employment opportunities and, 127–29, 152, 181, 187, 194–95, 202, 252; environmental impacts of, 18–20, 163, 181, 184–85, 189, 192–201, 204–9, 281, 287, 304n18; as expression of state power, 9, 20, 30–31, 33–34, 121, 136–40, 164, 181, 184–85, 193–94, 196–201, 279–83; infrastructure of, 9, 18, 20, 30–31, 118–19, *120*, 128, 181, 293, 306n1; land use by, 9, 163, 186–89, 197–200, 203–4, 269; local (mis)understandings,

20, 41, 118–22, 128–30, 164, 181, 184–89, 192–201, 203–6, 269, 273–74, 280–81; overview and history, 41, 123–31; relationship to marine park, 9, 18–20, 118–19, 163–64, 172–73, 186–87, 191, 197, 201–3, 208, 281 (*See also* Mnazi Bay-Ruvuma Estuary Marine Park); terrorist threat to, 291–92; violence in support of, 30–31, 121, 136–40, 181, 184–85, 283. *See also* gas wells; National Natural Gas Infrastructure Pipeline; power plants
Tanzania Social Action Fund (TASAF), 222, 225
Tanzania's People's Defense Force (TPDF), 32, 125–26, 138–40
TASAF (Tanzania Social Action Fund), 222, 225
TotalEnergies, 291, 308n14
tourism, 35–36, 57, 58. *See also* ecotourism
TPDC. *See* Tanzania Petroleum Development Corporation
TPDF (Tanzania's People's Defense Force), 32, 125–26, 138–40
transportation, 23, 23–24, 62, 130, 195, 253, 291
turtles, 86, 89, 97, 207

Uganda, 3, 9, 21, 50
Ujamaa: The Basis of African Socialism (Nyerere), 51
ujamaa era, 48, 50–56, 78, 80, 102, 140. *See also* villagization
UN Development Program (UNDP), 13–14, 18
UNDP (UN Development Program), 13–14, 18
ustawi. *See* well-being, human

VEMC (Village Environment Management Committee), 13
VICOBA (village community banking), 151, *151*, 306n7

Village Environment Management Committee (VEMC), 13
Village Land Act (1999), 152, 296n11
Village Liaison Committee (VLC), 13
villages, 12, 24, 53–55, 66–69, 71. *See also* villagization; individual villages
Villages Act (1975), 72
villagization, 53–56, 70–71
violence: directed towards marine park, 28–30, 136–40, *138*, 164–66, 247; insurgency and terrorism, 43, 261, 291–93
violence, state: associated with resource extraction, 30–31, 123, 142–43, 280–82; by marine park employees, 28–29, 93–94, 227–29, 297n15; against opposition parties, 60; police violence, 29; against protesters, 32–33, 121, 125–26, 138–40, 196–97; traumatic effects of, 115, 134, 138–40, 194, 200–1, 282–84
VLC (Village Liaison Committee), 13

Walley, Christine, 162–63
waMakonde. *See* Makonde people
War of Independence (Mozambique), 37, 299n37
waSwahili. *See* Swahili people
Watamu Marine National Park and Reserve, 4
Waziri (Msangamkuu village), **104–5**
well-being, human: access to cash and employment, 244–46; certainty and, 256–60; conservation efforts and, 7, 8, 42, 247–48, 269–74; education and, 263; freedom and capability, 34, 248–50, 251–52, 262–63, 285, 308n4, 310n12; gendered perceptions of, 310n11; harmed by gas project, 285–86; harmed by marine park, 84–85, 93–98, 285–86; key elements of, 262, 269–74, 309n4, 310n8, 310n9, 310n12; "life is hard," 76, 245, 267–68; local understandings of, 42, 250–62, 270–71; material aspects of, 72, 74, 77–79,

81, 252–55, 259, 266, 310n9, 310n10; relational aspects of, 253, 258, 259, 261, 262, 272, 310n11; scholarship regarding, 34–35, 42, 248–50, 253, 271–72, 299n35; social cohesion and, 77, 78–79; subjective aspects of, 271–72, 309n3; temporality of, 73–79, 255–56, 266–68

Wellbeing in Developing Countries Research group, 249

Wentworth Resources. *See* Artumas

West, Paige, 122

Willow, Anna, 21–22

Willow, Anna and Sara Wylie, 119, 144

Wind's Whisper, 64–65, 66

women: conservation activities of, 89, 186–87 (*See also* Bi Mkubwa); divorce and, 263–65, 299n39; effects of marine conservation on, 100, 105, 148–49, 157–70, 233–34, 238–39, 306n14; effects of *ujamaa* on, 78; fishing and gleaning by, 26, 105, 108, 111, 150, 233–34; focus group interviews of, 188–91, 254–55, 261, 266–68; food insecurity and, 109–12, 170, 271, 303n18; gas project and, 131; gendered perspectives of, 148–49, 167–70, 271, 306n14; land rights and, 104, 160–61, 167, 188–91, 197–98, 252, 261, 307n5, 307n6, 307n7; occupations of, 110, 135, 151–52, 292–93; villagization and, 55; WWF work with, 88, 151, 186, 187, 247, 252, 307n6

World Bank, 13, 16, 18, 56–57

World Wildlife Fund (WWF), 14, 137; conservation education by, 89, 91, 97–98, 150, 186, 187, 225, 247, 252

Wylie, Sara and Anna Willow, 119, 144

Youdelis, Megan, 219

youth: employment for, 124, 131–33, 169; hooliganism of, 168–70; politics of, 129–30; theft of coconuts by, 103–4, 106–7, 169–70. *See also* children

Yusuf (Msimbati village), **90–91, 199–200**

Zainabu (Msimbati village), **76, 133, 168, 190, 201, 229, 256–57, 263–64, 267, 268**

Zanzibar Declaration, 58

Zuhura (Msimbati village), **230**

ABOUT THE AUTHOR

Vinay Kamat is associate professor in the Department of Anthropology at the University of British Columbia, Canada. He is the author of *Silent Violence: Global Health, Malaria, and Child Survival in Tanzania* (2013), University of Arizona Press, and recipient of the Wenner-Gren Richard Carley Hunt Fellowship.